13

Story & Art by
Taeko Watanabe

Contents

Story Thus Far

It is the end of the Bakufu era, the 3rd year of Bunkyu (1863) in Kyoto. The Shinsengumi is a band of warriors formed to protect the Shogun.

Tominaga Sei, the daughter of a former Bakufu bushi, joined the Shinsengumi disguised as a boy by the name of Kamiya Seizaburo to avenge her father and brother. She has continued her training under the only person in the Shinsengumi who knows her true identity, Okita Soji, and she aspires to become a true *bushi*.

The Shinsengumi prove their worth through their success in the Ikedaya Affair and the *Kinmon no Hen*. Ito Kashitaro and his men join the Shinsengumi as part of the troop expansion. However, their disgust at the Bakufu drives them to plot to change the philosophy of the Shinsengumi.

Yamanami sympathizes with Ito and loses faith in the Bakufu when it mercilessly condemns the rebels of the Tengu-to. Unwilling to betray the Shinsegumi, Yamanami chooses seppuku. The mystery surrounding his sudden choice of death causes great anxiety in the rest of the troop as they prepare to move the headquarters to Nishi Honganji.

Characters

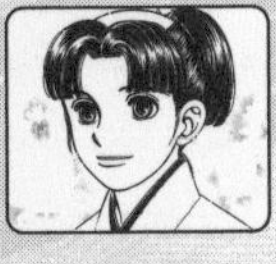

Tominaga Sei
She disguises herself as a boy to enter the Mibu-Roshi. She trains under Soji, aspiring to become a true *bushi*. But secretly, she is in love with Soji.

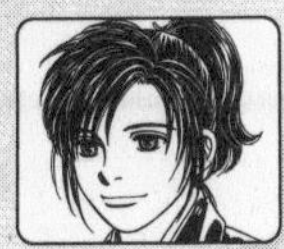

Okita Soji
Assistant vice captain of the Shinsengumi, and licensed master of the Ten'nen Rishin-Ryu. He supports the troop alongside Kondo and Hijikata and guides Seizaburo with a kind yet firm hand.

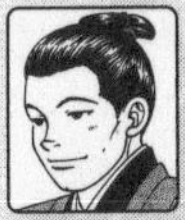

Kondo Isami
Captain of the Shinsengumi and fourth grandmaster of the Ten'nen Rishin-ryu. A passionate, warm and well-respected leader.

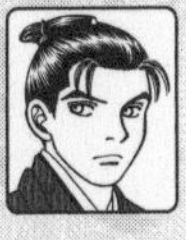

Hijikata Toshizo
Vice captain of the Shinsengumi. He commands both the group and himself with a rigid strictness. He is also known as the "Oni vice captain."

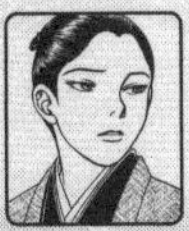

Ito Kashitaro
Councilor of the Shinsengumi. A skilled swordsman yet also an academic. A theorist with an inclination towards anti-Bakufu sentiments.

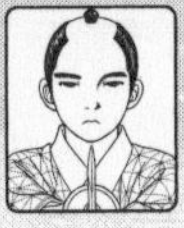

Saito Hajime
Assistant vice captain. He was a friend of Sei's older brother. Sei is attached to him in place of her lost brother.

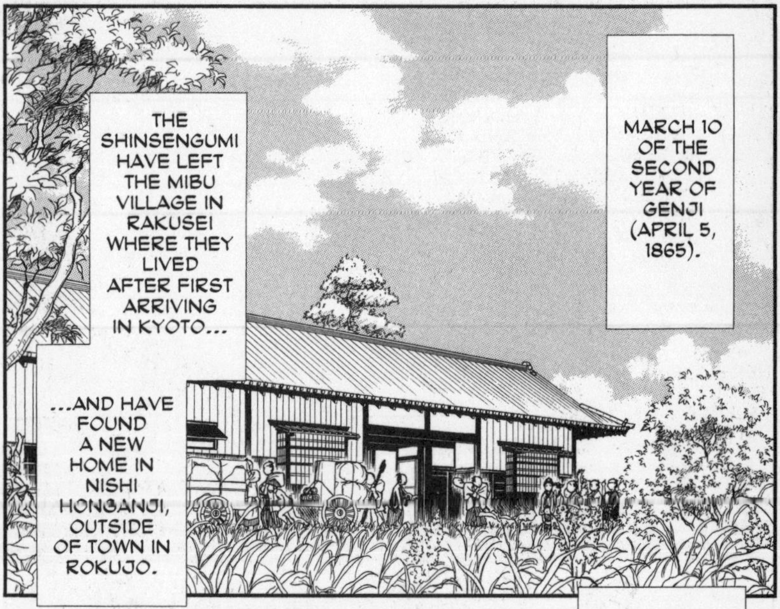
MARCH 10 OF THE SECOND YEAR OF GENJI (APRIL 5, 1865).
THE SHINSENGUMI HAVE LEFT THE MIBU VILLAGE IN RAKUSEI WHERE THEY LIVED AFTER FIRST ARRIVING IN KYOTO...
...AND HAVE FOUND A NEW HOME IN NISHI HONGANJI, OUTSIDE OF TOWN IN ROKUJO.
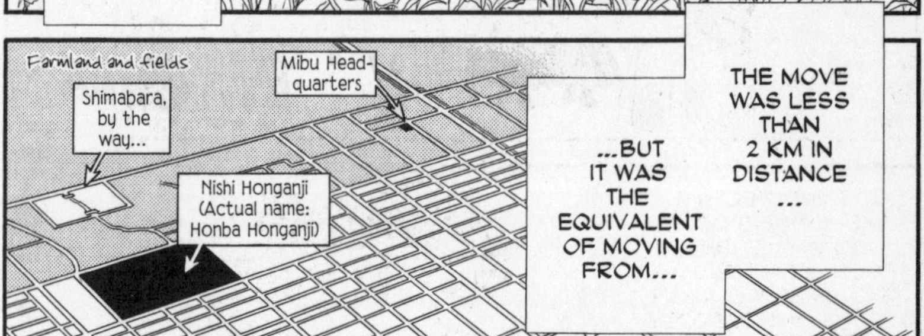
THE MOVE WAS LESS THAN 2 KM IN DISTANCE...
...BUT IT WAS THE EQUIVALENT OF MOVING FROM...
Mibu Head-quarters
Farmland and fields
Shimabara, by the way...
Nishi Honganji (Actual name: Honba Honganji)
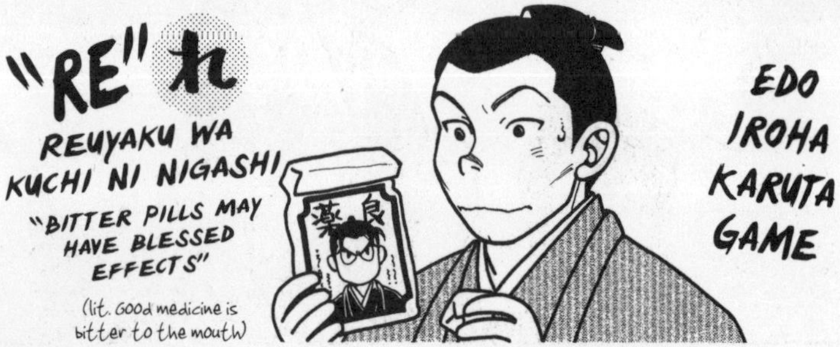
EDO IROHA KARUTA GAME
"RE" れ
REUYAKU WA KUCHI NI NIGASHI
"BITTER PILLS MAY HAVE BLESSED EFFECTS"
(lit. Good medicine is bitter to the mouth)

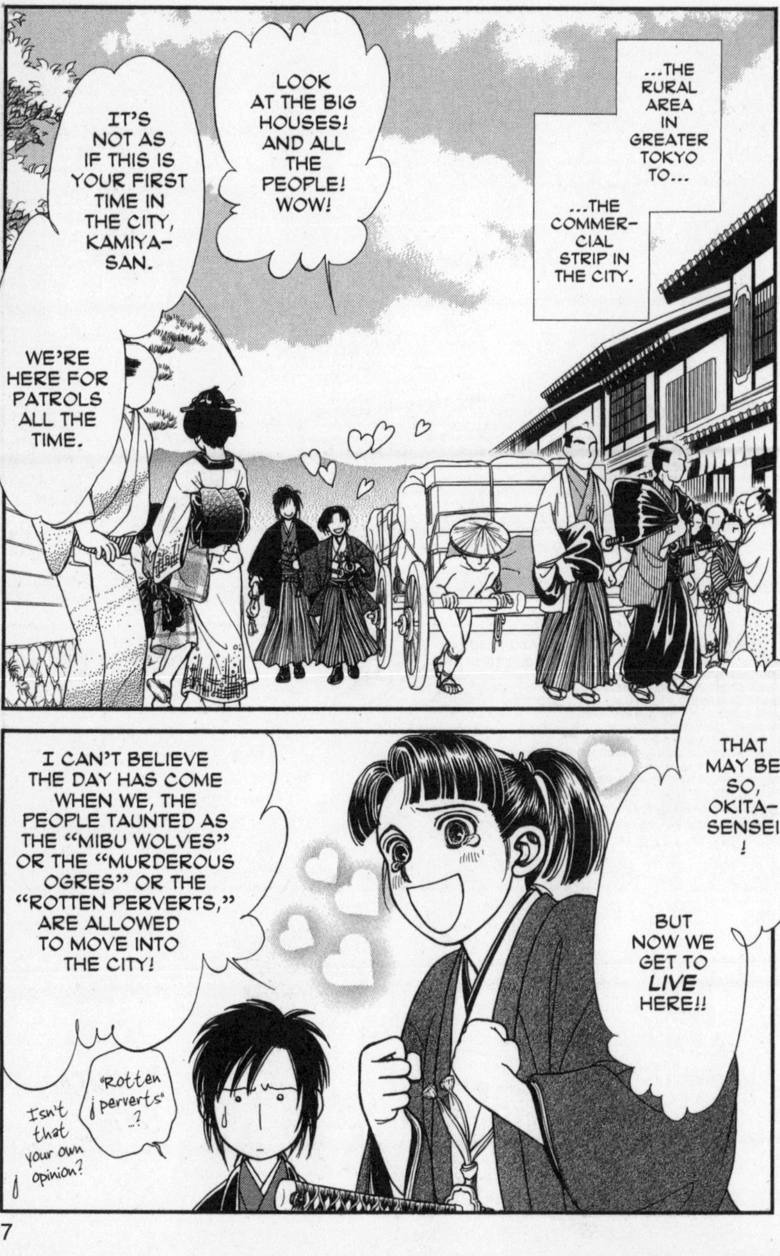
...THE RURAL AREA IN GREATER TOKYO TO...
...THE COMMERCIAL STRIP IN THE CITY.
LOOK AT THE BIG HOUSES! AND ALL THE PEOPLE! WOW!
IT'S NOT AS IF THIS IS YOUR FIRST TIME IN THE CITY, KAMIYA-SAN.
WE'RE HERE FOR PATROLS ALL THE TIME.
THAT MAY BE SO, OKITA-SENSEI!
BUT NOW WE GET TO *LIVE* HERE!!
I CAN'T BELIEVE THE DAY HAS COME WHEN WE, THE PEOPLE TAUNTED AS THE "MIBU WOLVES" OR THE "MURDEROUS OGRES" OR THE "ROTTEN PERVERTS," ARE ALLOWED TO MOVE INTO THE CITY!
"Rotten perverts" ...?
Isn't that your own opinion?

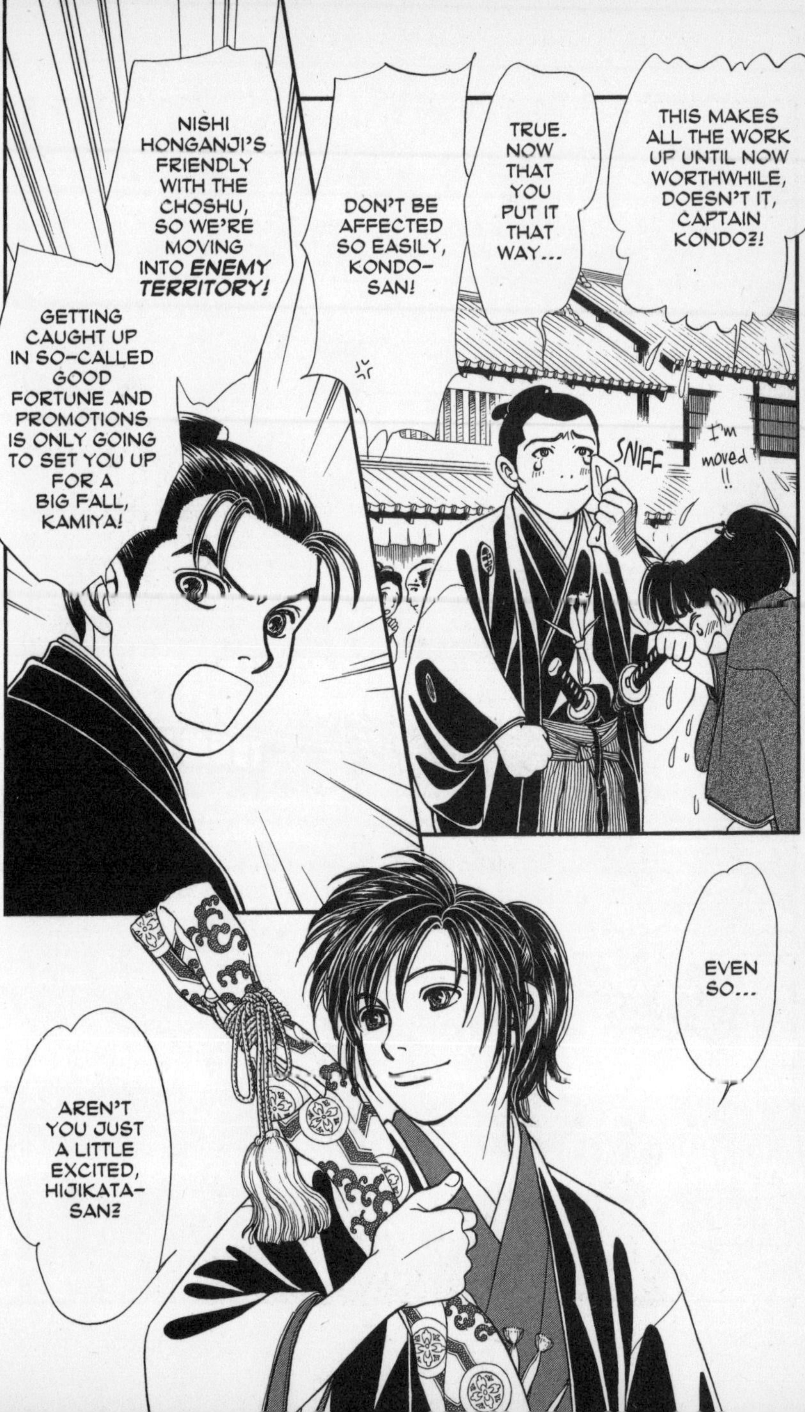
THIS MAKES ALL THE WORK UP UNTIL NOW WORTHWHILE, DOESN'T IT, CAPTAIN KONDO?!
TRUE. NOW THAT YOU PUT IT THAT WAY...
SNIFF
I'm moved!!
DON'T BE AFFECTED SO EASILY, KONDO-SAN!
NISHI HONGANJI'S FRIENDLY WITH THE CHOSHU, SO WE'RE MOVING INTO ENEMY TERRITORY!
GETTING CAUGHT UP IN SO-CALLED GOOD FORTUNE AND PROMOTIONS IS ONLY GOING TO SET YOU UP FOR A BIG FALL, KAMIYA!
EVEN SO...
AREN'T YOU JUST A LITTLE EXCITED, HIJIKATA-SAN?

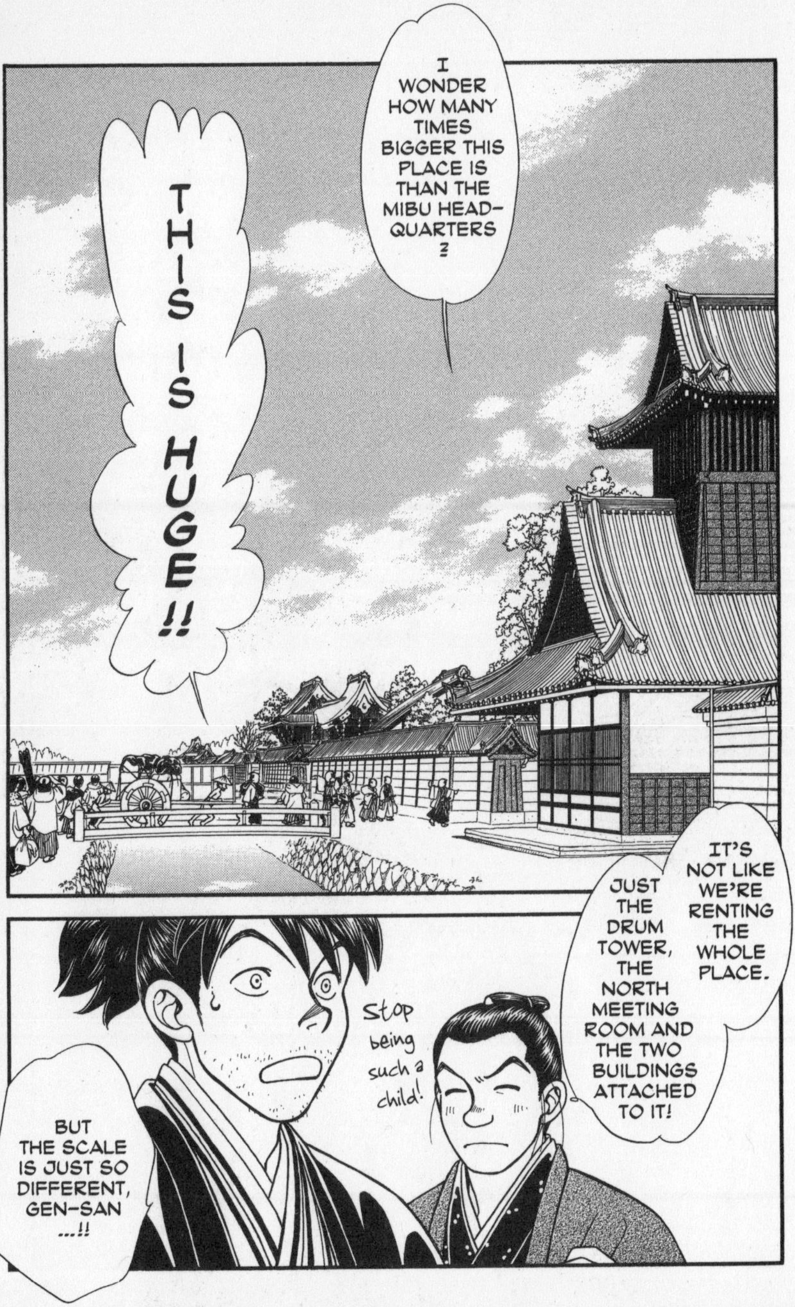
I WONDER HOW MANY TIMES BIGGER THIS PLACE IS THAN THE MIBU HEAD-QUARTERS ?
THIS IS HUGE!!
IT'S NOT LIKE WE'RE RENTING THE WHOLE PLACE.
JUST THE DRUM TOWER, THE NORTH MEETING ROOM AND THE TWO BUILDINGS ATTACHED TO IT!
Stop being such a child!
BUT THE SCALE IS JUST SO DIFFERENT, GEN-SAN ...!!

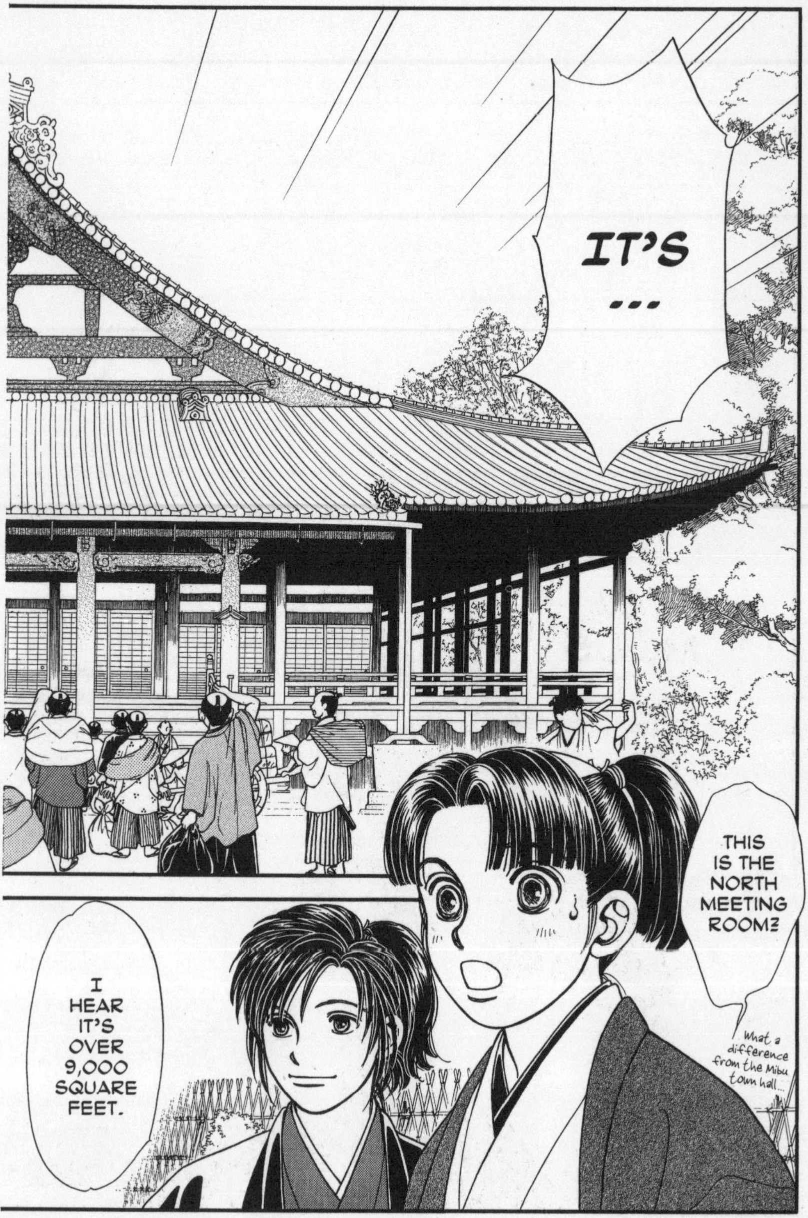
IT'S ...
THIS IS THE NORTH MEETING ROOM?
What a difference from the Mibu town hall...
I HEAR IT'S OVER 9,000 SQUARE FEET.

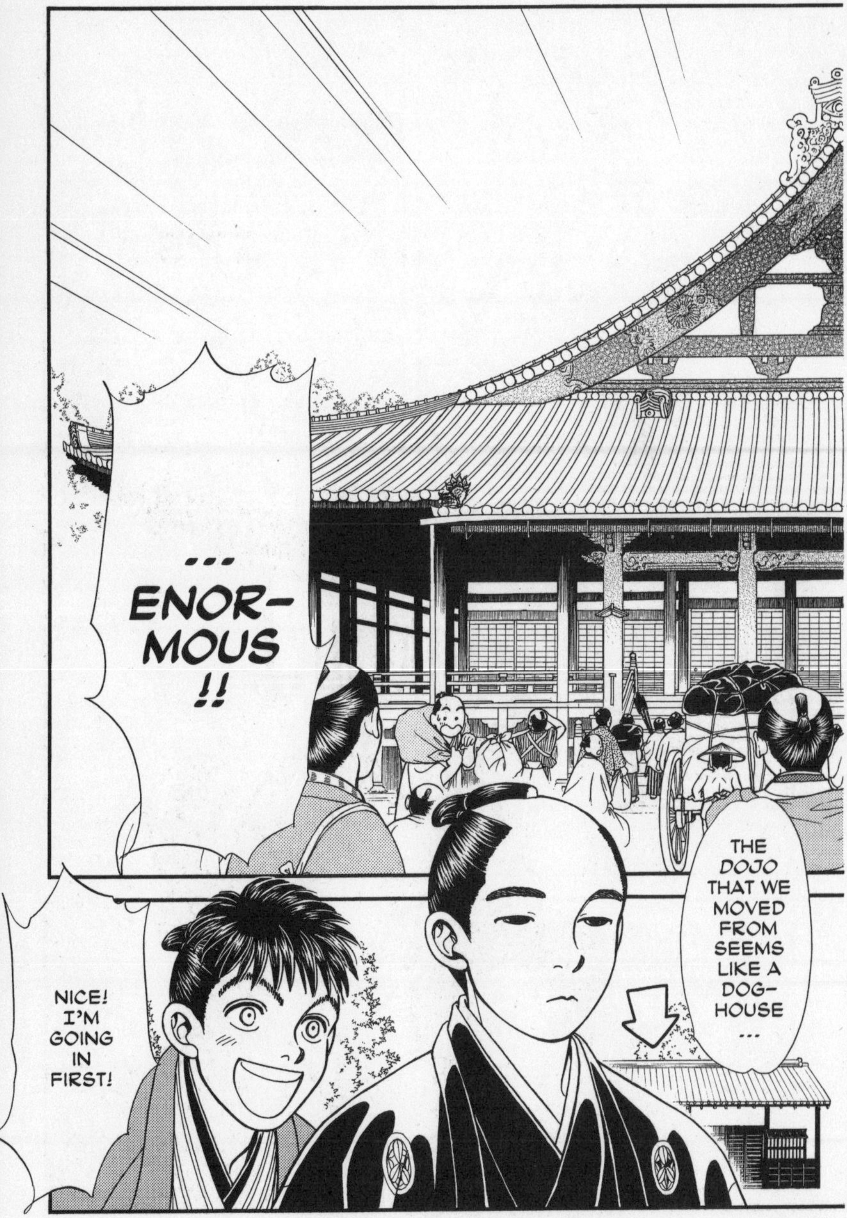
...ENORMOUS!!
THE *DOJO* THAT WE MOVED FROM SEEMS LIKE A DOGHOUSE...
NICE! I'M GOING IN FIRST!

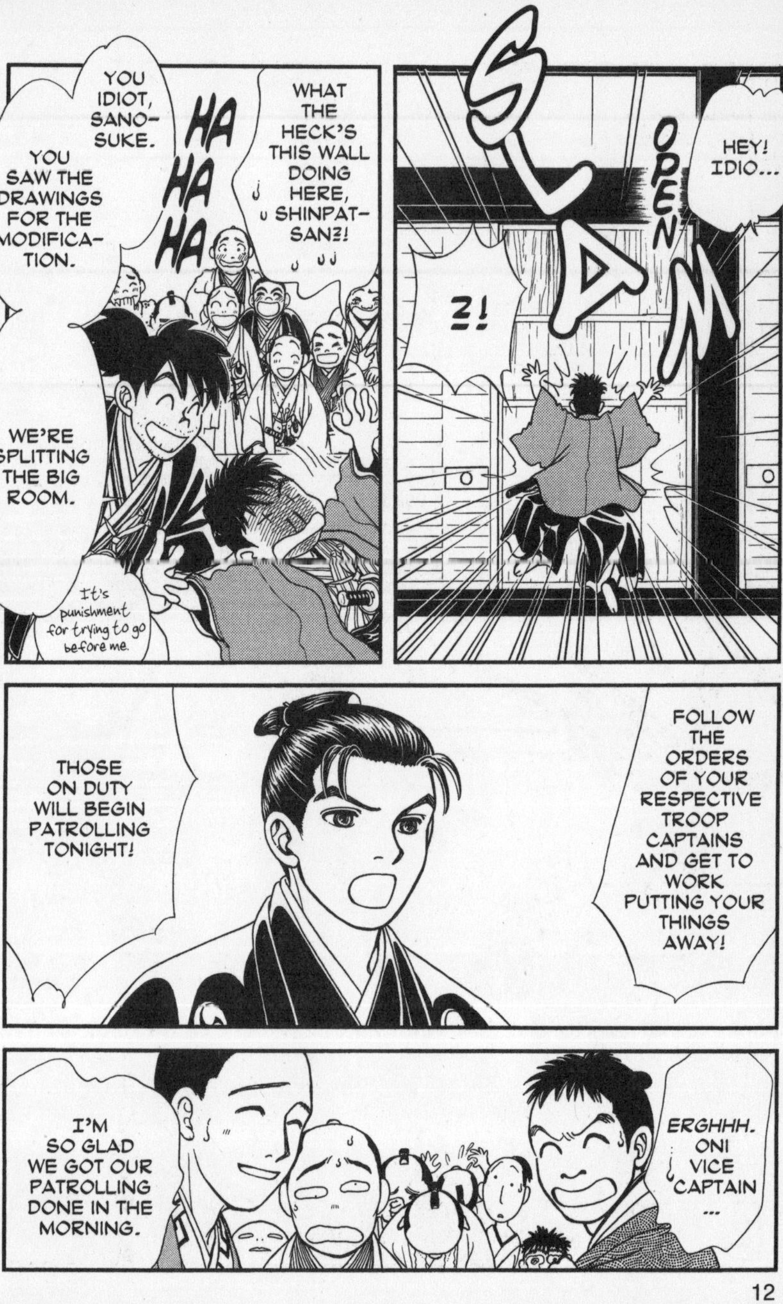

HEY! IDIO...
OPEN
SLAM
?!
WHAT THE HECK'S THIS WALL DOING HERE, SHINPAT-SAN?!
HA HA HA
YOU IDIOT, SANO-SUKE.
YOU SAW THE DRAWINGS FOR THE MODIFICA-TION.
WE'RE SPLITTING THE BIG ROOM.
It's punishment for trying to go before me.
FOLLOW THE ORDERS OF YOUR RESPECTIVE TROOP CAPTAINS AND GET TO WORK PUTTING YOUR THINGS AWAY!
THOSE ON DUTY WILL BEGIN PATROLLING TONIGHT!
ERGHHH. ONI VICE CAPTAIN ...
I'M SO GLAD WE GOT OUR PATROLLING DONE IN THE MORNING.

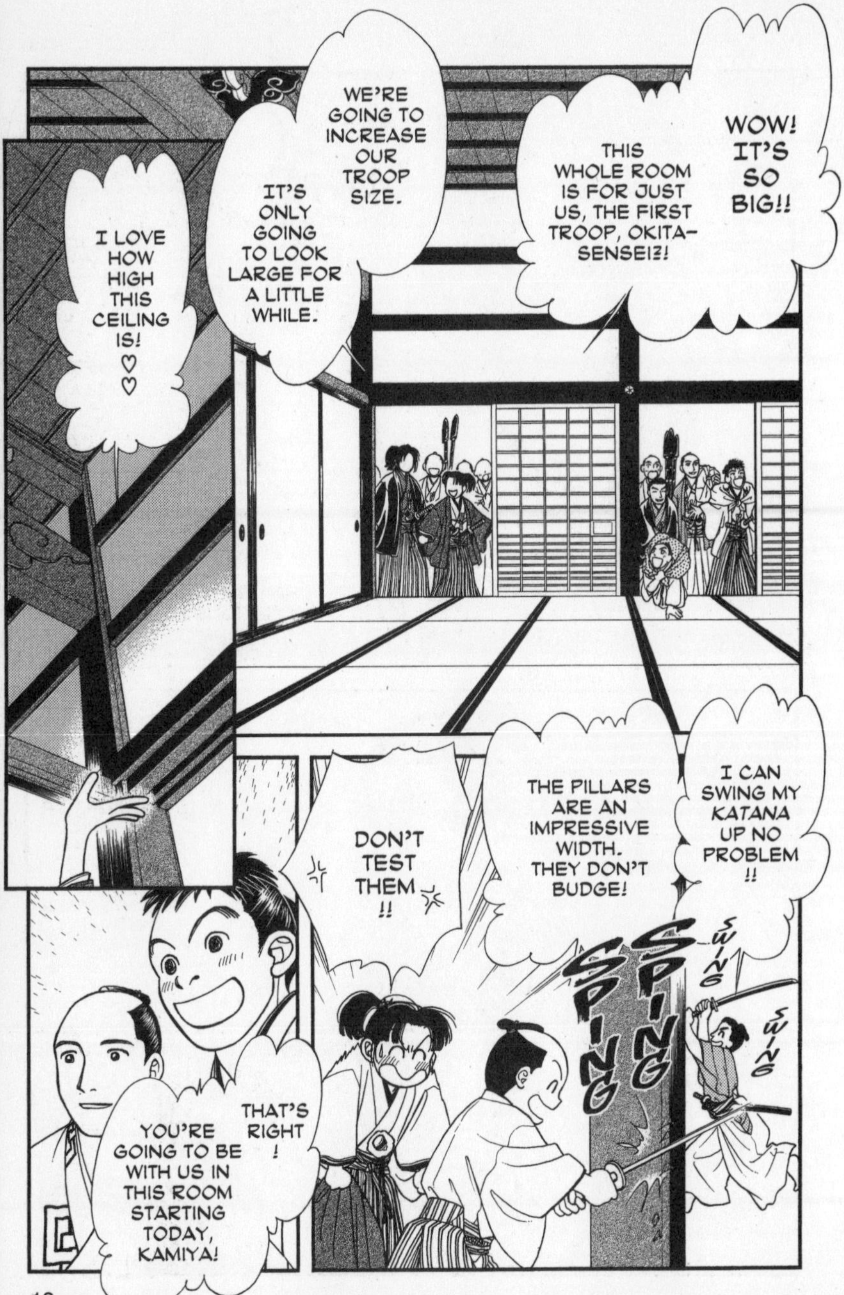
WOW! IT'S SO BIG!!
THIS WHOLE ROOM IS FOR JUST US, THE FIRST TROOP, OKITA-SENSEI?!
WE'RE GOING TO INCREASE OUR TROOP SIZE.
IT'S ONLY GOING TO LOOK LARGE FOR A LITTLE WHILE.
I LOVE HOW HIGH THIS CEILING IS! ♡ ♡
I CAN SWING MY KATANA UP NO PROBLEM !!
SWING
SWING
THE PILLARS ARE AN IMPRESSIVE WIDTH. THEY DON'T BUDGE!
SPING
SPING
DON'T TEST THEM !!
THAT'S RIGHT !
YOU'RE GOING TO BE WITH US IN THIS ROOM STARTING TODAY, KAMIYA!

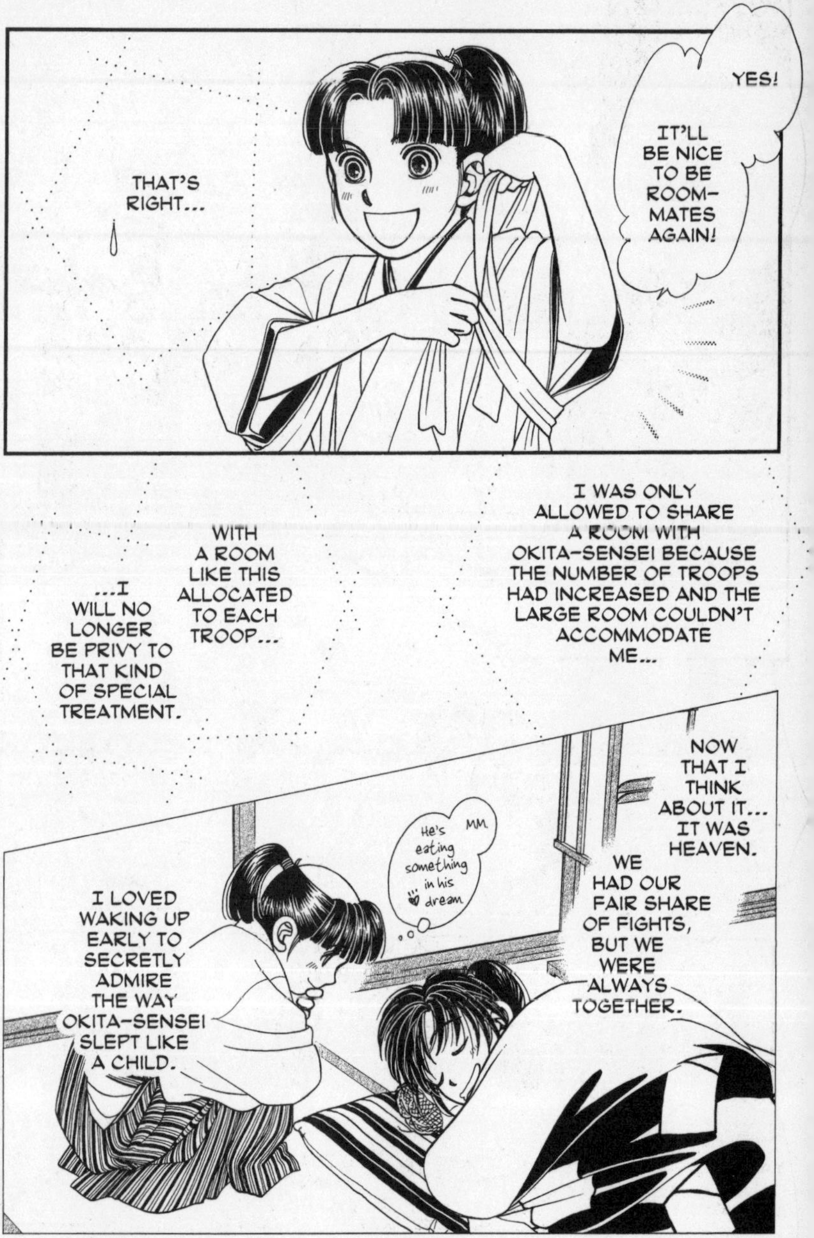
YES!
IT'LL BE NICE TO BE ROOM-MATES AGAIN!
THAT'S RIGHT...
I WAS ONLY ALLOWED TO SHARE A ROOM WITH OKITA-SENSEI BECAUSE THE NUMBER OF TROOPS HAD INCREASED AND THE LARGE ROOM COULDN'T ACCOMMODATE ME...
WITH A ROOM LIKE THIS ALLOCATED TO EACH TROOP...
...I WILL NO LONGER BE PRIVY TO THAT KIND OF SPECIAL TREATMENT.
NOW THAT I THINK ABOUT IT... IT WAS HEAVEN.
WE HAD OUR FAIR SHARE OF FIGHTS, BUT WE WERE ALWAYS TOGETHER.
MM.
He's eating something in his dream
I LOVED WAKING UP EARLY TO SECRETLY ADMIRE THE WAY OKITA-SENSEI SLEPT LIKE A CHILD.

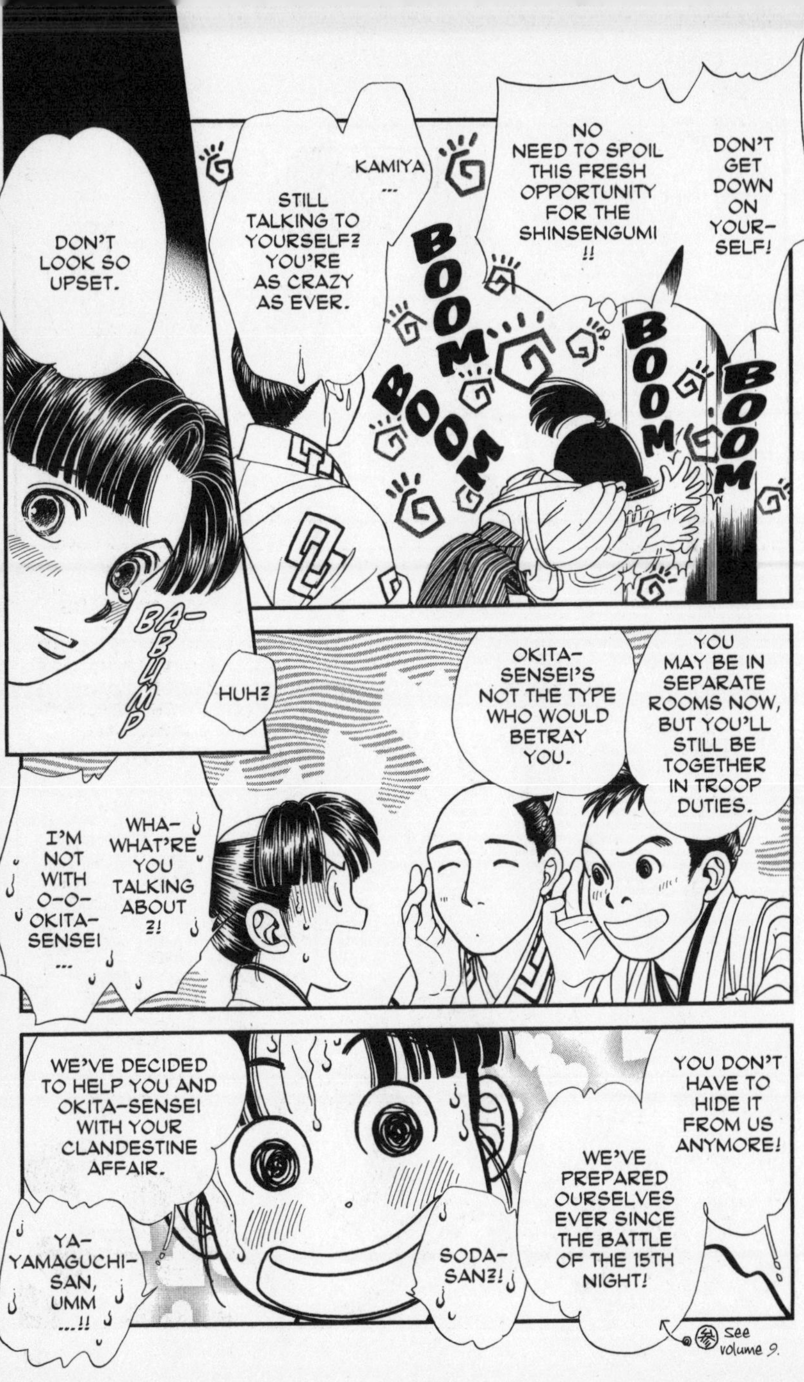
DON'T GET DOWN ON YOURSELF!
NO NEED TO SPOIL THIS FRESH OPPORTUNITY FOR THE SHINSENGUMI!!
KAMIYA...
STILL TALKING TO YOURSELF? YOU'RE AS CRAZY AS EVER.
BOOM
BOOM
BOOM
BOOM
DON'T LOOK SO UPSET.
BA-BUMP
HUH?
YOU MAY BE IN SEPARATE ROOMS NOW, BUT YOU'LL STILL BE TOGETHER IN TROOP DUTIES.
OKITA-SENSEI'S NOT THE TYPE WHO WOULD BETRAY YOU.
WHA-WHAT'RE YOU TALKING ABOUT?!
I'M NOT WITH O-O-OKITA-SENSEI...
YOU DON'T HAVE TO HIDE IT FROM US ANYMORE!
WE'VE PREPARED OURSELVES EVER SINCE THE BATTLE OF THE 15TH NIGHT!
See volume 9.
SODA-SAN?!
WE'VE DECIDED TO HELP YOU AND OKITA-SENSEI WITH YOUR CLANDESTINE AFFAIR.
YA-YAMAGUCHI-SAN, UMM...!!

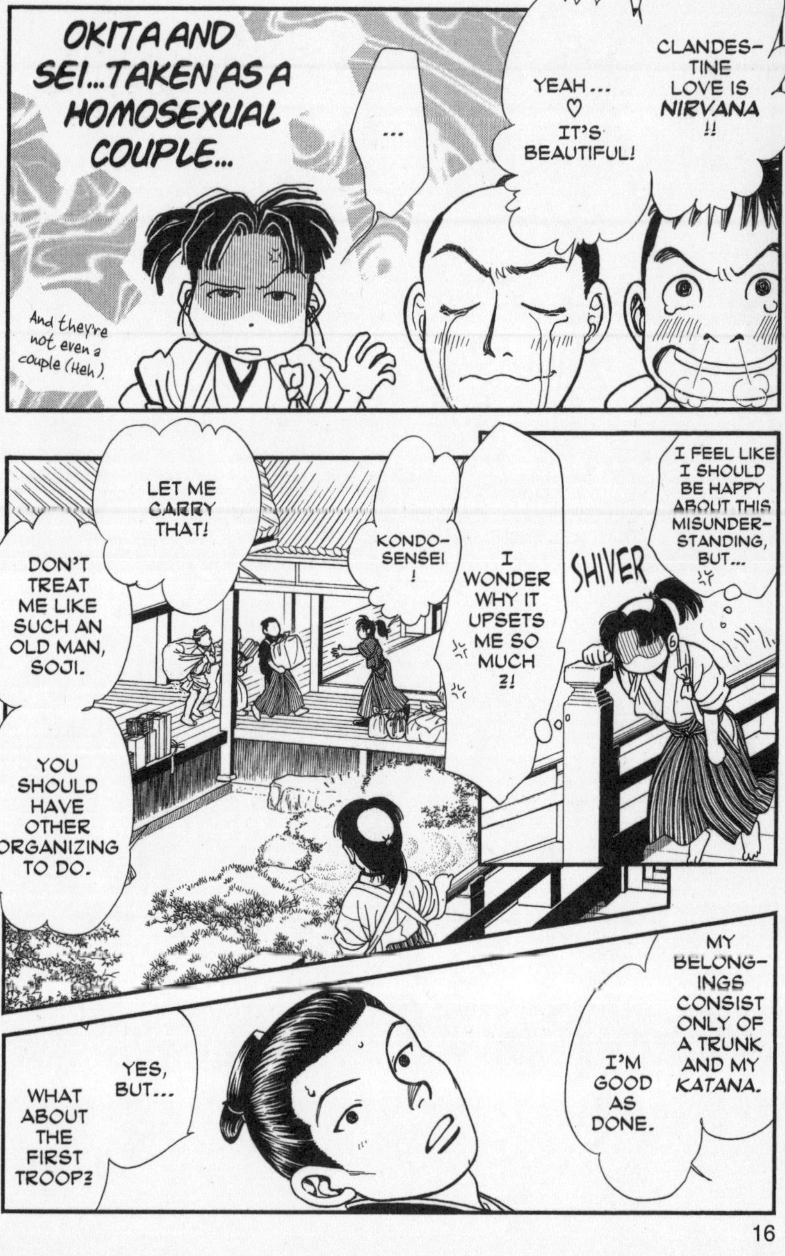
CLANDES-TINE LOVE IS NIRVANA !!
YEAH... ♡ IT'S BEAUTIFUL!
...
OKITA AND SEI...TAKEN AS A HOMOSEXUAL COUPLE...
And they're not even a couple (Heh).
I FEEL LIKE I SHOULD BE HAPPY ABOUT THIS MISUNDER-STANDING, BUT...
SHIVER
I WONDER WHY IT UPSETS ME SO MUCH?!
KONDO-SENSEI!
LET ME CARRY THAT!
DON'T TREAT ME LIKE SUCH AN OLD MAN, SOJI.
YOU SHOULD HAVE OTHER ORGANIZING TO DO.
MY BELONG-INGS CONSIST ONLY OF A TRUNK AND MY KATANA.
I'M GOOD AS DONE.
YES, BUT...
WHAT ABOUT THE FIRST TROOP?

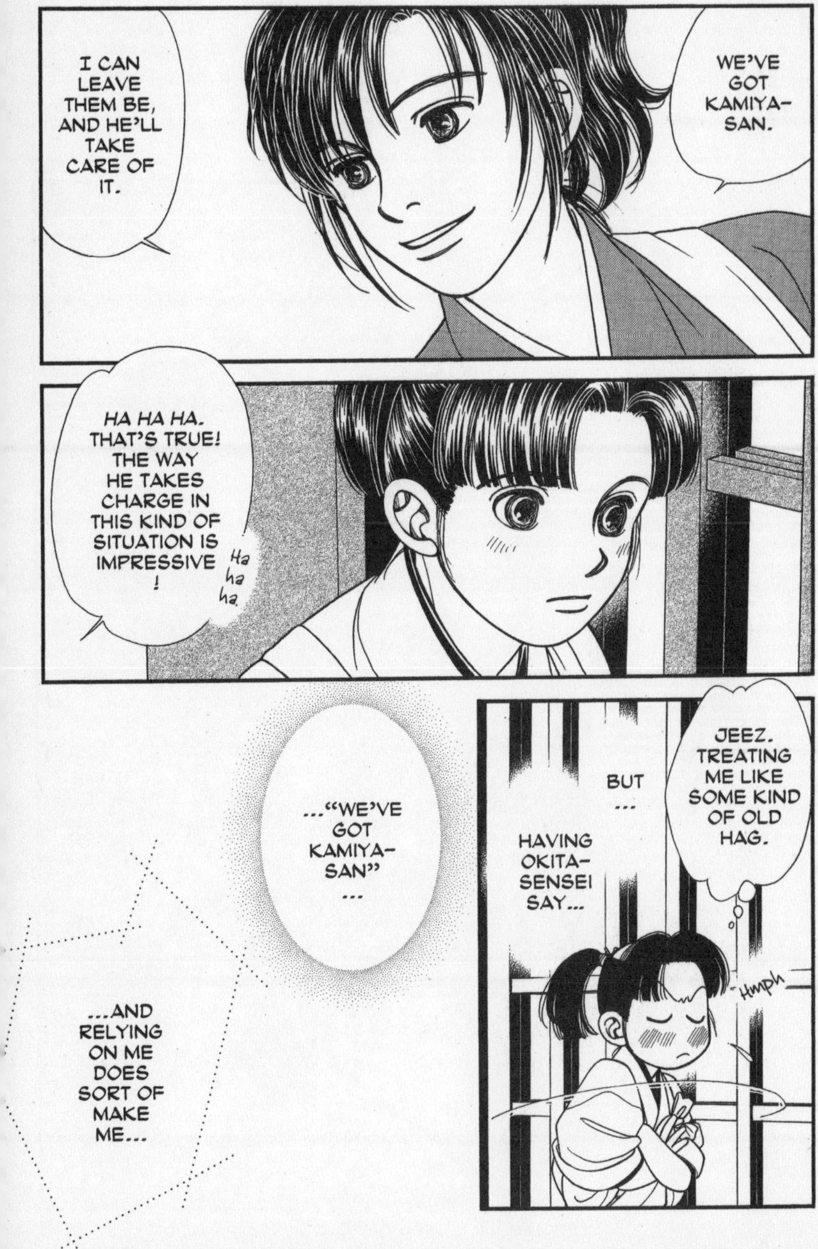
WE'VE GOT KAMIYA-SAN.
I CAN LEAVE THEM BE, AND HE'LL TAKE CARE OF IT.
HA HA HA. THAT'S TRUE! THE WAY HE TAKES CHARGE IN THIS KIND OF SITUATION IS IMPRESSIVE!
Ha ha ha.
JEEZ. TREATING ME LIKE SOME KIND OF OLD HAG.
Hmph
BUT ...
HAVING OKITA-SENSEI SAY...
..."WE'VE GOT KAMIYA-SAN" ...
...AND RELYING ON ME DOES SORT OF MAKE ME...

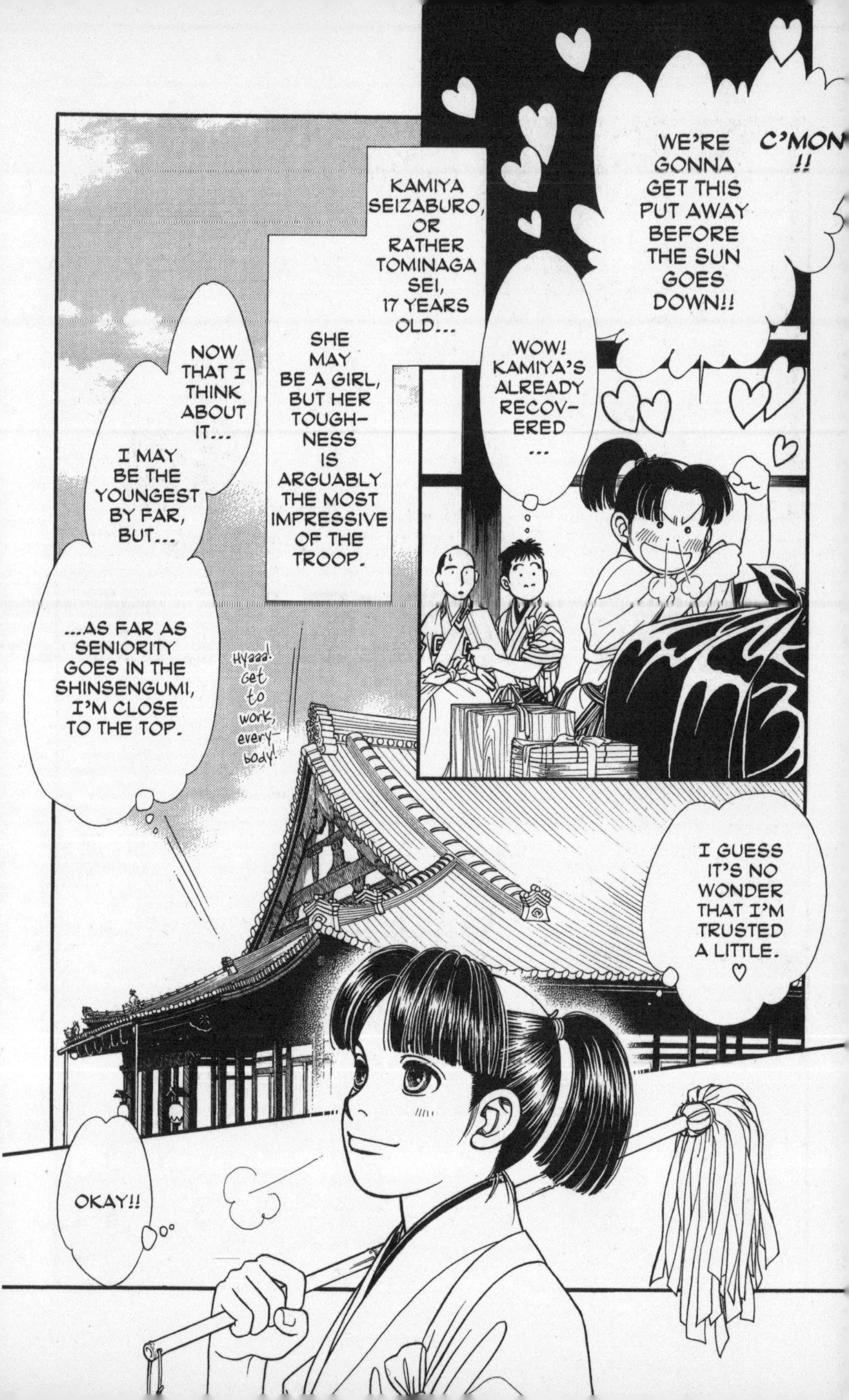
C'MON!!
WE'RE GONNA GET THIS PUT AWAY BEFORE THE SUN GOES DOWN!!
WOW! KAMIYA'S ALREADY RECOVERED...
KAMIYA SEIZABURO, OR RATHER TOMINAGA SEI, 17 YEARS OLD...
SHE MAY BE A GIRL, BUT HER TOUGHNESS IS ARGUABLY THE MOST IMPRESSIVE OF THE TROOP.
NOW THAT I THINK ABOUT IT...
I MAY BE THE YOUNGEST BY FAR, BUT...
...AS FAR AS SENIORITY GOES IN THE SHINSENGUMI, I'M CLOSE TO THE TOP.
Hyaaa! Get to work, everybody!
I GUESS IT'S NO WONDER THAT I'M TRUSTED A LITTLE. ♡
OKAY!!

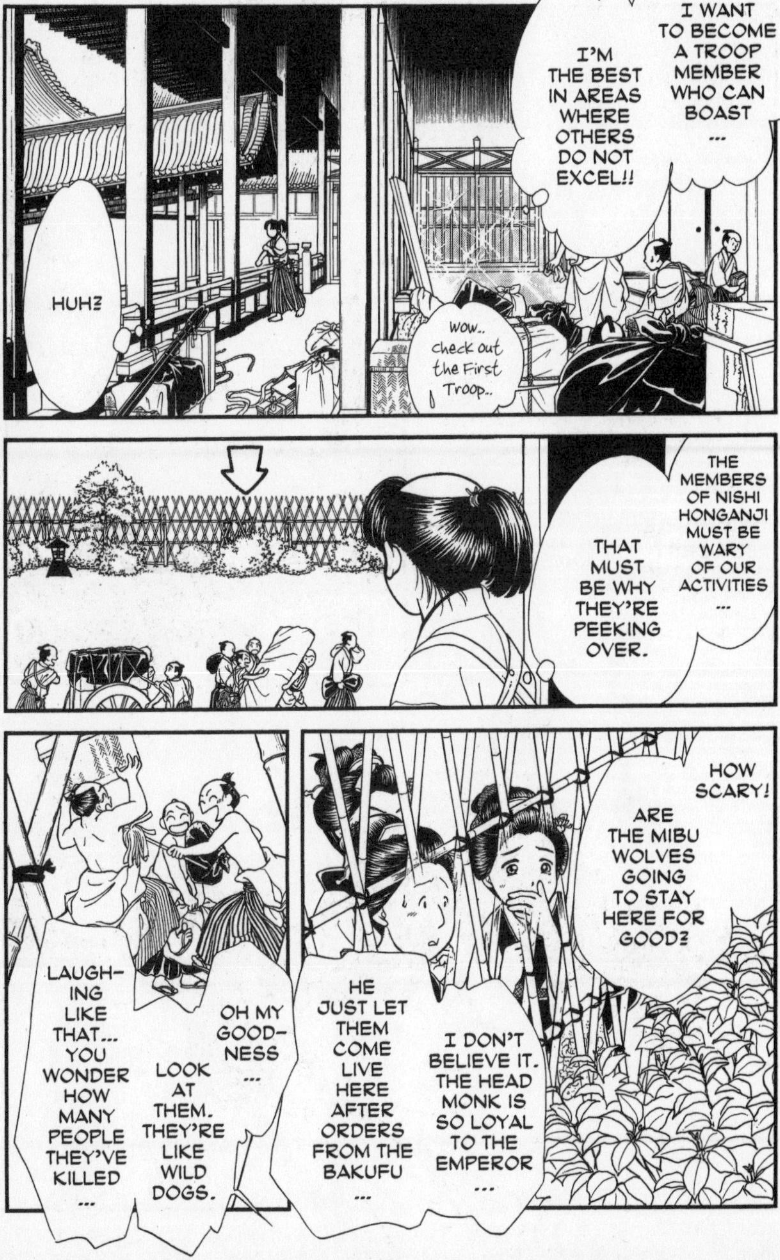
I WANT TO BECOME A TROOP MEMBER WHO CAN BOAST ...
I'M THE BEST IN AREAS WHERE OTHERS DO NOT EXCEL!!
wow.. check out the First Troop..
HUH?
THE MEMBERS OF NISHI HONGANJI MUST BE WARY OF OUR ACTIVITIES ...
THAT MUST BE WHY THEY'RE PEEKING OVER.
HOW SCARY!
ARE THE MIBU WOLVES GOING TO STAY HERE FOR GOOD?
I DON'T BELIEVE IT. THE HEAD MONK IS SO LOYAL TO THE EMPEROR ...
HE JUST LET THEM COME LIVE HERE AFTER ORDERS FROM THE BAKUFU ...
OH MY GOODNESS ...
LOOK AT THEM. THEY'RE LIKE WILD DOGS.
LAUGHING LIKE THAT... YOU WONDER HOW MANY PEOPLE THEY'VE KILLED ...

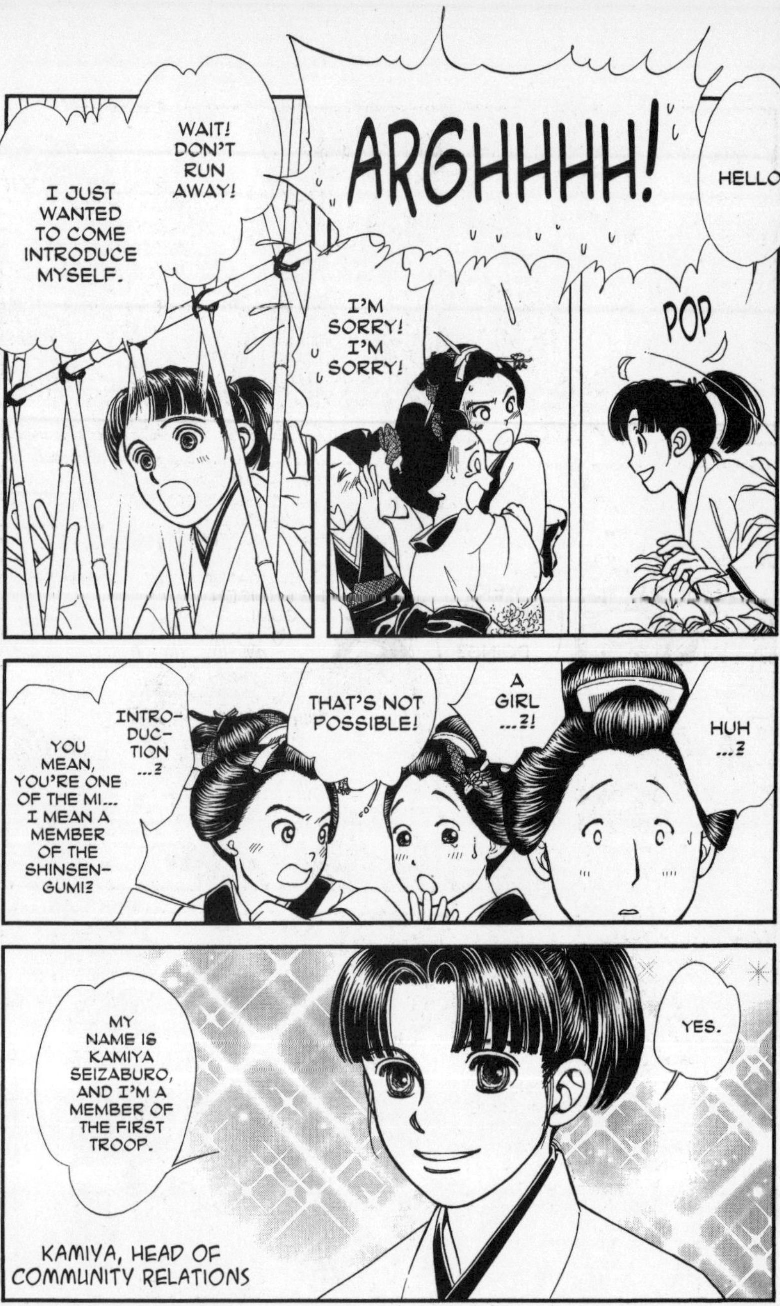
HELLO.
POP
ARGHHHH!
I'M SORRY! I'M SORRY!
WAIT! DON'T RUN AWAY!
I JUST WANTED TO COME INTRODUCE MYSELF.
HUH ...?
A GIRL ...?!
THAT'S NOT POSSIBLE!
INTRODUCTION ...?
YOU MEAN, YOU'RE ONE OF THE MI... I MEAN A MEMBER OF THE SHINSENGUMI?
YES.
MY NAME IS KAMIYA SEIZABURO, AND I'M A MEMBER OF THE FIRST TROOP.
KAMIYA, HEAD OF COMMUNITY RELATIONS

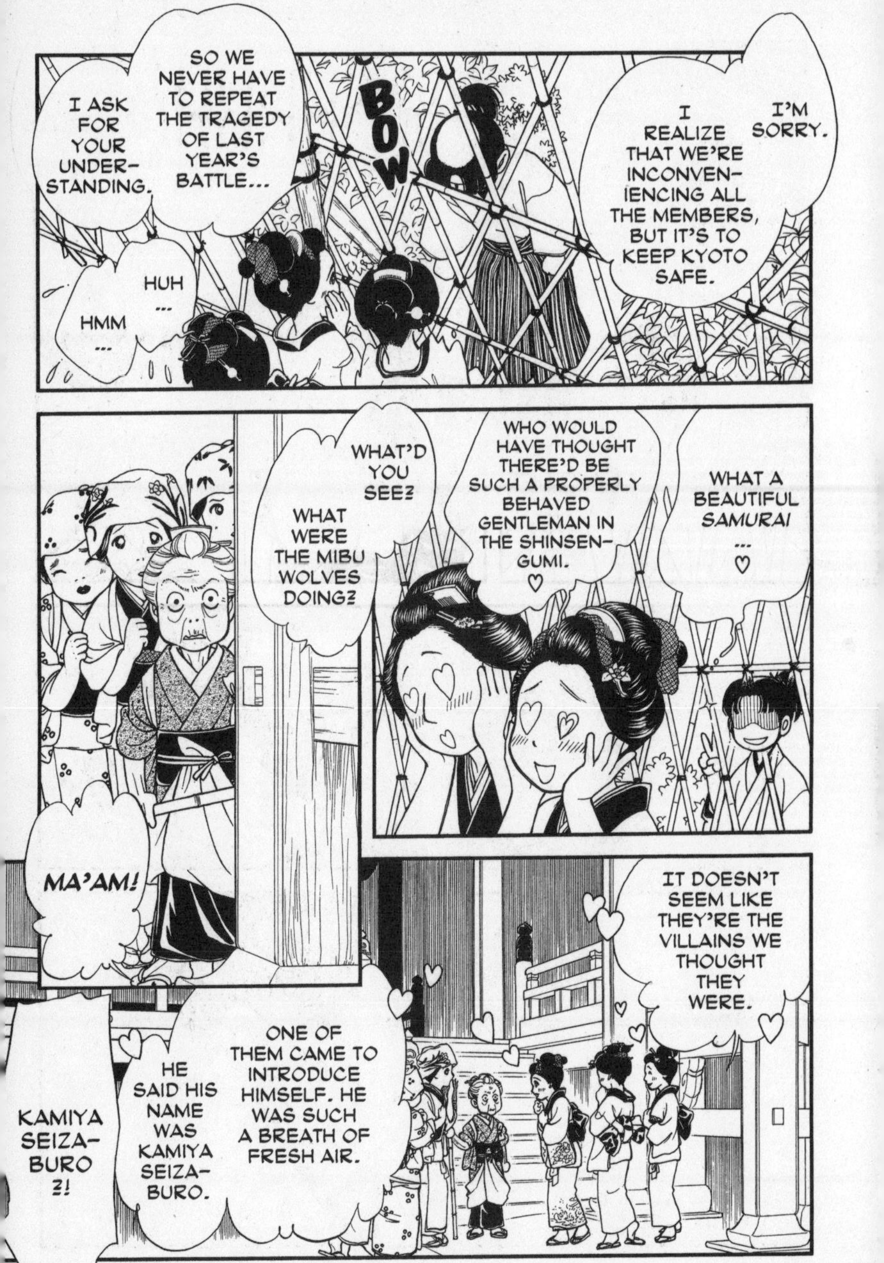
I'M SORRY.
I REALIZE THAT WE'RE INCONVEN-IENCING ALL THE MEMBERS, BUT IT'S TO KEEP KYOTO SAFE.
BOW
SO WE NEVER HAVE TO REPEAT THE TRAGEDY OF LAST YEAR'S BATTLE...
I ASK FOR YOUR UNDER-STANDING.
HUH ...
HMM ...
WHAT A BEAUTIFUL *SAMURAI* ... ♡
WHO WOULD HAVE THOUGHT THERE'D BE SUCH A PROPERLY BEHAVED GENTLEMAN IN THE SHINSEN-GUMI. ♡
WHAT'D YOU SEE?
WHAT WERE THE MIBU WOLVES DOING?
MA'AM!
IT DOESN'T SEEM LIKE THEY'RE THE VILLAINS WE THOUGHT THEY WERE.
ONE OF THEM CAME TO INTRODUCE HIMSELF. HE WAS SUCH A BREATH OF FRESH AIR.
HE SAID HIS NAME WAS KAMIYA SEIZA-BURO.
KAMIYA SEIZA-BURO ?!

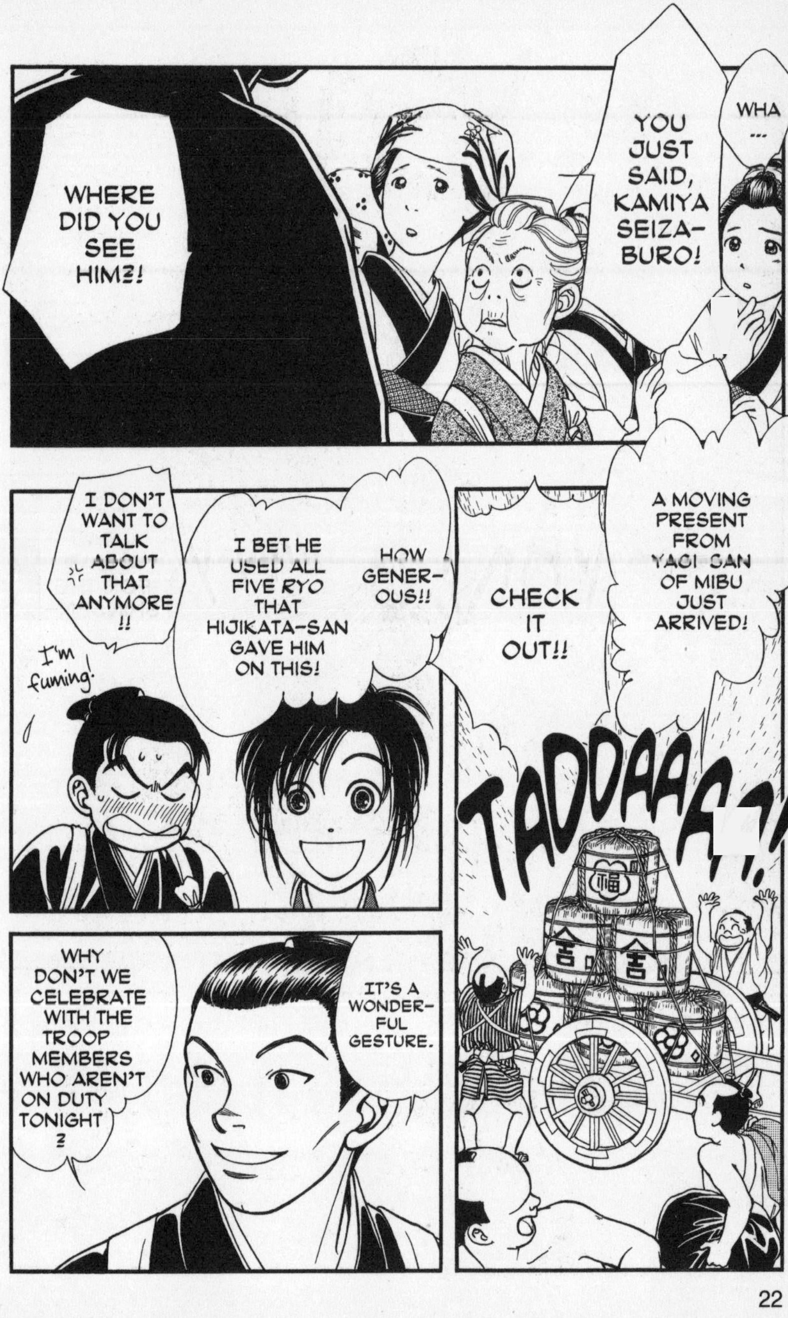
WHA ---
YOU JUST SAID, KAMIYA SEIZABURO!
WHERE DID YOU SEE HIM?!
A MOVING PRESENT FROM YAGI-SAN OF MIBU JUST ARRIVED!
CHECK IT OUT!!
TADDAAA ?!
HOW GENEROUS!!
I BET HE USED ALL FIVE RYO THAT HIJIKATA-SAN GAVE HIM ON THIS!
I DON'T WANT TO TALK ABOUT THAT ANYMORE!!
I'm fuming!
IT'S A WONDERFUL GESTURE.
WHY DON'T WE CELEBRATE WITH THE TROOP MEMBERS WHO AREN'T ON DUTY TONIGHT?

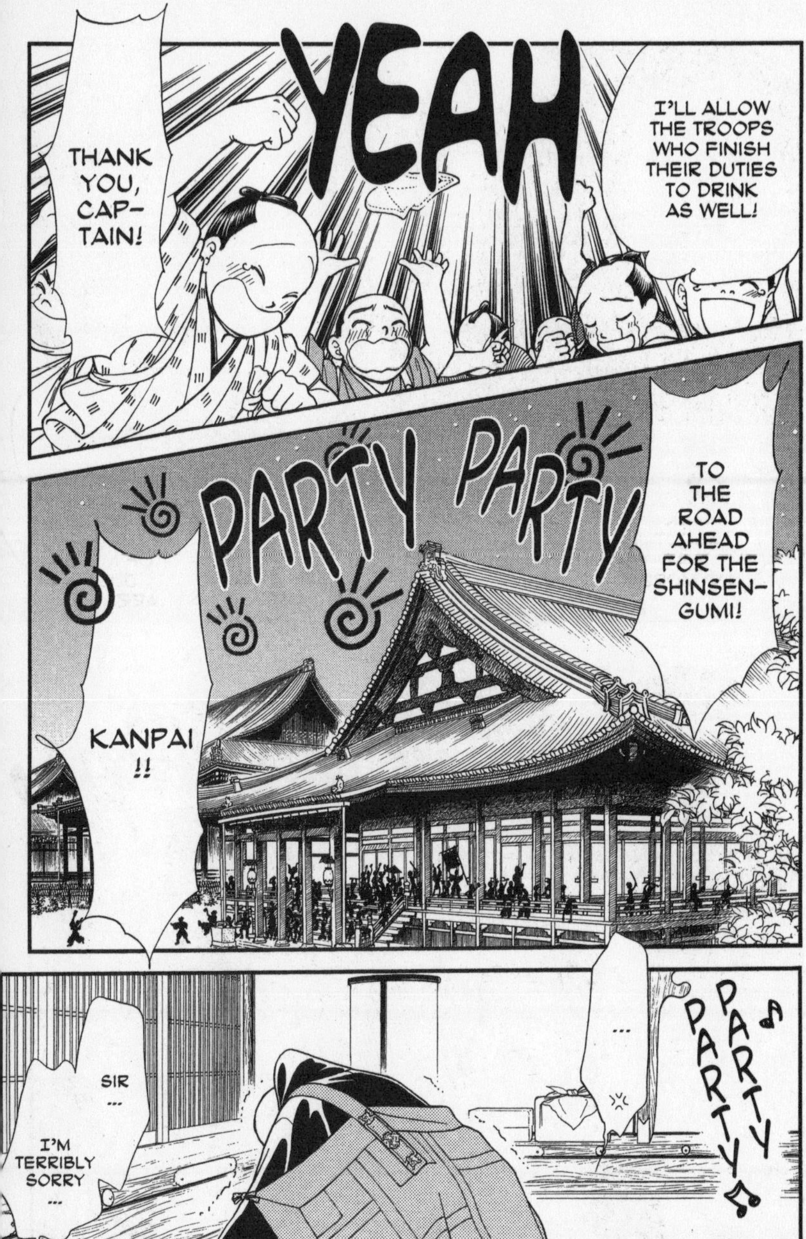
I'LL ALLOW THE TROOPS WHO FINISH THEIR DUTIES TO DRINK AS WELL!
YEAH
THANK YOU, CAP-TAIN!
TO THE ROAD AHEAD FOR THE SHINSEN-GUMI!
PARTY PARTY
KANPAI !!
PARTY PARTY
...
SIR ...
I'M TERRIBLY SORRY ...

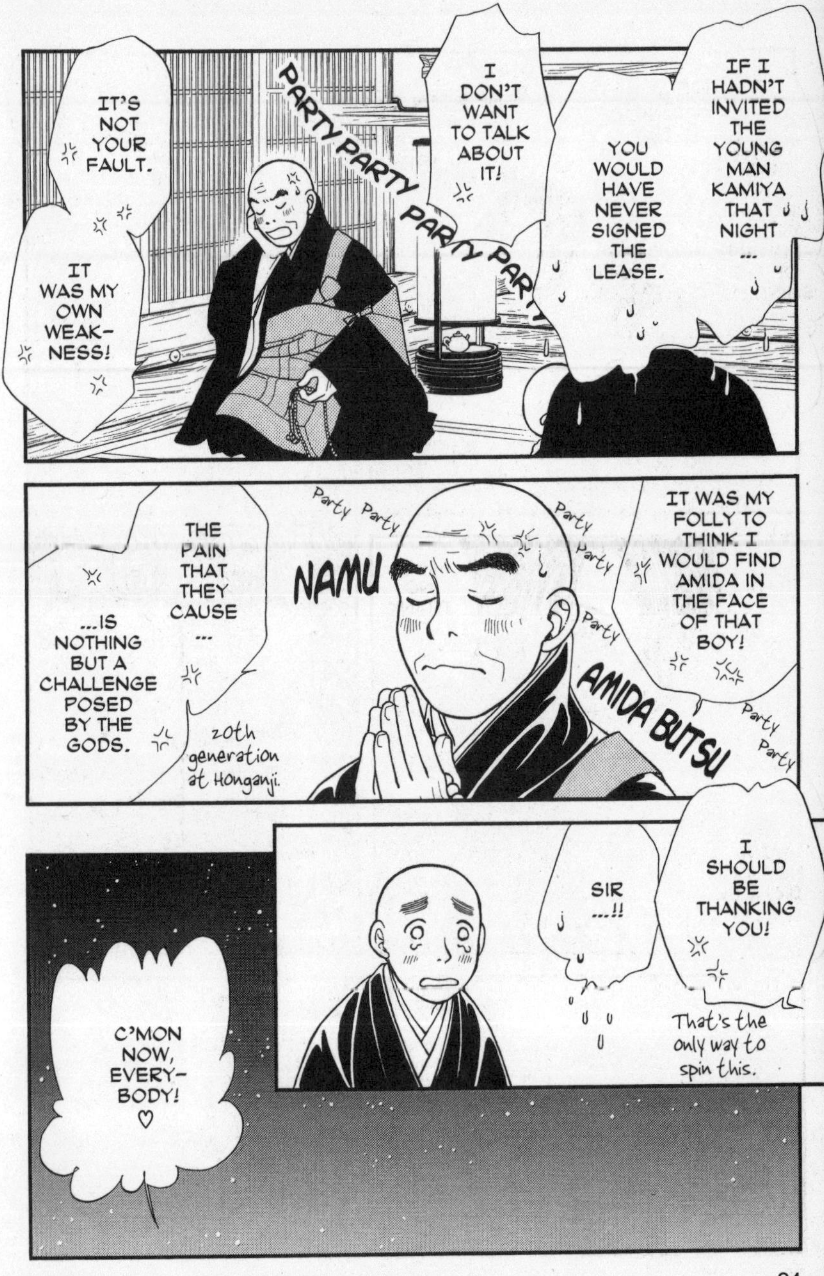
IF I HADN'T INVITED THE YOUNG MAN KAMIYA THAT NIGHT ...
YOU WOULD HAVE NEVER SIGNED THE LEASE.
I DON'T WANT TO TALK ABOUT IT!
PARTY PARTY PARTY PARTY PARTY
IT'S NOT YOUR FAULT.
IT WAS MY OWN WEAK-NESS!
IT WAS MY FOLLY TO THINK I WOULD FIND AMIDA IN THE FACE OF THAT BOY!
Party Party Party Party Party Party Party
NAMU AMIDA BUTSU
THE PAIN THAT THEY CAUSE ...
...IS NOTHING BUT A CHALLENGE POSED BY THE GODS.
20th generation at Honganji.
I SHOULD BE THANKING YOU!
That's the only way to spin this.
SIR ...!!
C'MON NOW, EVERY-BODY! ♡

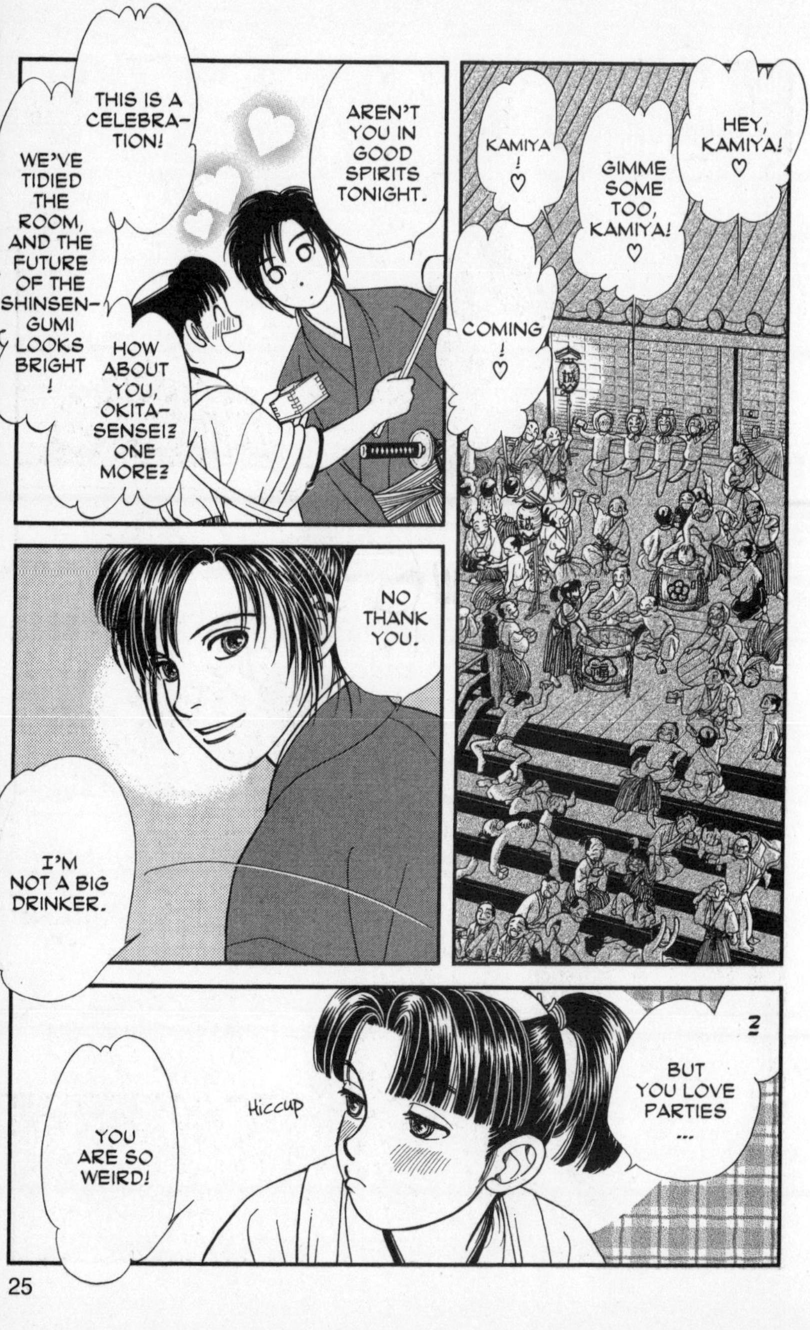
HEY, KAMIYA! ♡
GIMME SOME TOO, KAMIYA! ♡
KAMIYA! ♡
COMING! ♡
AREN'T YOU IN GOOD SPIRITS TONIGHT.
THIS IS A CELEBRA-TION!
WE'VE TIDIED THE ROOM, AND THE FUTURE OF THE SHINSEN-GUMI LOOKS BRIGHT!
HOW ABOUT YOU, OKITA-SENSEI? ONE MORE?
NO THANK YOU.
I'M NOT A BIG DRINKER.
? BUT YOU LOVE PARTIES ...
Hiccup
YOU ARE SO WEIRD!

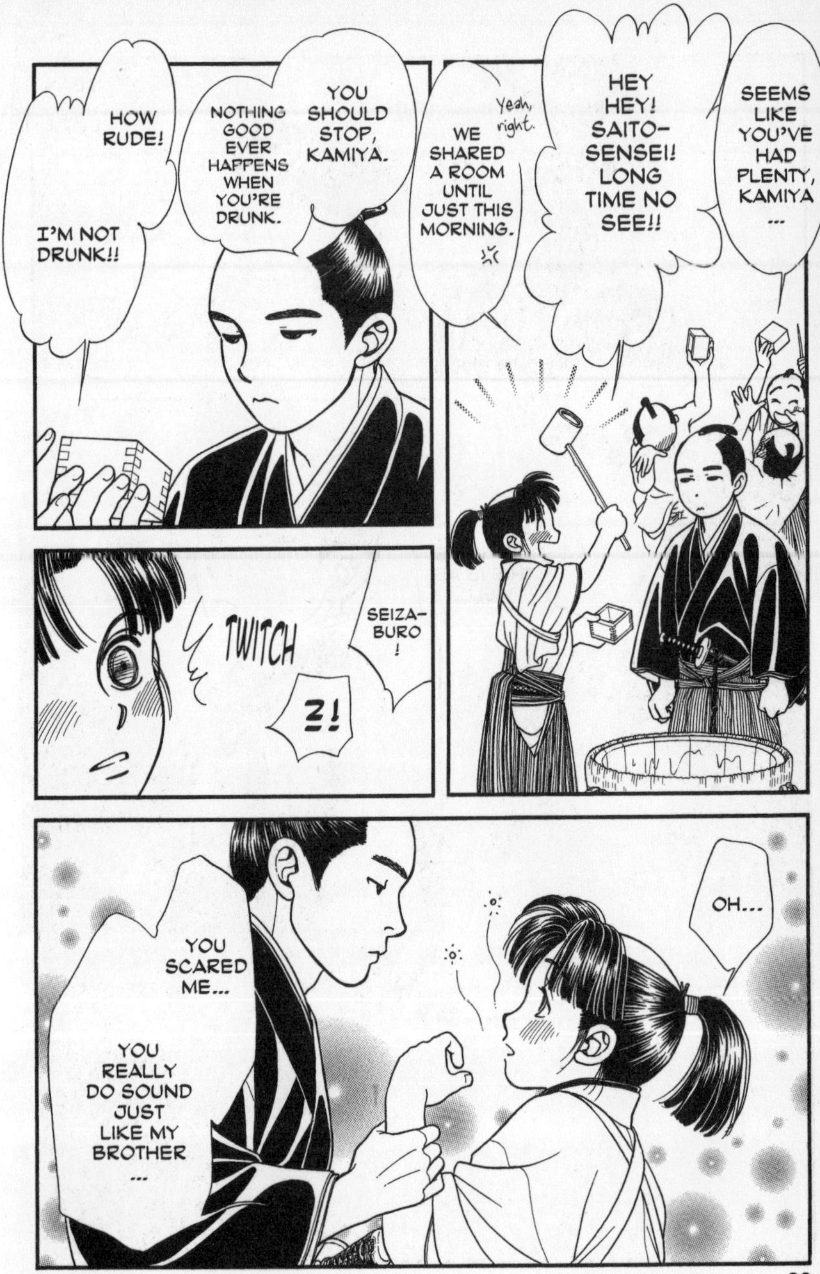
SEEMS LIKE YOU'VE HAD PLENTY, KAMIYA ...
HEY HEY! SAITO-SENSEI! LONG TIME NO SEE!!
WE SHARED A ROOM UNTIL JUST THIS MORNING.
Yeah, right.
YOU SHOULD STOP, KAMIYA.
NOTHING GOOD EVER HAPPENS WHEN YOU'RE DRUNK.
HOW RUDE!
I'M NOT DRUNK!!
SEIZABURO!
?!
TWITCH
OH...
YOU SCARED ME...
YOU REALLY DO SOUND JUST LIKE MY BROTHER ...

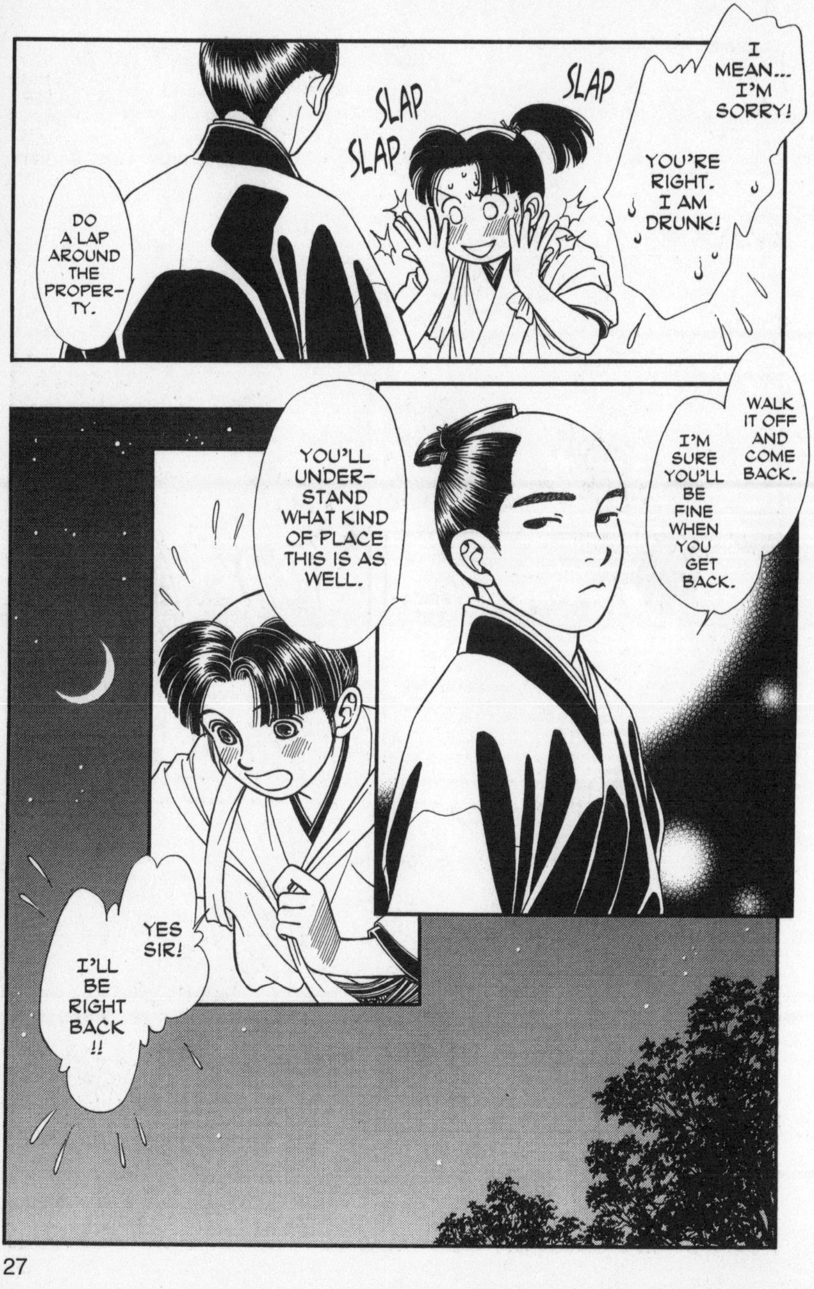
I MEAN... I'M SORRY!
YOU'RE RIGHT. I AM DRUNK!
SLAP
SLAP
SLAP
DO A LAP AROUND THE PROPER-TY.
WALK IT OFF AND COME BACK.
I'M SURE YOU'LL BE FINE WHEN YOU GET BACK.
YOU'LL UNDER-STAND WHAT KIND OF PLACE THIS IS AS WELL.
YES SIR!
I'LL BE RIGHT BACK!!

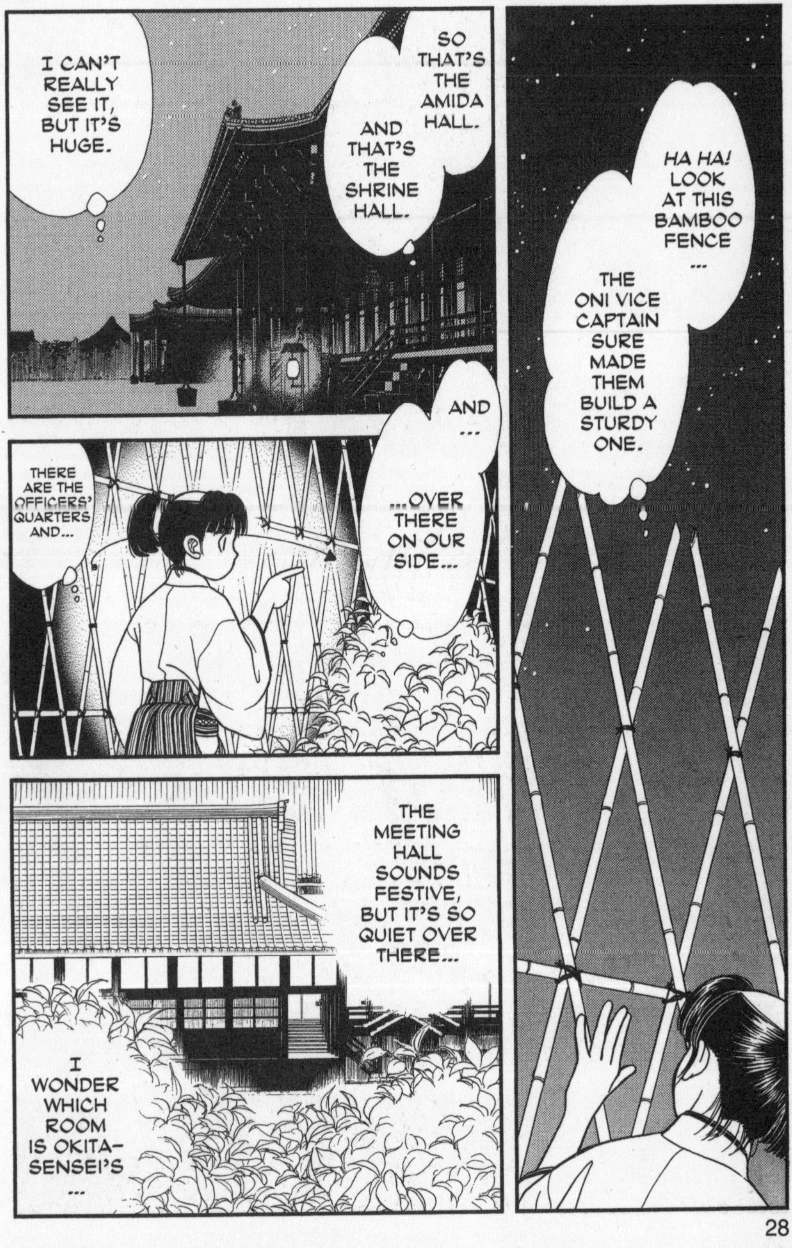
HA HA! LOOK AT THIS BAMBOO FENCE...
THE ONI VICE CAPTAIN SURE MADE THEM BUILD A STURDY ONE.
SO THAT'S THE AMIDA HALL.
AND THAT'S THE SHRINE HALL.
I CAN'T REALLY SEE IT, BUT IT'S HUGE.
AND...
...OVER THERE ON OUR SIDE...
THERE ARE THE OFFICERS' QUARTERS AND...
THE MEETING HALL SOUNDS FESTIVE, BUT IT'S SO QUIET OVER THERE...
I WONDER WHICH ROOM IS OKITA-SENSEI'S...

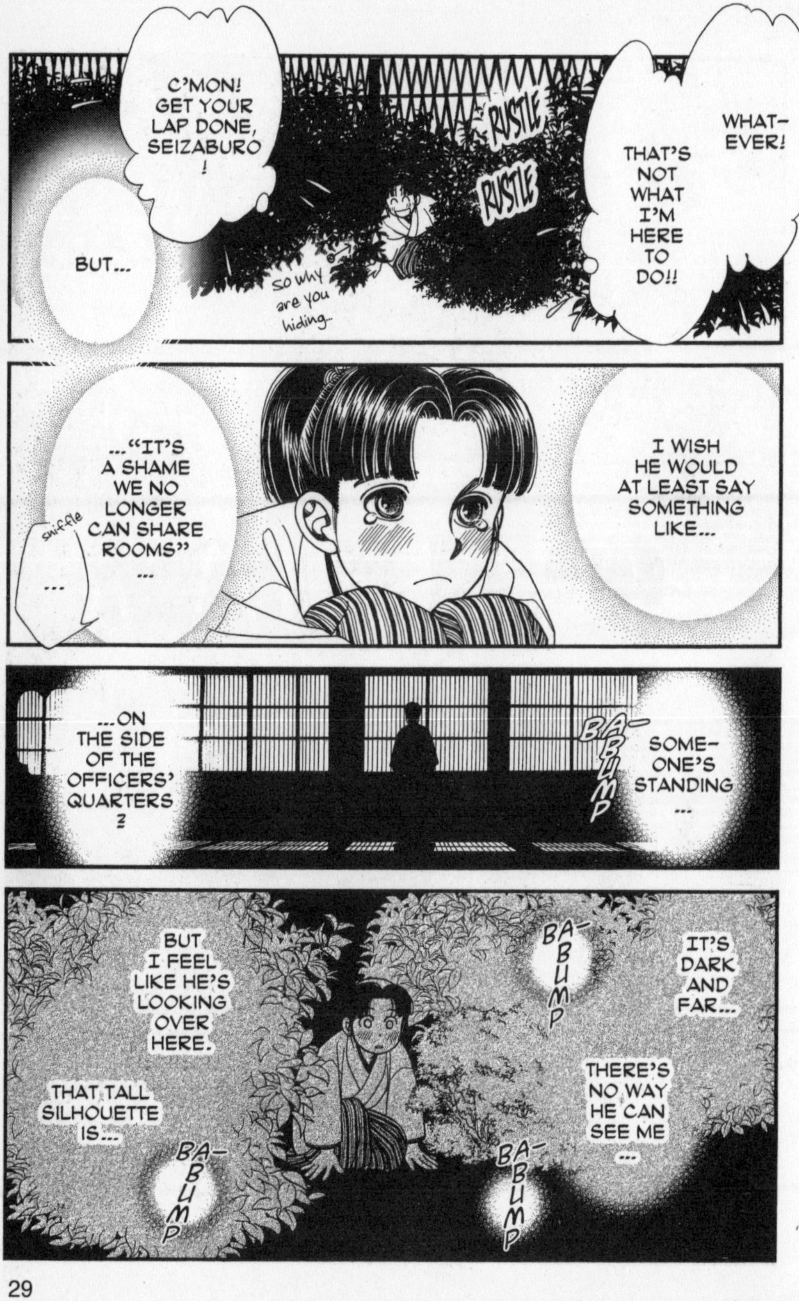
WHAT-EVER!
THAT'S NOT WHAT I'M HERE TO DO!!
RUSTLE
RUSTLE
so why are you hiding...
C'MON! GET YOUR LAP DONE, SEIZABURO!
BUT...
I WISH HE WOULD AT LEAST SAY SOMETHING LIKE...
..."IT'S A SHAME WE NO LONGER CAN SHARE ROOMS" ...
sniffle
...
SOME-ONE'S STANDING ...
BA-BUMP
...ON THE SIDE OF THE OFFICERS' QUARTERS?
IT'S DARK AND FAR...
BA-BUMP
THERE'S NO WAY HE CAN SEE ME ...
BA-BUMP
BUT I FEEL LIKE HE'S LOOKING OVER HERE.
THAT TALL SILHOUETTE IS...
BA-BUMP

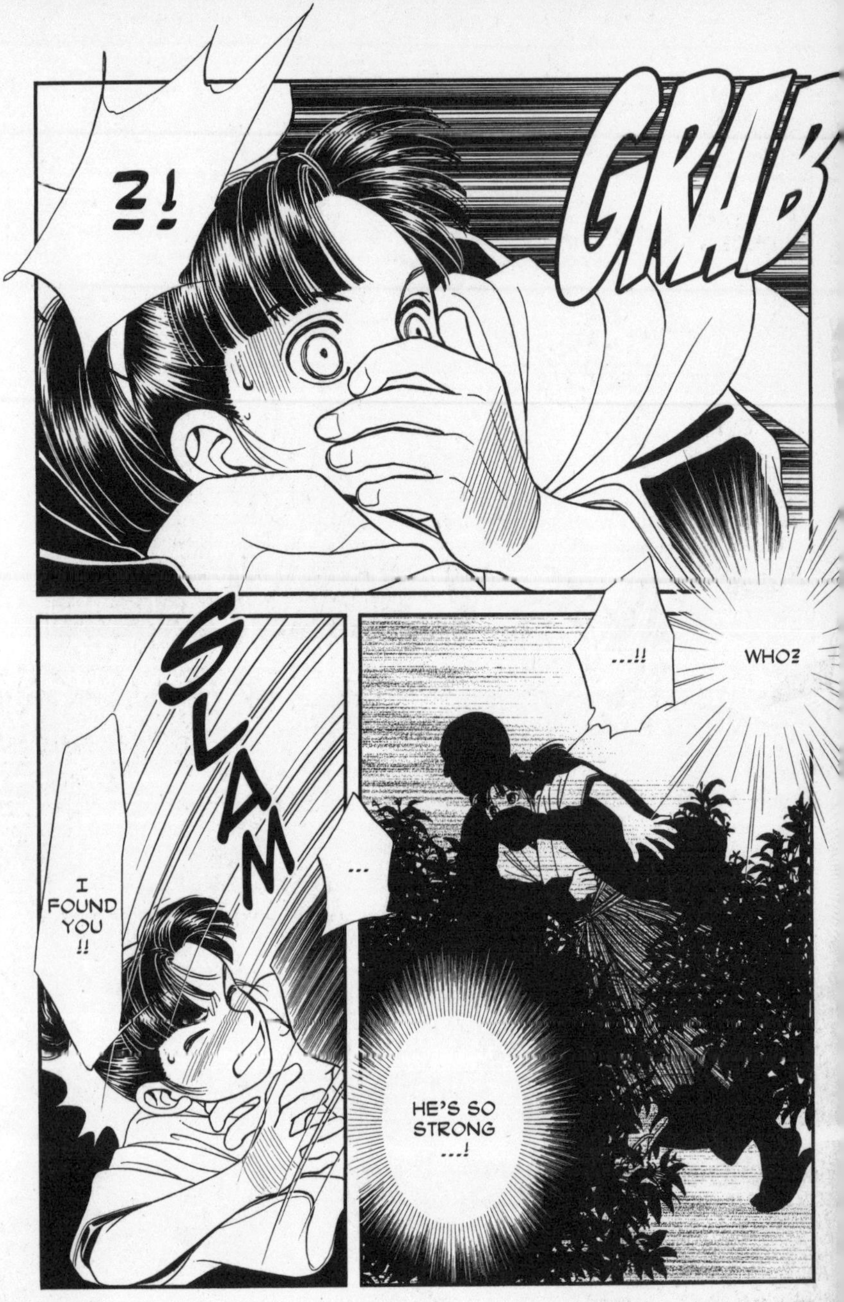
GRAB
?!
WHO?
...!!
...
HE'S SO STRONG ...!
SLAM
I FOUND YOU !!

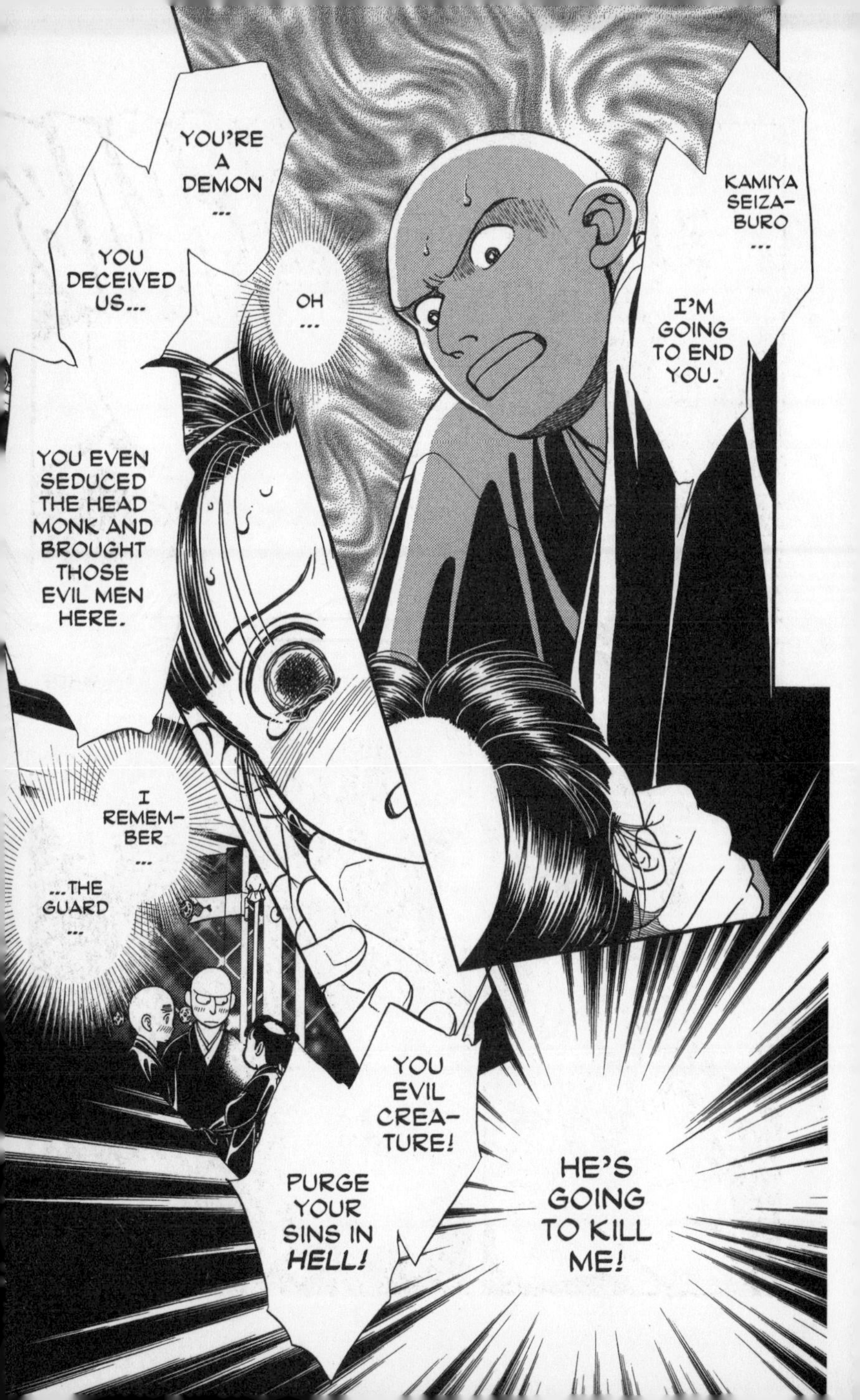
KAMIYA SEIZA-BURO ...
I'M GOING TO END YOU.
OH ...
YOU'RE A DEMON ...
YOU DECEIVED US...
YOU EVEN SEDUCED THE HEAD MONK AND BROUGHT THOSE EVIL MEN HERE.
I REMEM-BER ...
...THE GUARD ...
YOU EVIL CREA-TURE!
PURGE YOUR SINS IN *HELL!*
HE'S GOING TO KILL ME!

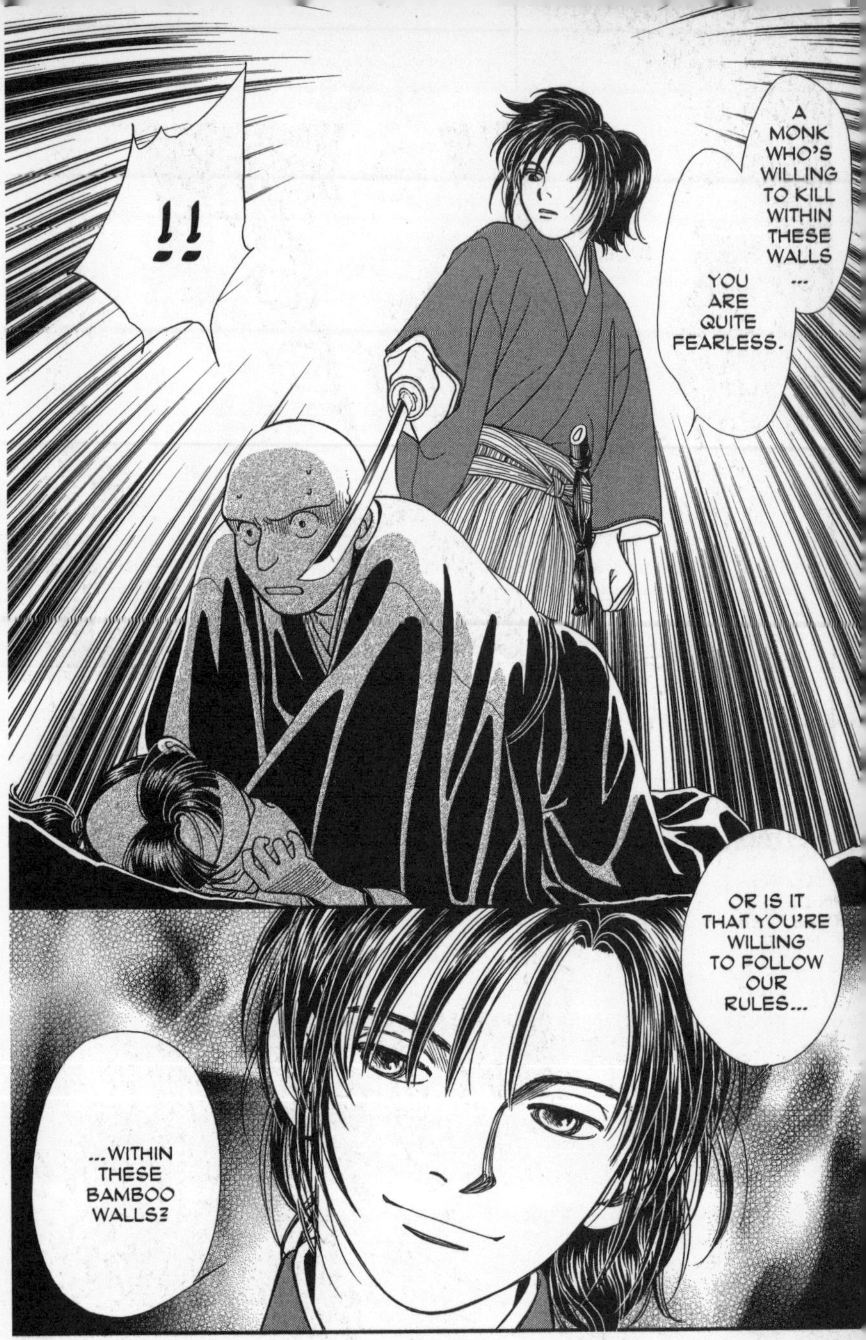
A MONK WHO'S WILLING TO KILL WITHIN THESE WALLS ... YOU ARE QUITE FEARLESS.
!!
OR IS IT THAT YOU'RE WILLING TO FOLLOW OUR RULES...
...WITHIN THESE BAMBOO WALLS?

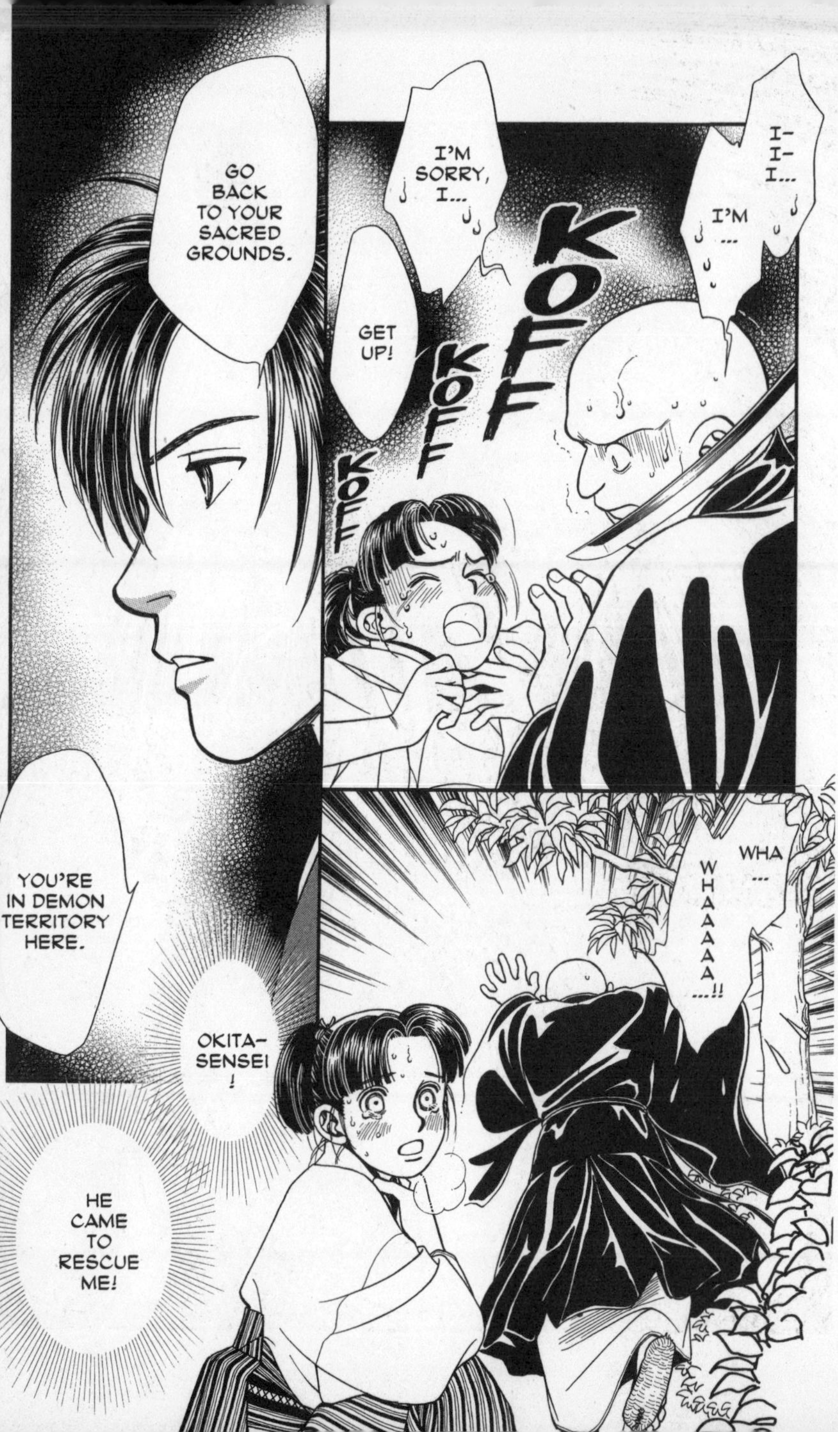
I-I-I...
I'M ...
I'M SORRY, I...
KOFF
KOFF
KOFF
KOFF
GET UP!
GO BACK TO YOUR SACRED GROUNDS.
YOU'RE IN DEMON TERRITORY HERE.
WHA ... WHAAAAAA ...!!
OKITA-SENSEI!
HE CAME TO RESCUE ME!

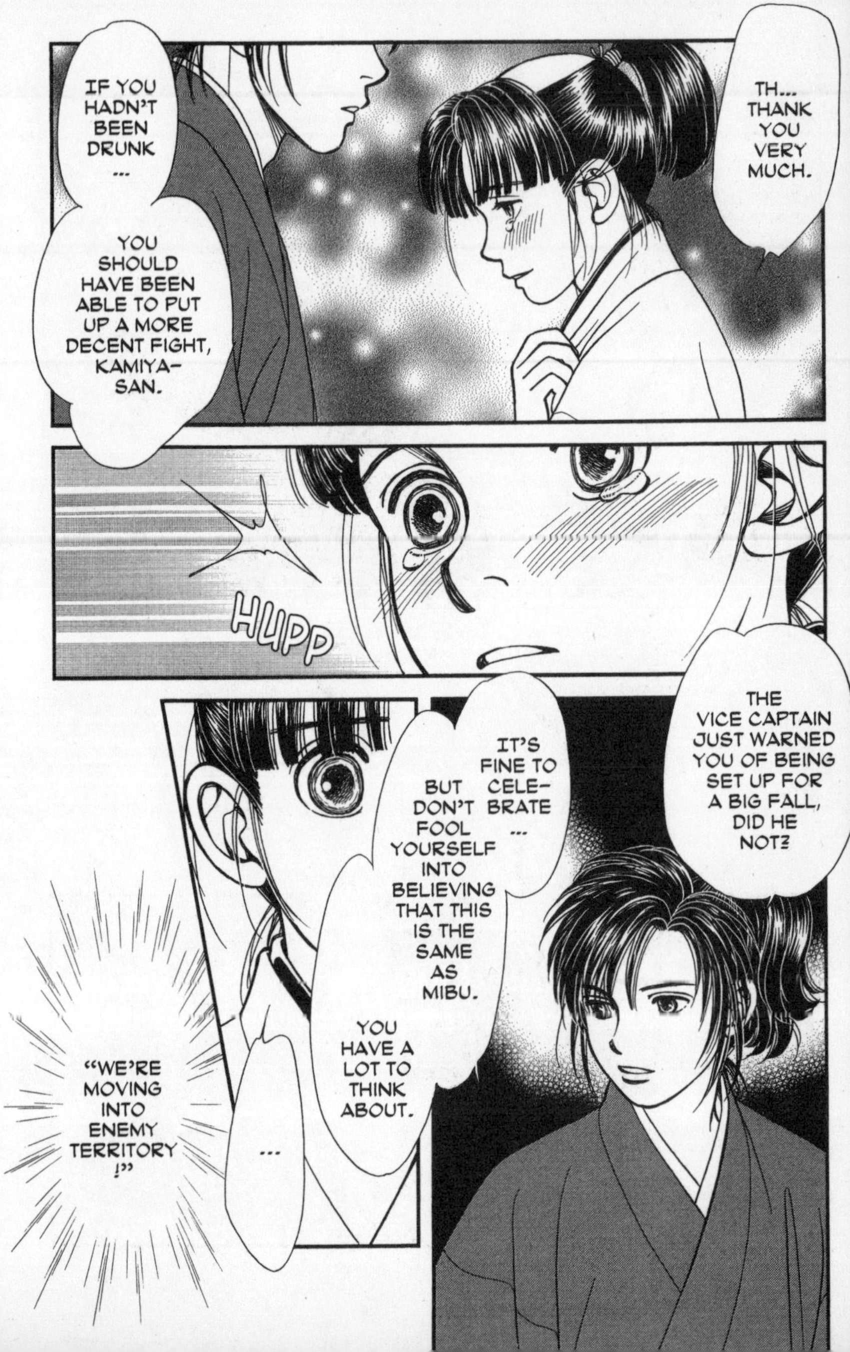
TH... THANK YOU VERY MUCH.
IF YOU HADN'T BEEN DRUNK ...
YOU SHOULD HAVE BEEN ABLE TO PUT UP A MORE DECENT FIGHT, KAMIYA-SAN.
HUPP
THE VICE CAPTAIN JUST WARNED YOU OF BEING SET UP FOR A BIG FALL, DID HE NOT?
IT'S FINE TO CELE-BRATE ...
BUT DON'T FOOL YOURSELF INTO BELIEVING THAT THIS IS THE SAME AS MIBU.
YOU HAVE A LOT TO THINK ABOUT.
...
"WE'RE MOVING INTO ENEMY TERRITORY!"

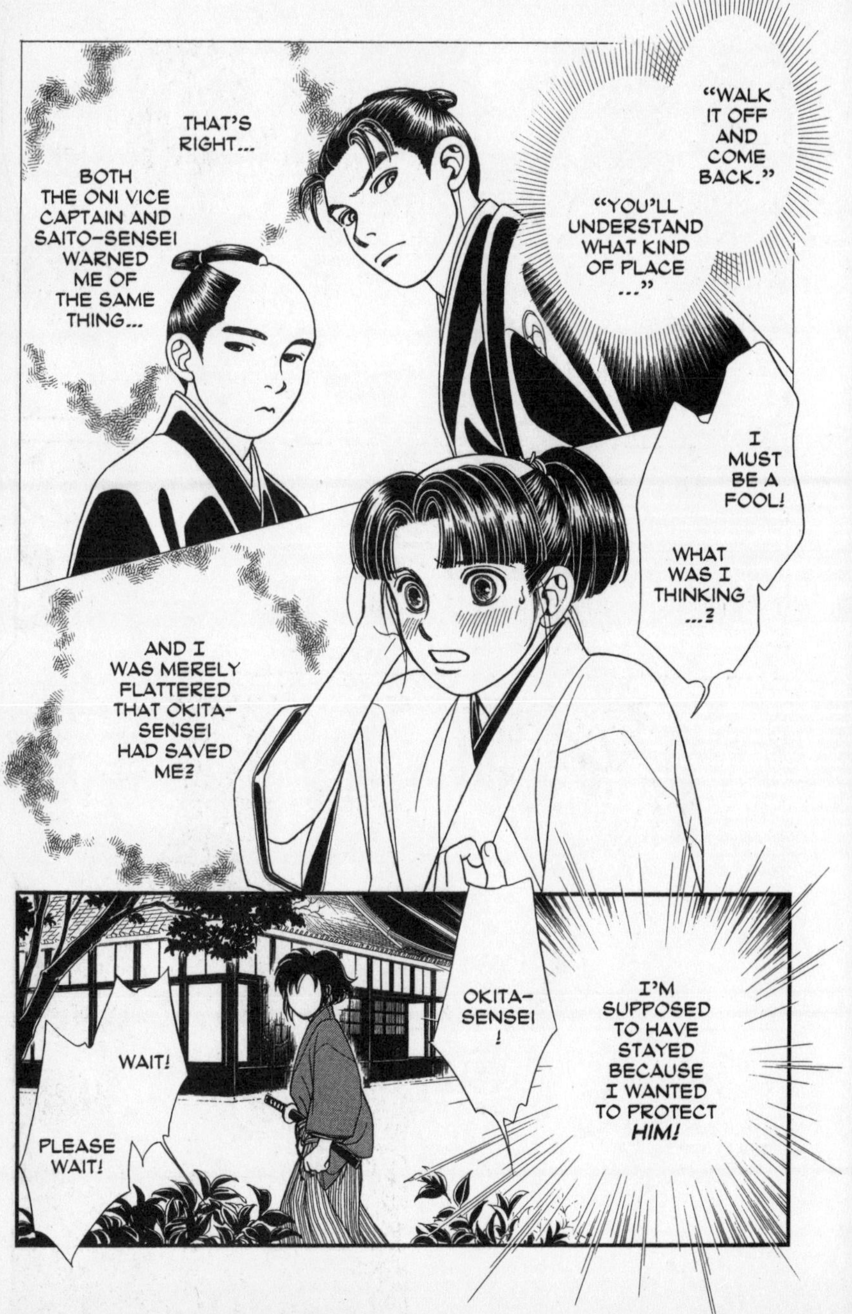
"WALK IT OFF AND COME BACK."
"YOU'LL UNDERSTAND WHAT KIND OF PLACE ..."
THAT'S RIGHT...
BOTH THE ONI VICE CAPTAIN AND SAITO-SENSEI WARNED ME OF THE SAME THING...
I MUST BE A FOOL!
WHAT WAS I THINKING ...?
AND I WAS MERELY FLATTERED THAT OKITA-SENSEI HAD SAVED ME?
I'M SUPPOSED TO HAVE STAYED BECAUSE I WANTED TO PROTECT *HIM!*
OKITA-SENSEI !
WAIT!
PLEASE WAIT!

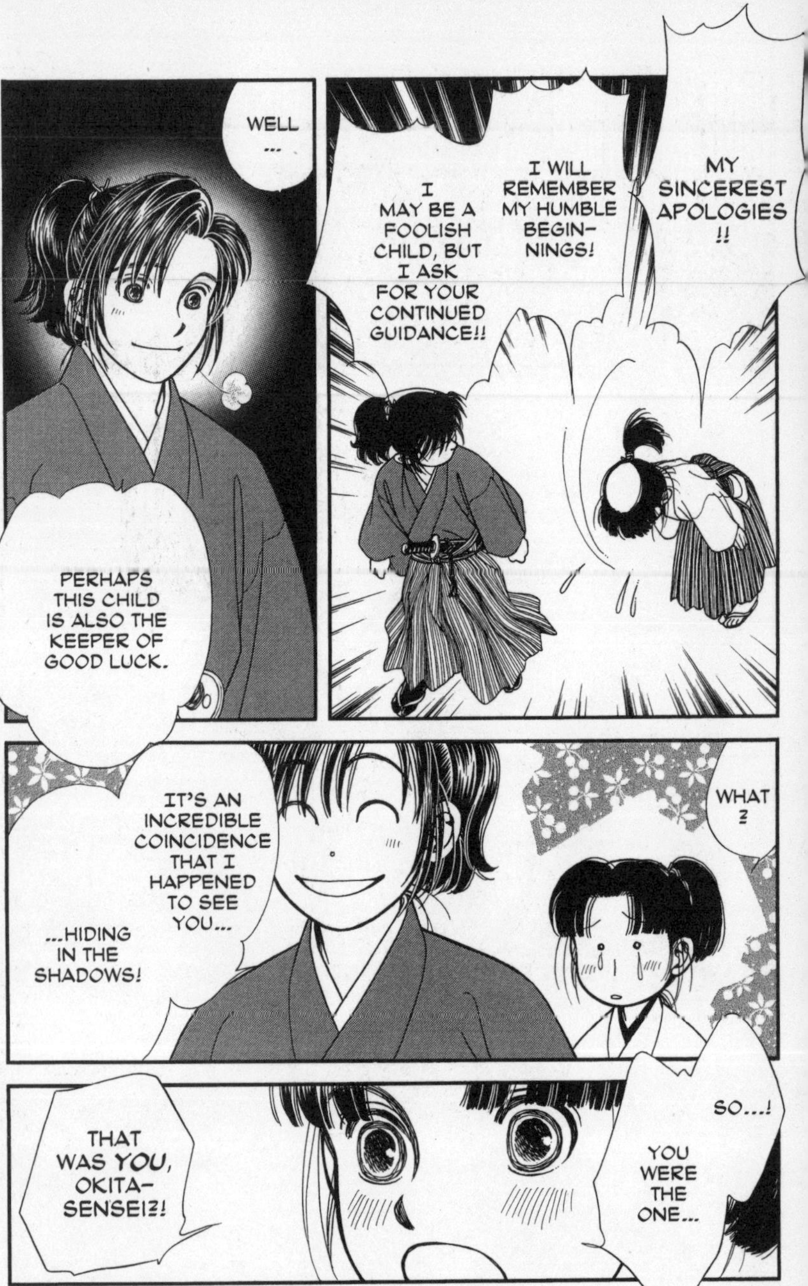
MY SINCEREST APOLOGIES!!
I WILL REMEMBER MY HUMBLE BEGINNINGS!
I MAY BE A FOOLISH CHILD, BUT I ASK FOR YOUR CONTINUED GUIDANCE!!
WELL...
PERHAPS THIS CHILD IS ALSO THE KEEPER OF GOOD LUCK.
WHAT?
IT'S AN INCREDIBLE COINCIDENCE THAT I HAPPENED TO SEE YOU...
...HIDING IN THE SHADOWS!
SO...!
YOU WERE THE ONE...
THAT WAS YOU, OKITA-SENSEI?!

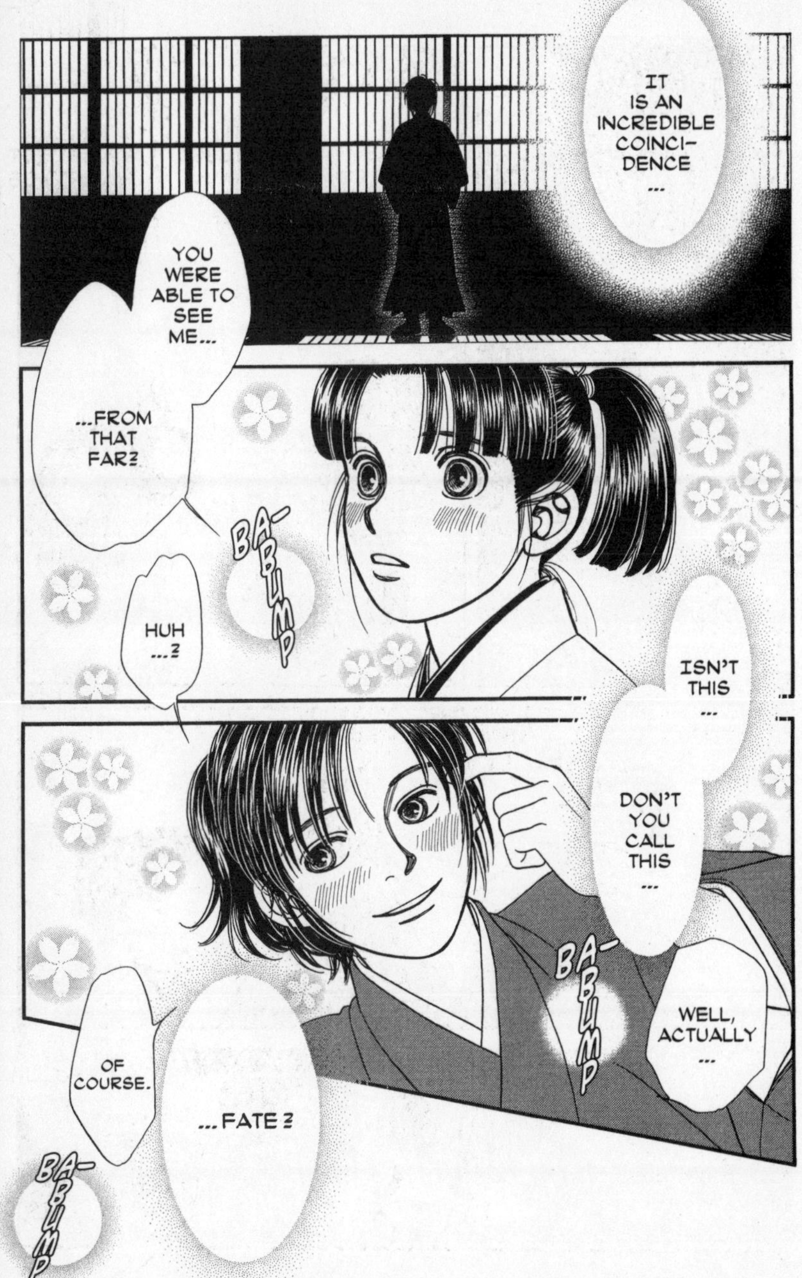
IT IS AN INCREDIBLE COINCIDENCE ...
YOU WERE ABLE TO SEE ME...
...FROM THAT FAR?
BA-BUMP
HUH ...?
ISN'T THIS ...
DON'T YOU CALL THIS ...
BA-BUMP
WELL, ACTUALLY ...
...FATE?
OF COURSE.
BA-BUMP

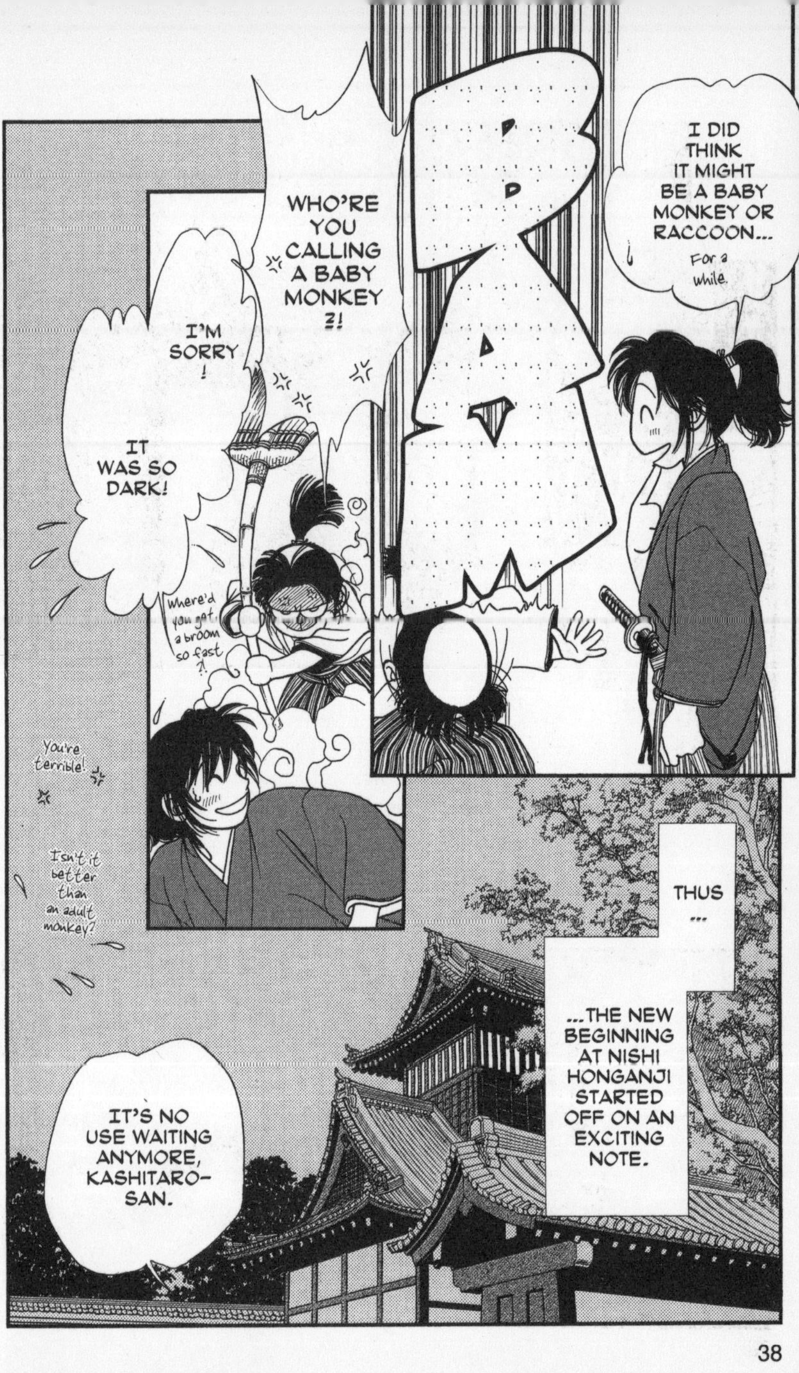
I DID THINK IT MIGHT BE A BABY MONKEY OR RACCOON...
For a while.
WHO'RE YOU CALLING A BABY MONKEY ?!
I'M SORRY!
IT WAS SO DARK!
Where'd you get a broom so fast ?!
You're terrible!
Isn't it better than an adult monkey?
THUS...
...THE NEW BEGINNING AT NISHI HONGANJI STARTED OFF ON AN EXCITING NOTE.
IT'S NO USE WAITING ANYMORE, KASHITARO-SAN.

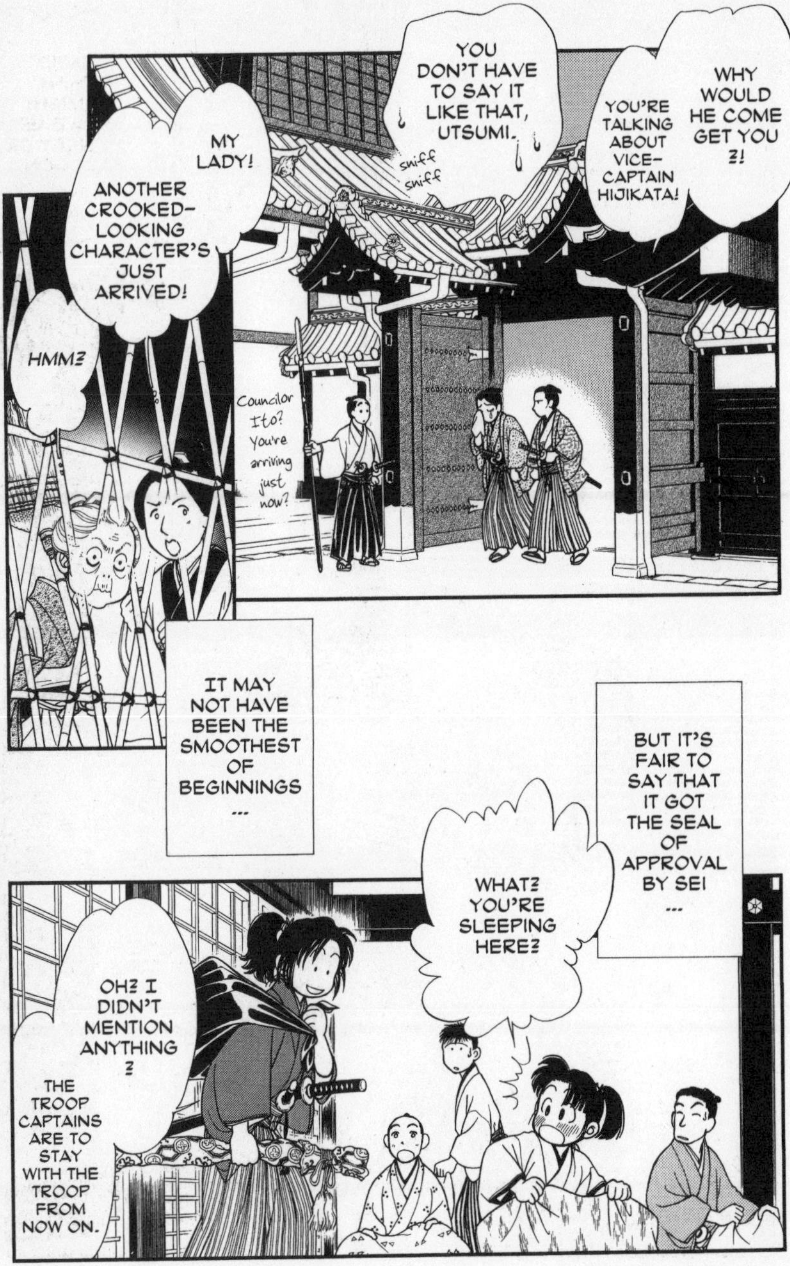
WHY WOULD HE COME GET YOU?!
YOU'RE TALKING ABOUT VICE-CAPTAIN HIJIKATA!
YOU DON'T HAVE TO SAY IT LIKE THAT, UTSUMI.
sniff sniff
Councilor Ito? You're arriving just now?
MY LADY!
ANOTHER CROOKED-LOOKING CHARACTER'S JUST ARRIVED!
HMM?
IT MAY NOT HAVE BEEN THE SMOOTHEST OF BEGINNINGS...
BUT IT'S FAIR TO SAY THAT IT GOT THE SEAL OF APPROVAL BY SEI...
WHAT? YOU'RE SLEEPING HERE?
OH? I DIDN'T MENTION ANYTHING?
THE TROOP CAPTAINS ARE TO STAY WITH THE TROOP FROM NOW ON.

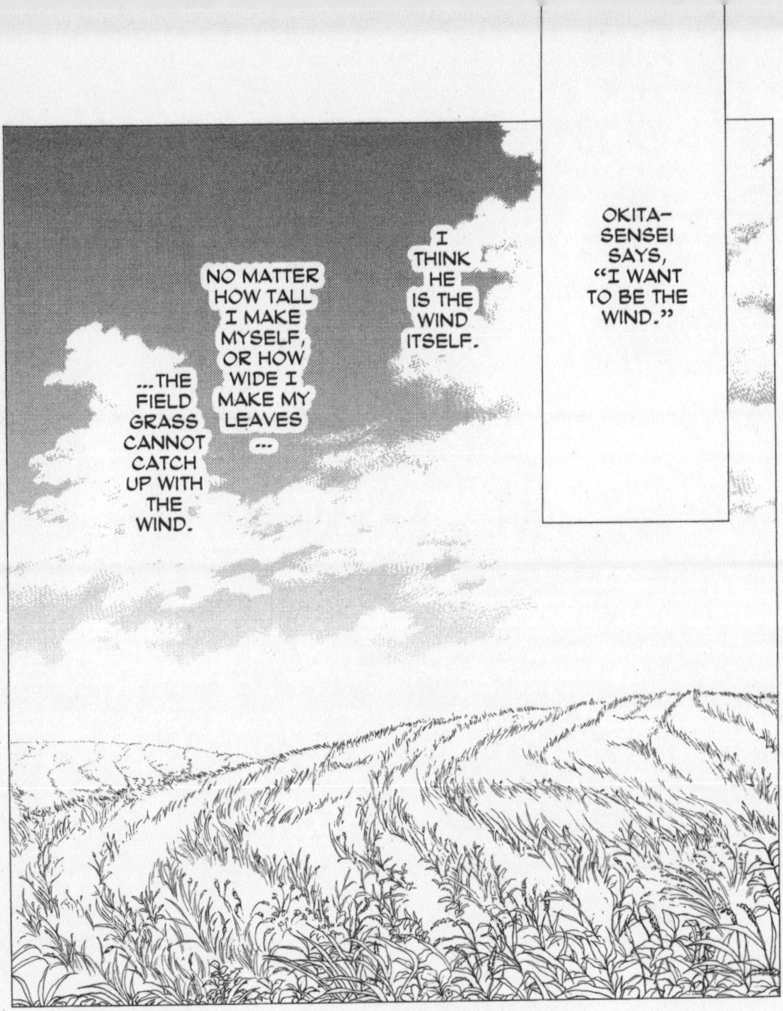
OKITA-SENSEI SAYS, "I WANT TO BE THE WIND."
I THINK HE IS THE WIND ITSELF.
NO MATTER HOW TALL I MAKE MYSELF, OR HOW WIDE I MAKE MY LEAVES ...
...THE FIELD GRASS CANNOT CATCH UP WITH THE WIND.

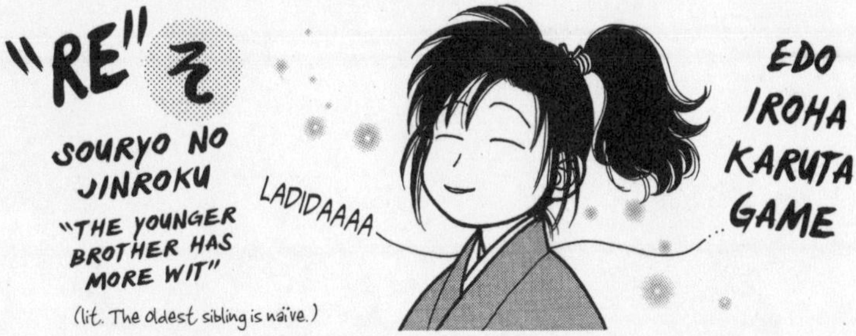
EDO IROHA KARUTA GAME
LADIDAAAA
"RE" れ
SOURYO NO JINROKU
"THE YOUNGER BROTHER HAS MORE WIT"
(lit. The oldest sibling is naïve.)

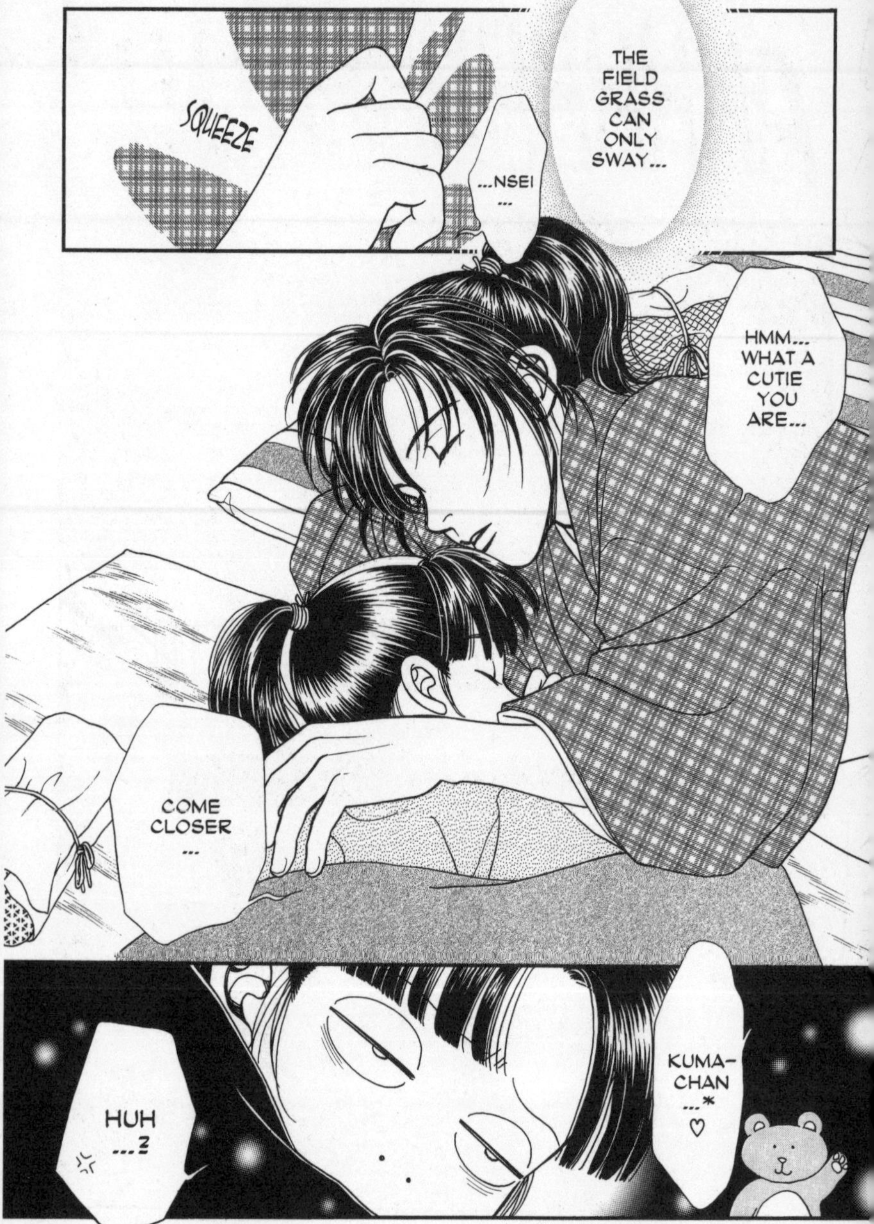
THE FIELD GRASS CAN ONLY SWAY...
...NSEI...
SQUEEZE
HMM... WHAT A CUTIE YOU ARE...
COME CLOSER...
KUMA-CHAN...* ♡
HUH...?

*Kuma means "bear" in Japanese.

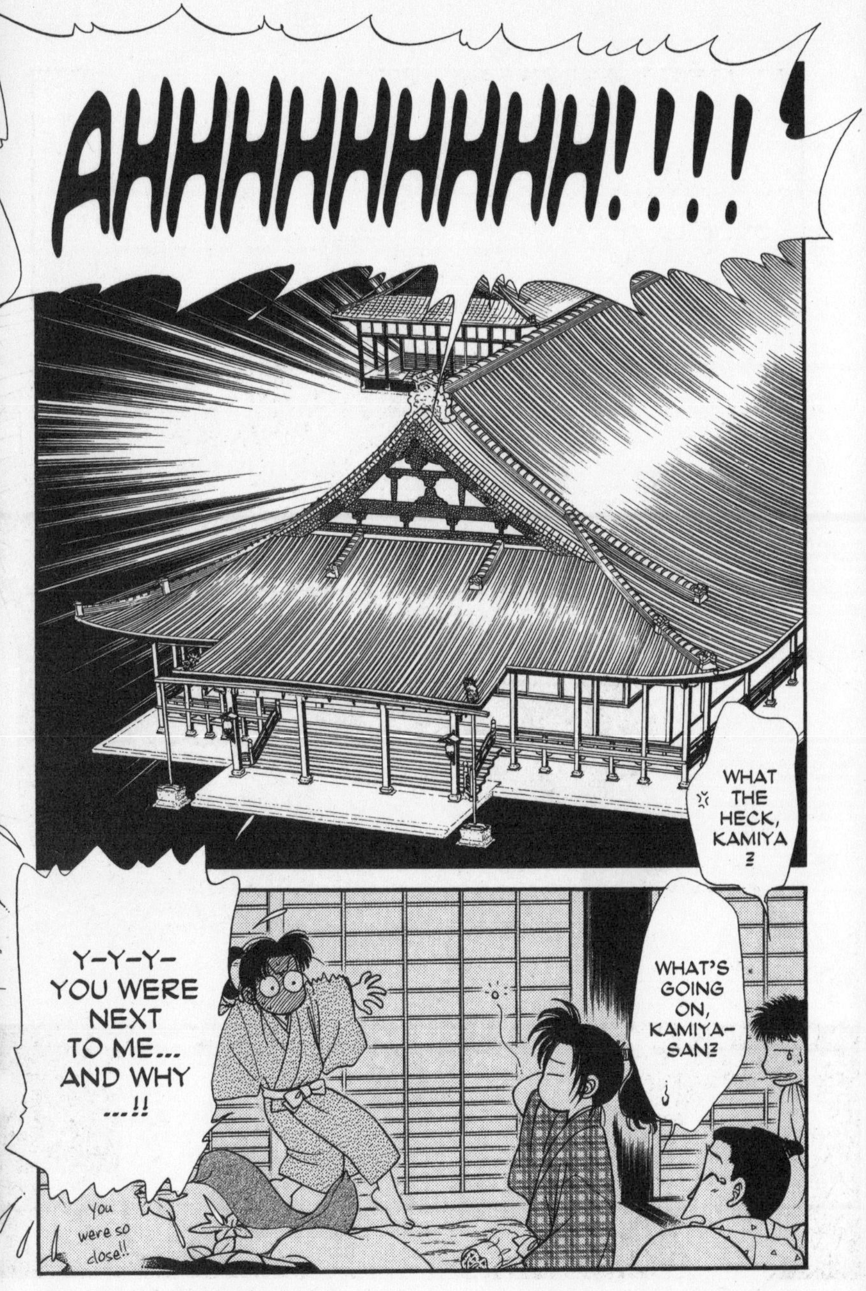
AHHHHHHHHHH!!!!
WHAT THE HECK, KAMIYA?
WHAT'S GOING ON, KAMIYA-SAN?
Y-Y-Y-YOU WERE NEXT TO ME... AND WHY ...!!
You were so close!!

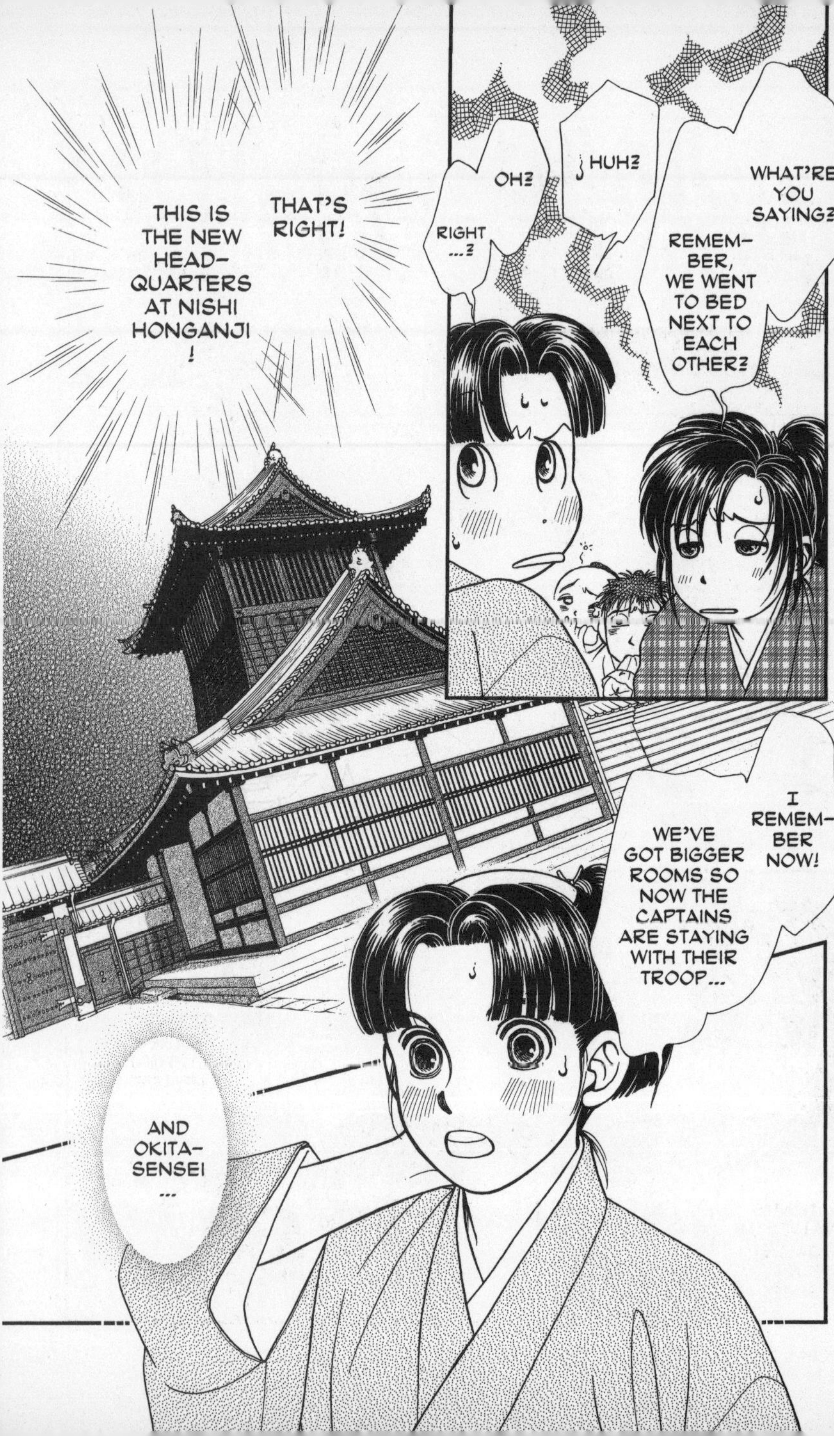
WHAT'RE YOU SAYING?
REMEMBER, WE WENT TO BED NEXT TO EACH OTHER?
HUH?
OH?
RIGHT ...?
THAT'S RIGHT!
THIS IS THE NEW HEADQUARTERS AT NISHI HONGANJI!
I REMEMBER NOW!
WE'VE GOT BIGGER ROOMS SO NOW THE CAPTAINS ARE STAYING WITH THEIR TROOP...
AND OKITA-SENSEI ...

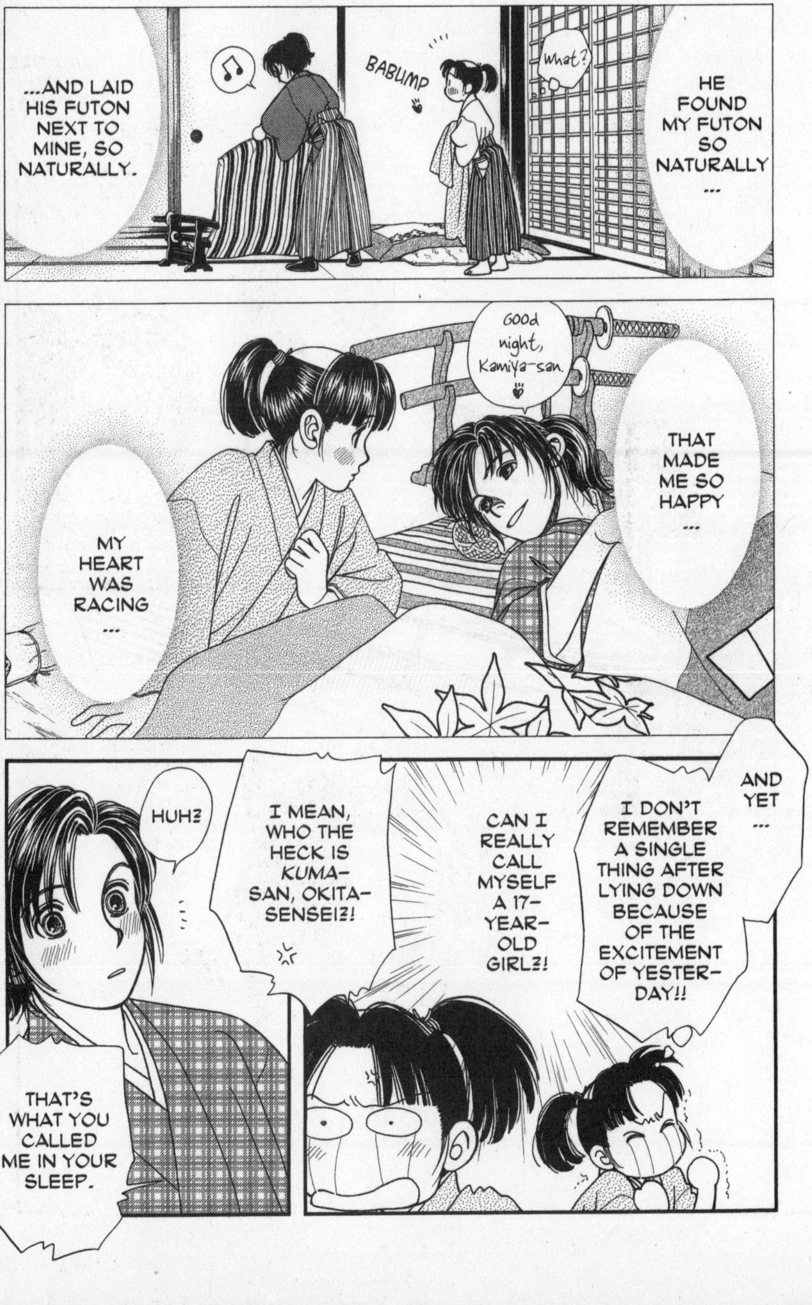
HE FOUND MY FUTON SO NATURALLY ...
What?
BABUMP
...AND LAID HIS FUTON NEXT TO MINE, SO NATURALLY.
THAT MADE ME SO HAPPY ...
Good night, Kamiya-san.
MY HEART WAS RACING ...
AND YET ...
I DON'T REMEMBER A SINGLE THING AFTER LYING DOWN BECAUSE OF THE EXCITEMENT OF YESTERDAY!!
CAN I REALLY CALL MYSELF A 17-YEAR-OLD GIRL?!
I MEAN, WHO THE HECK IS KUMA-SAN, OKITA-SENSEI?!
HUH?
THAT'S WHAT YOU CALLED ME IN YOUR SLEEP.

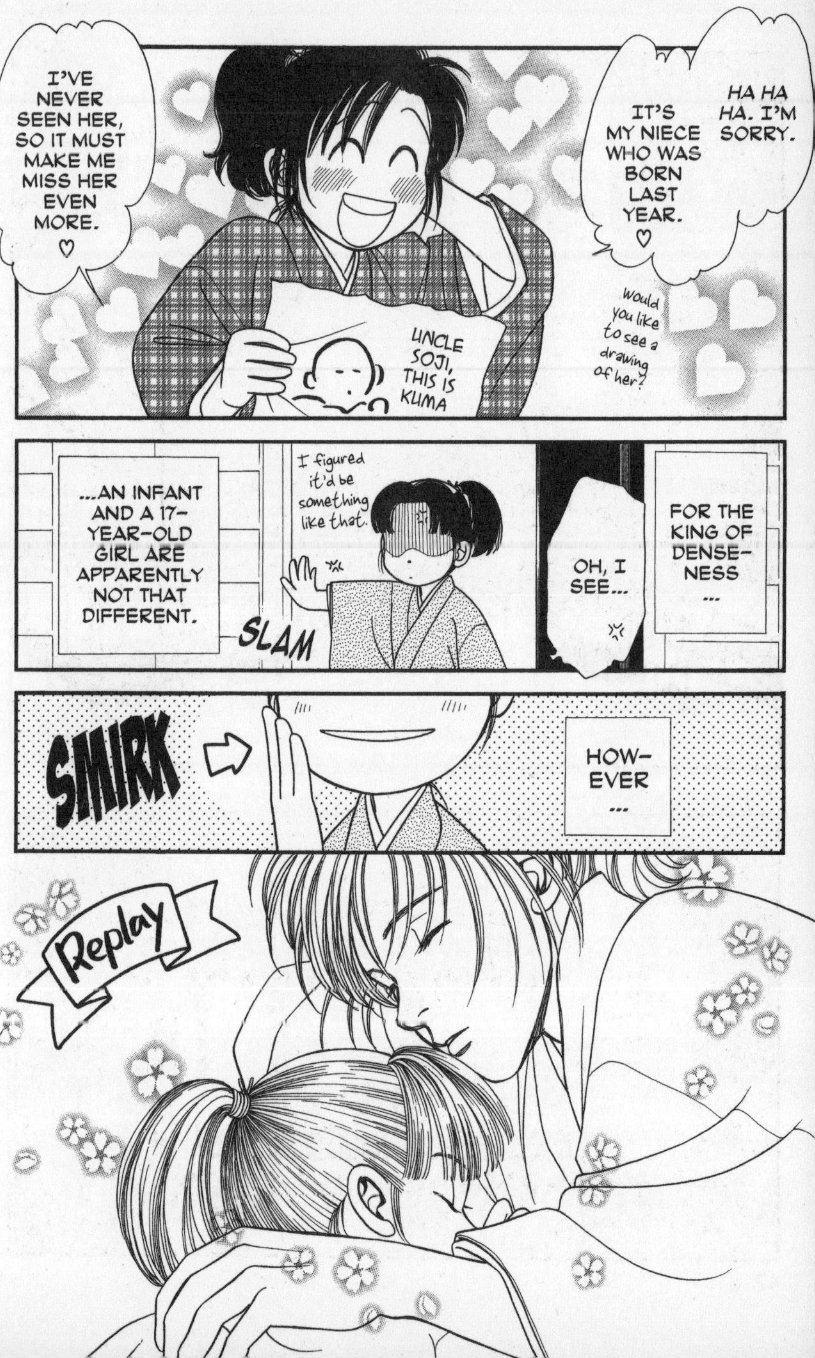
HA HA HA. I'M SORRY.
IT'S MY NIECE WHO WAS BORN LAST YEAR. ♡
Would you like to see a drawing of her?
UNCLE SOJI, THIS IS KUMA
I'VE NEVER SEEN HER, SO IT MUST MAKE ME MISS HER EVEN MORE. ♡
FOR THE KING OF DENSE-NESS ...
OH, I SEE...
I figured it'd be something like that.
SLAM
...AN INFANT AND A 17-YEAR-OLD GIRL ARE APPARENTLY NOT THAT DIFFERENT.
HOW-EVER ...
SMIRK
Replay

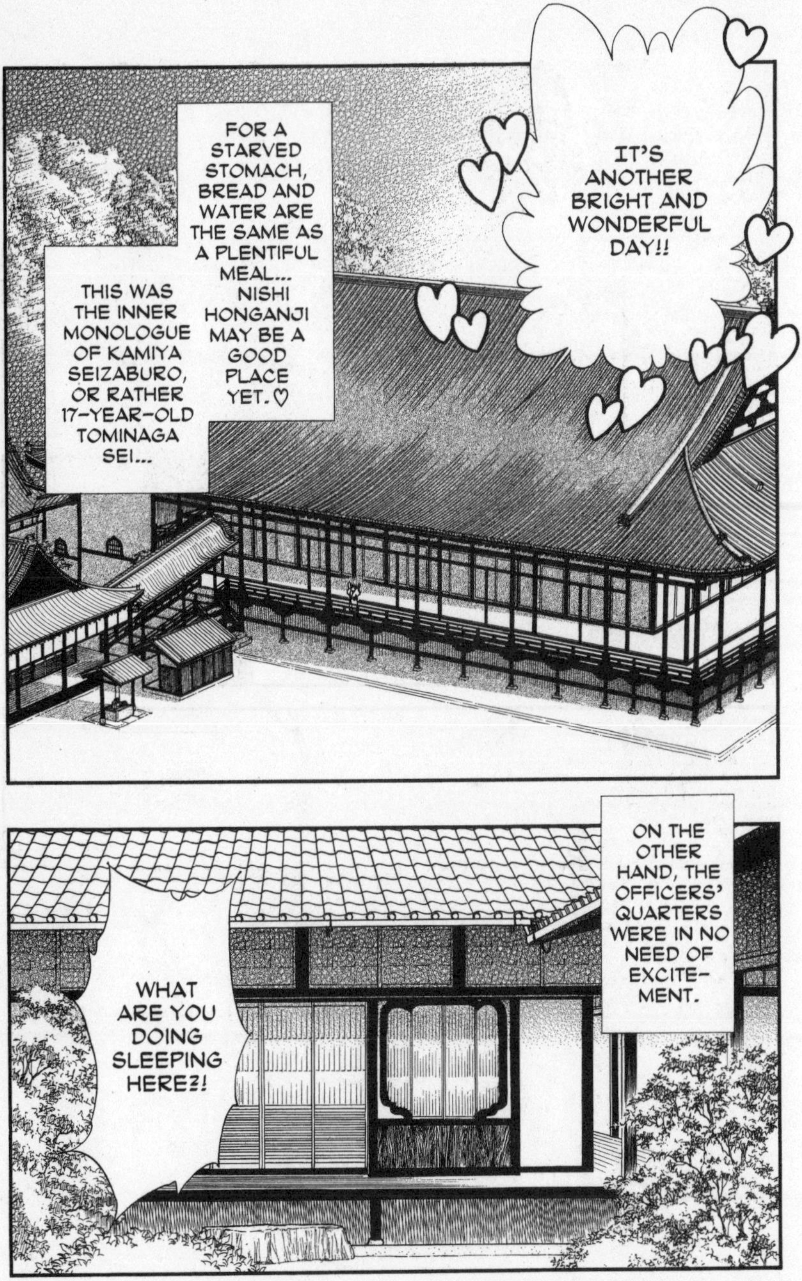
IT'S ANOTHER BRIGHT AND WONDERFUL DAY!!
FOR A STARVED STOMACH, BREAD AND WATER ARE THE SAME AS A PLENTIFUL MEAL... NISHI HONGANJI MAY BE A GOOD PLACE YET. ♡
THIS WAS THE INNER MONOLOGUE OF KAMIYA SEIZABURO, OR RATHER 17-YEAR-OLD TOMINAGA SEI...
ON THE OTHER HAND, THE OFFICERS' QUARTERS WERE IN NO NEED OF EXCITEMENT.
WHAT ARE YOU DOING SLEEPING HERE?!

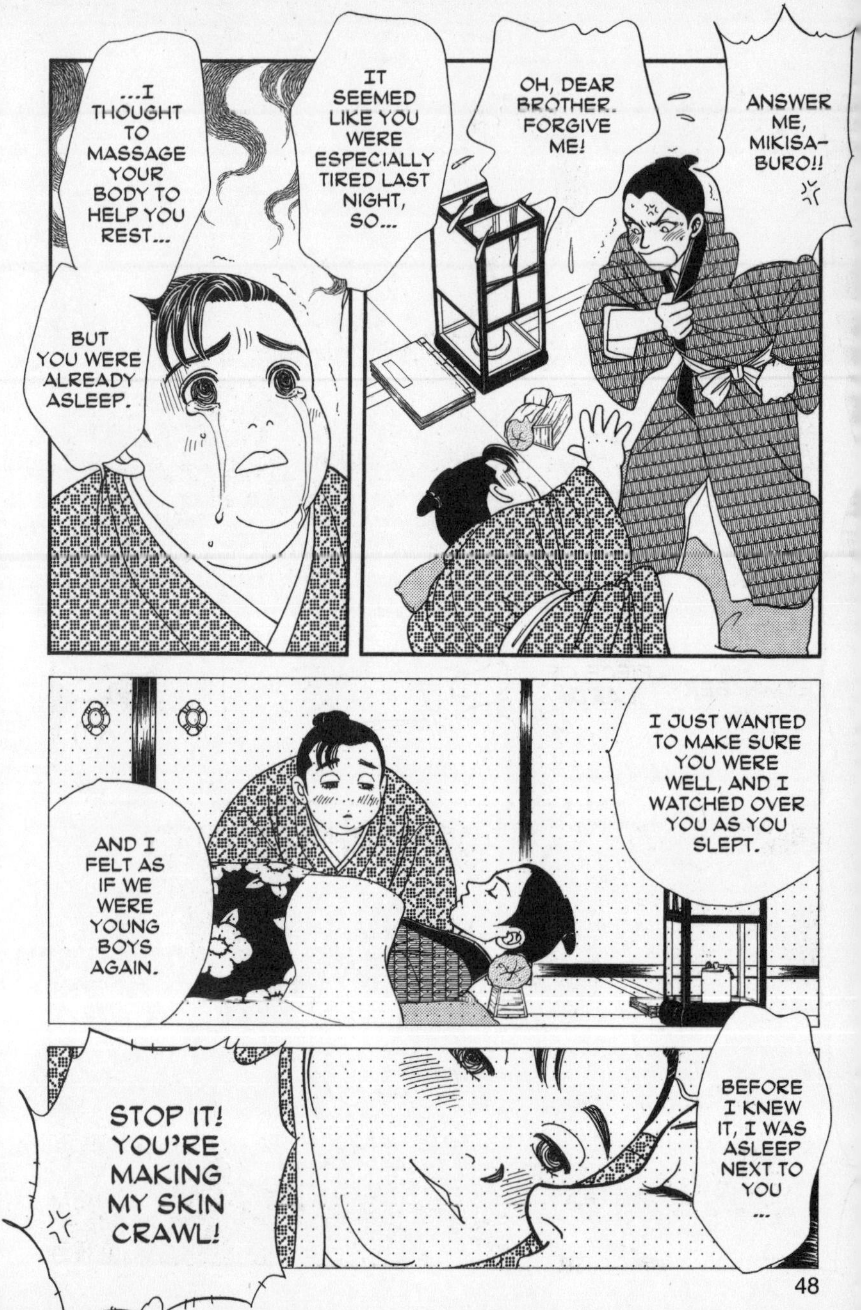

ANSWER ME, MIKISABURO!!
OH, DEAR BROTHER. FORGIVE ME!
IT SEEMED LIKE YOU WERE ESPECIALLY TIRED LAST NIGHT, SO...
...I THOUGHT TO MASSAGE YOUR BODY TO HELP YOU REST...
BUT YOU WERE ALREADY ASLEEP.
I JUST WANTED TO MAKE SURE YOU WERE WELL, AND I WATCHED OVER YOU AS YOU SLEPT.
AND I FELT AS IF WE WERE YOUNG BOYS AGAIN.
BEFORE I KNEW IT, I WAS ASLEEP NEXT TO YOU ...
STOP IT! YOU'RE MAKING MY SKIN CRAWL!

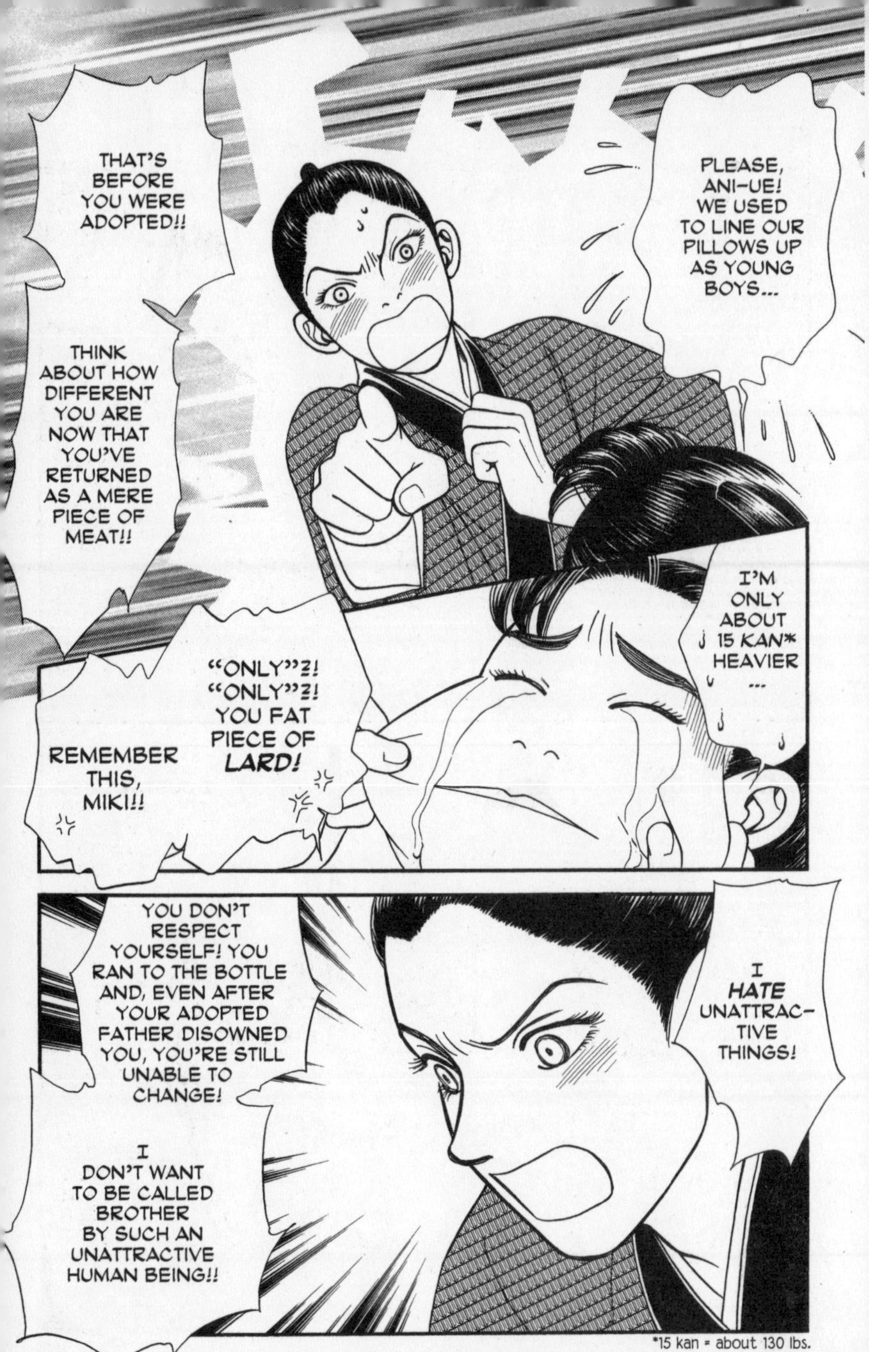
PLEASE, ANI-UE! WE USED TO LINE OUR PILLOWS UP AS YOUNG BOYS...
THAT'S BEFORE YOU WERE ADOPTED!!
THINK ABOUT HOW DIFFERENT YOU ARE NOW THAT YOU'VE RETURNED AS A MERE PIECE OF MEAT!!
I'M ONLY ABOUT 15 KAN* HEAVIER ...
"ONLY"?! "ONLY"?! YOU FAT PIECE OF LARD!
REMEMBER THIS, MIKI!!
I HATE UNATTRACTIVE THINGS!
YOU DON'T RESPECT YOURSELF! YOU RAN TO THE BOTTLE AND, EVEN AFTER YOUR ADOPTED FATHER DISOWNED YOU, YOU'RE STILL UNABLE TO CHANGE!
I DON'T WANT TO BE CALLED BROTHER BY SUCH AN UNATTRACTIVE HUMAN BEING!!

*15 kan = about 130 lbs.

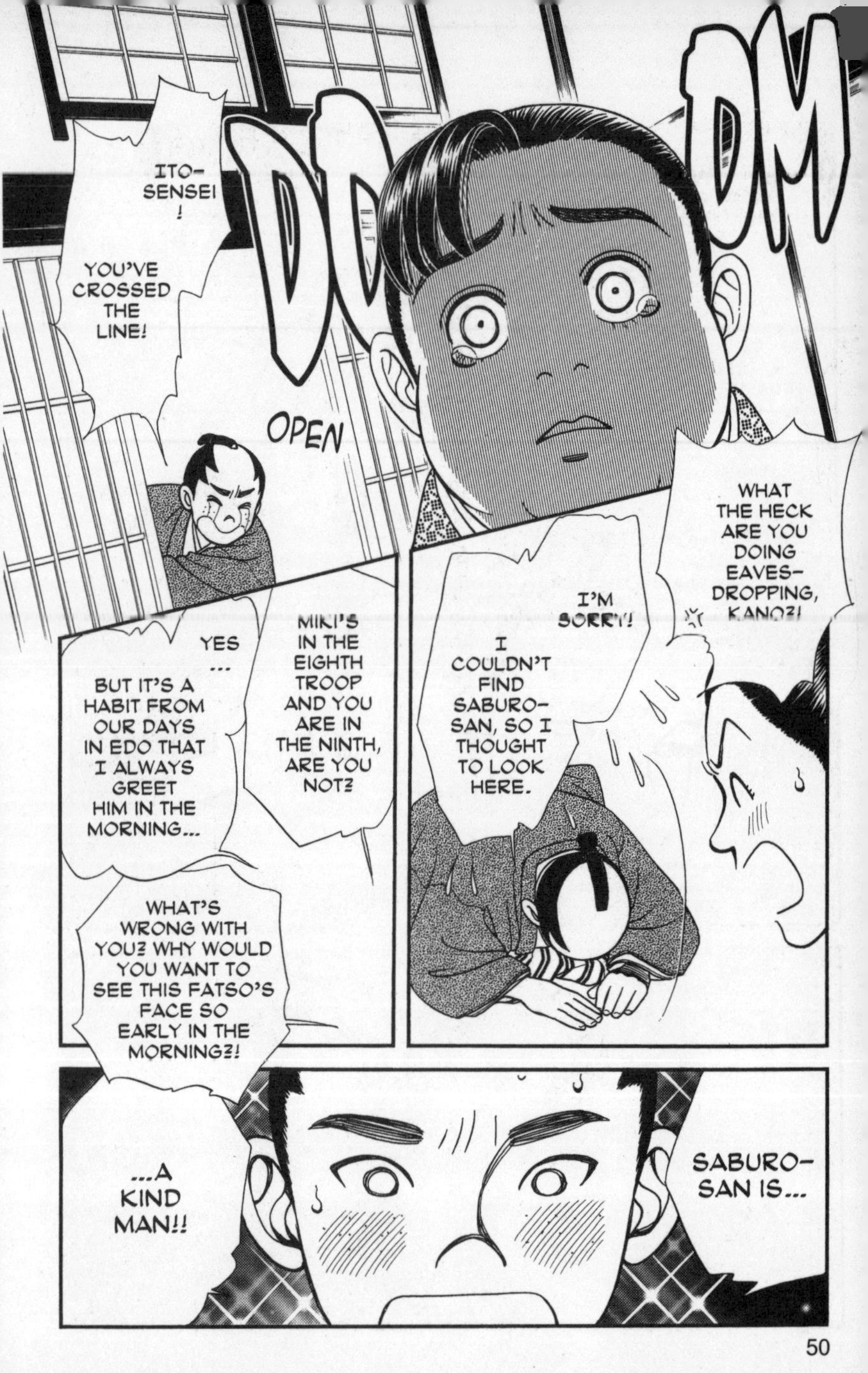
DM
DM
ITO-SENSEI!
YOU'VE CROSSED THE LINE!
OPEN
WHAT THE HECK ARE YOU DOING EAVESDROPPING, KANO?!
I'M SORRY!
I COULDN'T FIND SABURO-SAN, SO I THOUGHT TO LOOK HERE.
MIKI'S IN THE EIGHTH TROOP AND YOU ARE IN THE NINTH, ARE YOU NOT?
YES...
BUT IT'S A HABIT FROM OUR DAYS IN EDO THAT I ALWAYS GREET HIM IN THE MORNING...
WHAT'S WRONG WITH YOU? WHY WOULD YOU WANT TO SEE THIS FATSO'S FACE SO EARLY IN THE MORNING?!
SABURO-SAN IS...
...A KIND MAN!!

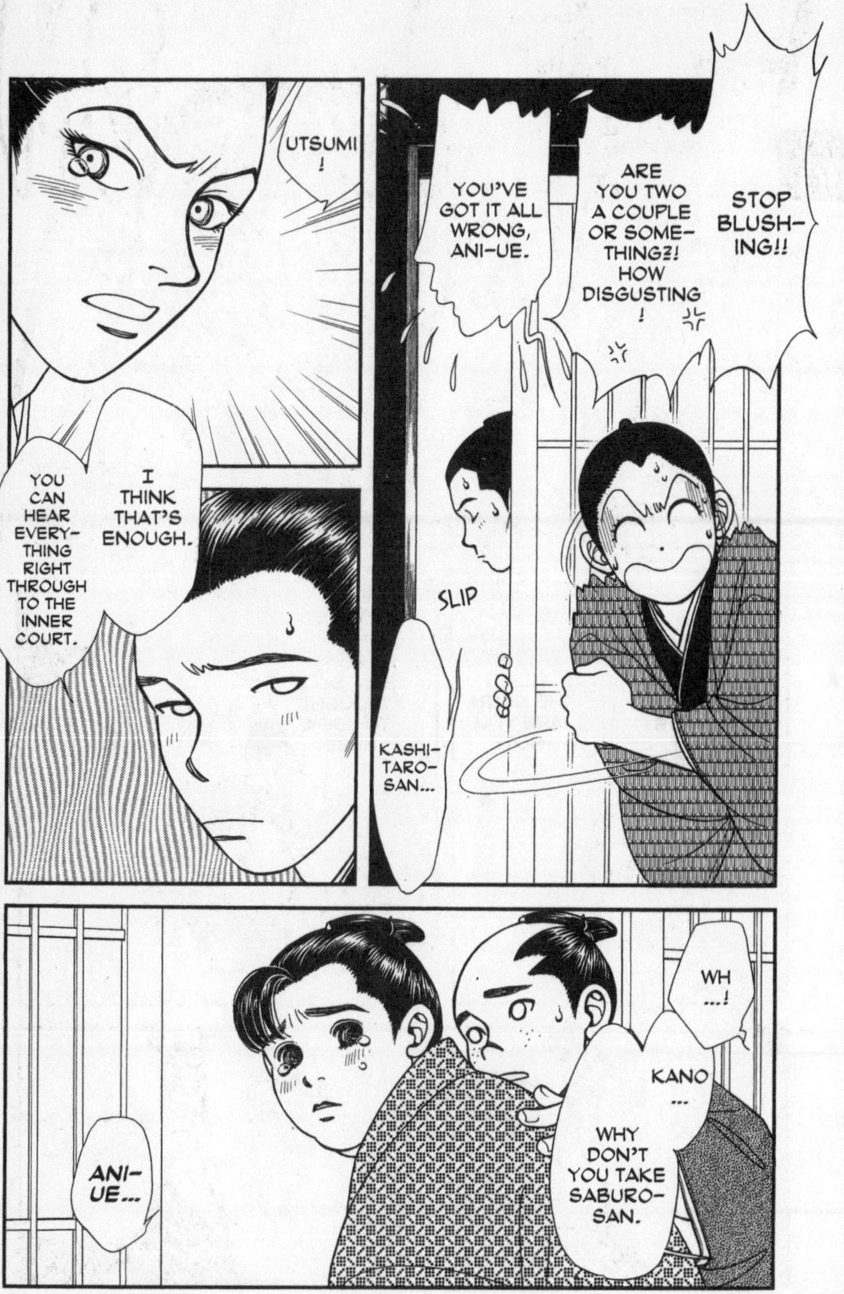
STOP BLUSHING!!
ARE YOU TWO A COUPLE OR SOMETHING?! HOW DISGUSTING!
YOU'VE GOT IT ALL WRONG, ANI-UE.
SLIP
KASHITARO-SAN...
UTSUMI!
I THINK THAT'S ENOUGH.
YOU CAN HEAR EVERYTHING RIGHT THROUGH TO THE INNER COURT.
WH...!
KANO...
WHY DON'T YOU TAKE SABURO-SAN.
ANI-UE...

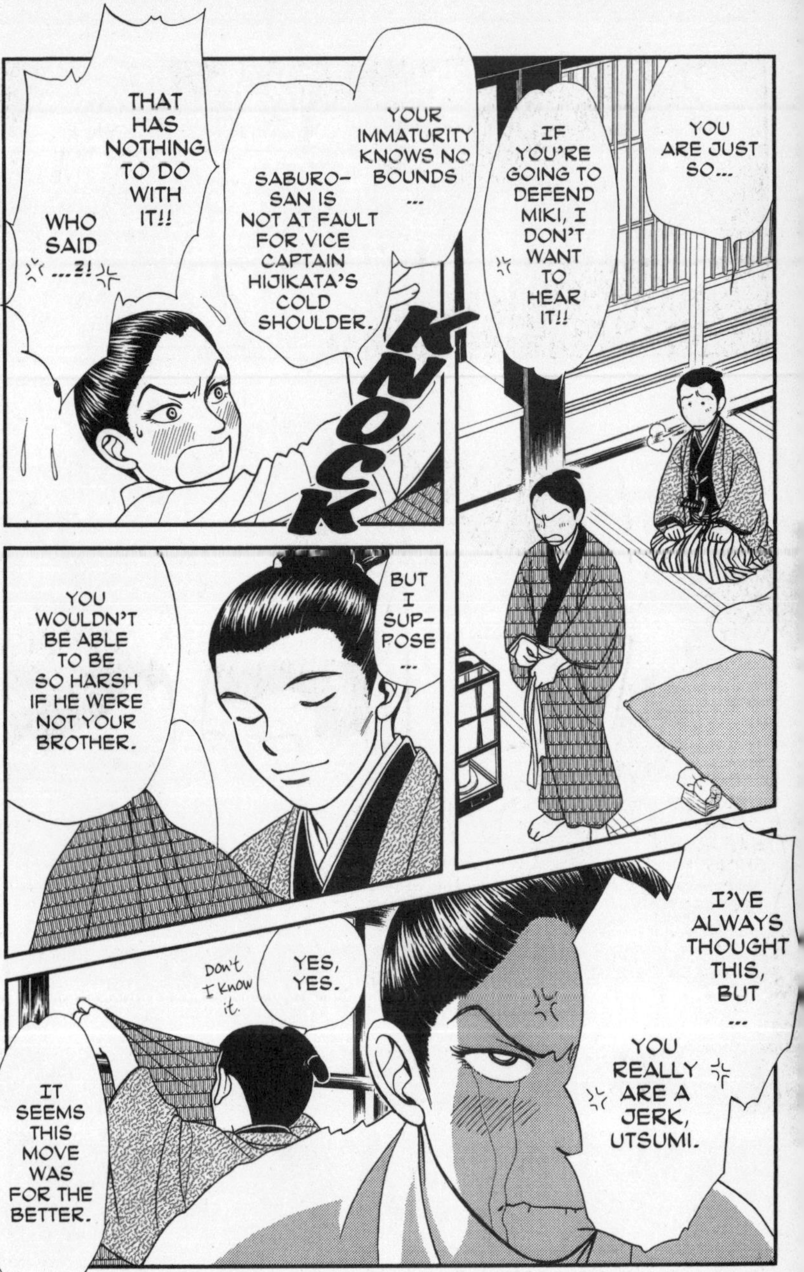
YOU ARE JUST SO...
IF YOU'RE GOING TO DEFEND MIKI, I DON'T WANT TO HEAR IT!!
YOUR IMMATURITY KNOWS NO BOUNDS ...
SABURO-SAN IS NOT AT FAULT FOR VICE CAPTAIN HIJIKATA'S COLD SHOULDER.
THAT HAS NOTHING TO DO WITH IT!!
WHO SAID ...?!
KNOCK
BUT I SUP-POSE ...
YOU WOULDN'T BE ABLE TO BE SO HARSH IF HE WERE NOT YOUR BROTHER.
I'VE ALWAYS THOUGHT THIS, BUT ...
YOU REALLY ARE A JERK, UTSUMI.
YES, YES.
Don't I know it.
IT SEEMS THIS MOVE WAS FOR THE BETTER.

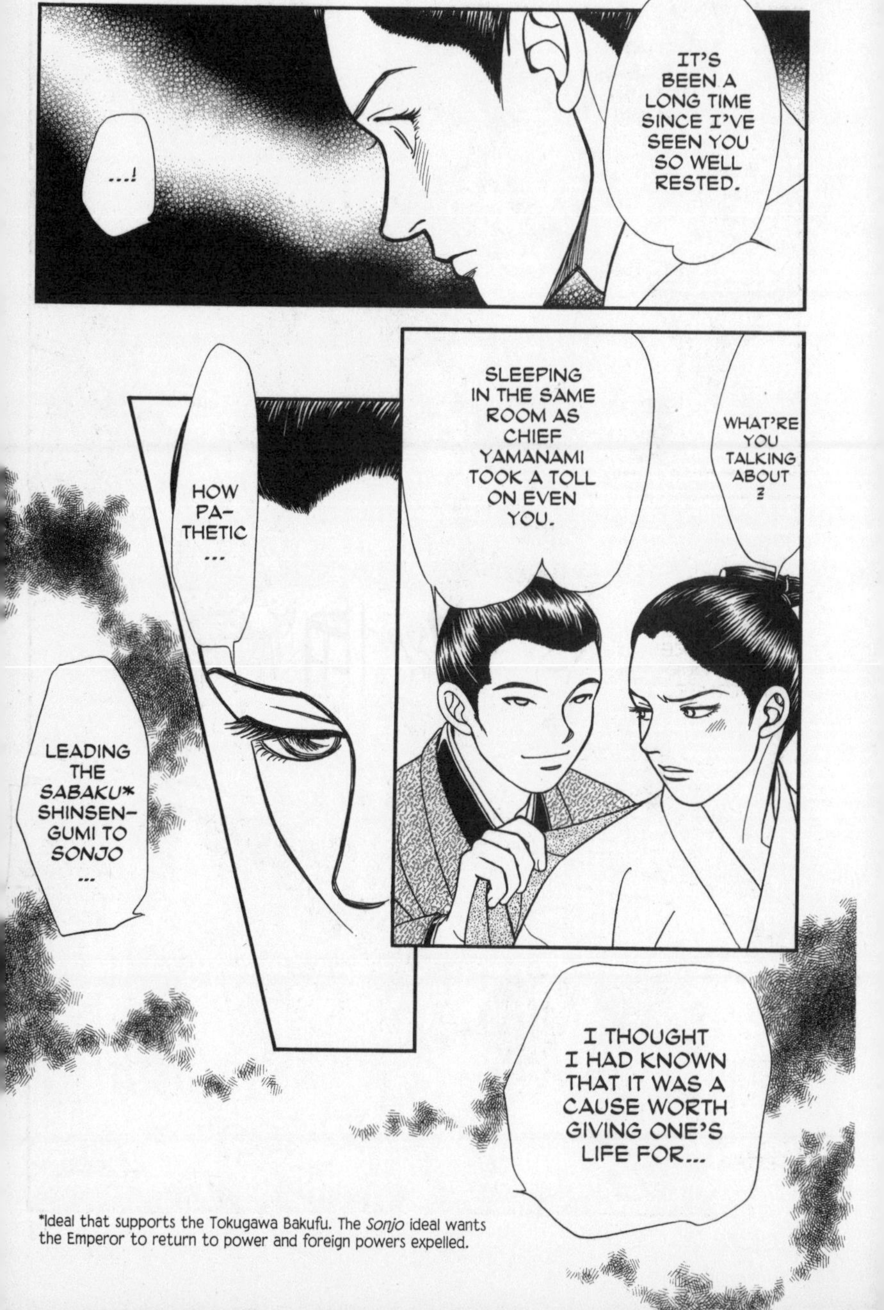
IT'S BEEN A LONG TIME SINCE I'VE SEEN YOU SO WELL RESTED.
...!
WHAT'RE YOU TALKING ABOUT?
SLEEPING IN THE SAME ROOM AS CHIEF YAMANAMI TOOK A TOLL ON EVEN YOU.
HOW PA-THETIC...
LEADING THE *SABAKU** SHINSEN-GUMI TO *SONJO*...
I THOUGHT I HAD KNOWN THAT IT WAS A CAUSE WORTH GIVING ONE'S LIFE FOR...

*Ideal that supports the Tokugawa Bakufu. The *Sonjo* ideal wants the Emperor to return to power and foreign powers expelled.

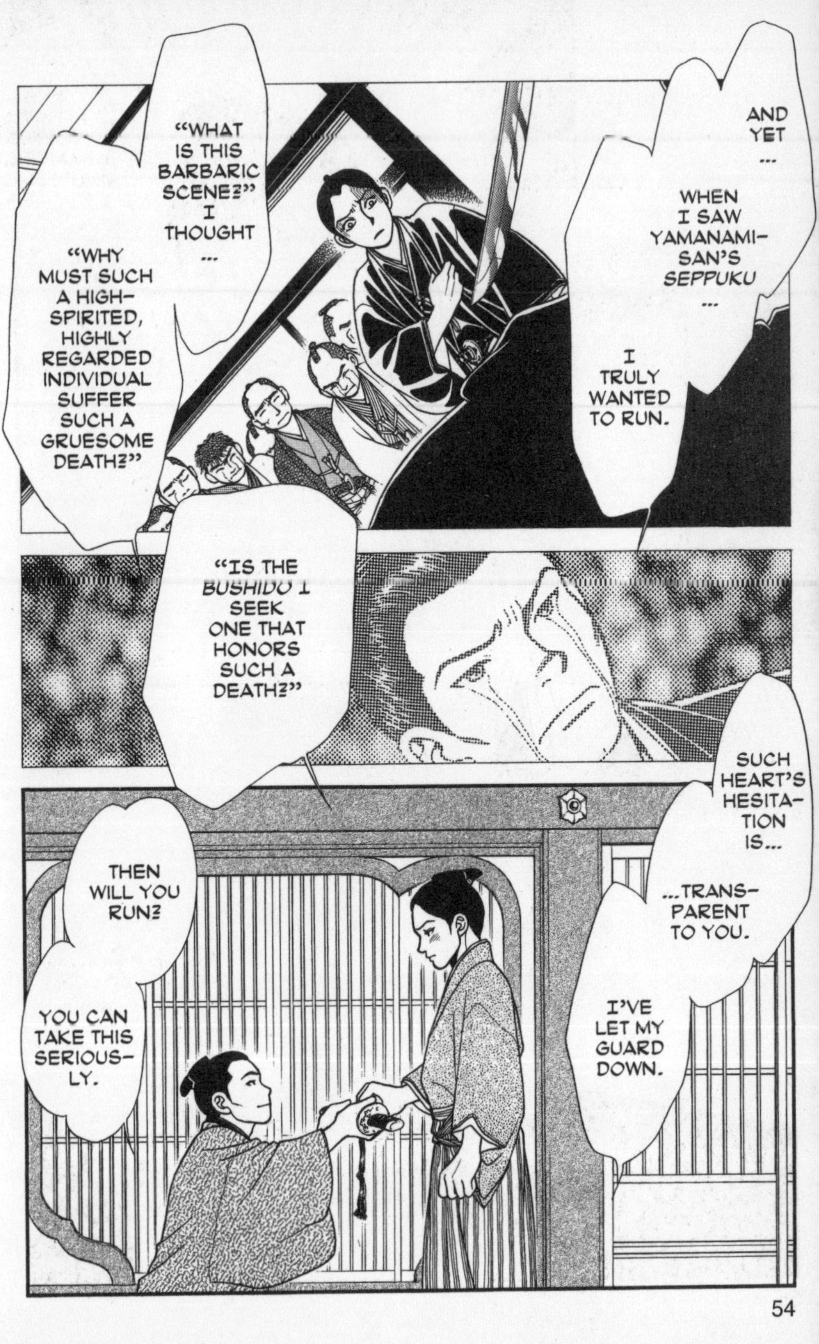
AND YET ... WHEN I SAW YAMANAMI-SAN'S SEPPUKU ...
I TRULY WANTED TO RUN.
"WHAT IS THIS BARBARIC SCENE?" I THOUGHT ...
"WHY MUST SUCH A HIGH-SPIRITED, HIGHLY REGARDED INDIVIDUAL SUFFER SUCH A GRUESOME DEATH?"
"IS THE BUSHIDO I SEEK ONE THAT HONORS SUCH A DEATH?"
SUCH HEART'S HESITATION IS...
...TRANSPARENT TO YOU.
I'VE LET MY GUARD DOWN.
THEN WILL YOU RUN?
YOU CAN TAKE THIS SERIOUSLY.

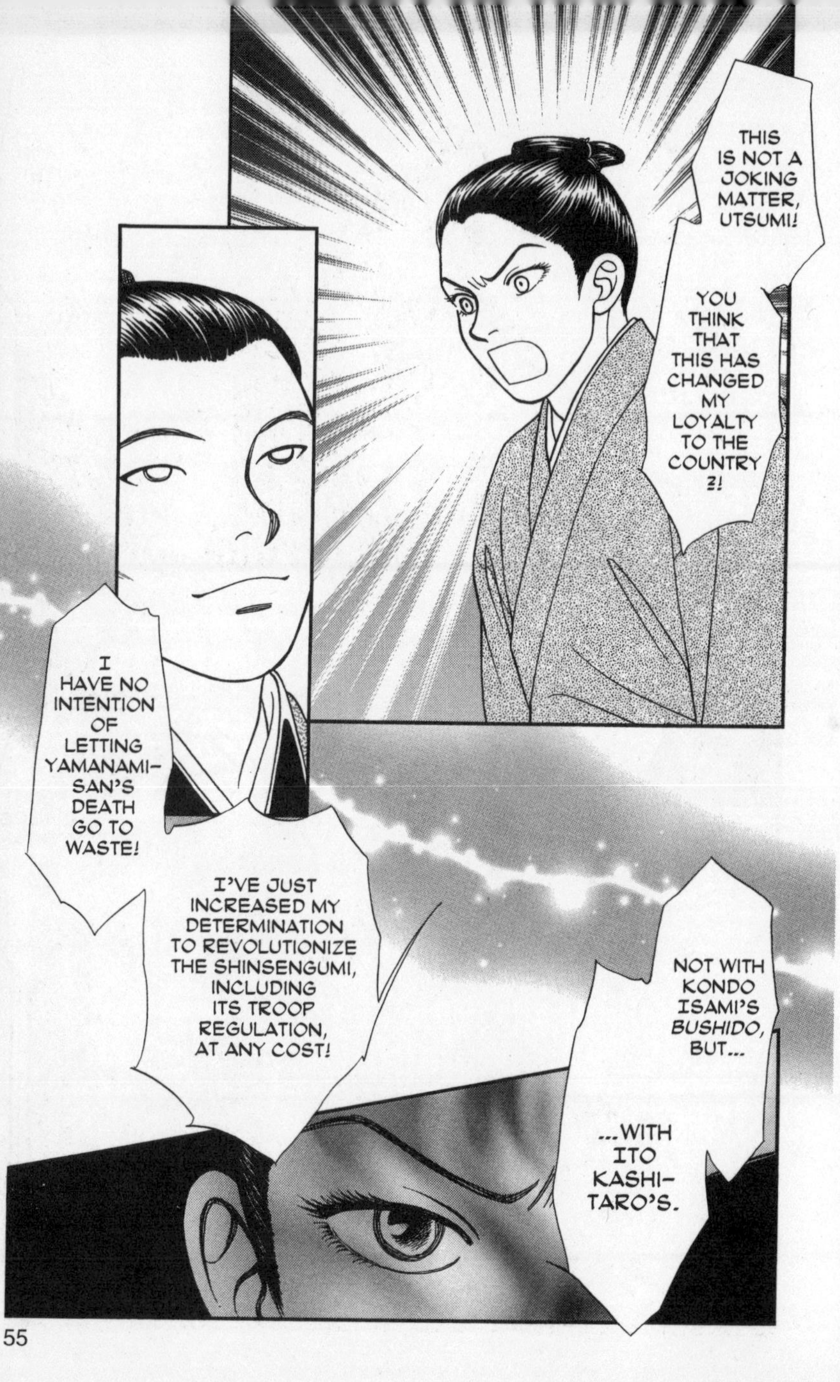
THIS IS NOT A JOKING MATTER, UTSUMI!
YOU THINK THAT THIS HAS CHANGED MY LOYALTY TO THE COUNTRY ?!
I HAVE NO INTENTION OF LETTING YAMANAMI-SAN'S DEATH GO TO WASTE!
I'VE JUST INCREASED MY DETERMINATION TO REVOLUTIONIZE THE SHINSENGUMI, INCLUDING ITS TROOP REGULATION, AT ANY COST!
NOT WITH KONDO ISAMI'S *BUSHIDO*, BUT...
...WITH ITO KASHI-TARO'S.

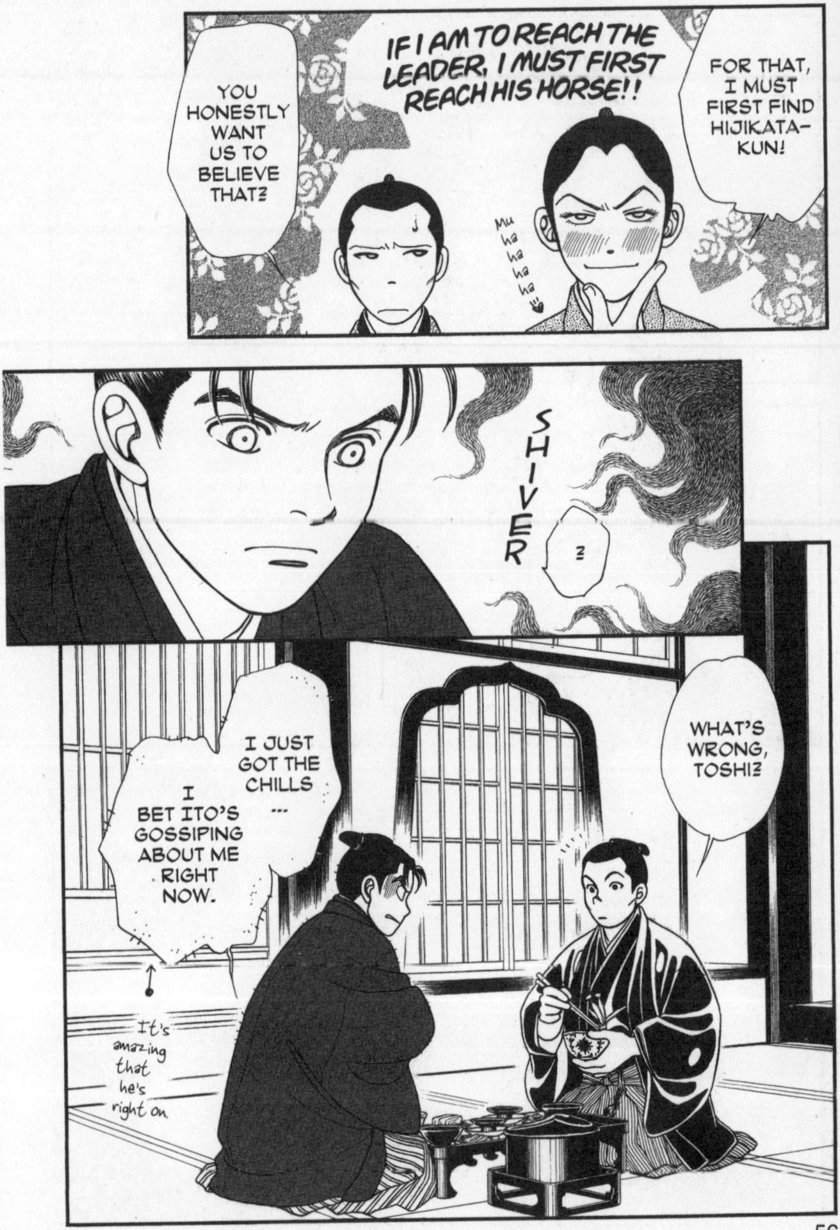
FOR THAT, I MUST FIRST FIND HIJIKATA-KUN!
IF I AM TO REACH THE LEADER, I MUST FIRST REACH HIS HORSE!!
Mu ha ha ha ha
YOU HONESTLY WANT US TO BELIEVE THAT?
SHIVER
?
WHAT'S WRONG, TOSHI?
I JUST GOT THE CHILLS...
I BET ITO'S GOSSIPING ABOUT ME RIGHT NOW.
It's amazing that he's right on.

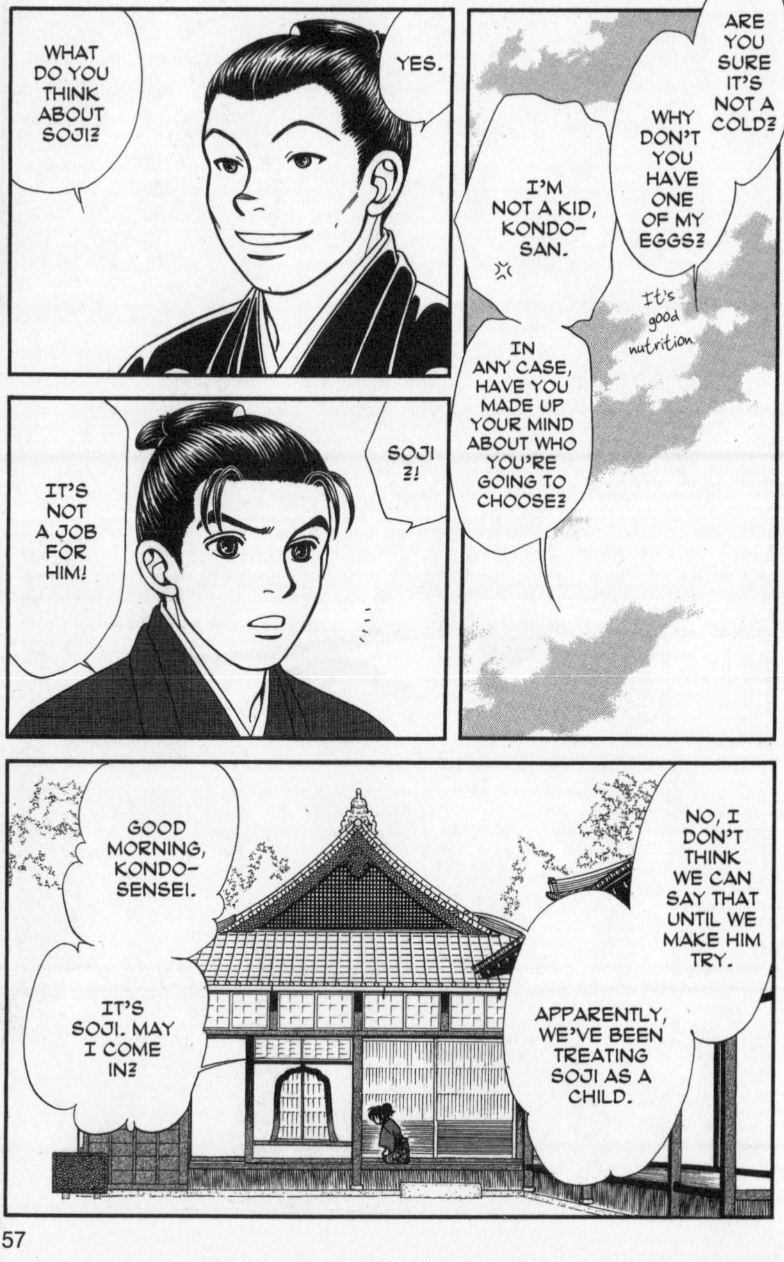
ARE YOU SURE IT'S NOT A COLD?
WHY DON'T YOU HAVE ONE OF MY EGGS?
It's good nutrition
I'M NOT A KID, KONDO-SAN.
IN ANY CASE, HAVE YOU MADE UP YOUR MIND ABOUT WHO YOU'RE GOING TO CHOOSE?
YES.
WHAT DO YOU THINK ABOUT SOJI?
SOJI?!
IT'S NOT A JOB FOR HIM!
NO, I DON'T THINK WE CAN SAY THAT UNTIL WE MAKE HIM TRY.
APPARENTLY, WE'VE BEEN TREATING SOJI AS A CHILD.
GOOD MORNING, KONDO-SENSEI.
IT'S SOJI. MAY I COME IN?

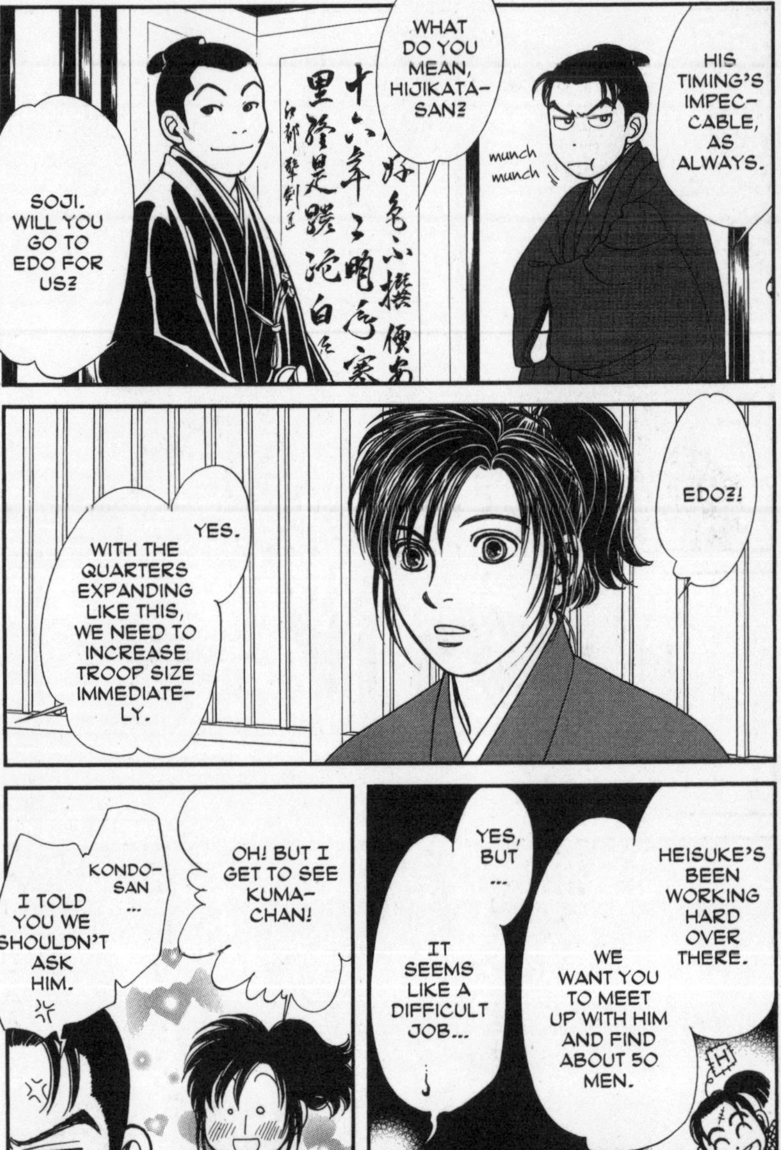
HIS TIMING'S IMPECCABLE, AS ALWAYS.
munch munch
WHAT DO YOU MEAN, HIJIKATA-SAN?
SOJI. WILL YOU GO TO EDO FOR US?
EDO?!
YES.
WITH THE QUARTERS EXPANDING LIKE THIS, WE NEED TO INCREASE TROOP SIZE IMMEDIATELY.
HEISUKE'S BEEN WORKING HARD OVER THERE.
WE WANT YOU TO MEET UP WITH HIM AND FIND ABOUT 50 MEN.
H
YES, BUT ...
IT SEEMS LIKE A DIFFICULT JOB...
OH! BUT I GET TO SEE KUMA-CHAN!
KONDO-SAN ...
I TOLD YOU WE SHOULDN'T ASK HIM.

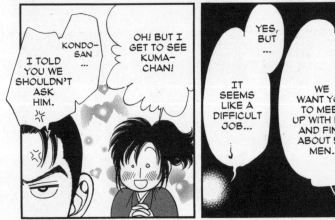

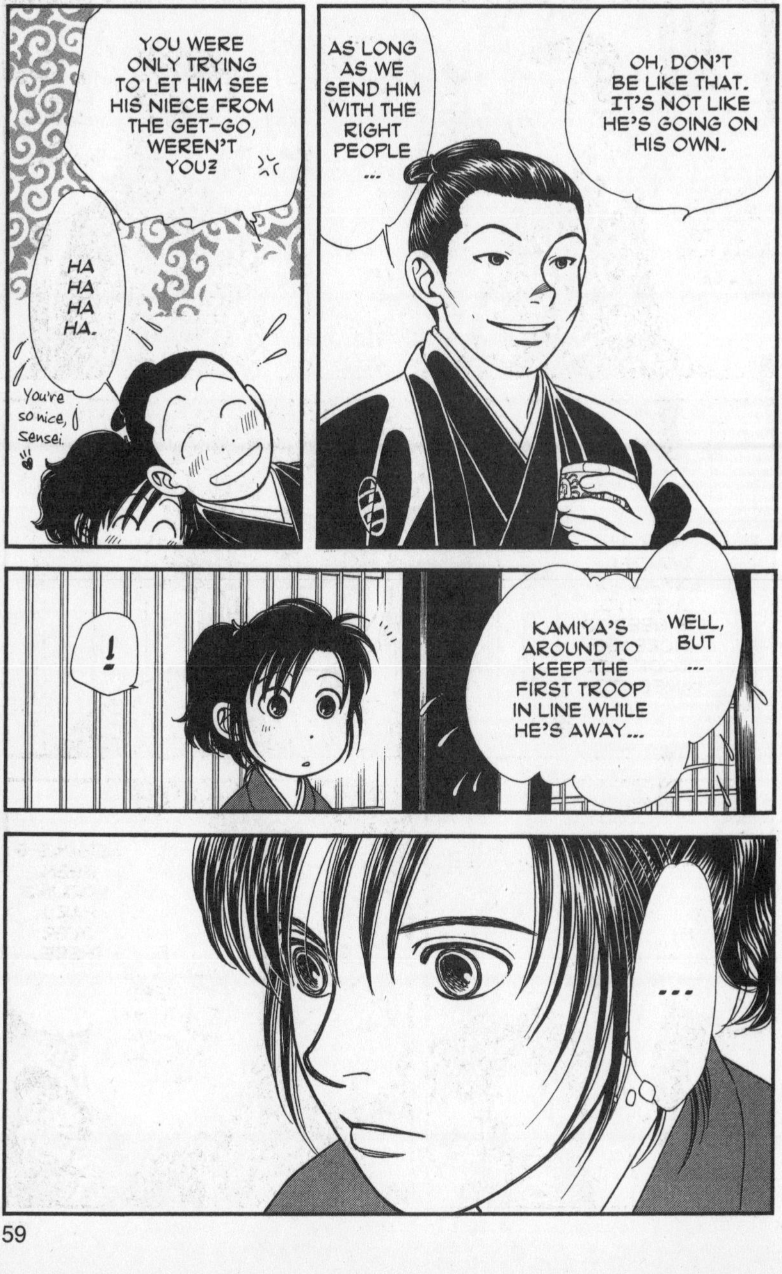
OH, DON'T BE LIKE THAT. IT'S NOT LIKE HE'S GOING ON HIS OWN.
AS LONG AS WE SEND HIM WITH THE RIGHT PEOPLE ...
YOU WERE ONLY TRYING TO LET HIM SEE HIS NIECE FROM THE GET-GO, WEREN'T YOU?
HA HA HA HA.
You're so nice, Sensei.
WELL, BUT ...
KAMIYA'S AROUND TO KEEP THE FIRST TROOP IN LINE WHILE HE'S AWAY...
!
...

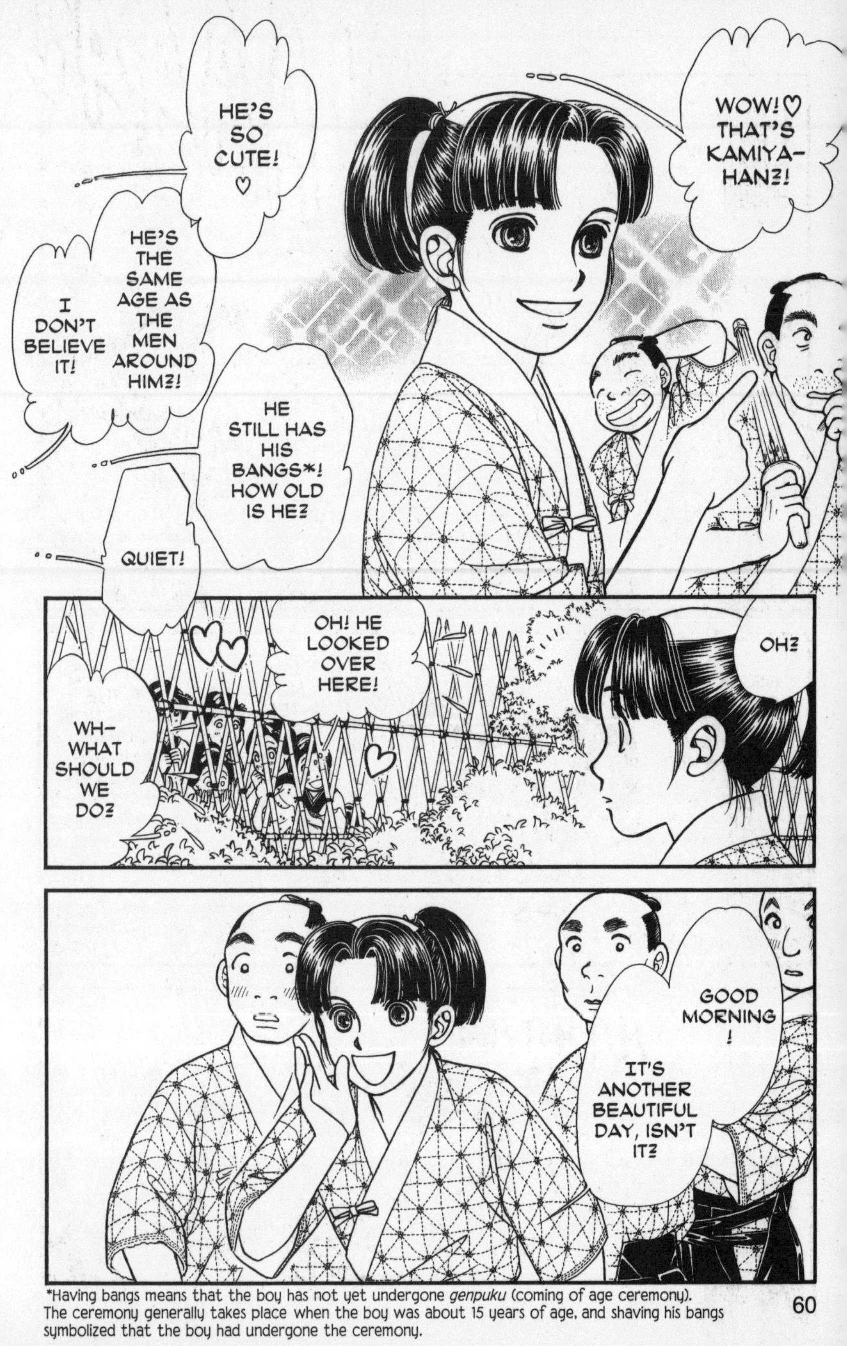
WOW! ♡ THAT'S KAMIYA-HAN?!
HE'S SO CUTE! ♡
HE STILL HAS HIS BANGS*! HOW OLD IS HE?
HE'S THE SAME AGE AS THE MEN AROUND HIM?!
I DON'T BELIEVE IT!
QUIET!
OH?
OH! HE LOOKED OVER HERE!
WH-WHAT SHOULD WE DO?
GOOD MORNING!
IT'S ANOTHER BEAUTIFUL DAY, ISN'T IT?

*Having bangs means that the boy has not yet undergone *genpuku* (coming of age ceremony). The ceremony generally takes place when the boy was about 15 years of age, and shaving his bangs symbolized that the boy had undergone the ceremony.

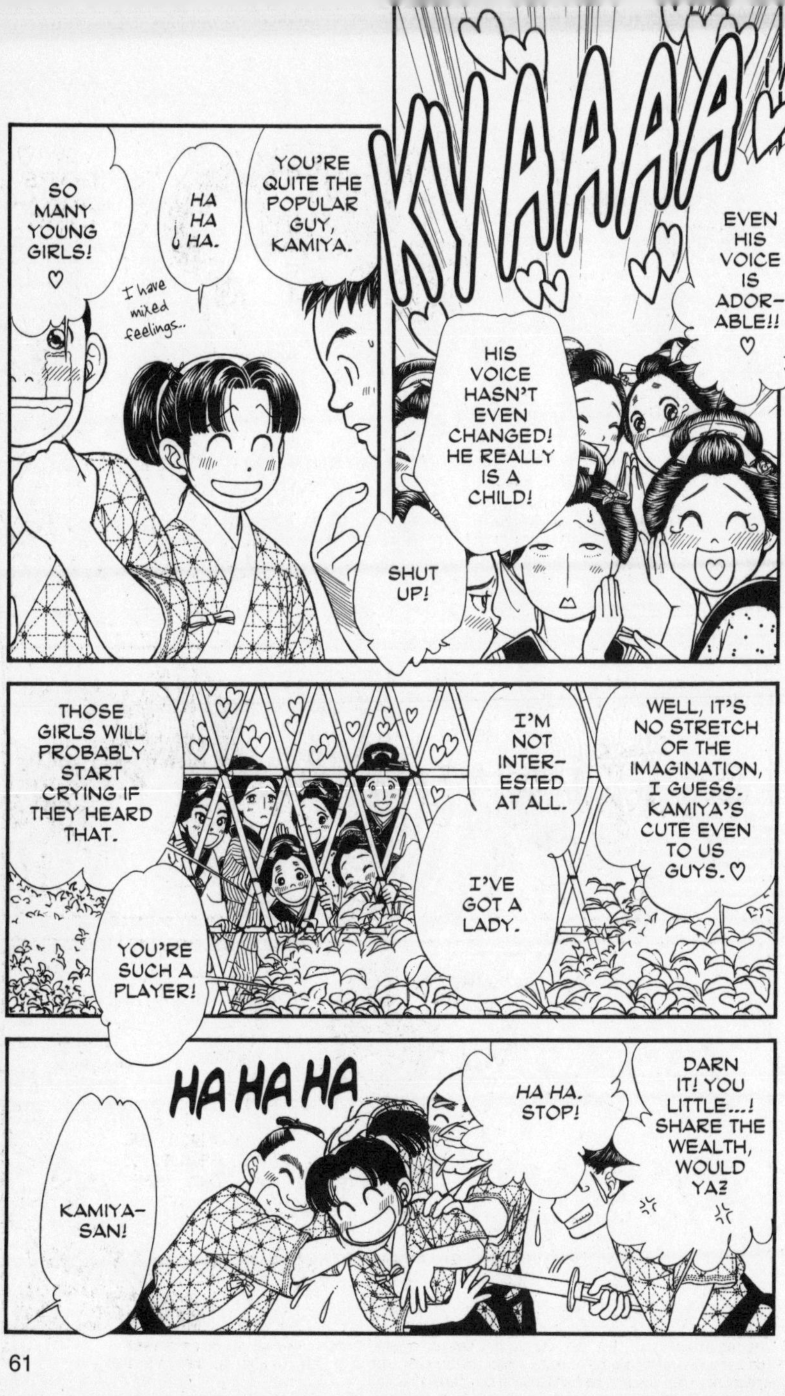
KYAAAA!!
EVEN HIS VOICE IS ADORABLE!! ♡
HIS VOICE HASN'T EVEN CHANGED! HE REALLY IS A CHILD!
SHUT UP!
YOU'RE QUITE THE POPULAR GUY, KAMIYA.
HA HA HA.
SO MANY YOUNG GIRLS! ♡
I have mixed feelings...
WELL, IT'S NO STRETCH OF THE IMAGINATION, I GUESS. KAMIYA'S CUTE EVEN TO US GUYS. ♡
I'M NOT INTERESTED AT ALL.
I'VE GOT A LADY.
THOSE GIRLS WILL PROBABLY START CRYING IF THEY HEARD THAT.
YOU'RE SUCH A PLAYER!
DARN IT! YOU LITTLE...! SHARE THE WEALTH, WOULD YA?
HA HA. STOP!
HA HA HA
KAMIYA-SAN!

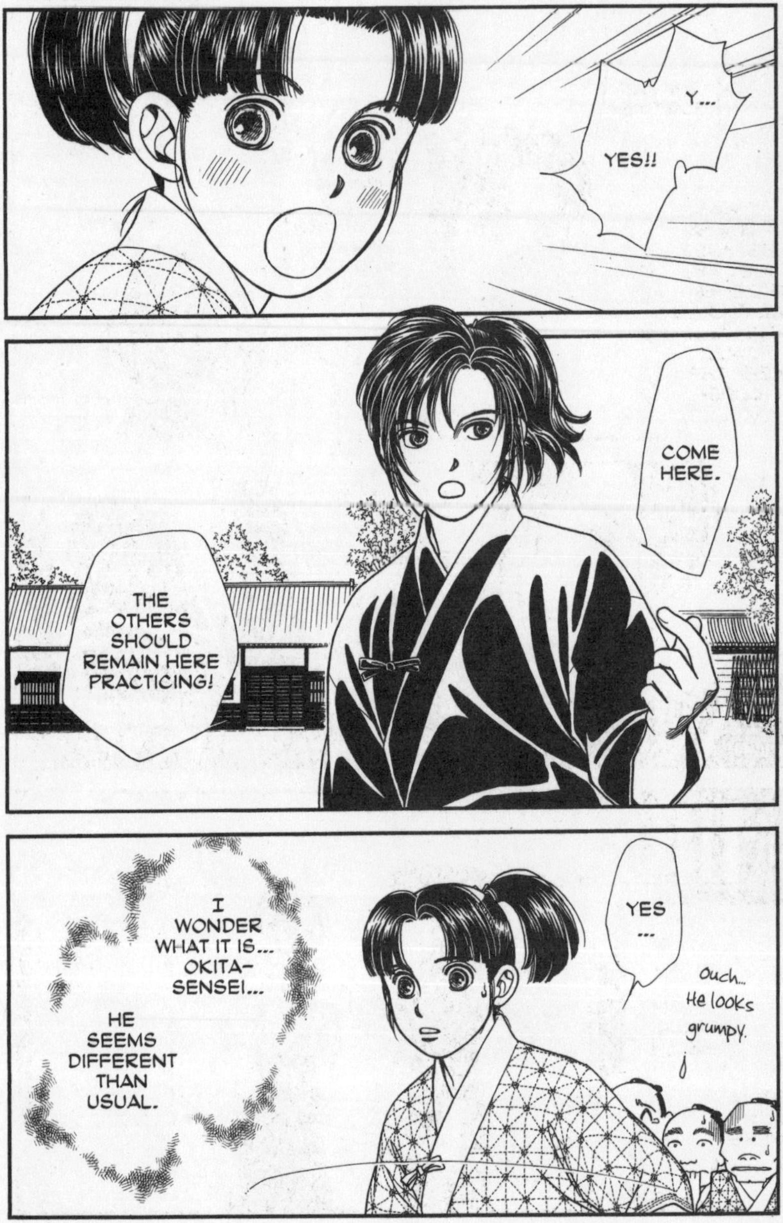
Y...
YES!!
COME HERE.
THE OTHERS SHOULD REMAIN HERE PRACTICING!
YES ...
Ouch... He looks grumpy.
I WONDER WHAT IT IS... OKITA-SENSEI...
HE SEEMS DIFFERENT THAN USUAL.

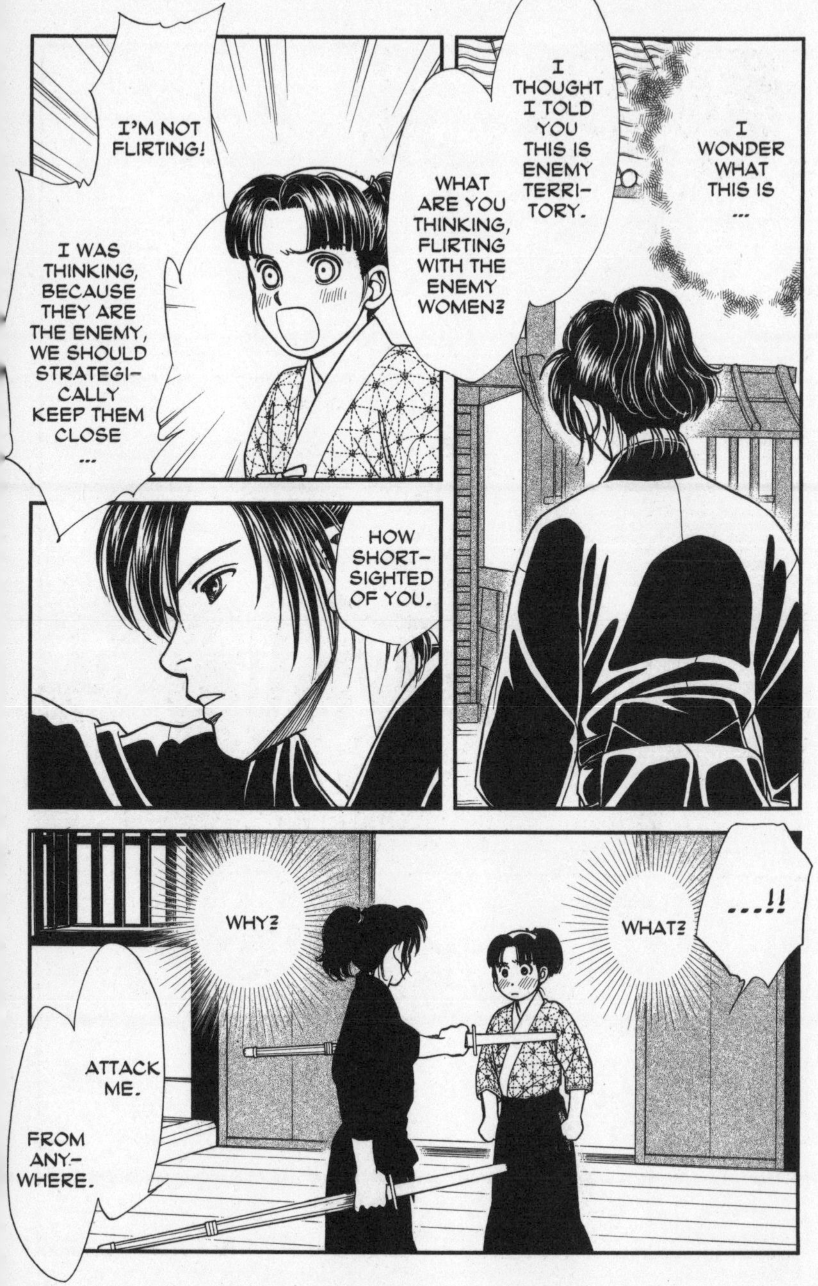
I WONDER WHAT THIS IS ...
I THOUGHT I TOLD YOU THIS IS ENEMY TERRITORY.
WHAT ARE YOU THINKING, FLIRTING WITH THE ENEMY WOMEN?
I'M NOT FLIRTING!
I WAS THINKING, BECAUSE THEY ARE THE ENEMY, WE SHOULD STRATEGICALLY KEEP THEM CLOSE ...
HOW SHORT-SIGHTED OF YOU.
...!!
WHAT?
WHY?
ATTACK ME.
FROM ANYWHERE.

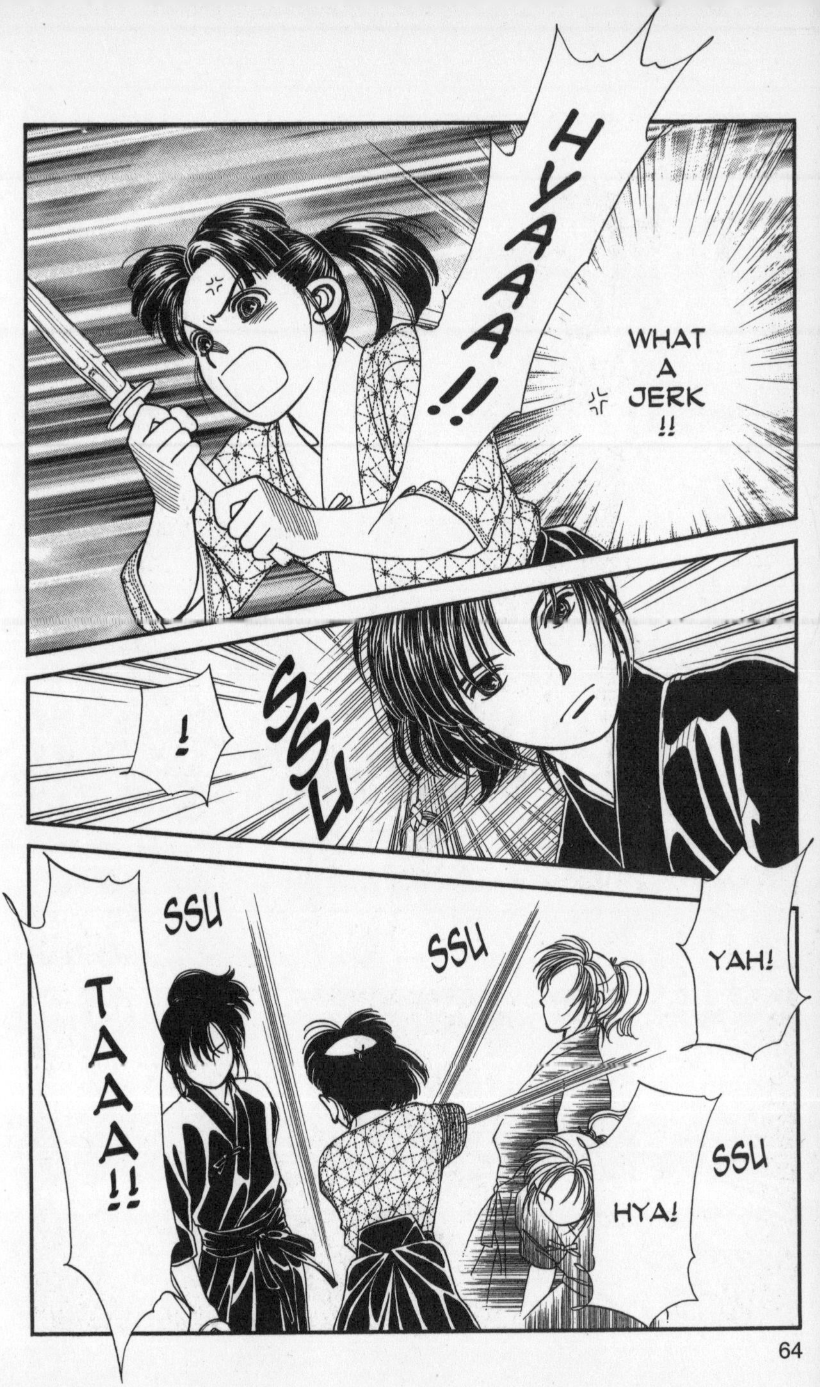
HYAAAA!!
WHAT A JERK !!
SSSU
!
YAH!
SSU
HYA!
SSU
SSU
TAAA!!

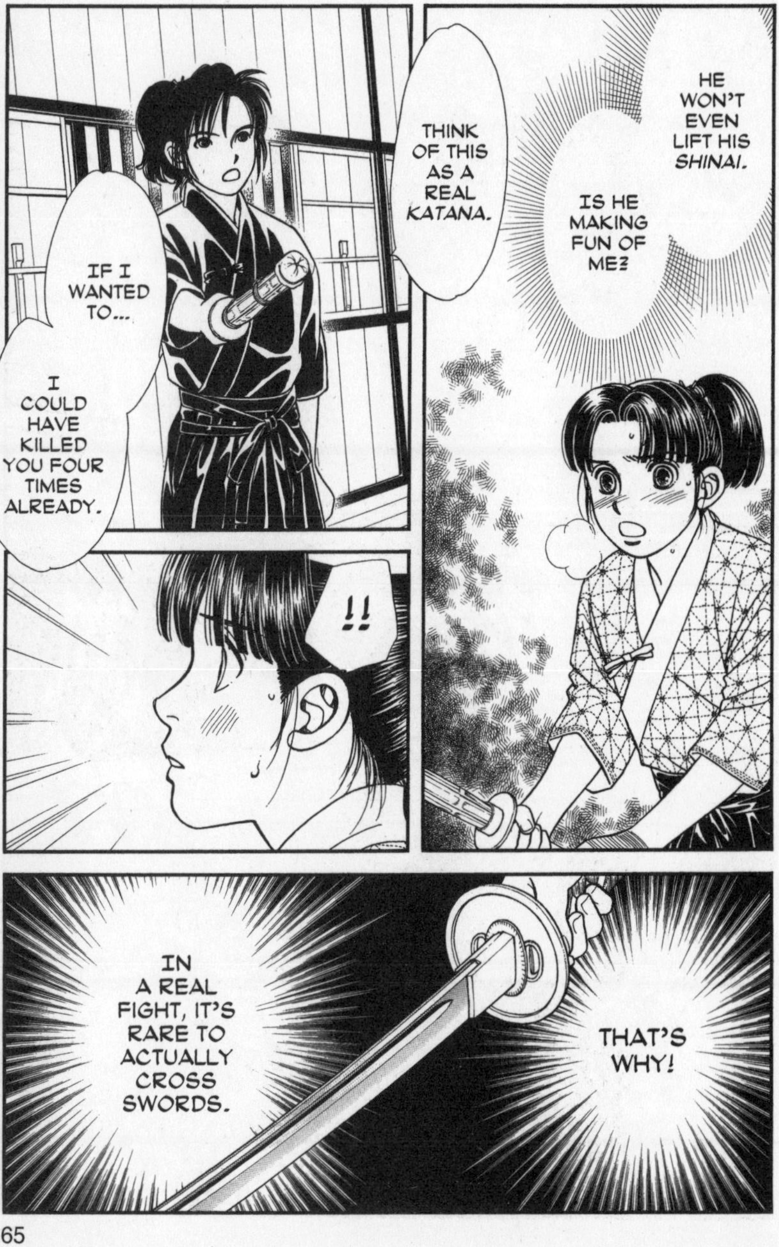
HE WON'T EVEN LIFT HIS *SHINAI*.
IS HE MAKING FUN OF ME?
THINK OF THIS AS A REAL *KATANA*.
IF I WANTED TO...
I COULD HAVE KILLED YOU FOUR TIMES ALREADY.
!!
THAT'S WHY!
IN A REAL FIGHT, IT'S RARE TO ACTUALLY CROSS SWORDS.

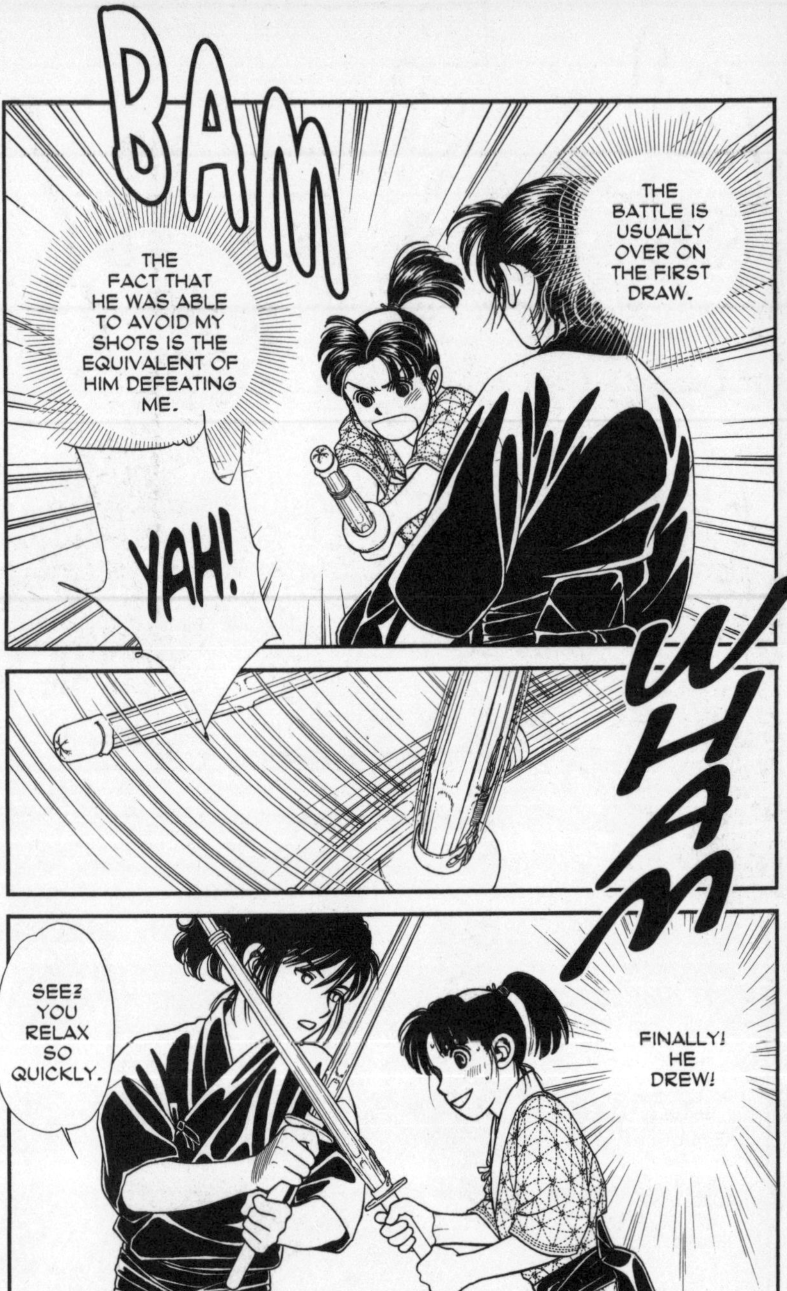
BAM
THE BATTLE IS USUALLY OVER ON THE FIRST DRAW.
THE FACT THAT HE WAS ABLE TO AVOID MY SHOTS IS THE EQUIVALENT OF HIM DEFEATING ME.
YAH!
WHAM
FINALLY! HE DREW!
SEE? YOU RELAX SO QUICKLY.

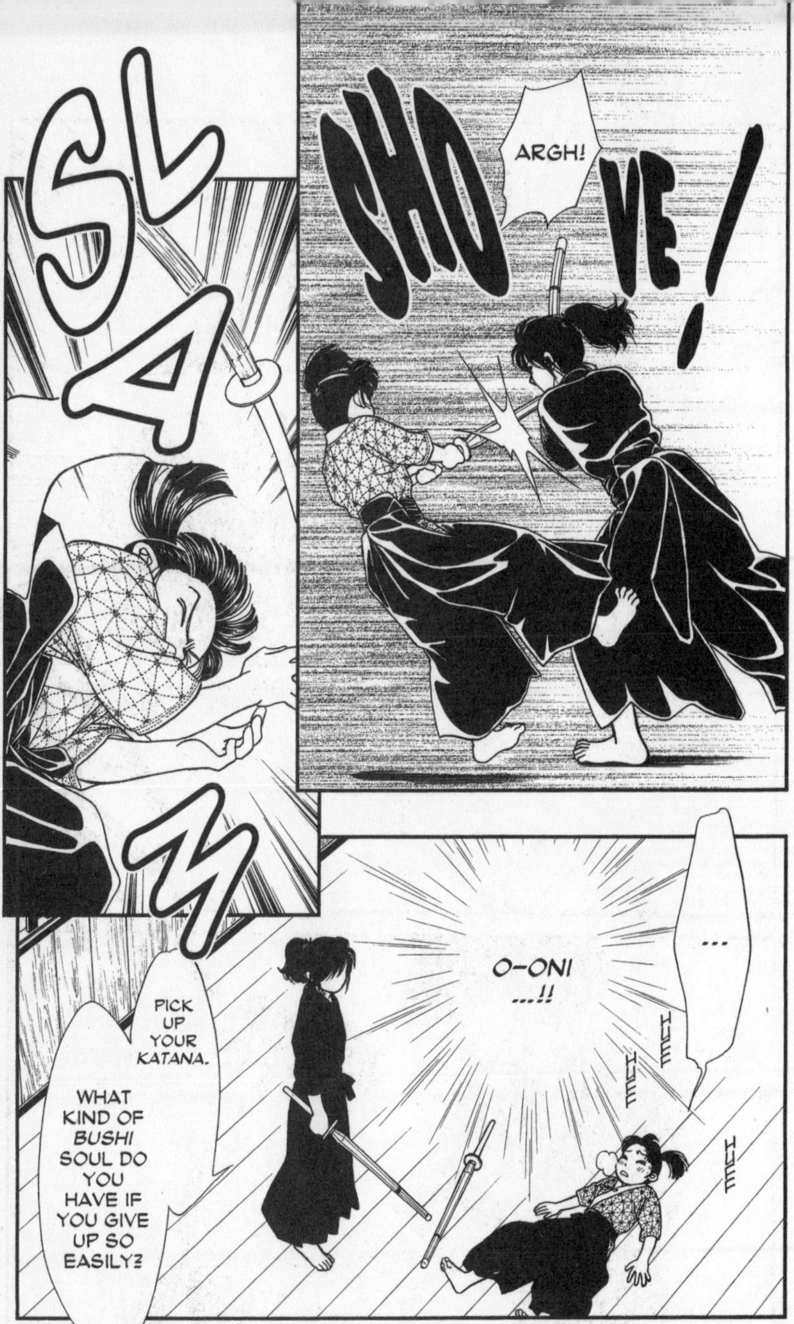
ARGH!
SHOVE!
SLAM
...
HUFF HUFF
HUFF
O-ONI ...!!
PICK UP YOUR KATANA.
WHAT KIND OF *BUSHI* SOUL DO YOU HAVE IF YOU GIVE UP SO EASILY?

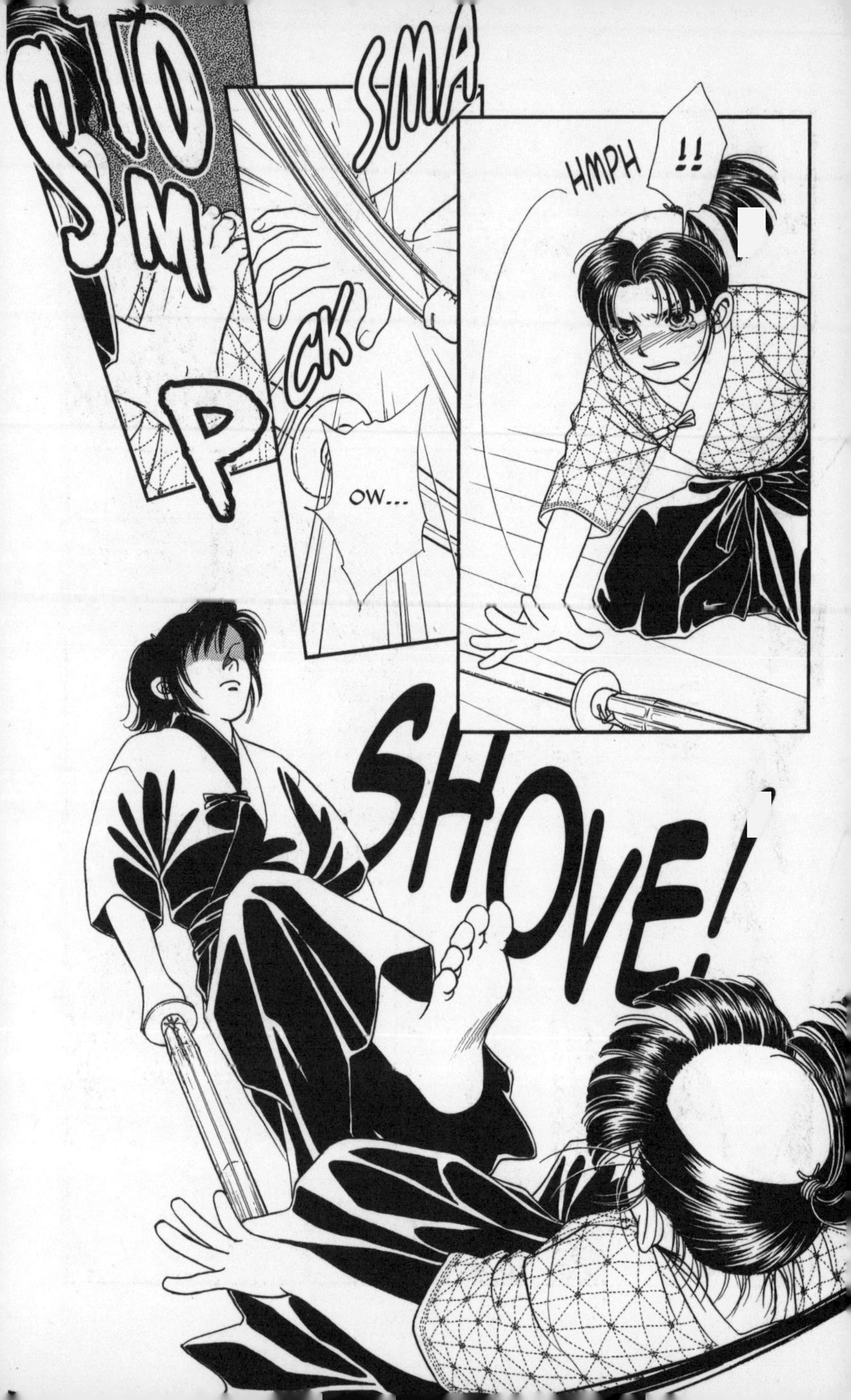
HMPH
!!
SMACK
OW...
STOMP
SHOVE!

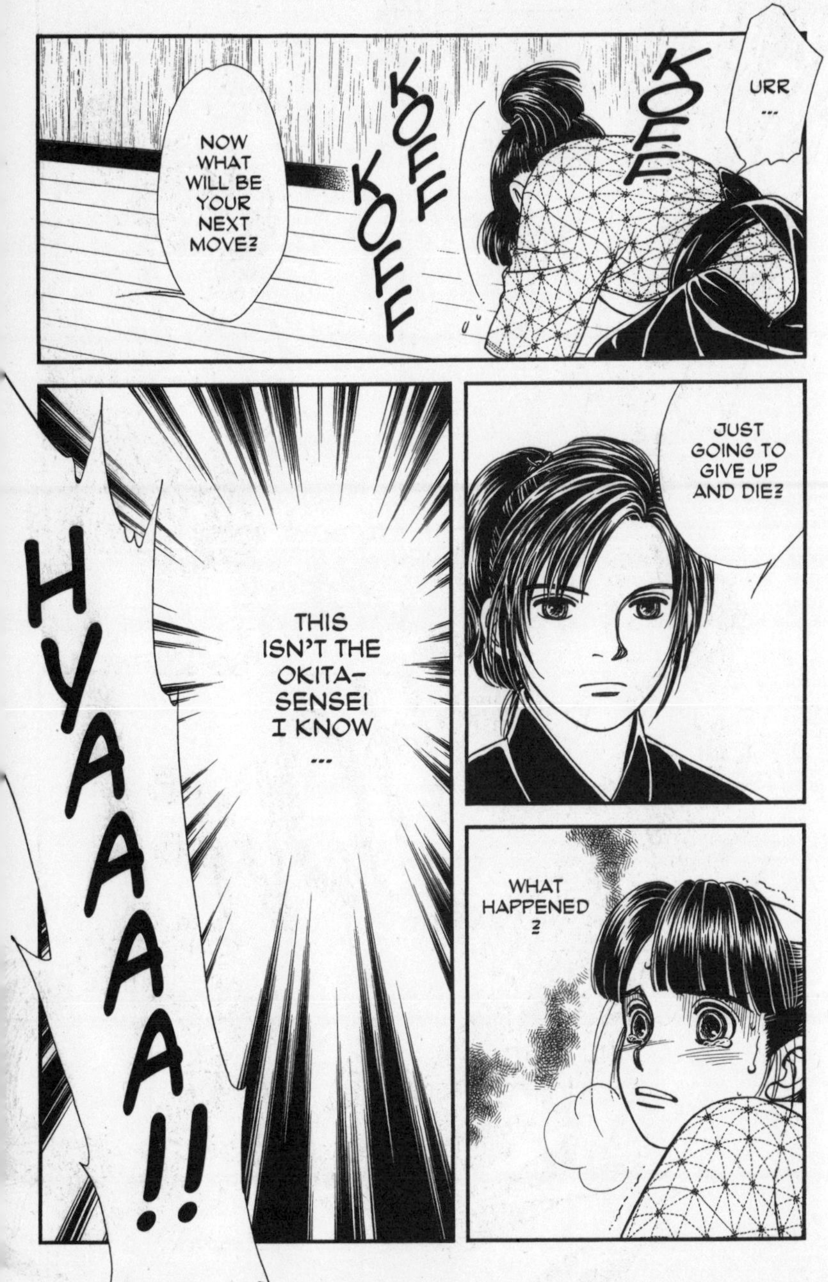
URR ...
KOFF KOFF
KOFF KOFF
NOW WHAT WILL BE YOUR NEXT MOVE?
JUST GOING TO GIVE UP AND DIE?
WHAT HAPPENED ?
THIS ISN'T THE OKITA-SENSEI I KNOW ...
HYAAAAA!!

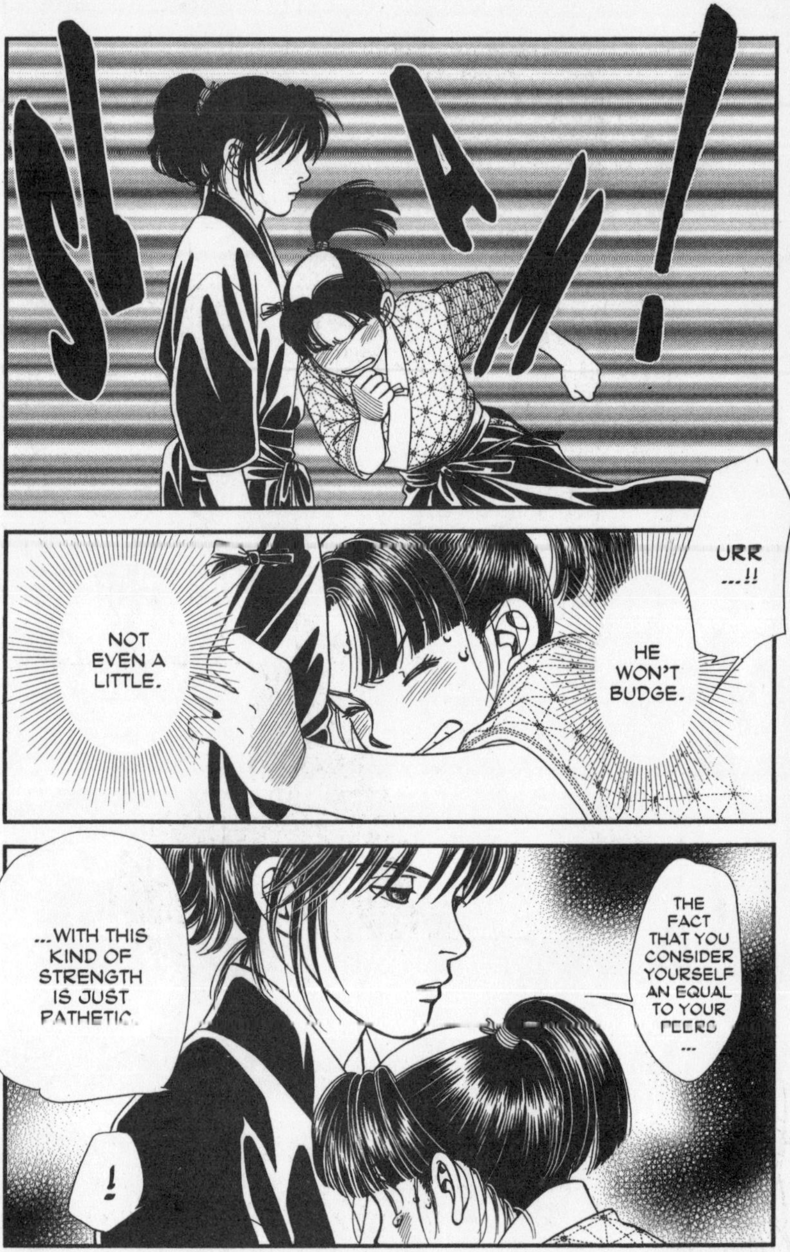
SLAM!
URR ...!!
HE WON'T BUDGE.
NOT EVEN A LITTLE.
THE FACT THAT YOU CONSIDER YOURSELF AN EQUAL TO YOUR PEERS ...
...WITH THIS KIND OF STRENGTH IS JUST PATHETIC.
!

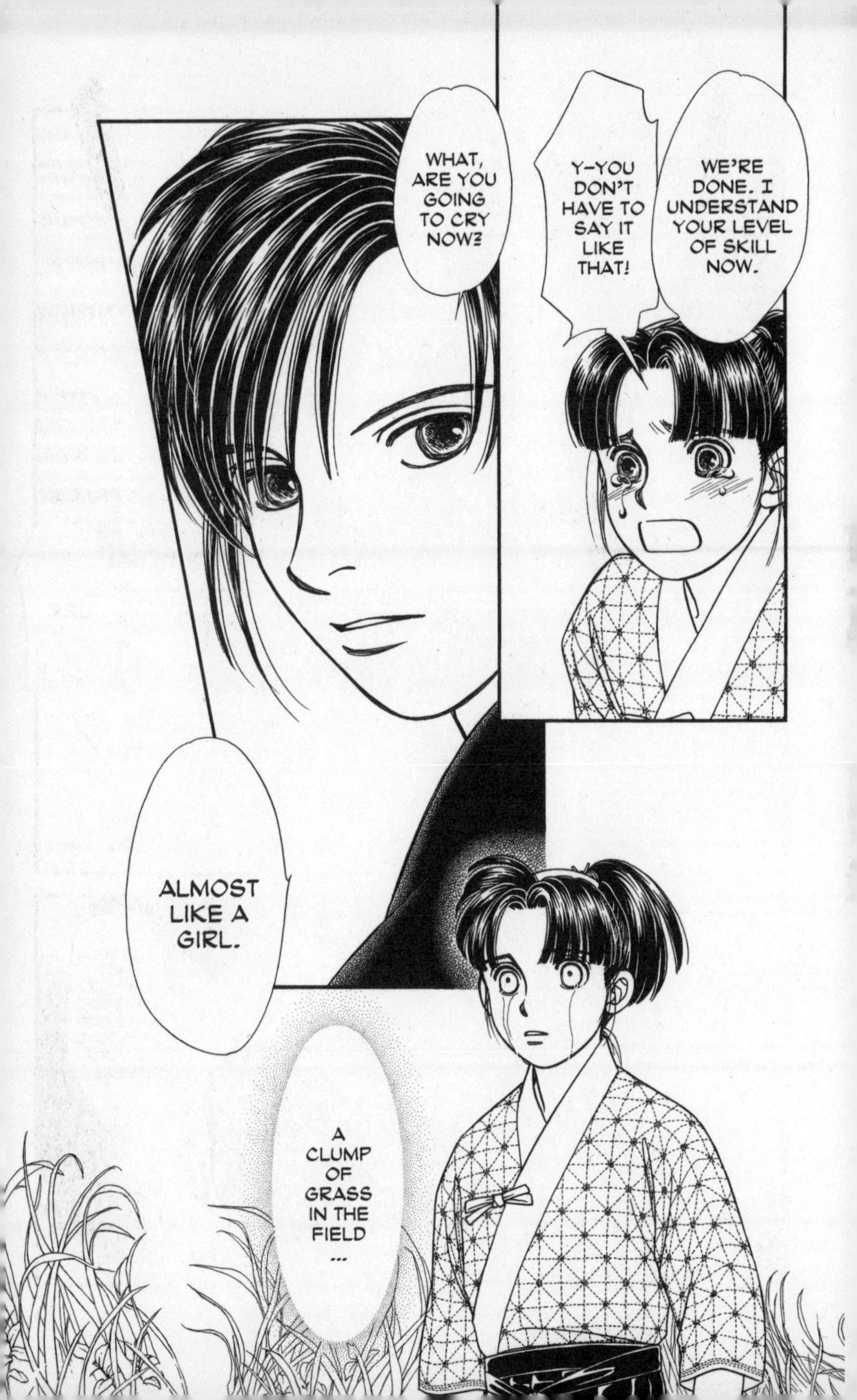
WE'RE DONE. I UNDERSTAND YOUR LEVEL OF SKILL NOW.
Y-YOU DON'T HAVE TO SAY IT LIKE THAT!
WHAT, ARE YOU GOING TO CRY NOW?
ALMOST LIKE A GIRL.
A CLUMP OF GRASS IN THE FIELD ...

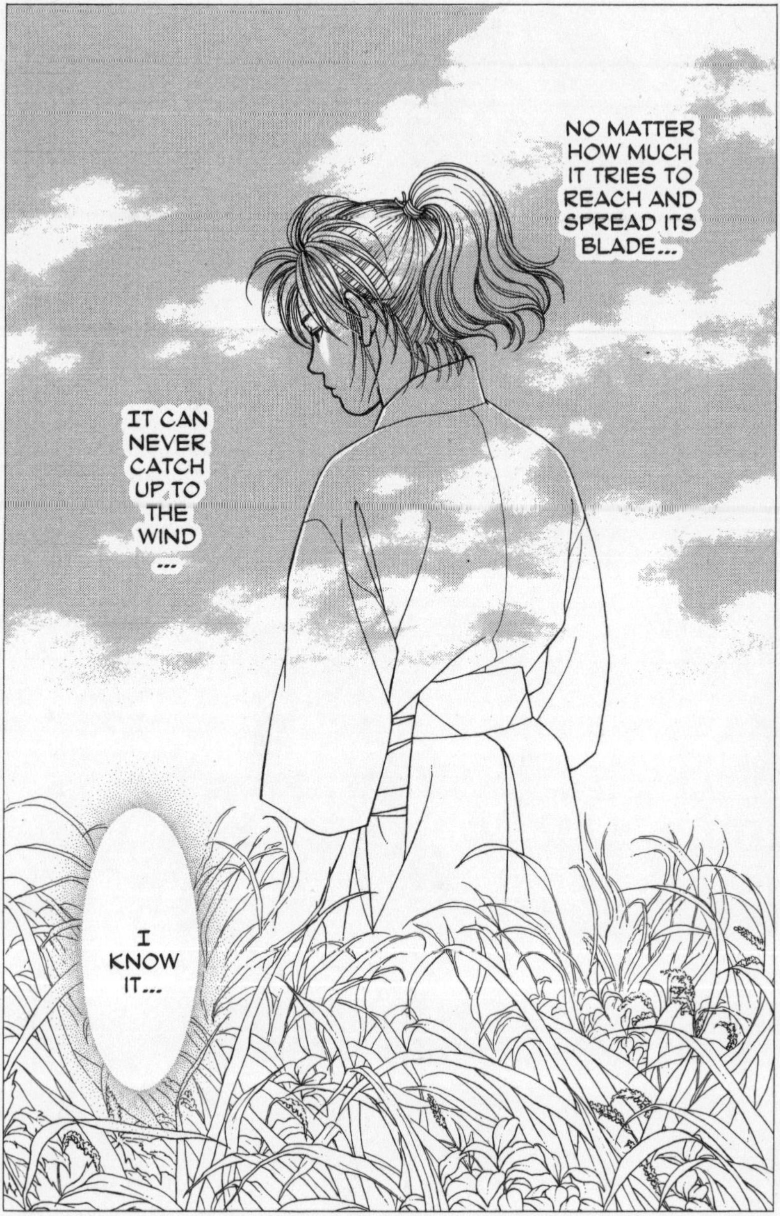
NO MATTER HOW MUCH IT TRIES TO REACH AND SPREAD ITS BLADE...
IT CAN NEVER CATCH UP TO THE WIND ...
I KNOW IT...

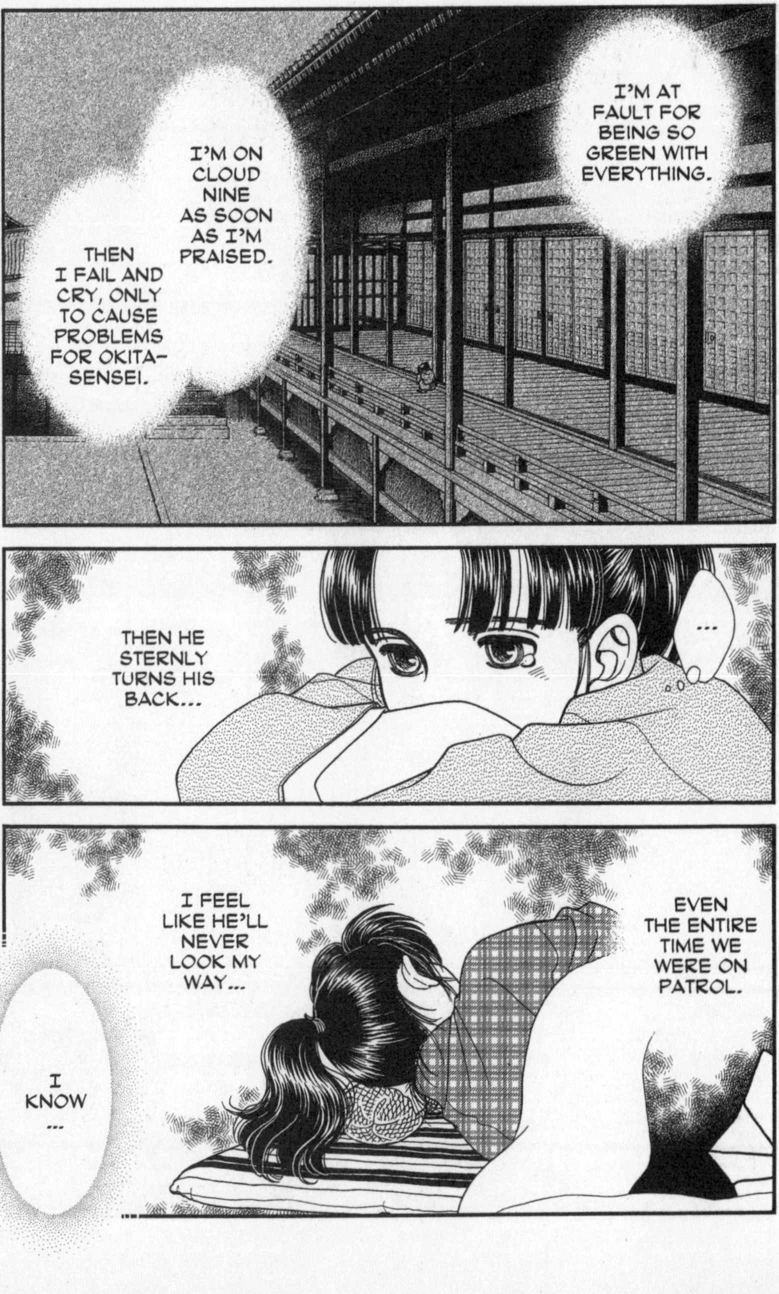
I'M AT FAULT FOR BEING SO GREEN WITH EVERYTHING.
I'M ON CLOUD NINE AS SOON AS I'M PRAISED.
THEN I FAIL AND CRY, ONLY TO CAUSE PROBLEMS FOR OKITA-SENSEI.
...
THEN HE STERNLY TURNS HIS BACK...
EVEN THE ENTIRE TIME WE WERE ON PATROL.
I FEEL LIKE HE'LL NEVER LOOK MY WAY...
I KNOW...

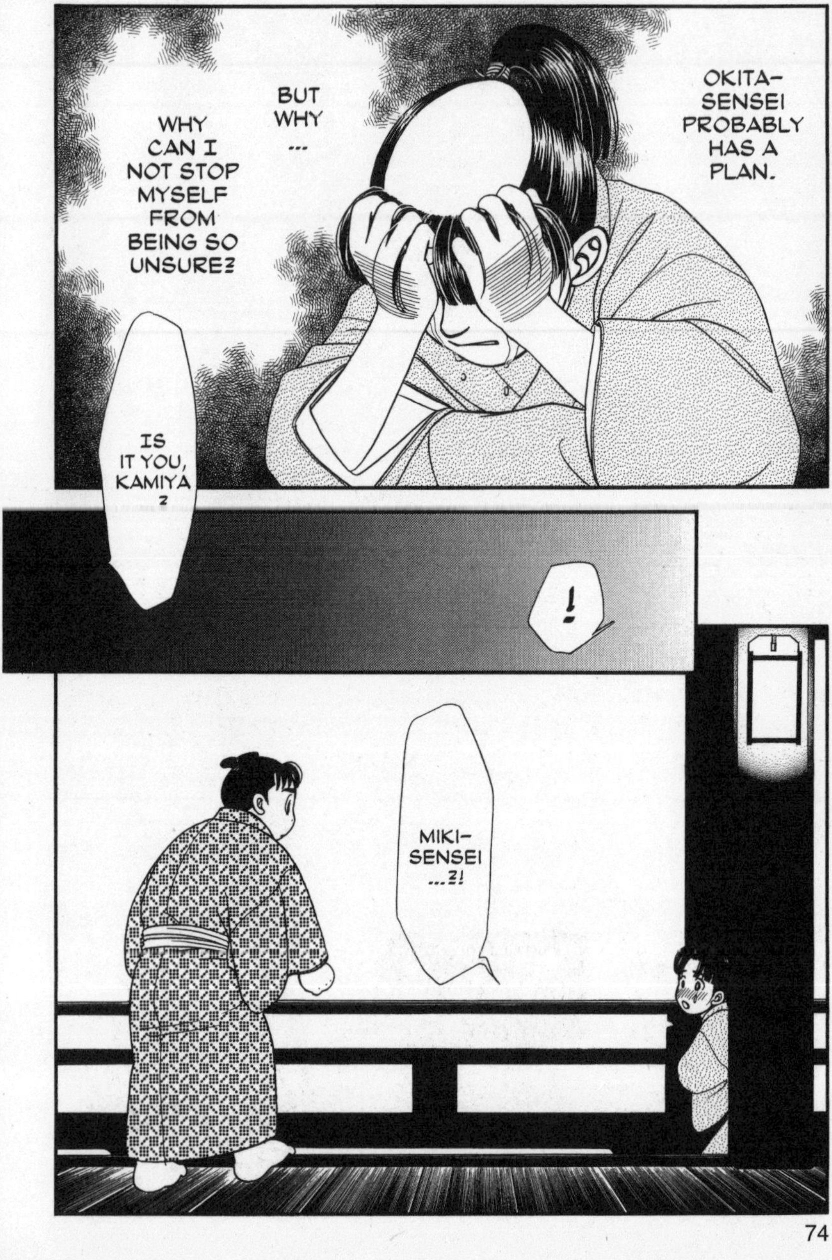
OKITA-SENSEI PROBABLY HAS A PLAN.
BUT WHY ...
WHY CAN I NOT STOP MYSELF FROM BEING SO UNSURE?
IS IT YOU, KAMIYA?
!
MIKI-SENSEI ...?!

"TSU" つ

TSUKIYO NI
KAMA O NUKARERU

"IDLENESS IS
THE DEVIL'S
WORKSHOP"

(lit. An iron pot stolen
on a full moon)

DRIVE
OFF
THIEVES
HARADA

EDO
IROHA
KARUTA
GAME

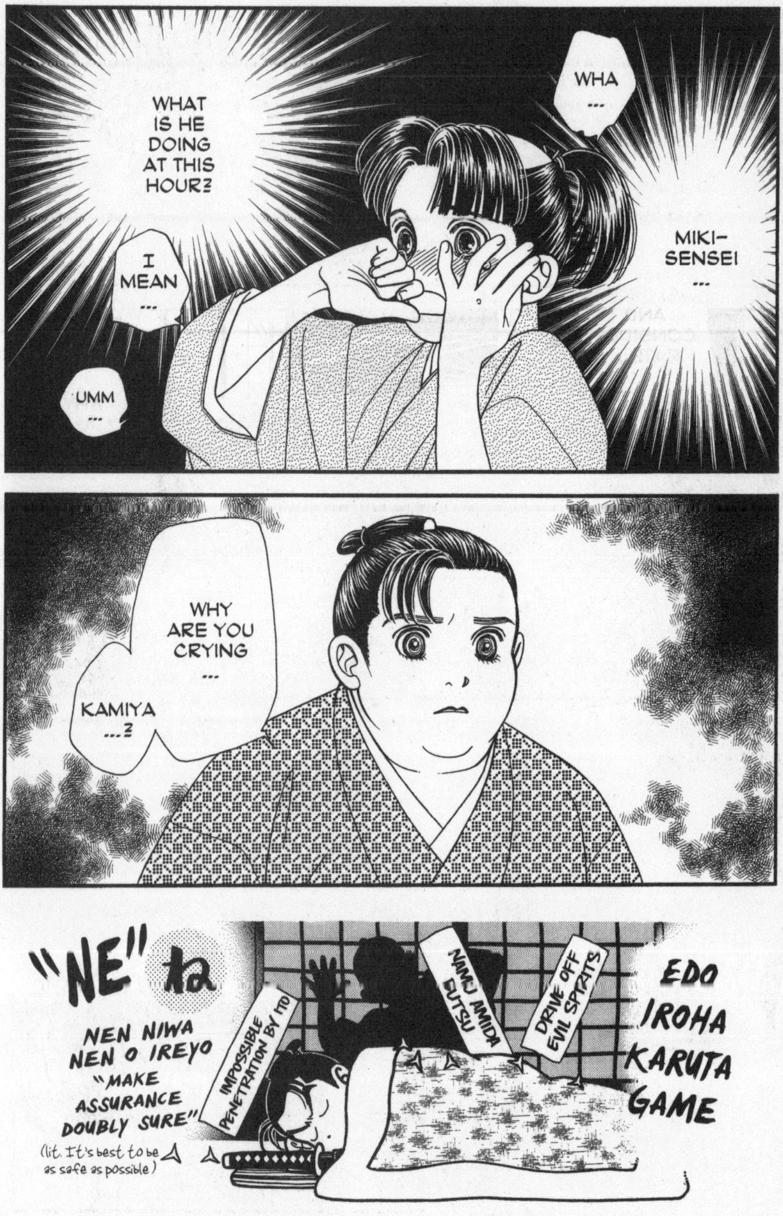
WHA ...
MIKI-SENSEI ...
WHAT IS HE DOING AT THIS HOUR?
I MEAN ...
UMM ...
WHY ARE YOU CRYING ...
KAMIYA ...?
EDO IROHA KARUTA GAME
DRIVE OFF EVIL SPIRITS
NAMU AMIDA BUTSU
IMPOSSIBLE PENETRATION BY ITO
"NE" ね
NEN NIWA NEN O IREYO
"MAKE ASSURANCE DOUBLY SURE"
(lit. It's best to be as safe as possible)

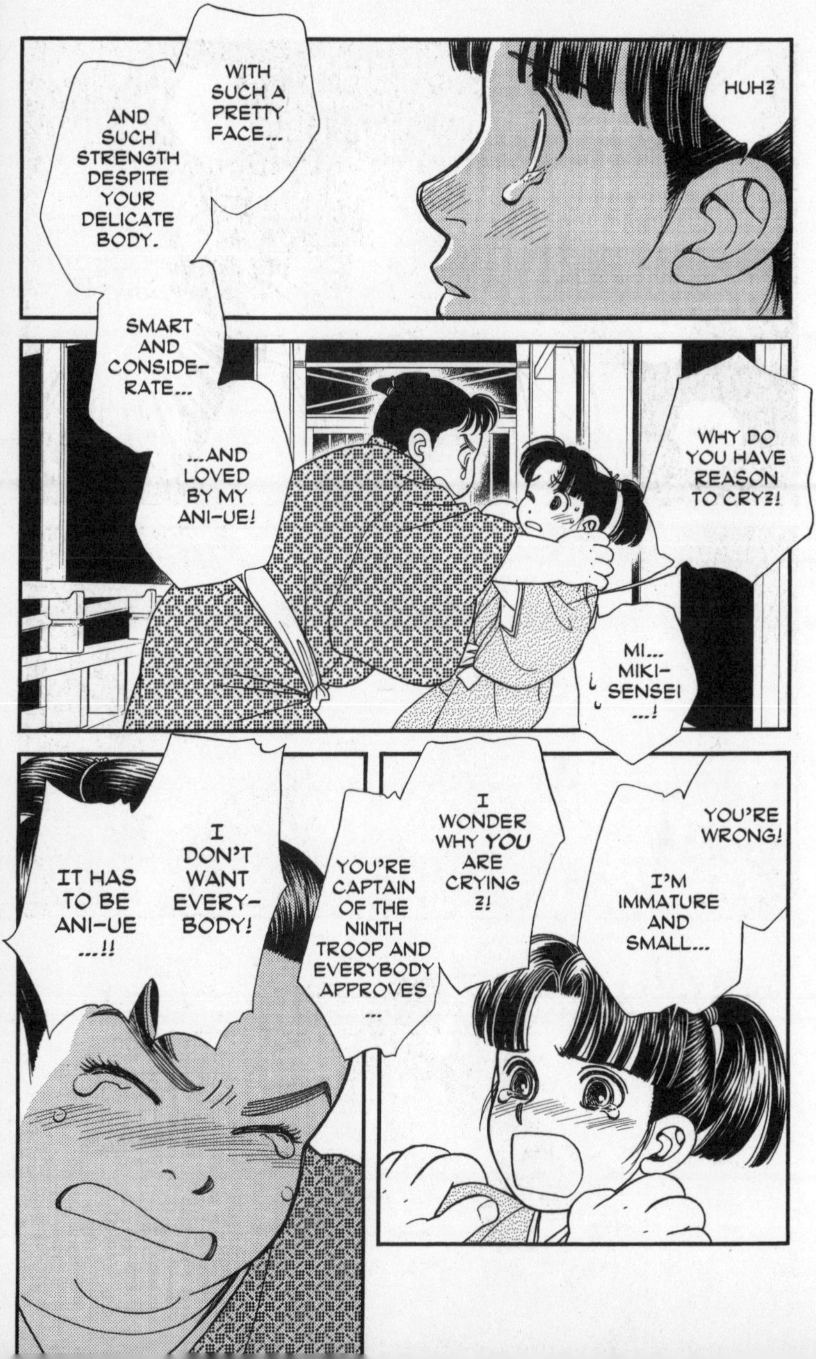
HUH?
WITH SUCH A PRETTY FACE...
AND SUCH STRENGTH DESPITE YOUR DELICATE BODY.
SMART AND CONSIDE-RATE...
...AND LOVED BY MY ANI-UE!
WHY DO YOU HAVE REASON TO CRY?!
MI... MIKI-SENSEI ...!
YOU'RE WRONG!
I'M IMMATURE AND SMALL...
I WONDER WHY *YOU* ARE CRYING ?!
YOU'RE CAPTAIN OF THE NINTH TROOP AND EVERYBODY APPROVES ...
I DON'T WANT EVERY-BODY!
IT HAS TO BE ANI-UE ...!!

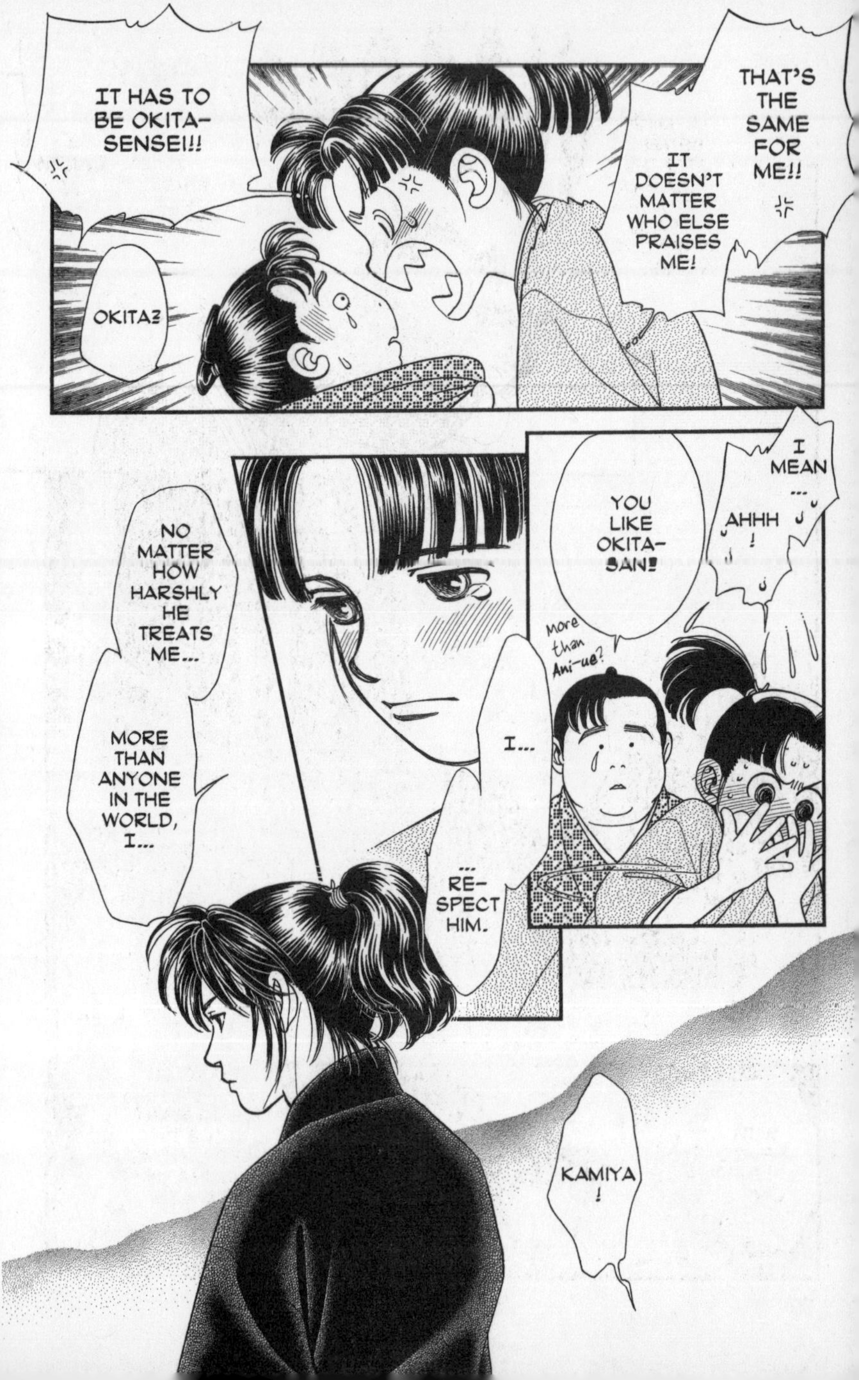
THAT'S THE SAME FOR ME!!
IT DOESN'T MATTER WHO ELSE PRAISES ME!
IT HAS TO BE OKITA-SENSEI!!!
OKITA?
I MEAN... AHHH!
YOU LIKE OKITA-SAN!
More than Ani-ue?
NO MATTER HOW HARSHLY HE TREATS ME...
MORE THAN ANYONE IN THE WORLD, I...
I...
...RE-SPECT HIM.
KAMIYA!

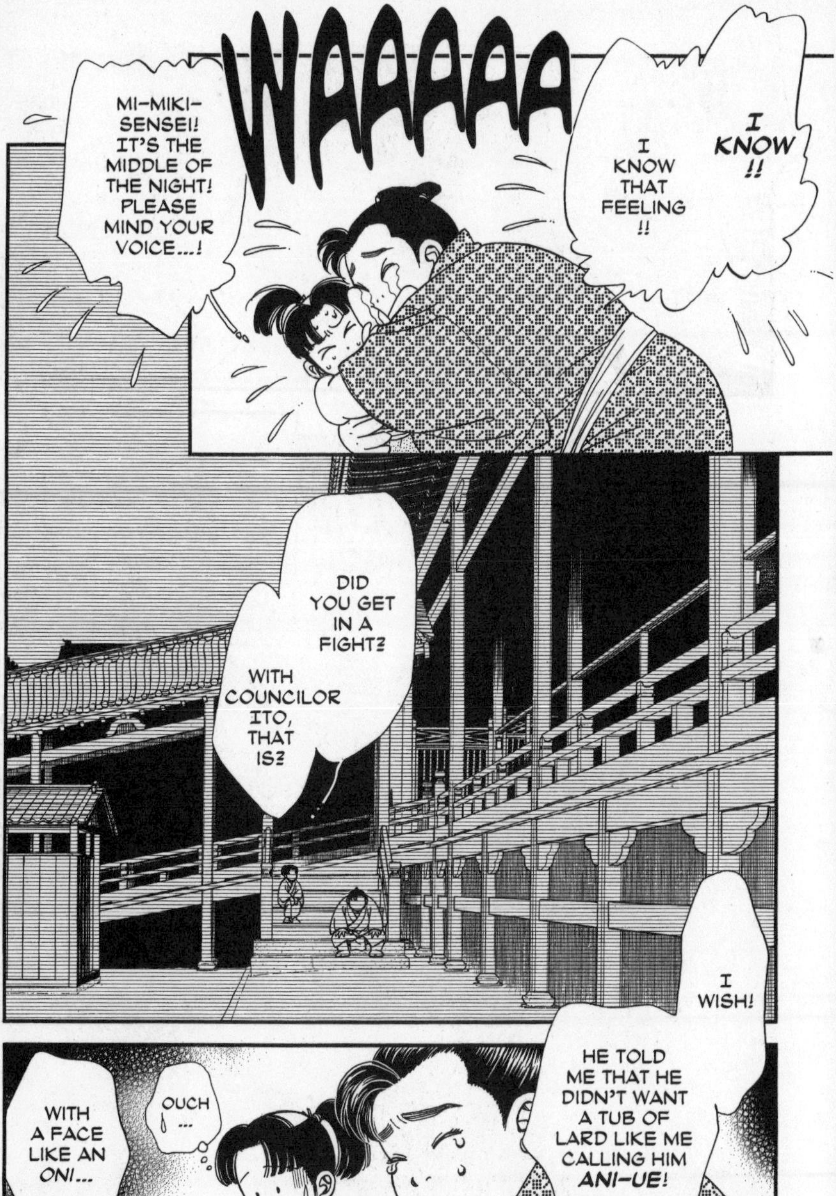
WAAAAA
I KNOW!!
I KNOW THAT FEELING!!
MI-MIKI-SENSEI! IT'S THE MIDDLE OF THE NIGHT! PLEASE MIND YOUR VOICE...!
DID YOU GET IN A FIGHT?
WITH COUNCILOR ITO, THAT IS?
I WISH!
HE TOLD ME THAT HE DIDN'T WANT A TUB OF LARD LIKE ME CALLING HIM *ANI-UE*!
OUCH...
WITH A FACE LIKE AN *ONI*...

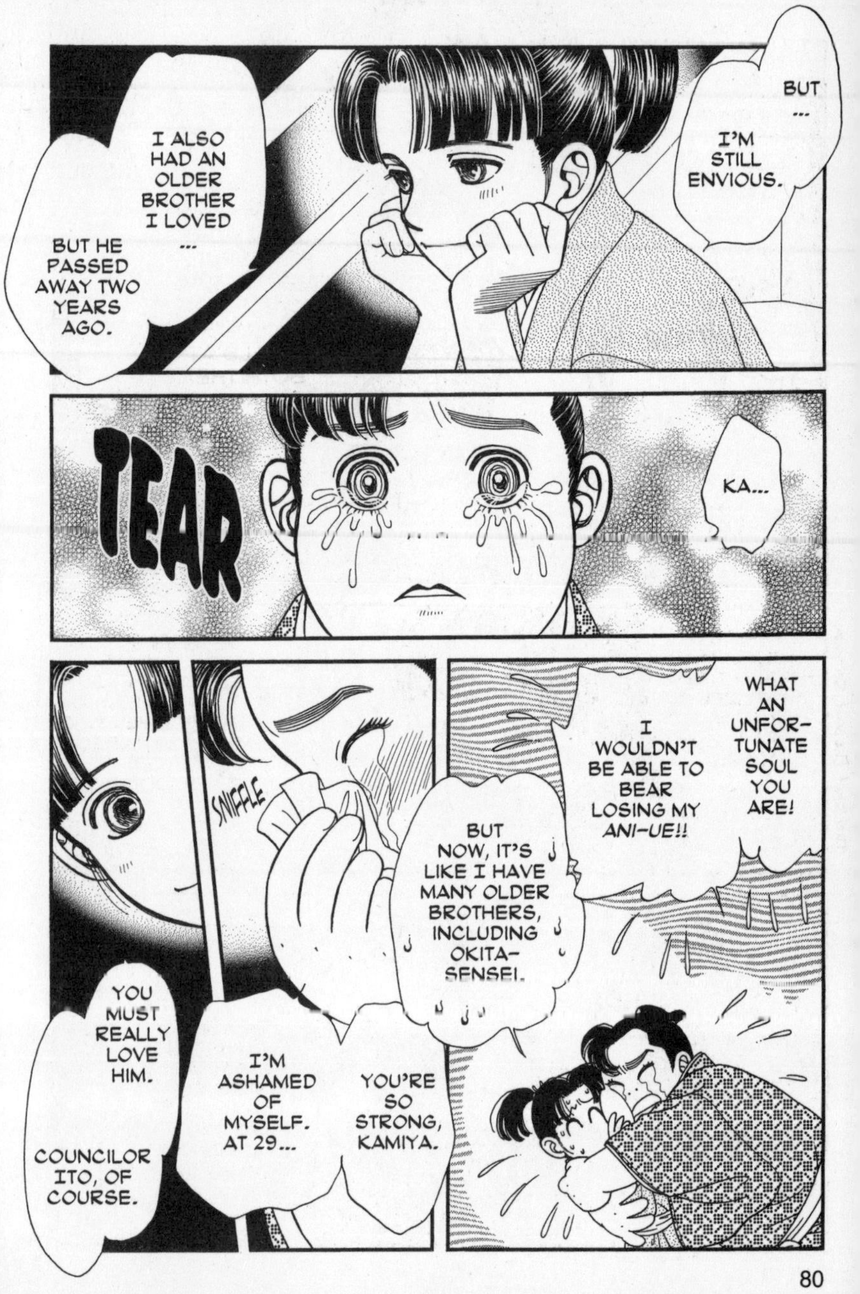
BUT ... I'M STILL ENVIOUS.
I ALSO HAD AN OLDER BROTHER I LOVED ...
BUT HE PASSED AWAY TWO YEARS AGO.
KA...
TEAR
WHAT AN UNFOR-TUNATE SOUL YOU ARE!
I WOULDN'T BE ABLE TO BEAR LOSING MY *ANI-UE*!!
BUT NOW, IT'S LIKE I HAVE MANY OLDER BROTHERS, INCLUDING OKITA-SENSEI.
SNIFFLE
YOU'RE SO STRONG, KAMIYA.
I'M ASHAMED OF MYSELF. AT 29...
YOU MUST REALLY LOVE HIM.
COUNCILOR ITO, OF COURSE.

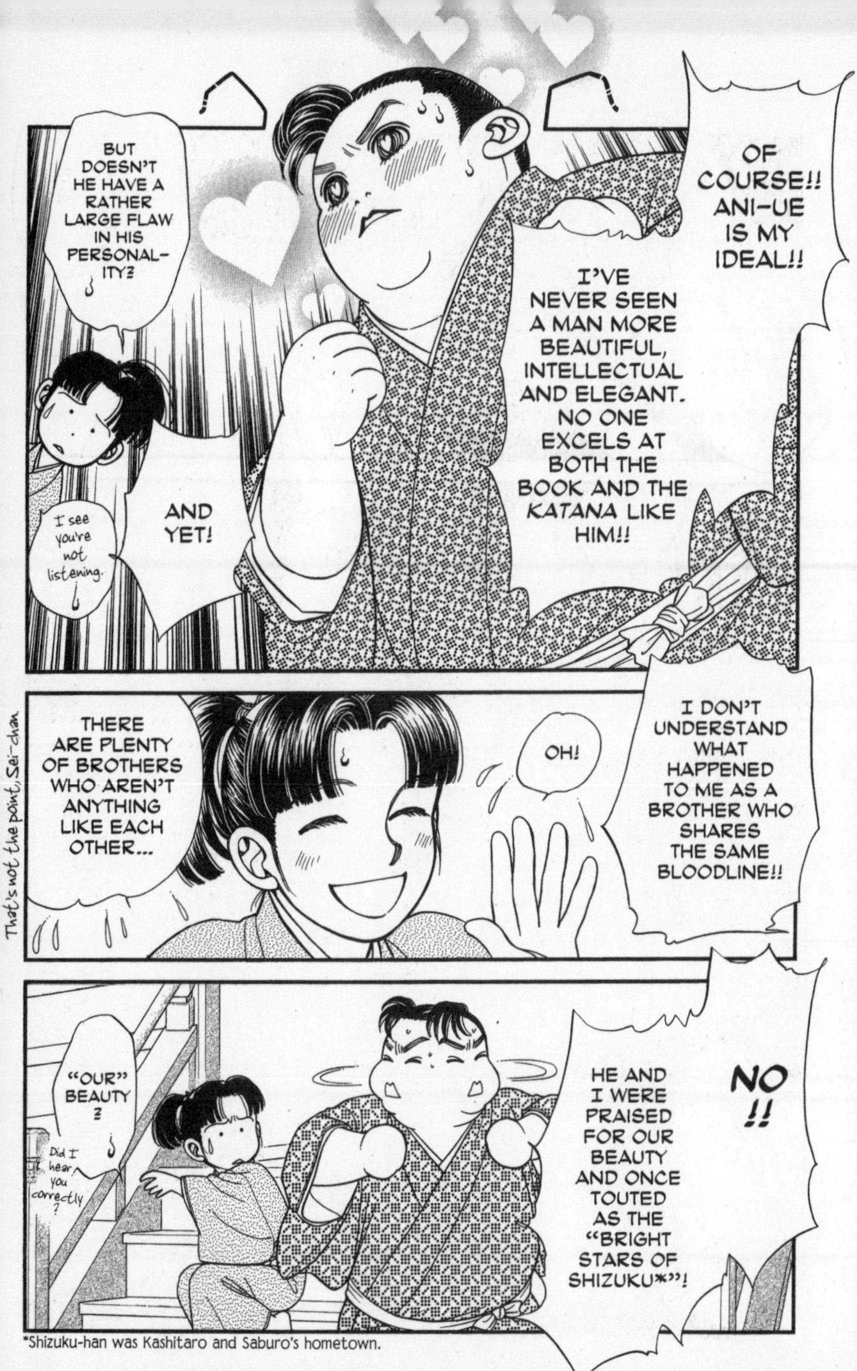
OF COURSE!! ANI-UE IS MY IDEAL!!
I'VE NEVER SEEN A MAN MORE BEAUTIFUL, INTELLECTUAL AND ELEGANT. NO ONE EXCELS AT BOTH THE BOOK AND THE *KATANA* LIKE HIM!!
AND YET!
BUT DOESN'T HE HAVE A RATHER LARGE FLAW IN HIS PERSONAL-ITY?
I see you're not listening.
I DON'T UNDERSTAND WHAT HAPPENED TO ME AS A BROTHER WHO SHARES THE SAME BLOODLINE!!
OH!
THERE ARE PLENTY OF BROTHERS WHO AREN'T ANYTHING LIKE EACH OTHER...
That's not the point, Sei-chan.
NO!!
HE AND I WERE PRAISED FOR OUR BEAUTY AND ONCE TOUTED AS THE "BRIGHT STARS OF SHIZUKU*"!
"OUR" BEAUTY?
Did I hear you correctly?

*Shizuku-han was Kashitaro and Saburo's hometown.

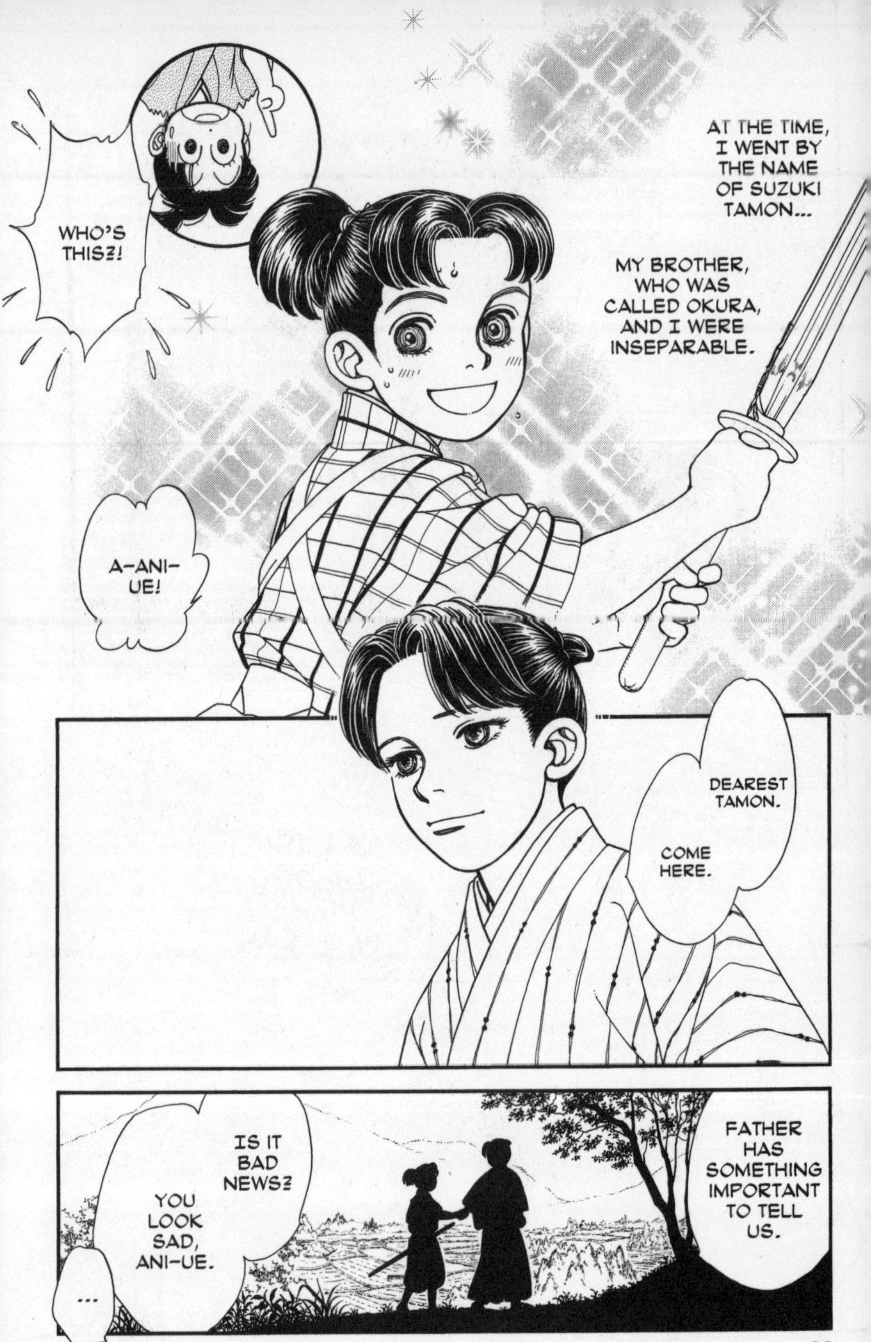
AT THE TIME, I WENT BY THE NAME OF SUZUKI TAMON...
MY BROTHER, WHO WAS CALLED OKURA, AND I WERE INSEPARABLE.
WHO'S THIS?!
A-ANI-UE!
DEAREST TAMON.
COME HERE.
FATHER HAS SOMETHING IMPORTANT TO TELL US.
IS IT BAD NEWS?
YOU LOOK SAD, ANI-UE.
...

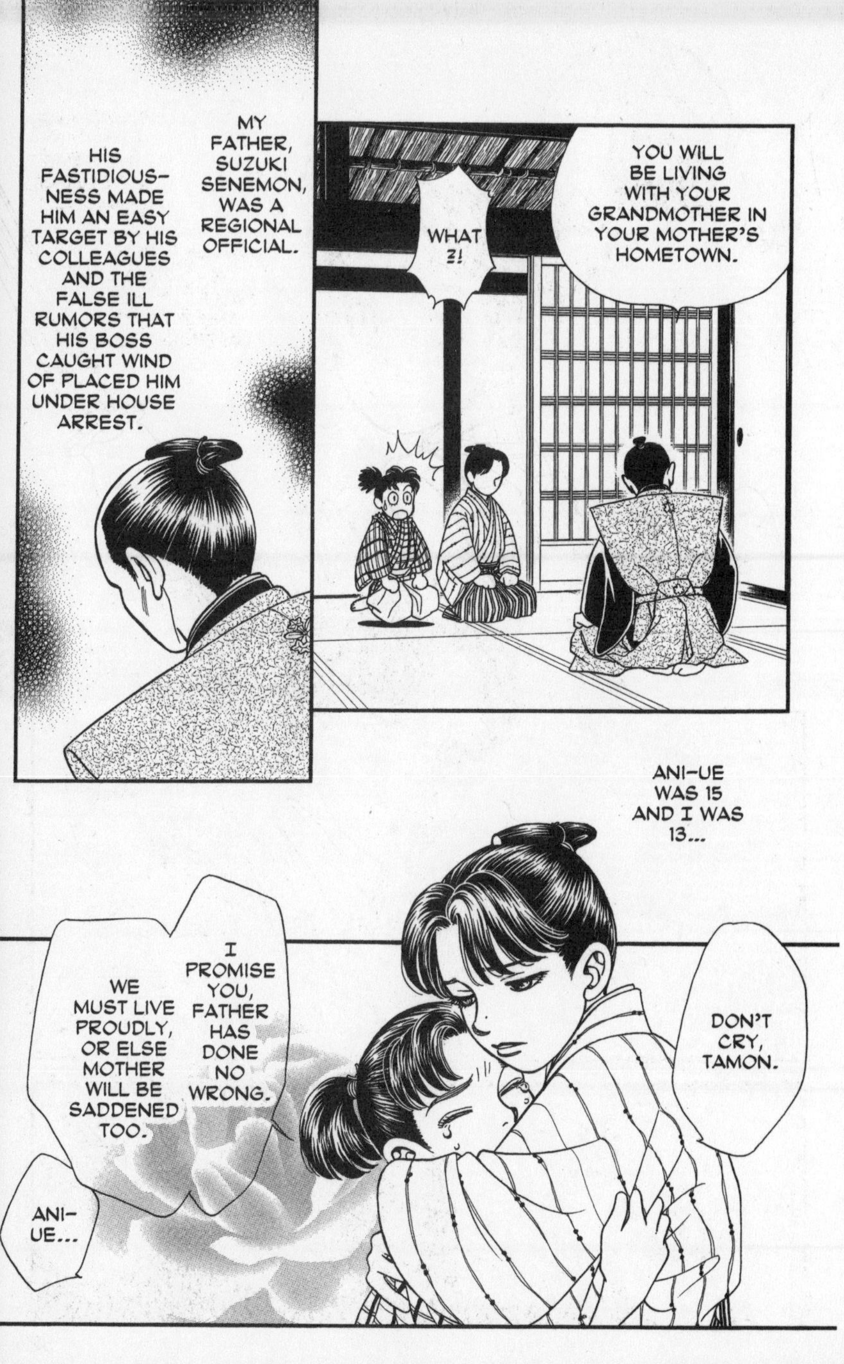
YOU WILL BE LIVING WITH YOUR GRANDMOTHER IN YOUR MOTHER'S HOMETOWN.
WHAT?!
MY FATHER, SUZUKI SENEMON, WAS A REGIONAL OFFICIAL.
HIS FASTIDIOUSNESS MADE HIM AN EASY TARGET BY HIS COLLEAGUES AND THE FALSE ILL RUMORS THAT HIS BOSS CAUGHT WIND OF PLACED HIM UNDER HOUSE ARREST.
ANI-UE WAS 15 AND I WAS 13...
DON'T CRY, TAMON.
I PROMISE YOU, FATHER HAS DONE NO WRONG.
WE MUST LIVE PROUDLY, OR ELSE MOTHER WILL BE SADDENED TOO.
ANI-UE...

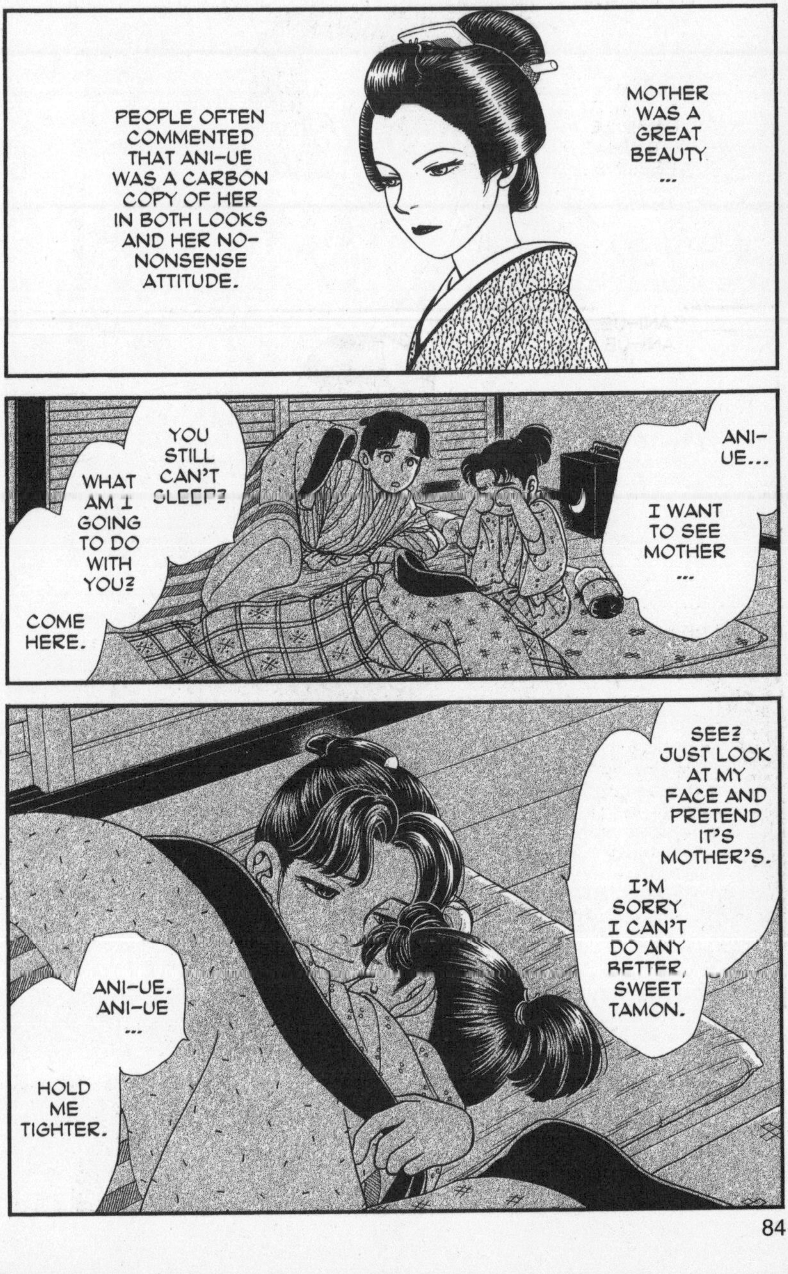
MOTHER WAS A GREAT BEAUTY...
PEOPLE OFTEN COMMENTED THAT ANI-UE WAS A CARBON COPY OF HER IN BOTH LOOKS AND HER NO-NONSENSE ATTITUDE.
ANI-UE...
I WANT TO SEE MOTHER...
YOU STILL CAN'T SLEEP?
WHAT AM I GOING TO DO WITH YOU?
COME HERE.
SEE? JUST LOOK AT MY FACE AND PRETEND IT'S MOTHER'S.
I'M SORRY I CAN'T DO ANY BETTER, SWEET TAMON.
ANI-UE. ANI-UE...
HOLD ME TIGHTER.

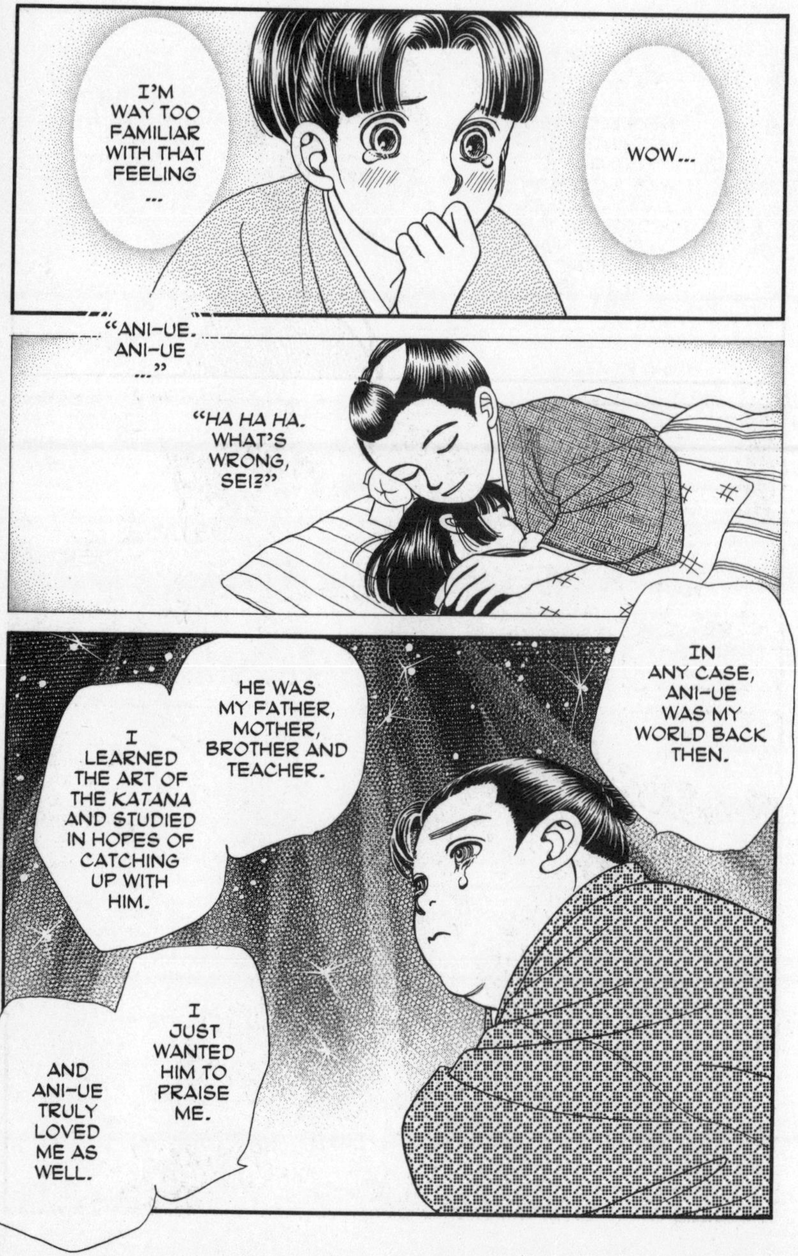
WOW...
I'M WAY TOO FAMILIAR WITH THAT FEELING ...
"ANI-UE. ANI-UE ..."
"HA HA HA. WHAT'S WRONG, SEI?"
IN ANY CASE, ANI-UE WAS MY WORLD BACK THEN.
HE WAS MY FATHER, MOTHER, BROTHER AND TEACHER.
I LEARNED THE ART OF THE *KATANA* AND STUDIED IN HOPES OF CATCHING UP WITH HIM.
I JUST WANTED HIM TO PRAISE ME.
AND ANI-UE TRULY LOVED ME AS WELL.

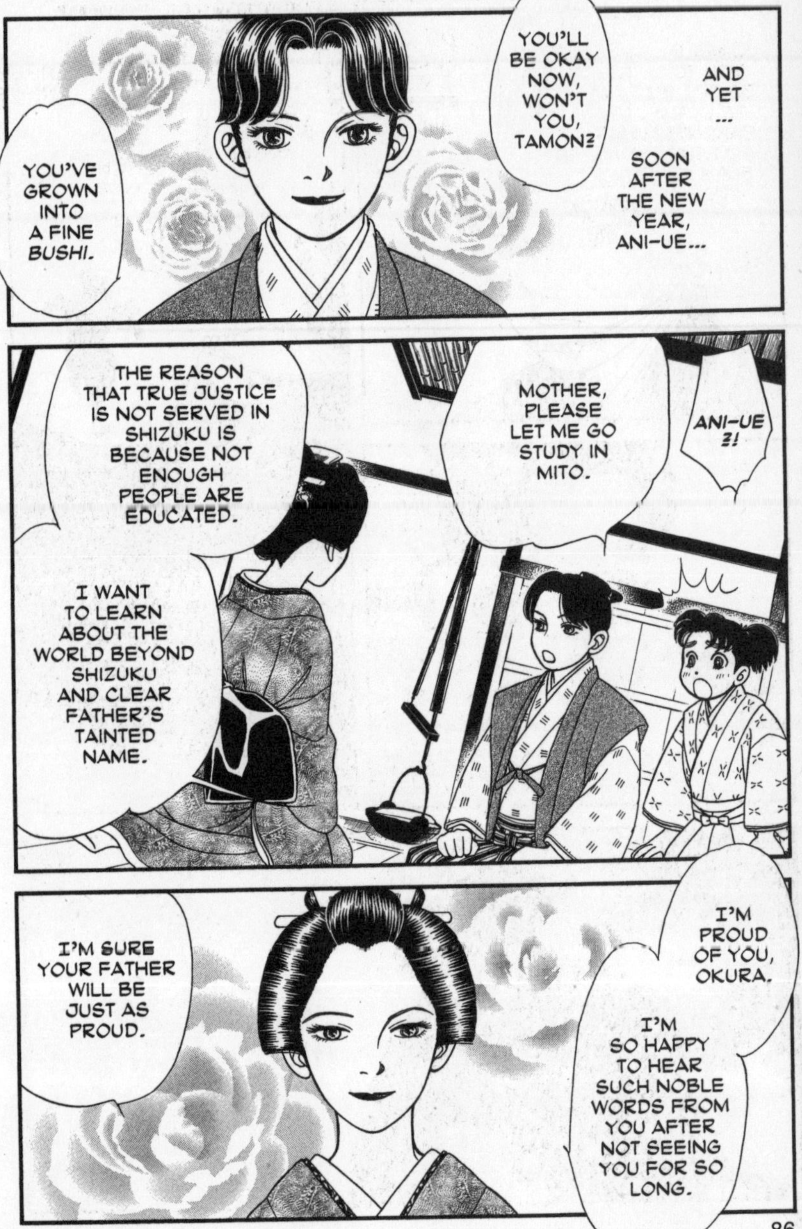
AND YET ... SOON AFTER THE NEW YEAR, ANI-UE...
YOU'LL BE OKAY NOW, WON'T YOU, TAMON?
YOU'VE GROWN INTO A FINE *BUSHI*.
ANI-UE?!
MOTHER, PLEASE LET ME GO STUDY IN MITO.
THE REASON THAT TRUE JUSTICE IS NOT SERVED IN SHIZUKU IS BECAUSE NOT ENOUGH PEOPLE ARE EDUCATED.
I WANT TO LEARN ABOUT THE WORLD BEYOND SHIZUKU AND CLEAR FATHER'S TAINTED NAME.
I'M PROUD OF YOU, OKURA.
I'M SO HAPPY TO HEAR SUCH NOBLE WORDS FROM YOU AFTER NOT SEEING YOU FOR SO LONG.
I'M SURE YOUR FATHER WILL BE JUST AS PROUD.

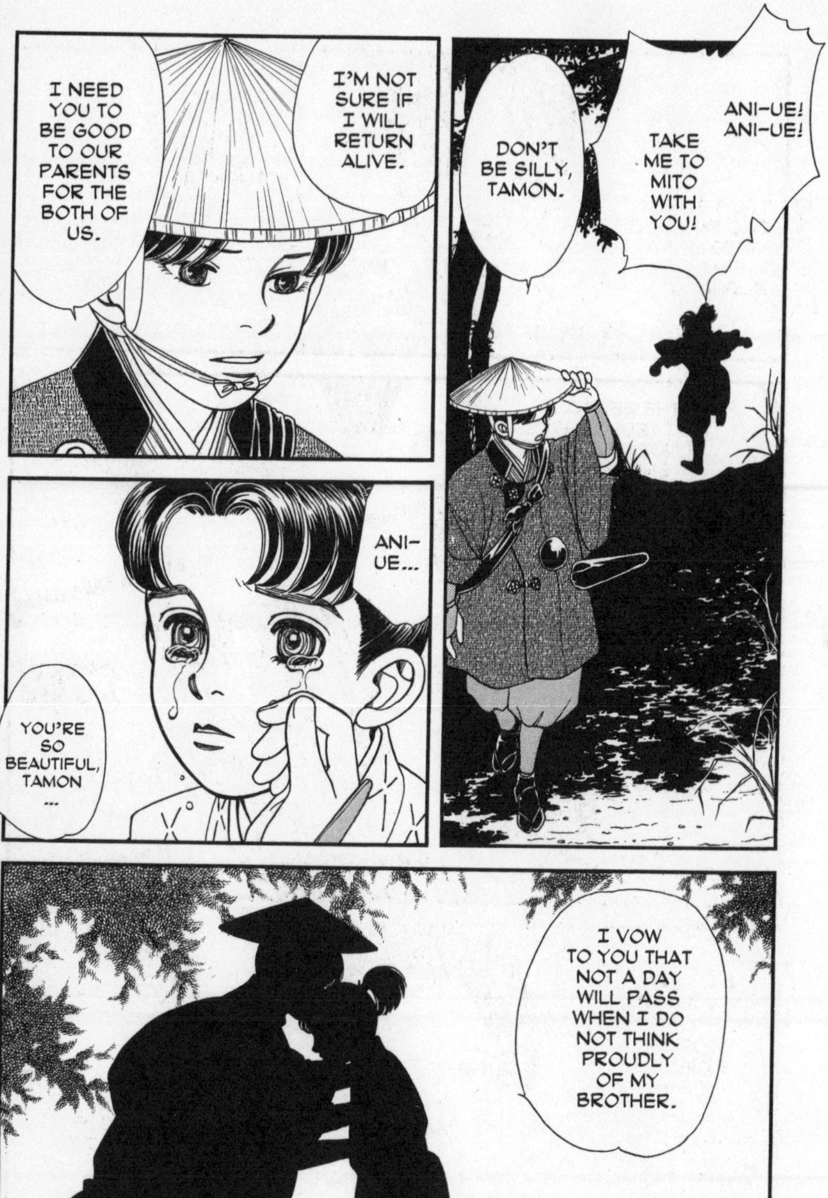
ANI-UE! ANI-UE!
TAKE ME TO MITO WITH YOU!
DON'T BE SILLY, TAMON.
I'M NOT SURE IF I WILL RETURN ALIVE.
I NEED YOU TO BE GOOD TO OUR PARENTS FOR THE BOTH OF US.
ANI-UE...
YOU'RE SO BEAUTIFUL, TAMON ...
I VOW TO YOU THAT NOT A DAY WILL PASS WHEN I DO NOT THINK PROUDLY OF MY BROTHER.

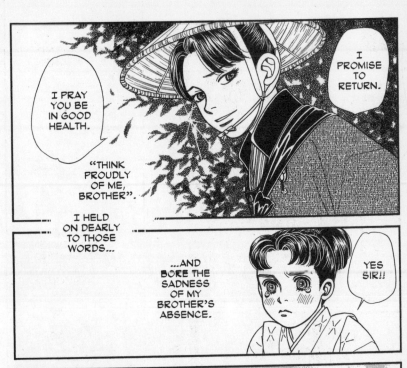

I PROMISE TO RETURN.
I PRAY YOU BE IN GOOD HEALTH.
"THINK PROUDLY OF ME, BROTHER".
I HELD ON DEARLY TO THOSE WORDS...
YES SIR!!
...AND BORE THE SADNESS OF MY BROTHER'S ABSENCE.
MY FATHER WAS EVENTUALLY RELEASED FROM HOUSE ARREST AND STARTED A SMALL PRIVATE SCHOOL.
MY FATHER'S LOYALTY AND PASSION SOON EARNED HIM RAVE REVIEWS.
I WORKED TO POLISH MYSELF WHILE HELPING HIM WITH HIS ENDEAV-OR.
I WANTED TO FEEL CLOSER TO ANI-UE THAT WAY.

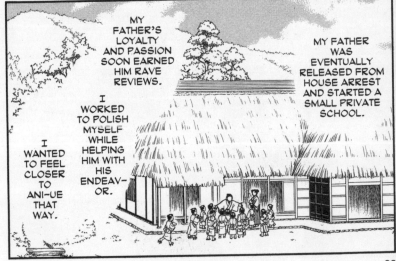

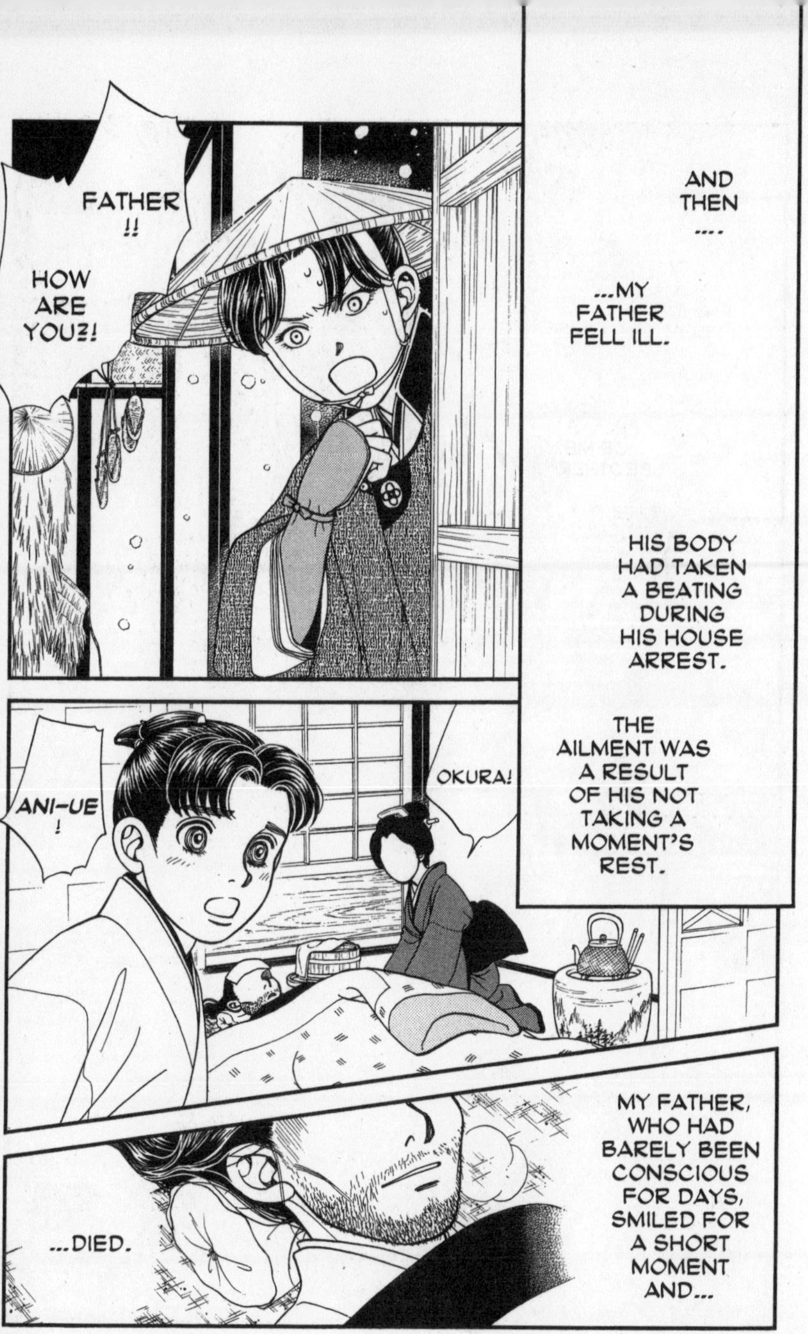
AND THEN ....
...MY FATHER FELL ILL.
HIS BODY HAD TAKEN A BEATING DURING HIS HOUSE ARREST.
THE AILMENT WAS A RESULT OF HIS NOT TAKING A MOMENT'S REST.
FATHER !!
HOW ARE YOU?!
OKURA!
ANI-UE !
MY FATHER, WHO HAD BARELY BEEN CONSCIOUS FOR DAYS, SMILED FOR A SHORT MOMENT AND...
...DIED.

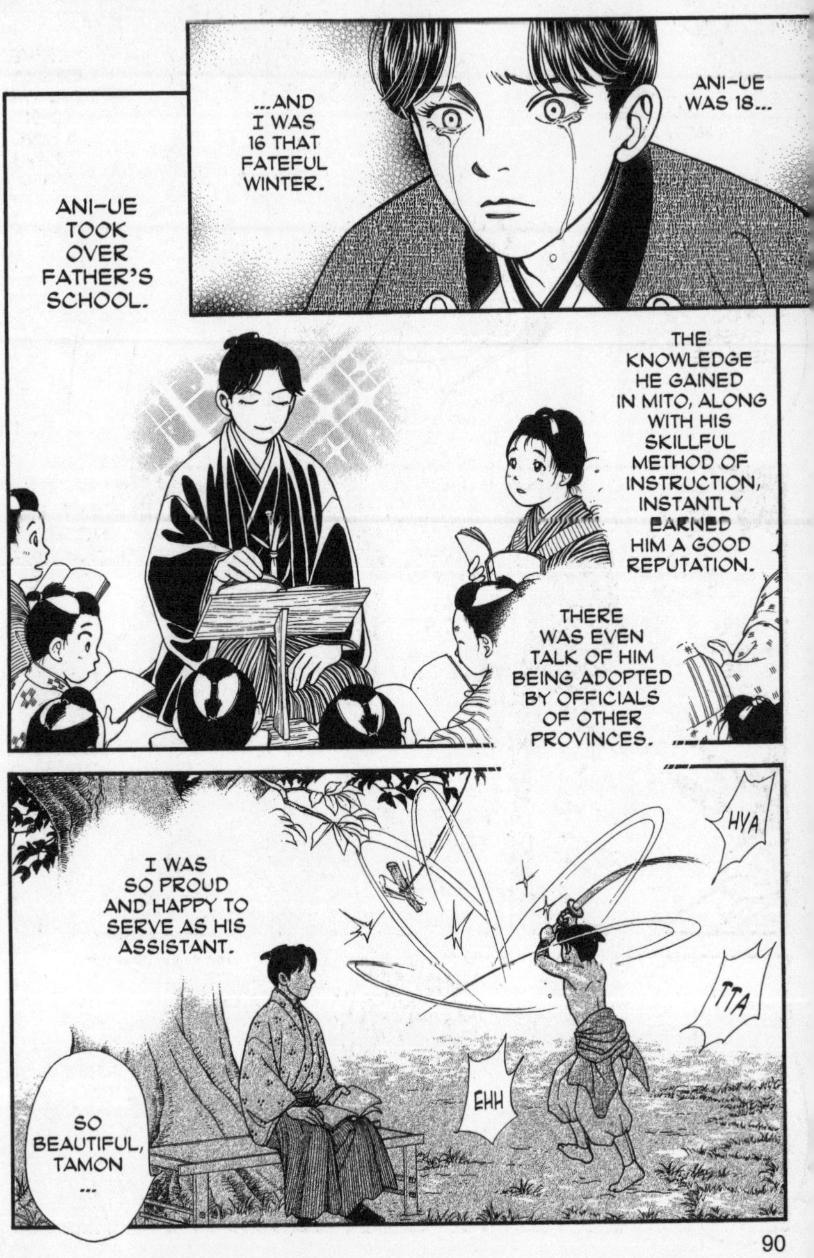
ANI-UE WAS 18...
...AND I WAS 16 THAT FATEFUL WINTER.
ANI-UE TOOK OVER FATHER'S SCHOOL.
THE KNOWLEDGE HE GAINED IN MITO, ALONG WITH HIS SKILLFUL METHOD OF INSTRUCTION, INSTANTLY EARNED HIM A GOOD REPUTATION.
THERE WAS EVEN TALK OF HIM BEING ADOPTED BY OFFICIALS OF OTHER PROVINCES.
HYA
TTA
I WAS SO PROUD AND HAPPY TO SERVE AS HIS ASSISTANT.
EHH
SO BEAUTIFUL, TAMON ...

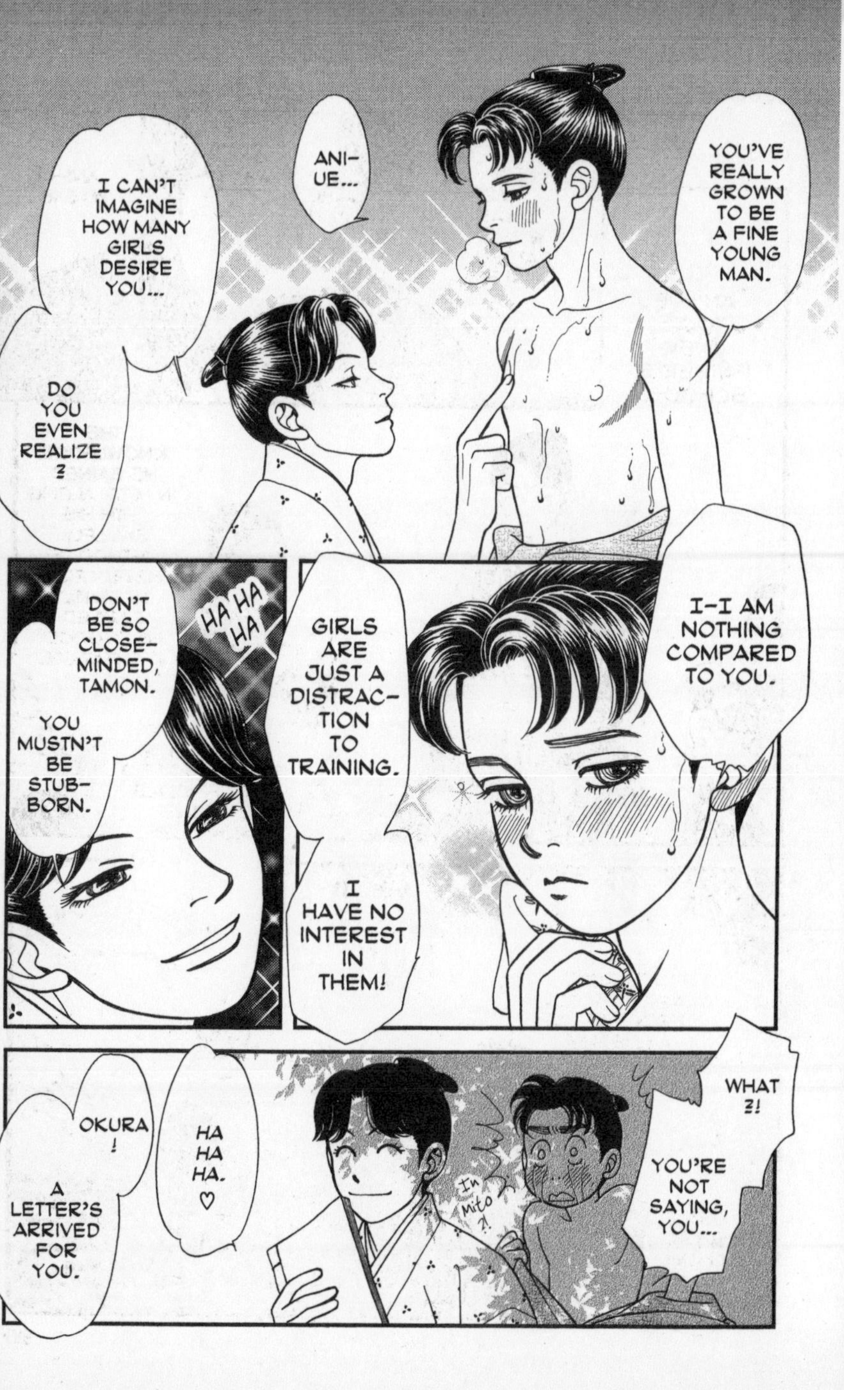
YOU'VE REALLY GROWN TO BE A FINE YOUNG MAN.
ANI-UE...
I CAN'T IMAGINE HOW MANY GIRLS DESIRE YOU...
DO YOU EVEN REALIZE?
I-I AM NOTHING COMPARED TO YOU.
GIRLS ARE JUST A DISTRACTION TO TRAINING.
I HAVE NO INTEREST IN THEM!
HA HA HA
DON'T BE SO CLOSE-MINDED, TAMON.
YOU MUSTN'T BE STUBBORN.
WHAT?!
YOU'RE NOT SAYING, YOU...
In Mito?!
HA HA HA. ♡
OKURA!
A LETTER'S ARRIVED FOR YOU.

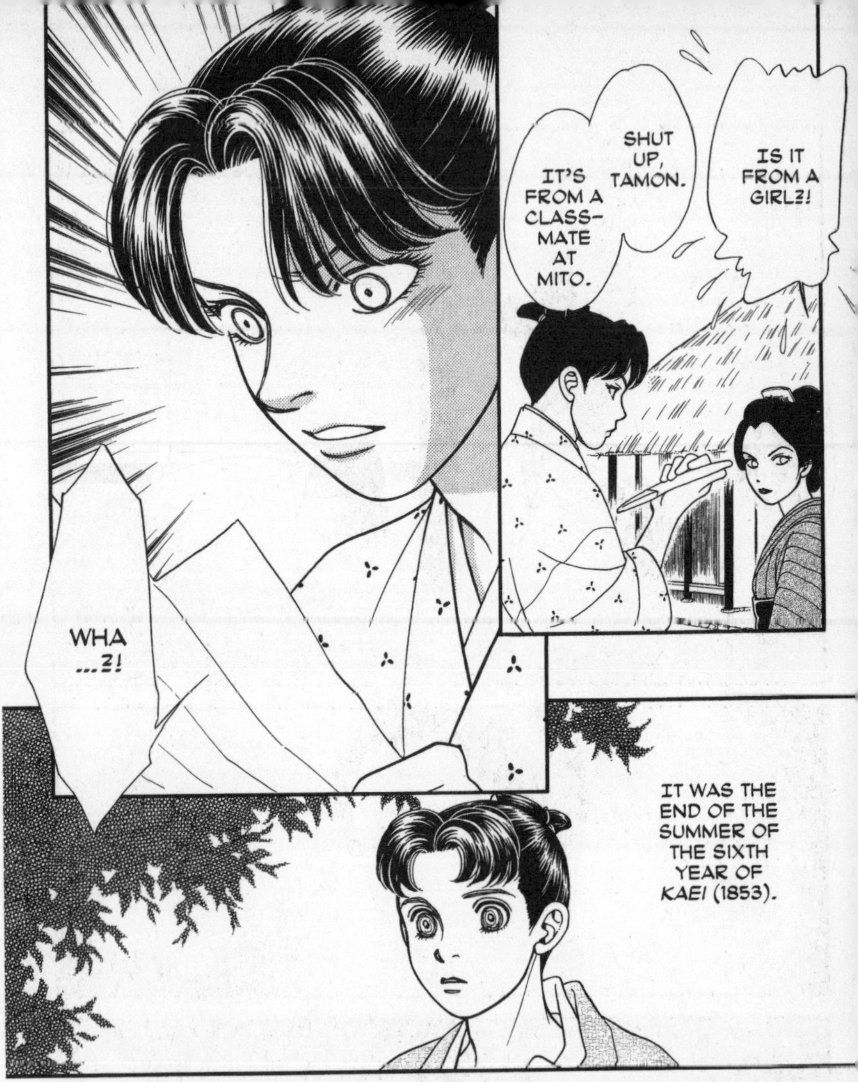
IS IT FROM A GIRL?!
SHUT UP, TAMON.
IT'S FROM A CLASSMATE AT MITO.
WHA ...?!
IT WAS THE END OF THE SUMMER OF THE SIXTH YEAR OF *KAEI* (1853).
THE LETTER WAS NOTIFYING HIM OF THE ARRIVAL OF THE BLACK SHIPS.*

*American Commodore Perry's fleet arriving to negotiate trade with Japan.

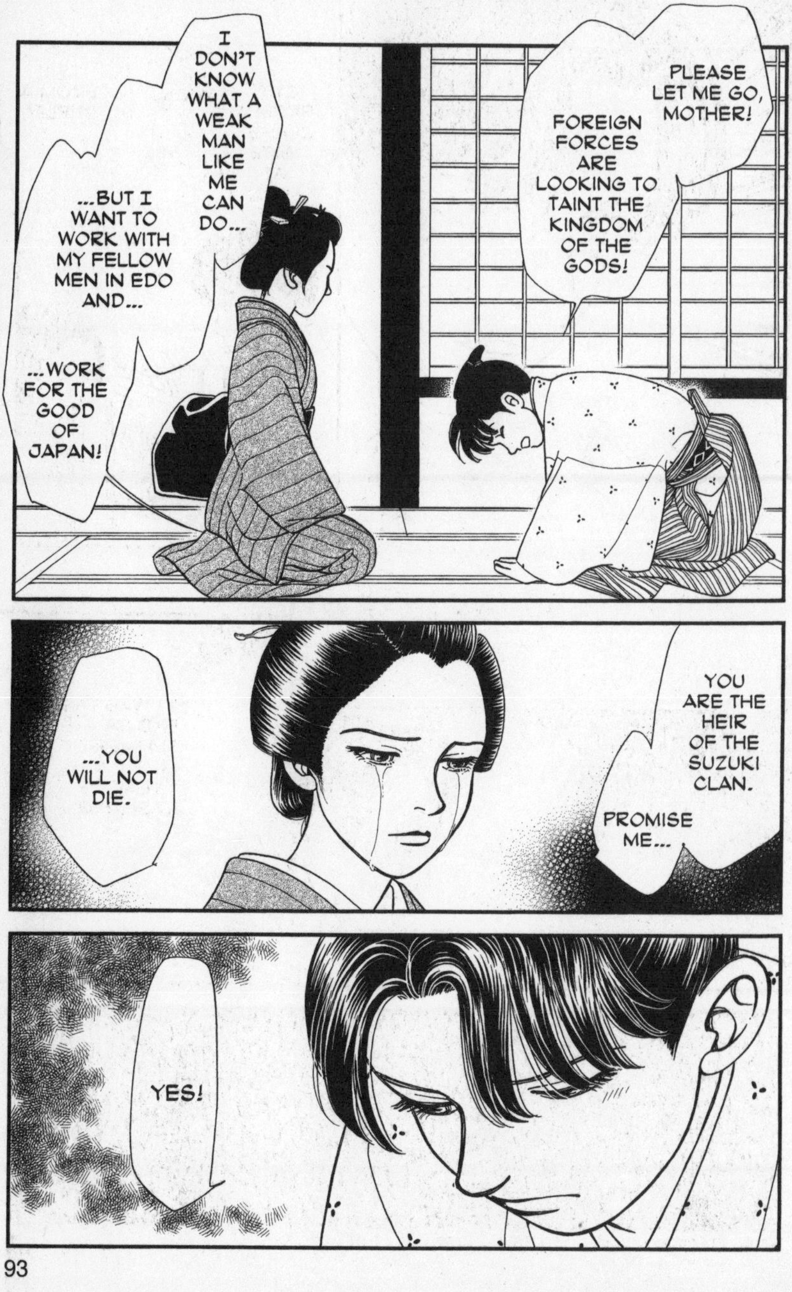
PLEASE LET ME GO, MOTHER!
FOREIGN FORCES ARE LOOKING TO TAINT THE KINGDOM OF THE GODS!
I DON'T KNOW WHAT A WEAK MAN LIKE ME CAN DO...
...BUT I WANT TO WORK WITH MY FELLOW MEN IN EDO AND...
...WORK FOR THE GOOD OF JAPAN!
YOU ARE THE HEIR OF THE SUZUKI CLAN.
PROMISE ME...
...YOU WILL NOT DIE.
YES!

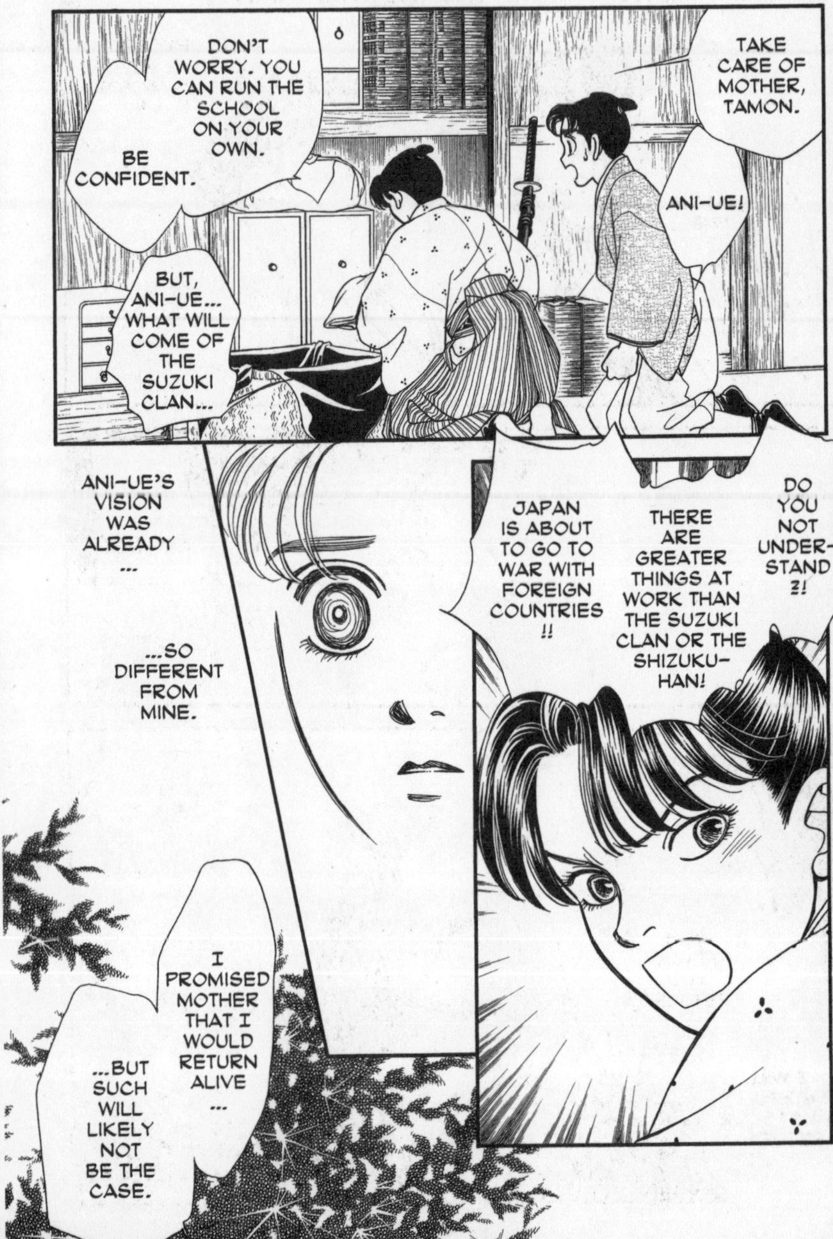
TAKE CARE OF MOTHER, TAMON.
ANI-UE!
DON'T WORRY. YOU CAN RUN THE SCHOOL ON YOUR OWN.
BE CONFIDENT.
BUT, ANI-UE... WHAT WILL COME OF THE SUZUKI CLAN...
DO YOU NOT UNDERSTAND ?!
THERE ARE GREATER THINGS AT WORK THAN THE SUZUKI CLAN OR THE SHIZUKU-HAN!
JAPAN IS ABOUT TO GO TO WAR WITH FOREIGN COUNTRIES !!
ANI-UE'S VISION WAS ALREADY ...
...SO DIFFERENT FROM MINE.
I PROMISED MOTHER THAT I WOULD RETURN ALIVE ...
...BUT SUCH WILL LIKELY NOT BE THE CASE.

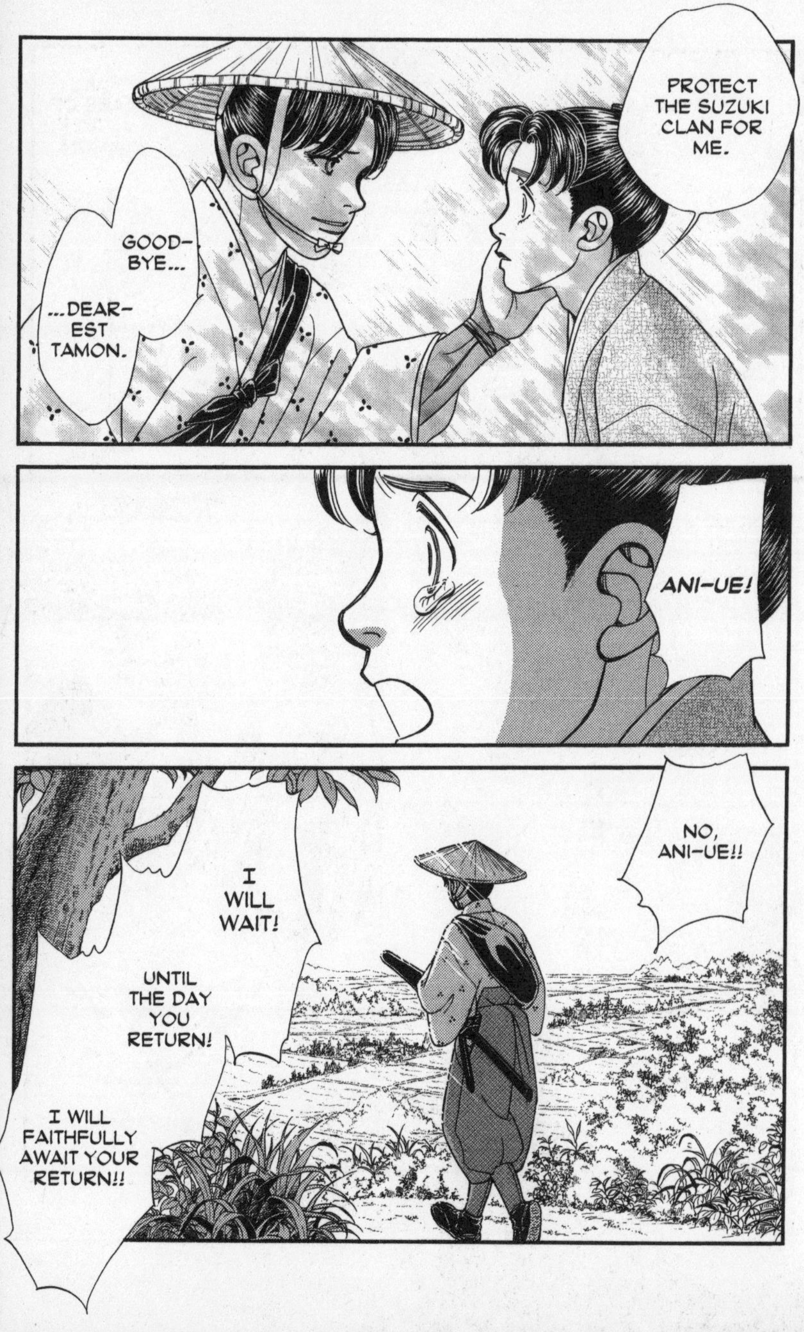
PROTECT THE SUZUKI CLAN FOR ME.
GOOD-BYE...
...DEAR-EST TAMON.
ANI-UE!
NO, ANI-UE!!
I WILL WAIT!
UNTIL THE DAY YOU RETURN!
I WILL FAITHFULLY AWAIT YOUR RETURN!!

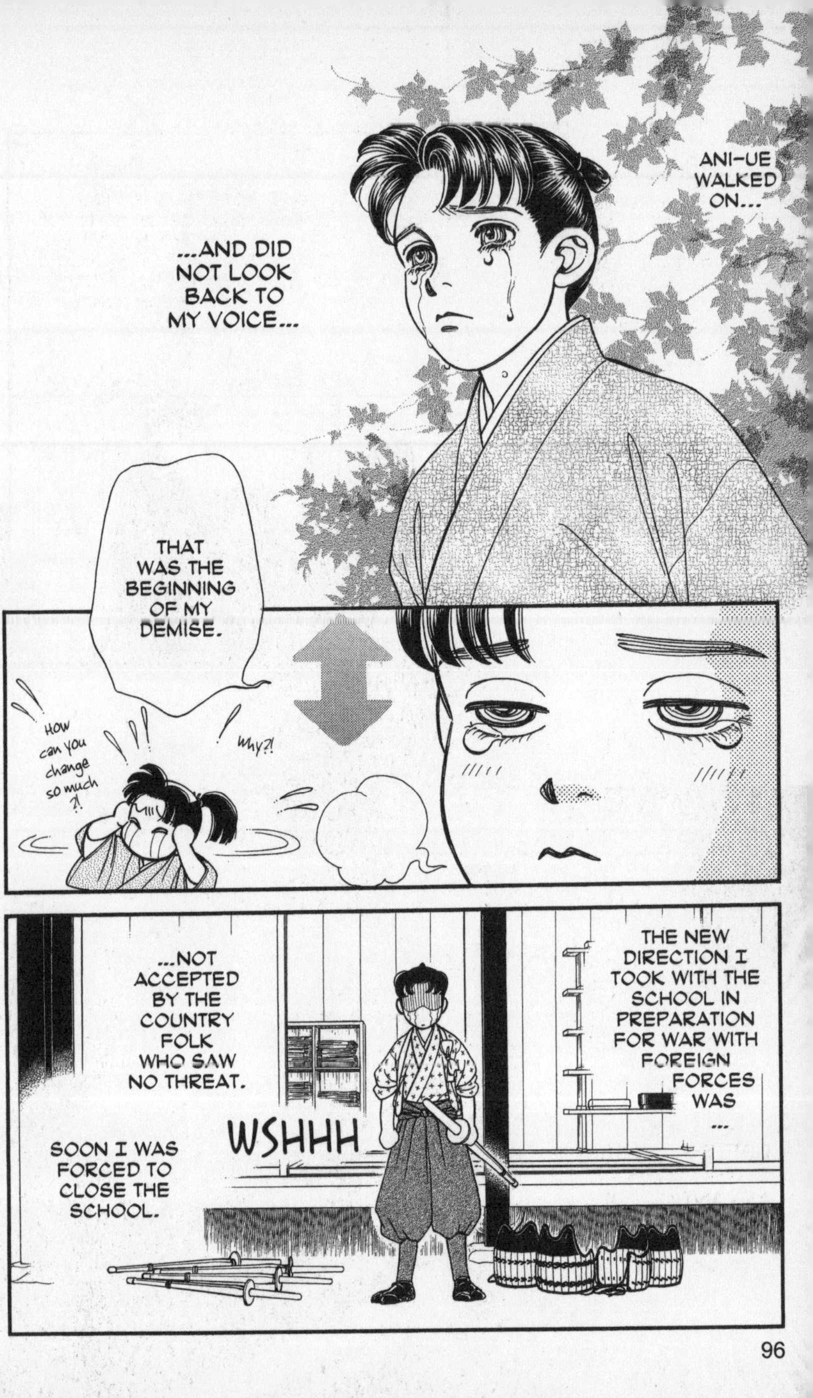
ANI-UE WALKED ON...
...AND DID NOT LOOK BACK TO MY VOICE...
THAT WAS THE BEGINNING OF MY DEMISE.
Why?!
How can you change so much?!
THE NEW DIRECTION I TOOK WITH THE SCHOOL IN PREPARATION FOR WAR WITH FOREIGN FORCES WAS ...
...NOT ACCEPTED BY THE COUNTRY FOLK WHO SAW NO THREAT.
WSHHH
SOON I WAS FORCED TO CLOSE THE SCHOOL.

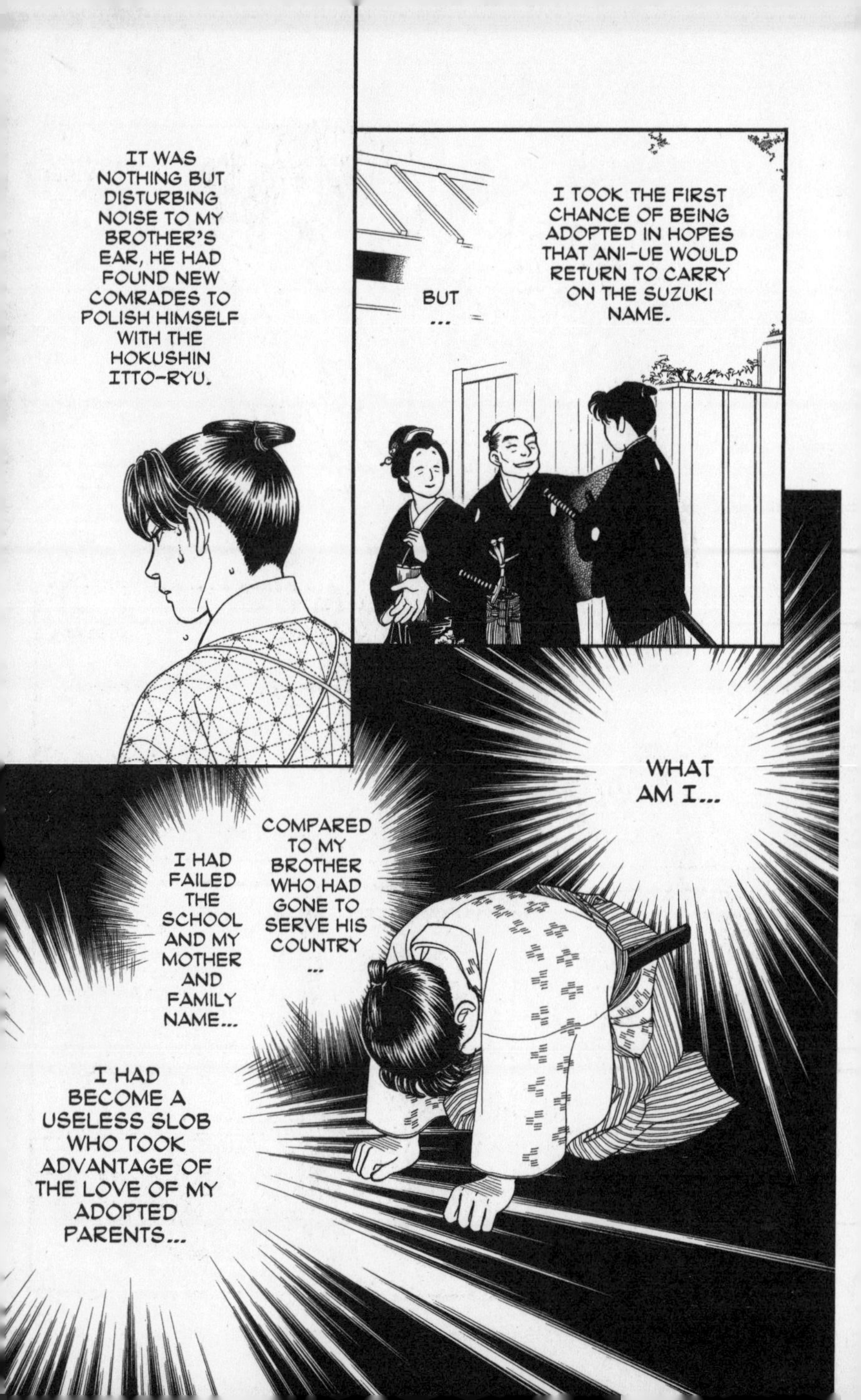
I TOOK THE FIRST CHANCE OF BEING ADOPTED IN HOPES THAT ANI-UE WOULD RETURN TO CARRY ON THE SUZUKI NAME.
BUT ...
IT WAS NOTHING BUT DISTURBING NOISE TO MY BROTHER'S EAR, HE HAD FOUND NEW COMRADES TO POLISH HIMSELF WITH THE HOKUSHIN ITTO-RYU.
WHAT AM I...
COMPARED TO MY BROTHER WHO HAD GONE TO SERVE HIS COUNTRY ...
I HAD FAILED THE SCHOOL AND MY MOTHER AND FAMILY NAME...
I HAD BECOME A USELESS SLOB WHO TOOK ADVANTAGE OF THE LOVE OF MY ADOPTED PARENTS...

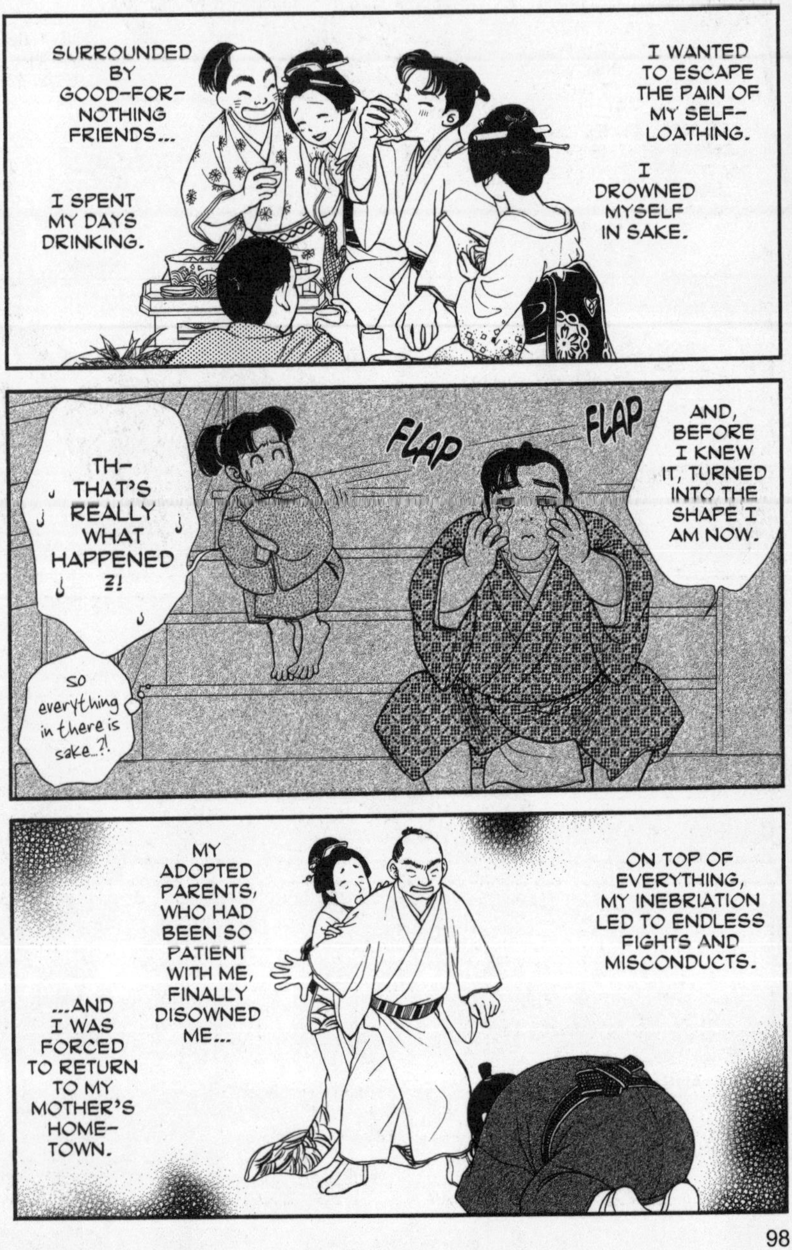
I WANTED TO ESCAPE THE PAIN OF MY SELF-LOATHING.
I DROWNED MYSELF IN SAKE.
SURROUNDED BY GOOD-FOR-NOTHING FRIENDS...
I SPENT MY DAYS DRINKING.
AND, BEFORE I KNEW IT, TURNED INTO THE SHAPE I AM NOW.
FLAP
FLAP
TH-THAT'S REALLY WHAT HAPPENED?!
so everything in there is sake...?!
ON TOP OF EVERYTHING, MY INEBRIATION LED TO ENDLESS FIGHTS AND MISCONDUCTS.
MY ADOPTED PARENTS, WHO HAD BEEN SO PATIENT WITH ME, FINALLY DISOWNED ME...
...AND I WAS FORCED TO RETURN TO MY MOTHER'S HOMETOWN.

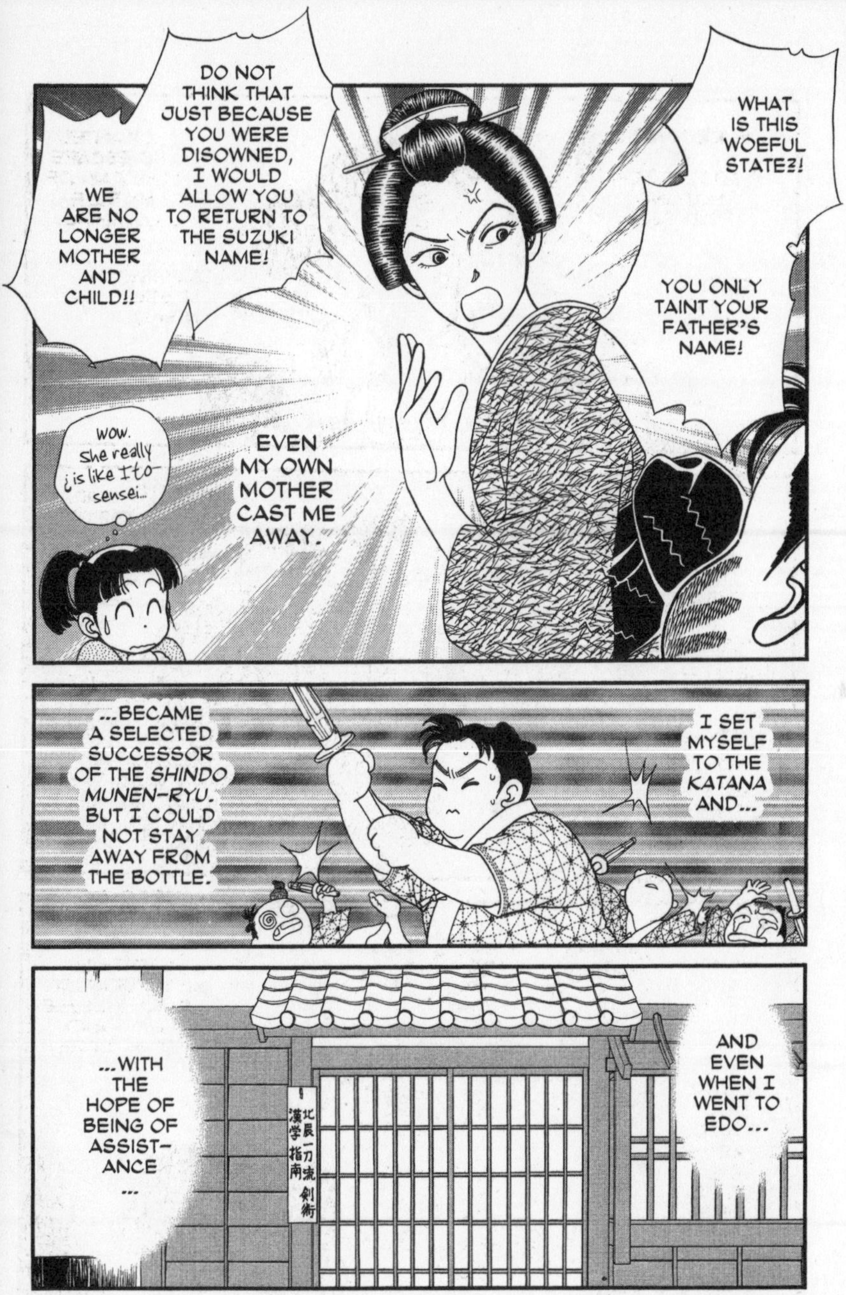
WHAT IS THIS WOEFUL STATE?!
YOU ONLY TAINT YOUR FATHER'S NAME!
DO NOT THINK THAT JUST BECAUSE YOU WERE DISOWNED, I WOULD ALLOW YOU TO RETURN TO THE SUZUKI NAME!
WE ARE NO LONGER MOTHER AND CHILD!!
EVEN MY OWN MOTHER CAST ME AWAY.
Wow. She really is like Ito-sensei...
I SET MYSELF TO THE KATANA AND...
...BECAME A SELECTED SUCCESSOR OF THE *SHINDO MUNEN-RYU*. BUT I COULD NOT STAY AWAY FROM THE BOTTLE.
AND EVEN WHEN I WENT TO EDO...
北辰一刀流剣術
漢学指南
...WITH THE HOPE OF BEING OF ASSIST-ANCE...

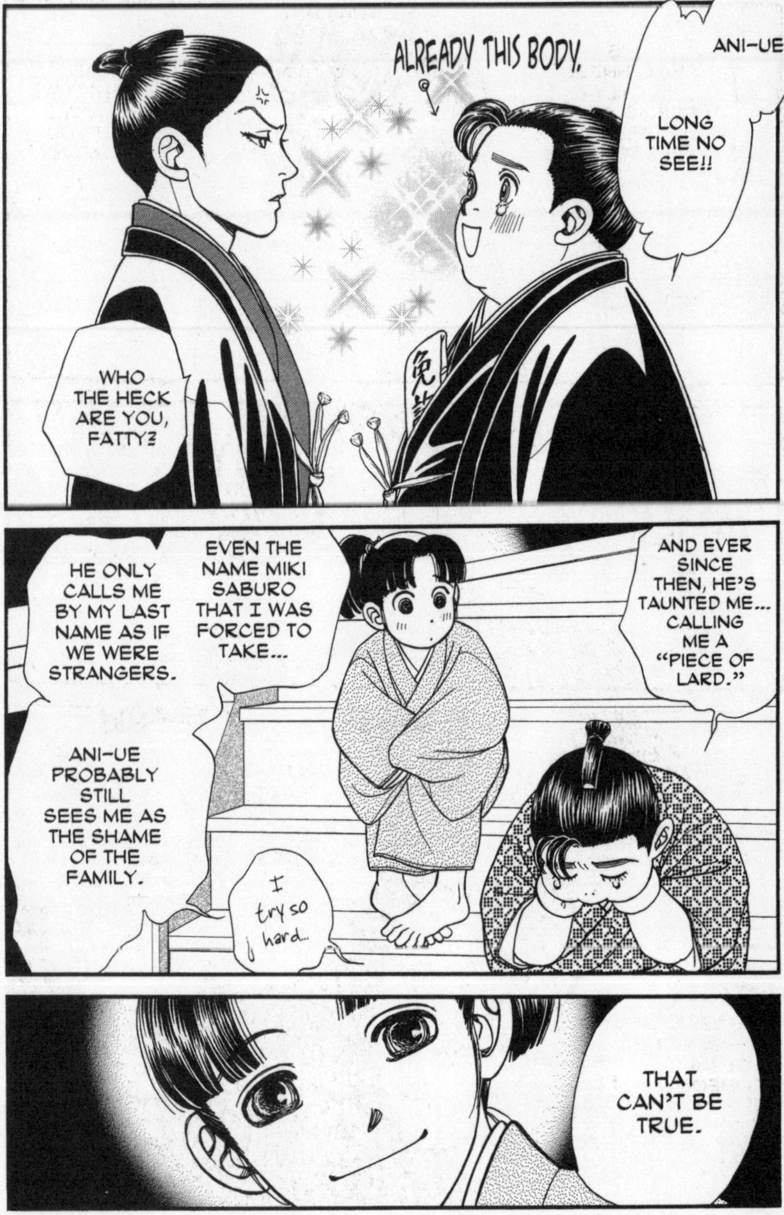
ANI-UE!
LONG TIME NO SEE!!
ALREADY THIS BODY.
WHO THE HECK ARE YOU, FATTY?
AND EVER SINCE THEN, HE'S TAUNTED ME... CALLING ME A "PIECE OF LARD."
EVEN THE NAME MIKI SABURO THAT I WAS FORCED TO TAKE...
HE ONLY CALLS ME BY MY LAST NAME AS IF WE WERE STRANGERS.
ANI-UE PROBABLY STILL SEES ME AS THE SHAME OF THE FAMILY.
I try so hard...
THAT CAN'T BE TRUE.

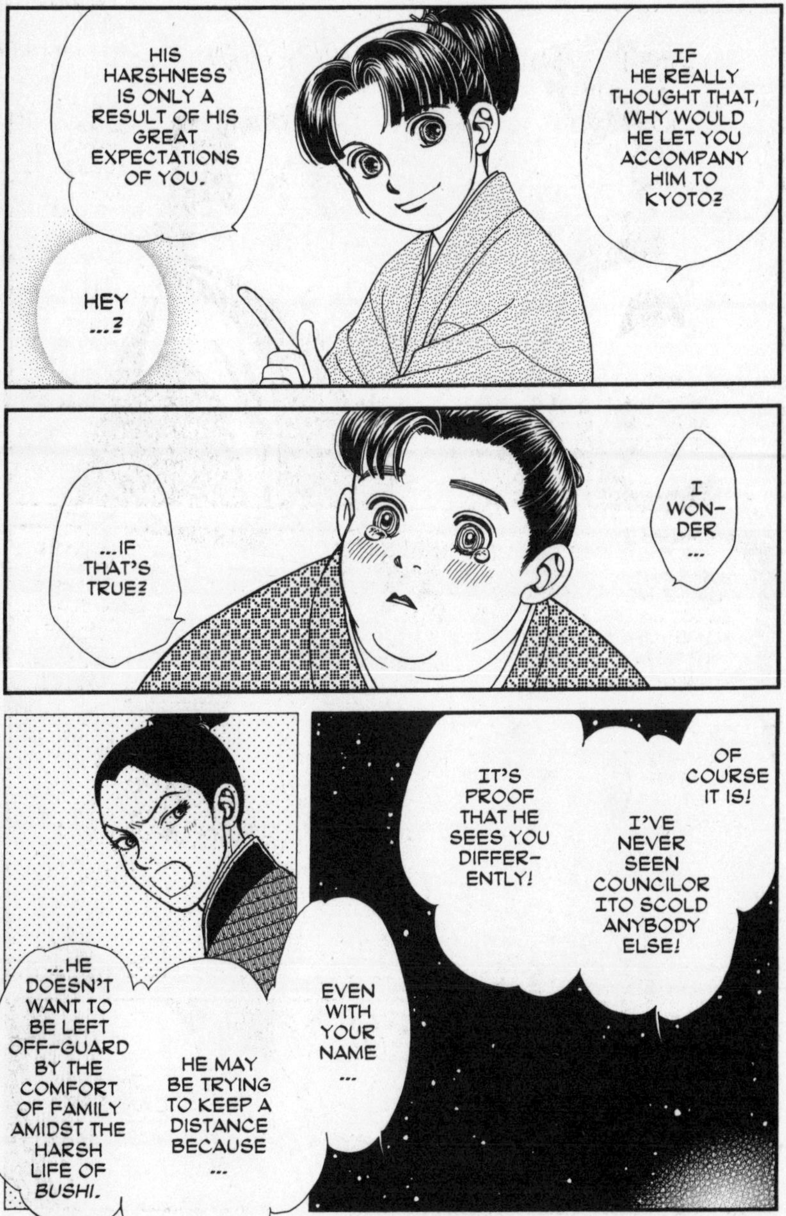
IF HE REALLY THOUGHT THAT, WHY WOULD HE LET YOU ACCOMPANY HIM TO KYOTO?
HIS HARSHNESS IS ONLY A RESULT OF HIS GREAT EXPECTATIONS OF YOU.
HEY ...?
I WON-DER ...
...IF THAT'S TRUE?
OF COURSE IT IS!
IT'S PROOF THAT HE SEES YOU DIFFER-ENTLY!
I'VE NEVER SEEN COUNCILOR ITO SCOLD ANYBODY ELSE!
EVEN WITH YOUR NAME ...
HE MAY BE TRYING TO KEEP A DISTANCE BECAUSE ...
...HE DOESN'T WANT TO BE LEFT OFF-GUARD BY THE COMFORT OF FAMILY AMIDST THE HARSH LIFE OF *BUSHI*.

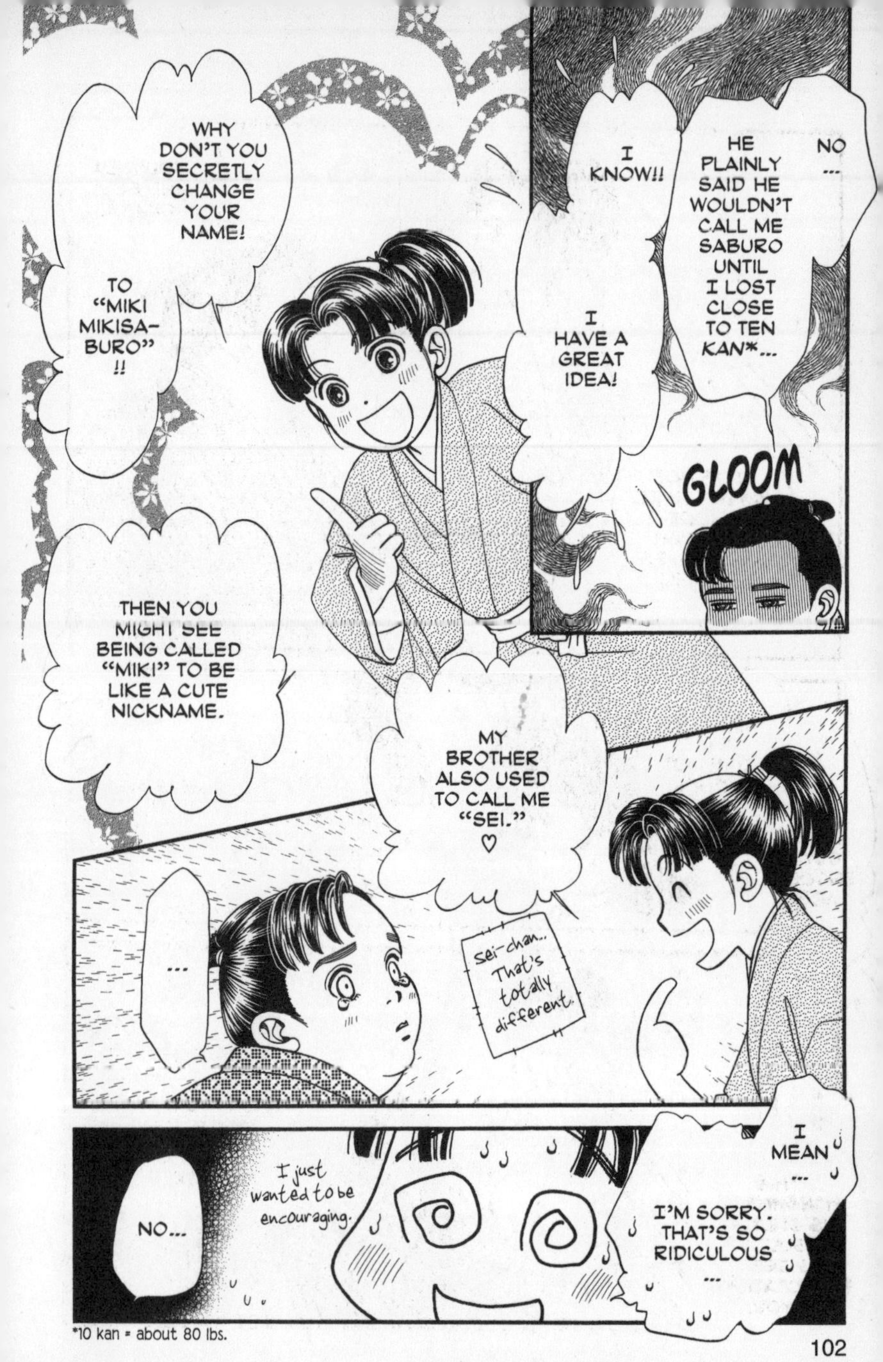
NO ...
HE PLAINLY SAID HE WOULDN'T CALL ME SABURO UNTIL I LOST CLOSE TO TEN KAN*...
GLOOM
I KNOW!!
I HAVE A GREAT IDEA!
WHY DON'T YOU SECRETLY CHANGE YOUR NAME!
TO "MIKI MIKISA-BURO"!!
THEN YOU MIGHT SEE BEING CALLED "MIKI" TO BE LIKE A CUTE NICKNAME.
MY BROTHER ALSO USED TO CALL ME "SEI." ♡
...
Sei-chan.. That's totally different.
I MEAN ...
I'M SORRY. THAT'S SO RIDICULOUS ...
I just wanted to be encouraging.
NO...

*10 kan = about 80 lbs.

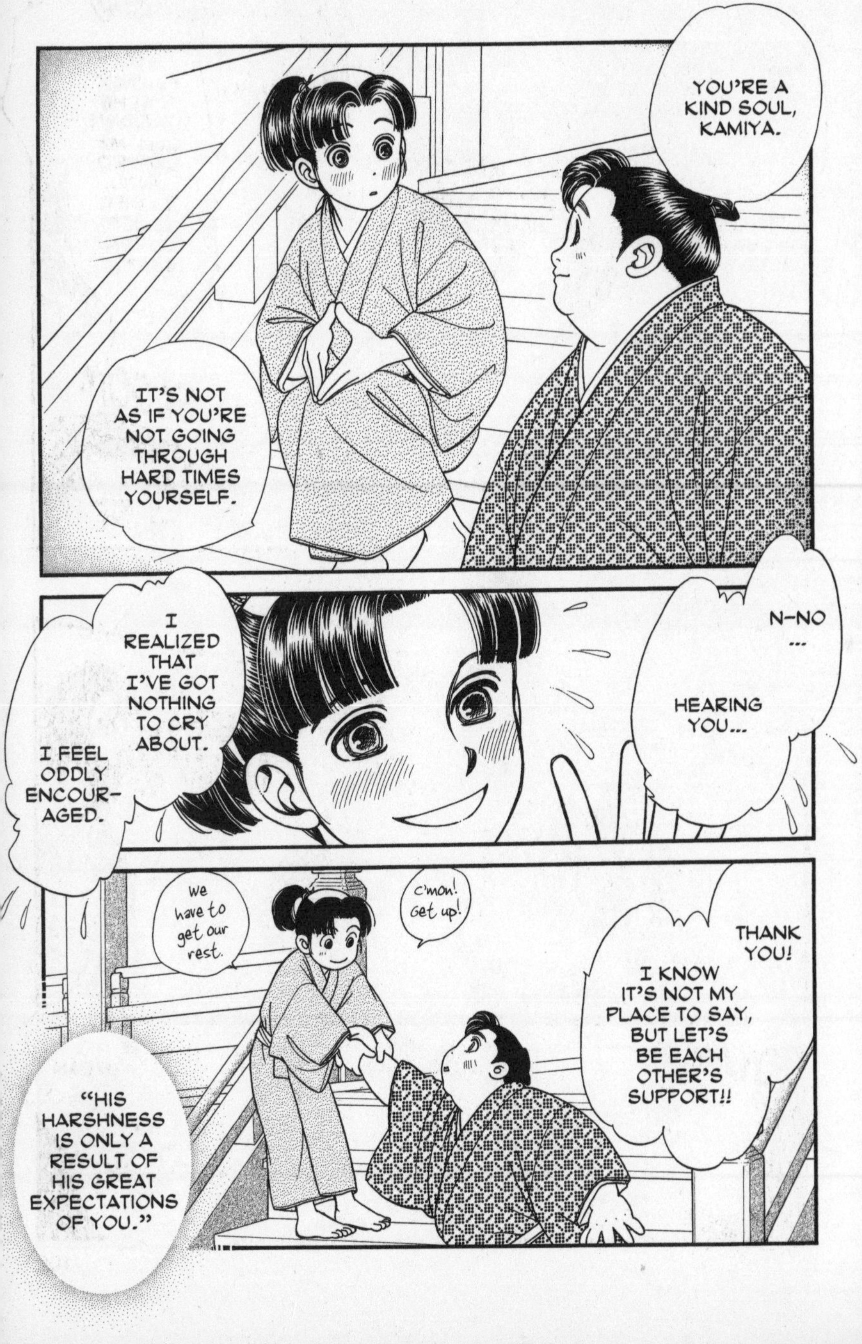

YOU'RE A KIND SOUL, KAMIYA.
IT'S NOT AS IF YOU'RE NOT GOING THROUGH HARD TIMES YOURSELF.
N-NO...
HEARING YOU...
I REALIZED THAT I'VE GOT NOTHING TO CRY ABOUT.
I FEEL ODDLY ENCOUR-AGED.
THANK YOU!
I KNOW IT'S NOT MY PLACE TO SAY, BUT LET'S BE EACH OTHER'S SUPPORT!!
C'mon! Get up!
We have to get our rest.
"HIS HARSHNESS IS ONLY A RESULT OF HIS GREAT EXPECTATIONS OF YOU."

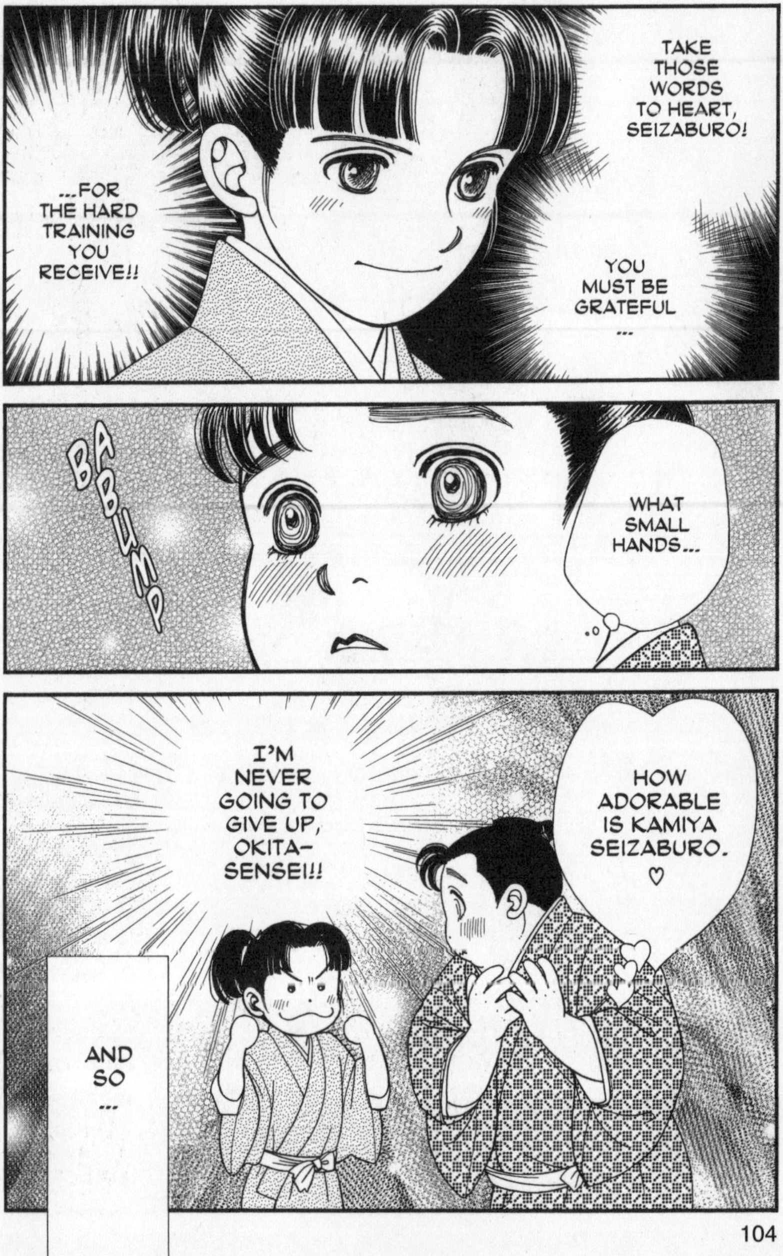
TAKE THOSE WORDS TO HEART, SEIZABURO!
YOU MUST BE GRATEFUL...
...FOR THE HARD TRAINING YOU RECEIVE!!
WHAT SMALL HANDS...
BABUMP
HOW ADORABLE IS KAMIYA SEIZABURO. ♡
I'M NEVER GOING TO GIVE UP, OKITA-SENSEI!!
AND SO...

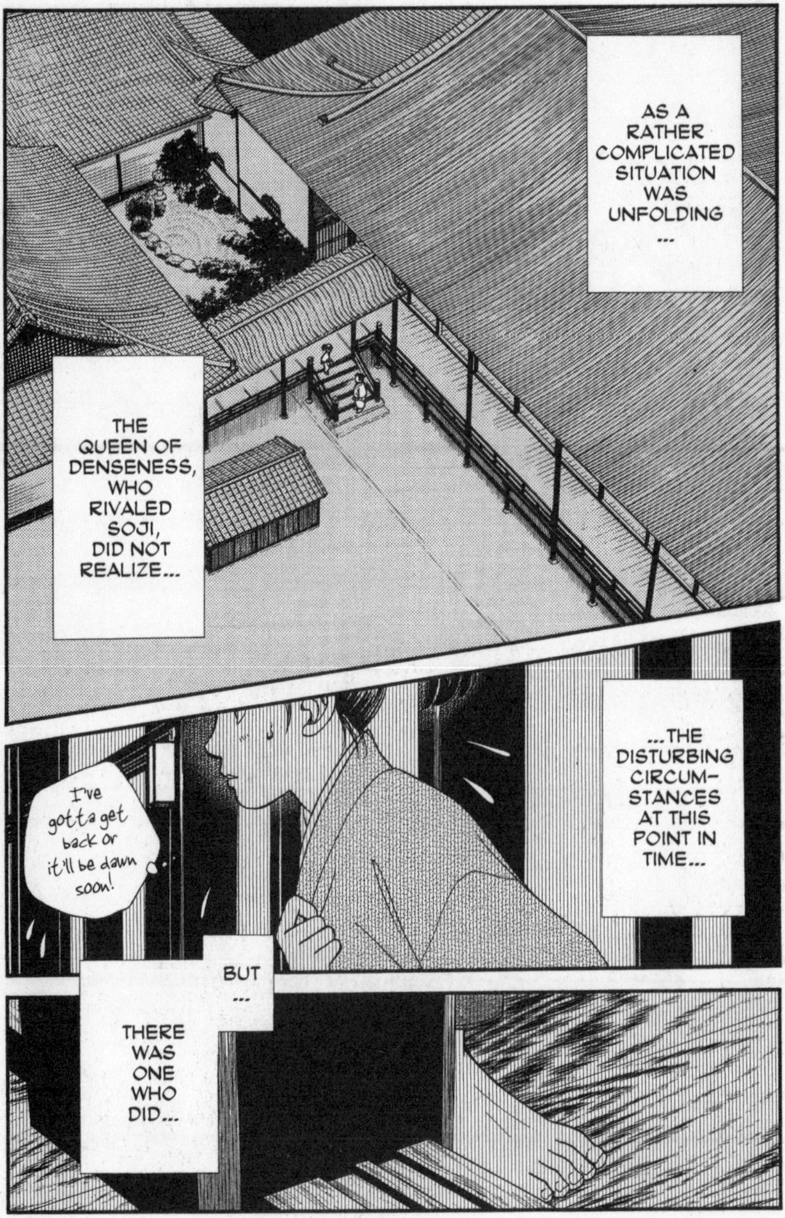
AS A RATHER COMPLICATED SITUATION WAS UNFOLDING...
THE QUEEN OF DENSENESS, WHO RIVALED SOJI, DID NOT REALIZE...
...THE DISTURBING CIRCUMSTANCES AT THIS POINT IN TIME...
I've gotta get back or it'll be dawn soon!
BUT...
THERE WAS ONE WHO DID...

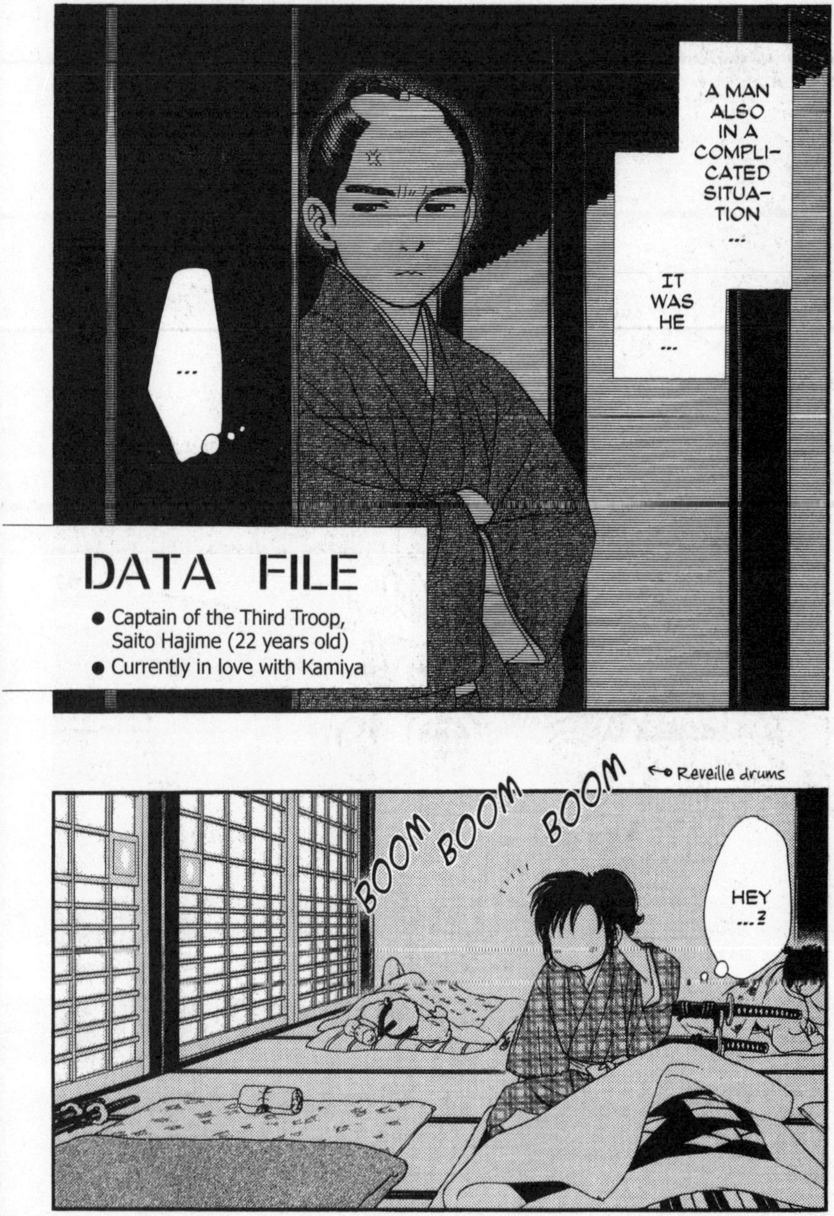
A MAN ALSO IN A COMPLICATED SITUATION...
IT WAS HE...
...
DATA FILE
● Captain of the Third Troop, Saito Hajime (22 years old)
● Currently in love with Kamiya
BOOM BOOM BOOM
← Reveille drums
HEY...?

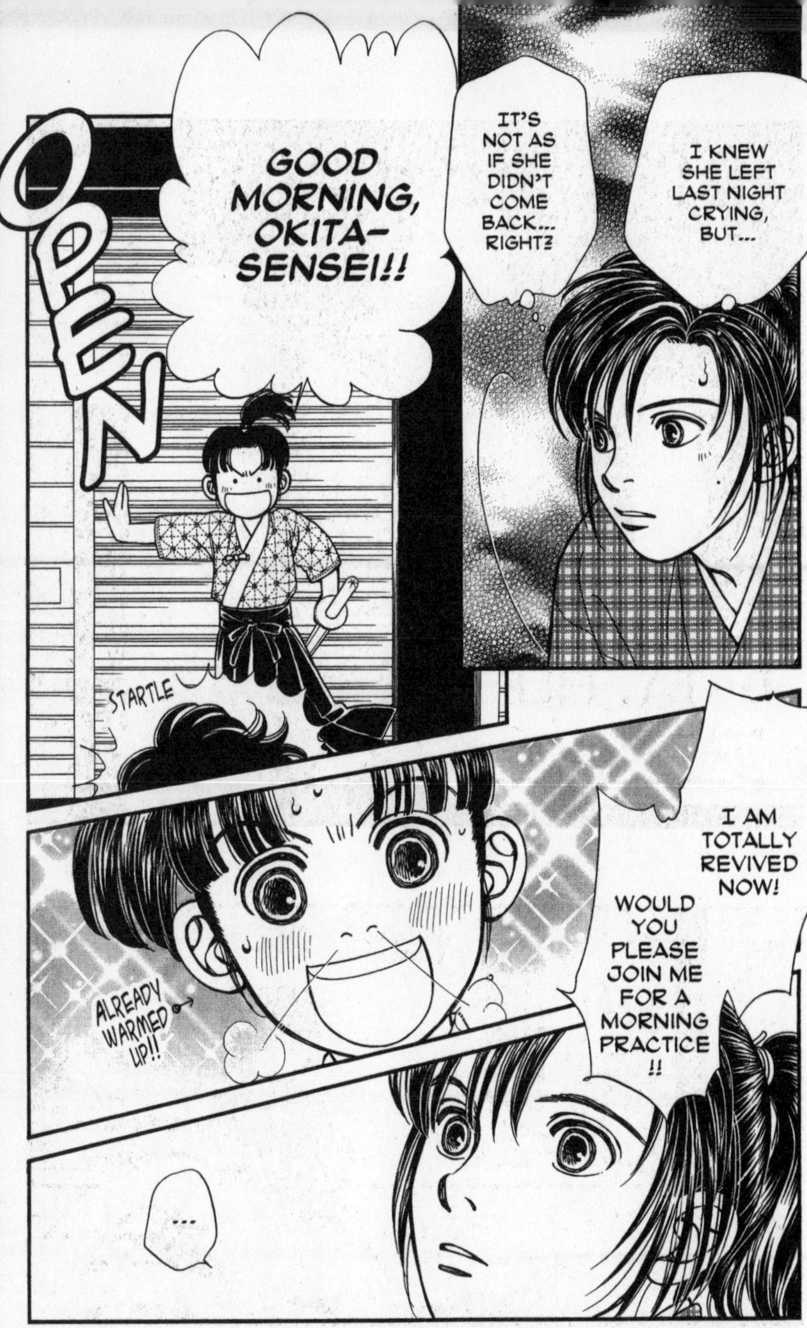
I KNEW SHE LEFT LAST NIGHT CRYING, BUT...
IT'S NOT AS IF SHE DIDN'T COME BACK... RIGHT?
OPEN
GOOD MORNING, OKITA-SENSEI!!
STARTLE
I AM TOTALLY REVIVED NOW!
WOULD YOU PLEASE JOIN ME FOR A MORNING PRACTICE!!
ALREADY WARMED UP!!
...

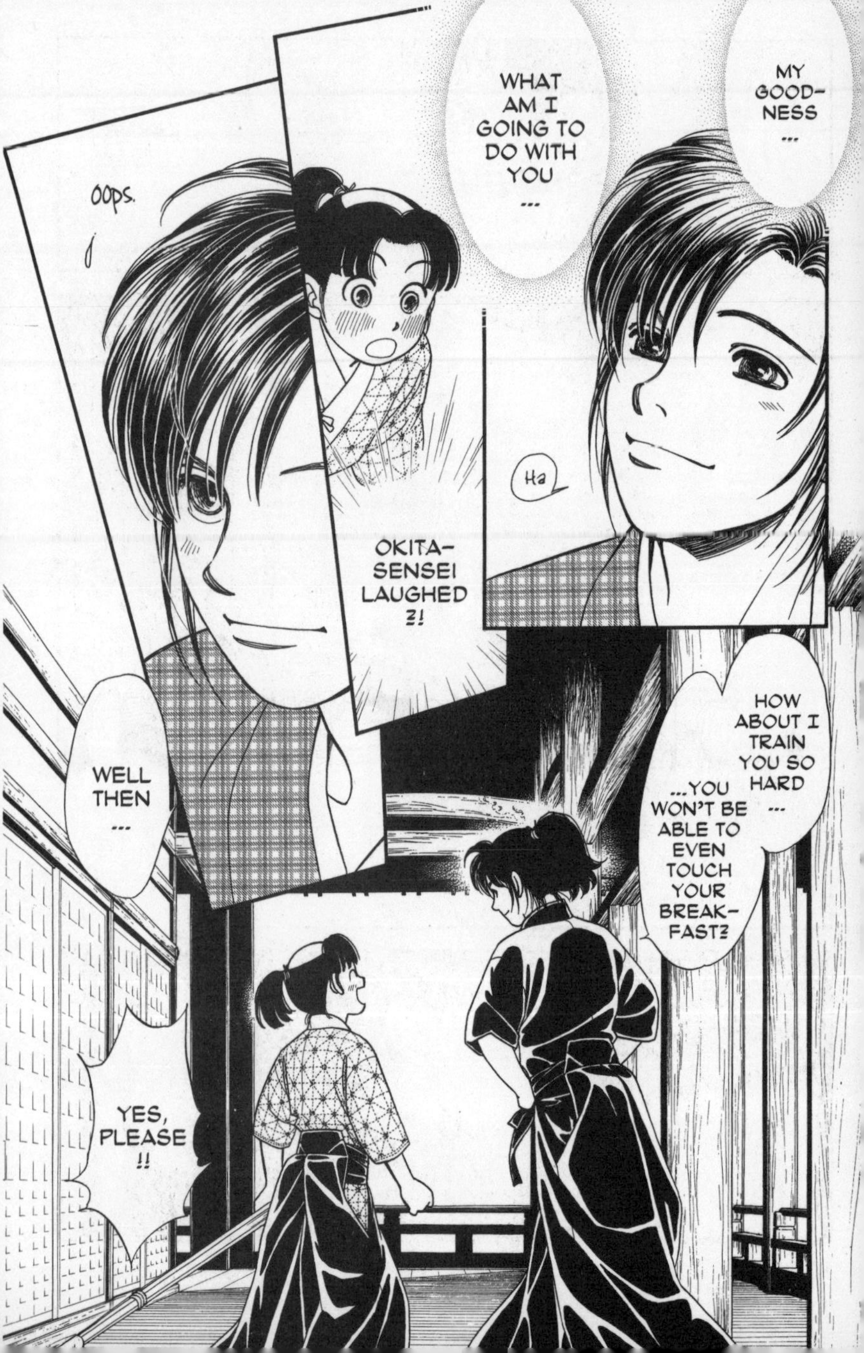
MY GOOD-NESS ...
WHAT AM I GOING TO DO WITH YOU ...
Ha
OKITA-SENSEI LAUGHED ?!
oops.
WELL THEN ...
HOW ABOUT I TRAIN YOU SO HARD ...
...YOU WON'T BE ABLE TO EVEN TOUCH YOUR BREAK-FAST?
YES, PLEASE !!

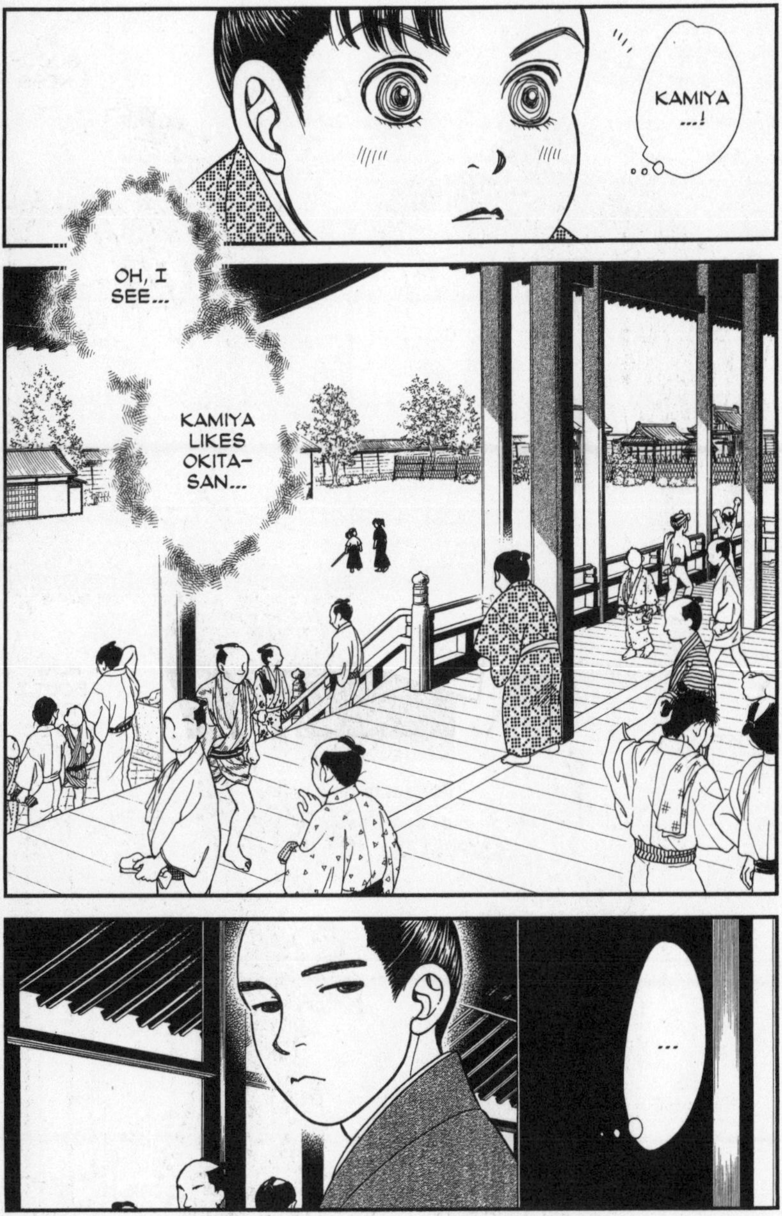
KAMIYA ...!
OH, I SEE...
KAMIYA LIKES OKITA-SAN...
...

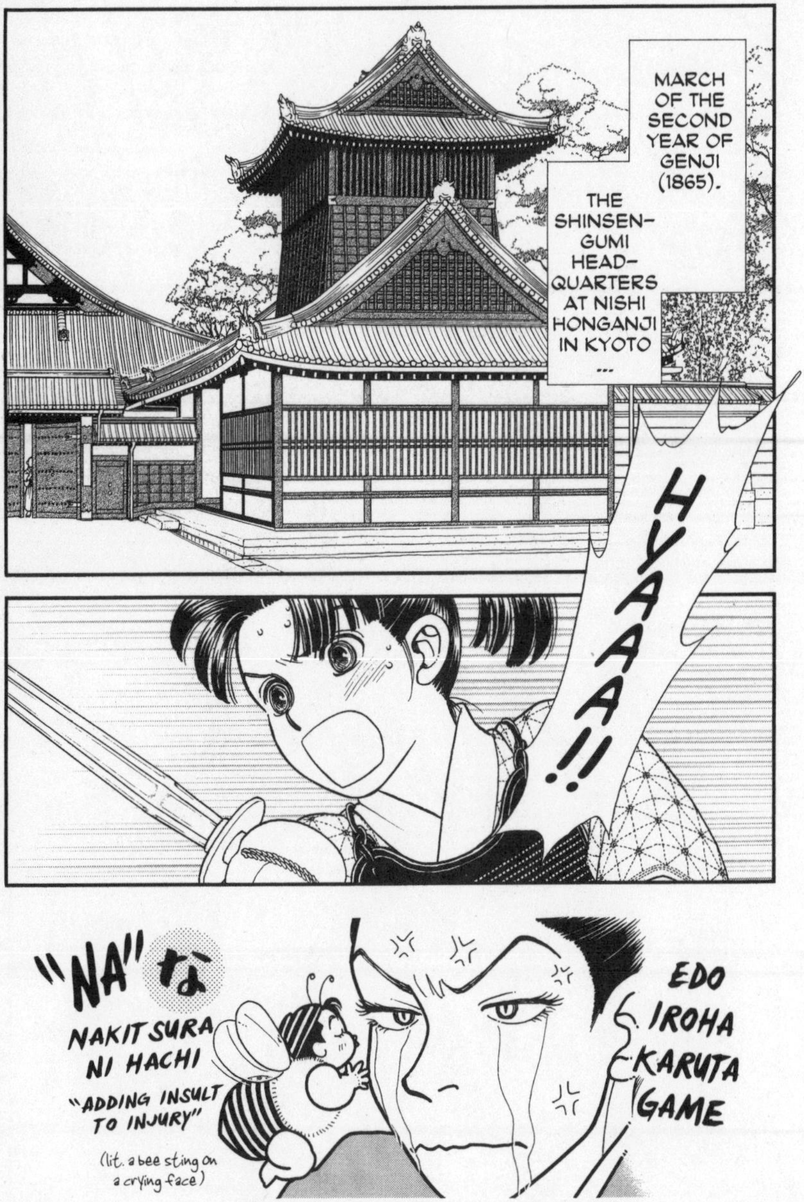
MARCH OF THE SECOND YEAR OF GENJI (1865).
THE SHINSEN-GUMI HEAD-QUARTERS AT NISHI HONGANJI IN KYOTO ...
HYAAAA!!
EDO IROHA KARUTA GAME
"NA" な
NAKIT SURA NI HACHI
"ADDING INSULT TO INJURY"
(lit. a bee sting on a crying face)

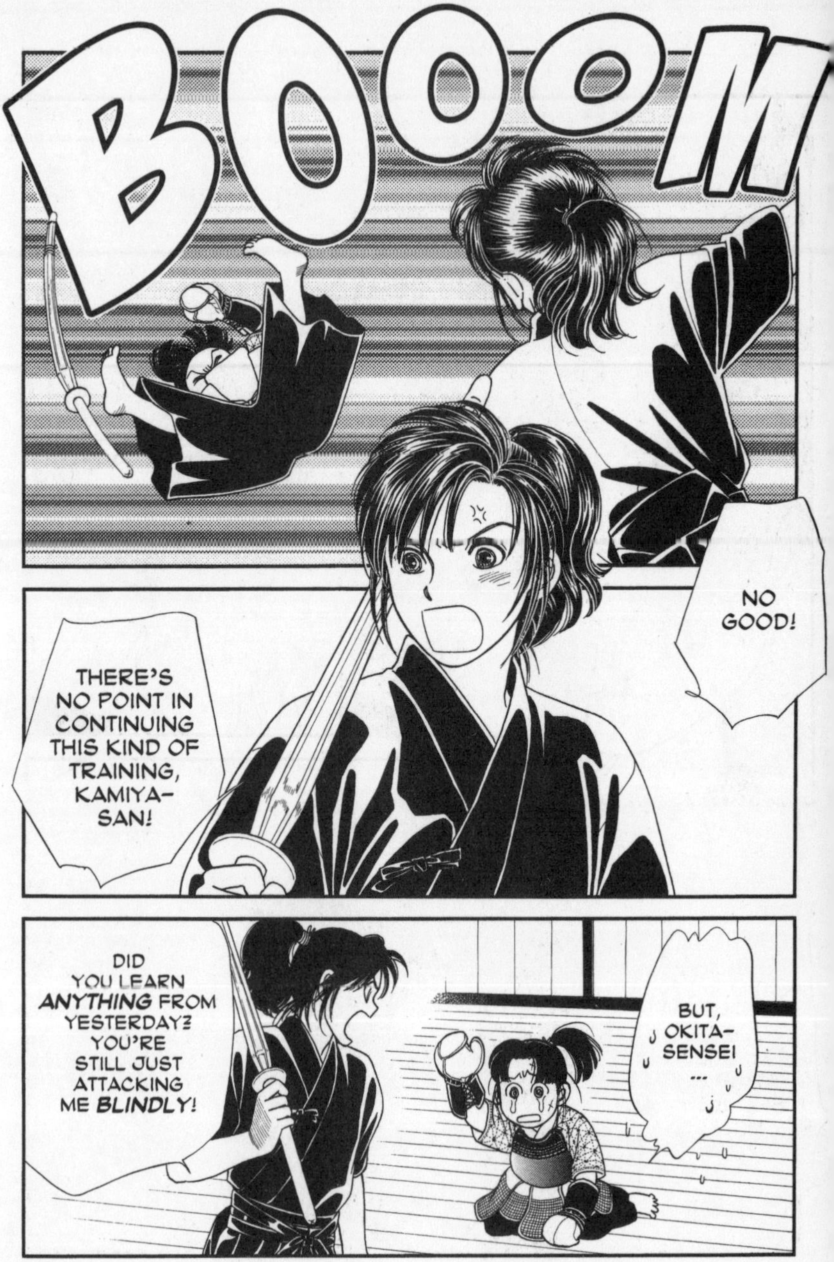
BOOOM
NO GOOD!
THERE'S NO POINT IN CONTINUING THIS KIND OF TRAINING, KAMIYA-SAN!
BUT, OKITA-SENSEI ...
DID YOU LEARN **ANYTHING** FROM YESTERDAY? YOU'RE STILL JUST ATTACKING ME ***BLINDLY***!

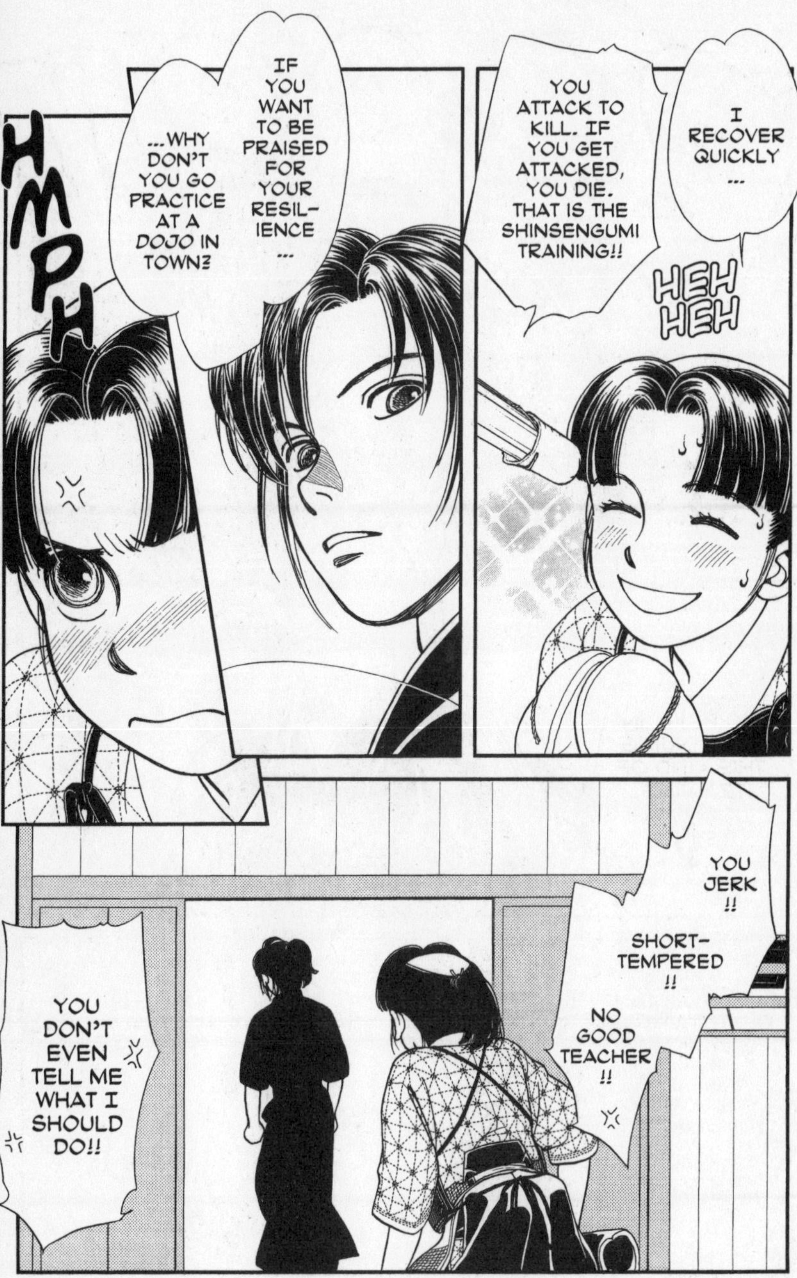
I RECOVER QUICKLY...
YOU ATTACK TO KILL. IF YOU GET ATTACKED, YOU DIE. THAT IS THE SHINSENGUMI TRAINING!!
HEH HEH
IF YOU WANT TO BE PRAISED FOR YOUR RESILIENCE...
...WHY DON'T YOU GO PRACTICE AT A *DOJO* IN TOWN?
HMPH
YOU JERK!! SHORT-TEMPERED!! NO GOOD TEACHER!!
YOU DON'T EVEN TELL ME WHAT I SHOULD DO!!

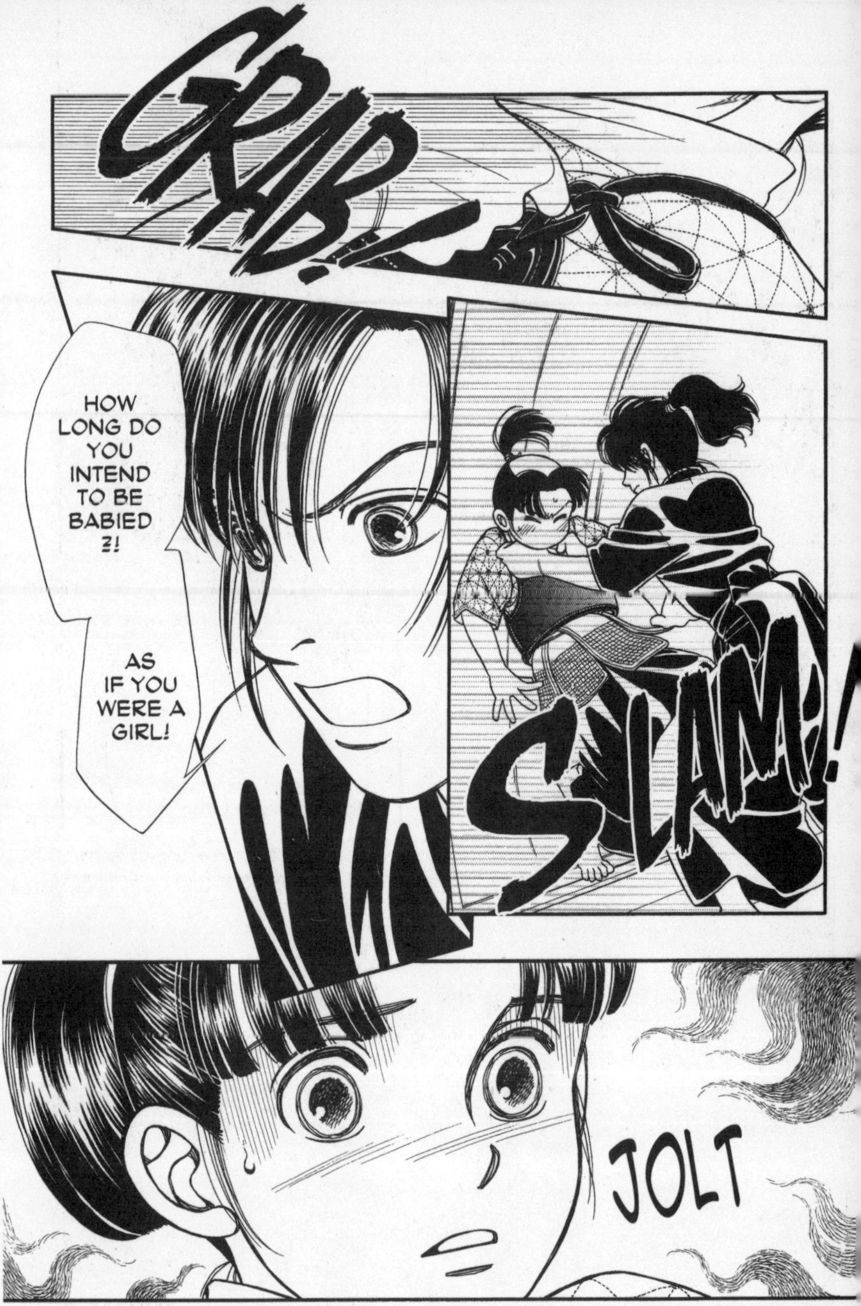
GRAB!
SLAM!!
HOW LONG DO YOU INTEND TO BE BABIED ?!
AS IF YOU WERE A GIRL!
JOLT

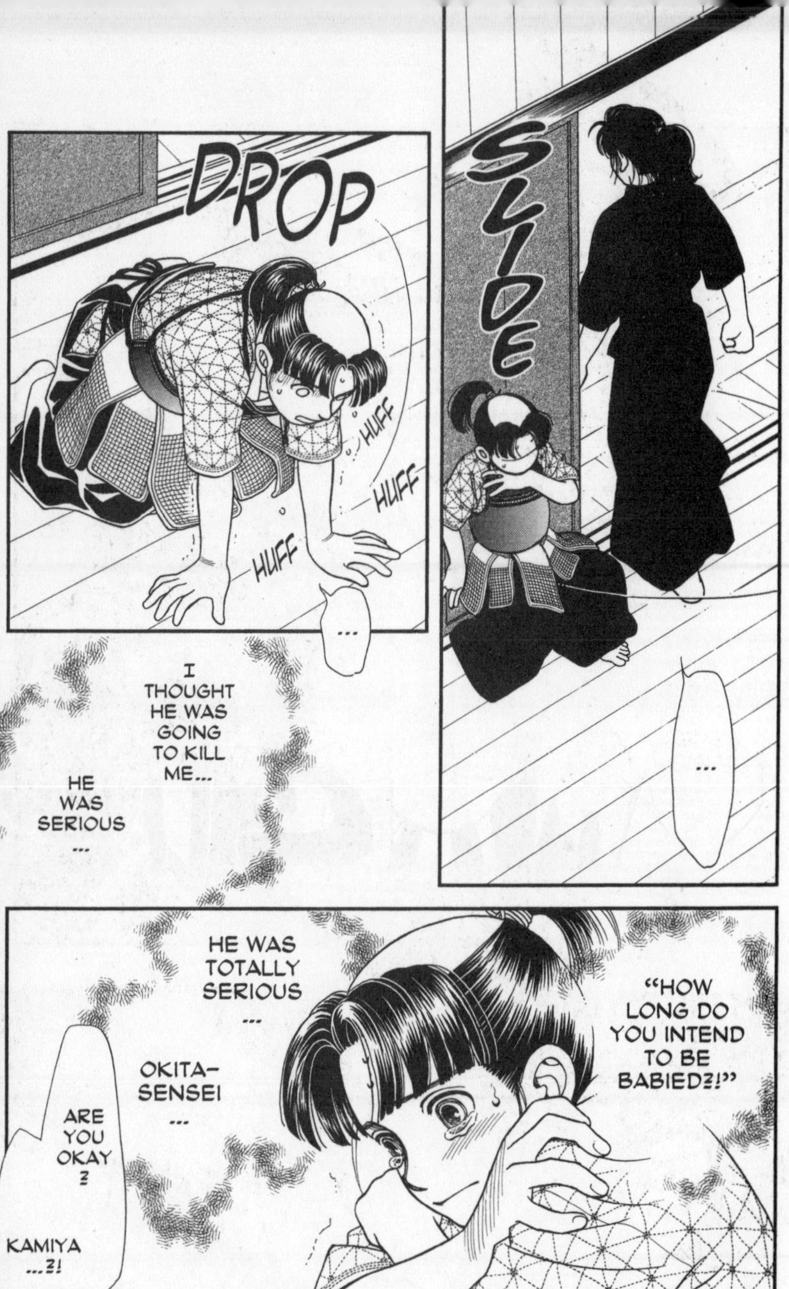
SLIDE
...
DROP
HUFF
HUFF
HUFF
...
I THOUGHT HE WAS GOING TO KILL ME...
HE WAS SERIOUS...
"HOW LONG DO YOU INTEND TO BE BABIED?!"
HE WAS TOTALLY SERIOUS...
OKITA-SENSEI...
ARE YOU OKAY?
KAMIYA...?!

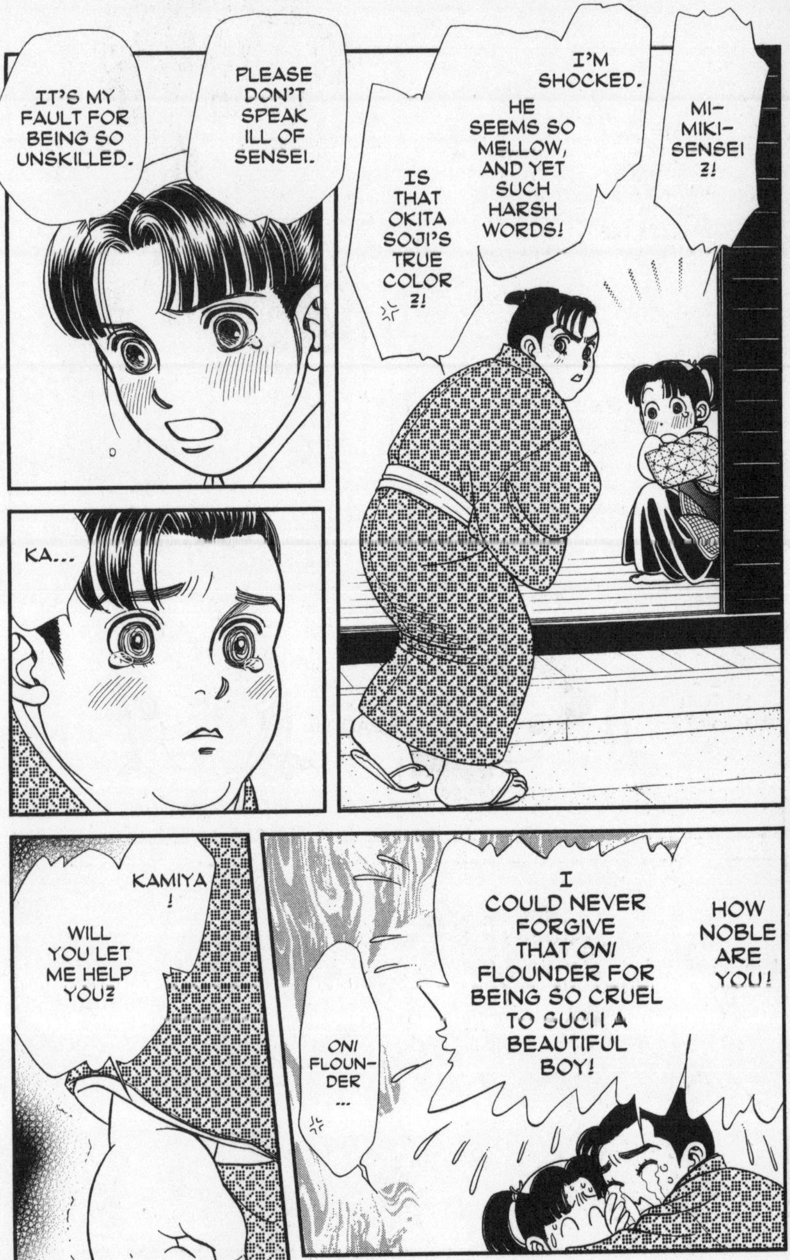
MI-MIKI-SENSEI?!
I'M SHOCKED.
HE SEEMS SO MELLOW, AND YET SUCH HARSH WORDS!
IS THAT OKITA SOJI'S TRUE COLOR?!
PLEASE DON'T SPEAK ILL OF SENSEI.
IT'S MY FAULT FOR BEING SO UNSKILLED.
KA...
HOW NOBLE ARE YOU!
I COULD NEVER FORGIVE THAT *ONI* FLOUNDER FOR BEING SO CRUEL TO SUCH A BEAUTIFUL BOY!
ONI FLOUNDER...
KAMIYA!
WILL YOU LET ME HELP YOU?

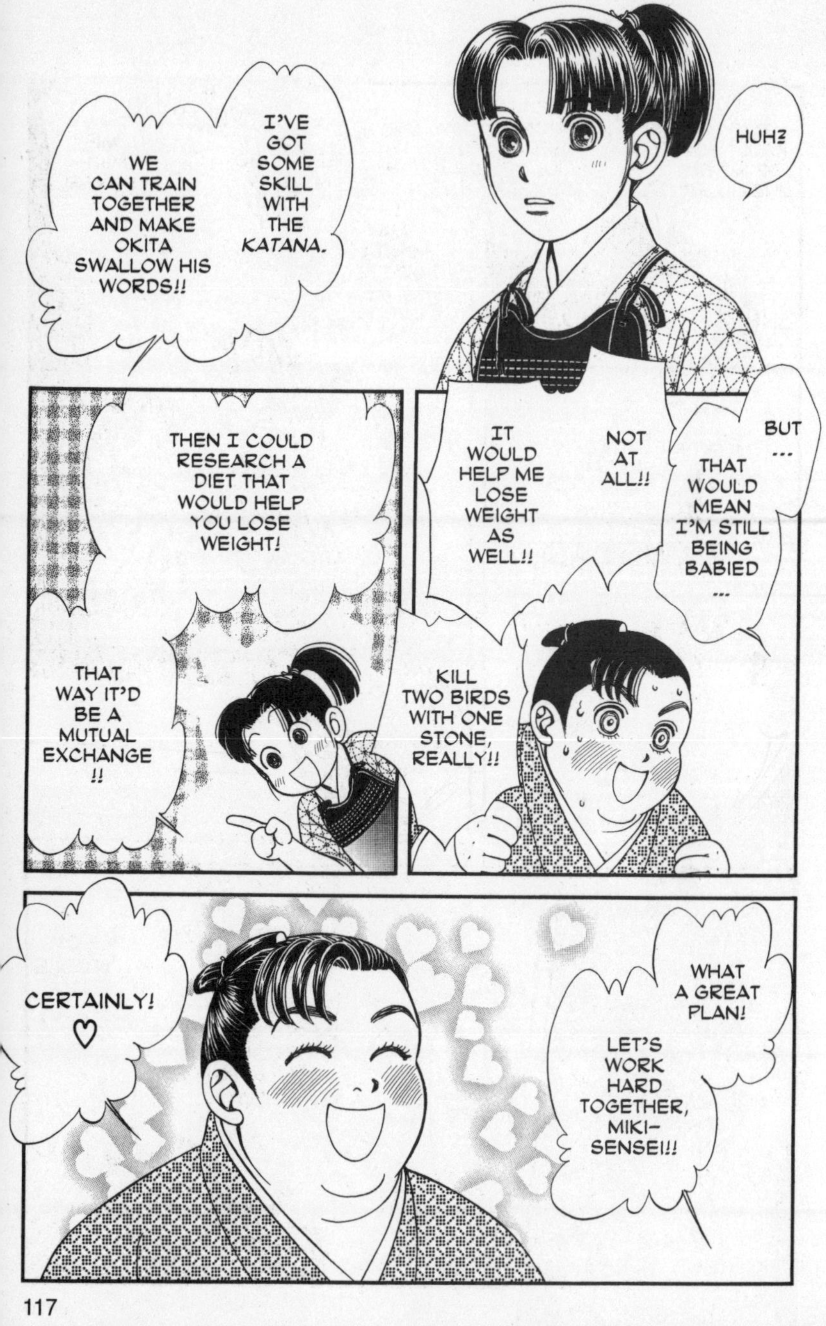
HUH?
I'VE GOT SOME SKILL WITH THE *KATANA*.
WE CAN TRAIN TOGETHER AND MAKE OKITA SWALLOW HIS WORDS!!
BUT... THAT WOULD MEAN I'M STILL BEING BABIED...
NOT AT ALL!!
IT WOULD HELP ME LOSE WEIGHT AS WELL!!
KILL TWO BIRDS WITH ONE STONE, REALLY!!
THEN I COULD RESEARCH A DIET THAT WOULD HELP YOU LOSE WEIGHT!
THAT WAY IT'D BE A MUTUAL EXCHANGE!!
WHAT A GREAT PLAN!
LET'S WORK HARD TOGETHER, MIKI-SENSEI!!
CERTAINLY! ♡

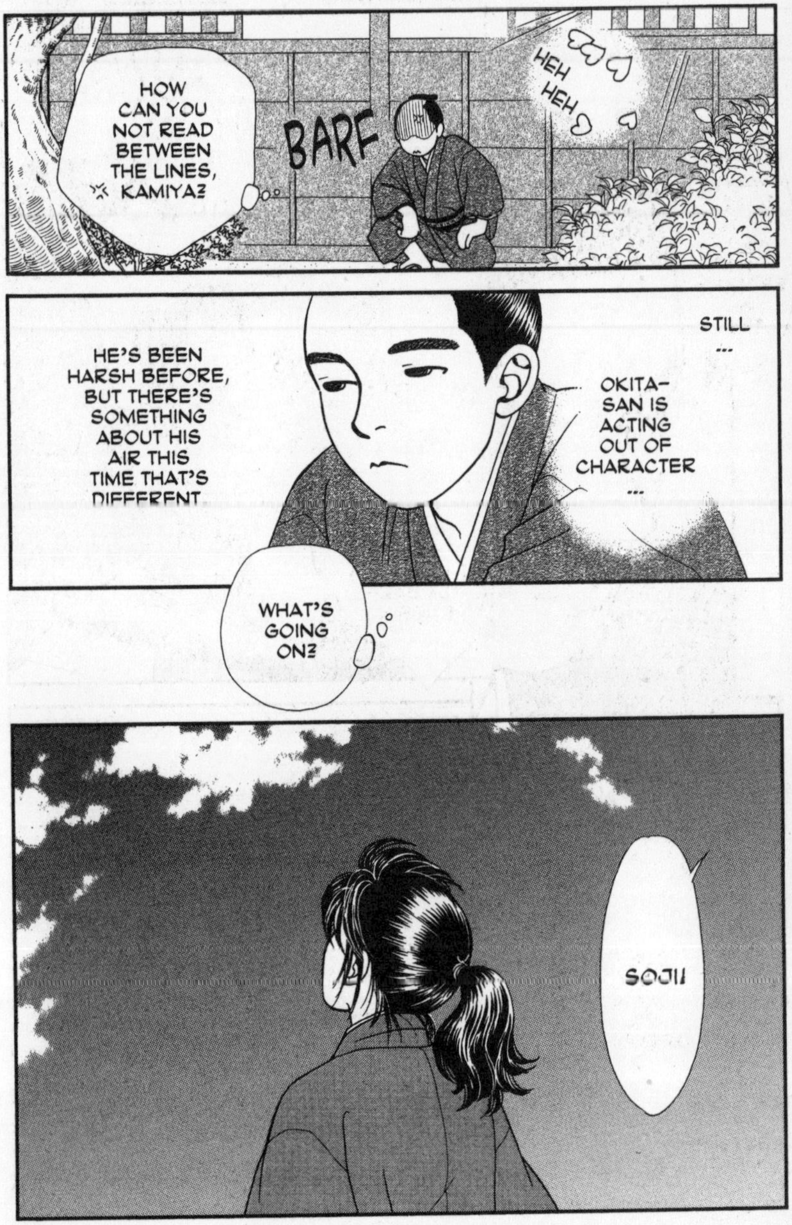
HEH HEH
BARF
HOW CAN YOU NOT READ BETWEEN THE LINES, KAMIYA?
STILL...
OKITA-SAN IS ACTING OUT OF CHARACTER...
HE'S BEEN HARSH BEFORE, BUT THERE'S SOMETHING ABOUT HIS AIR THIS TIME THAT'S DIFFERENT
WHAT'S GOING ON?
SOJI!

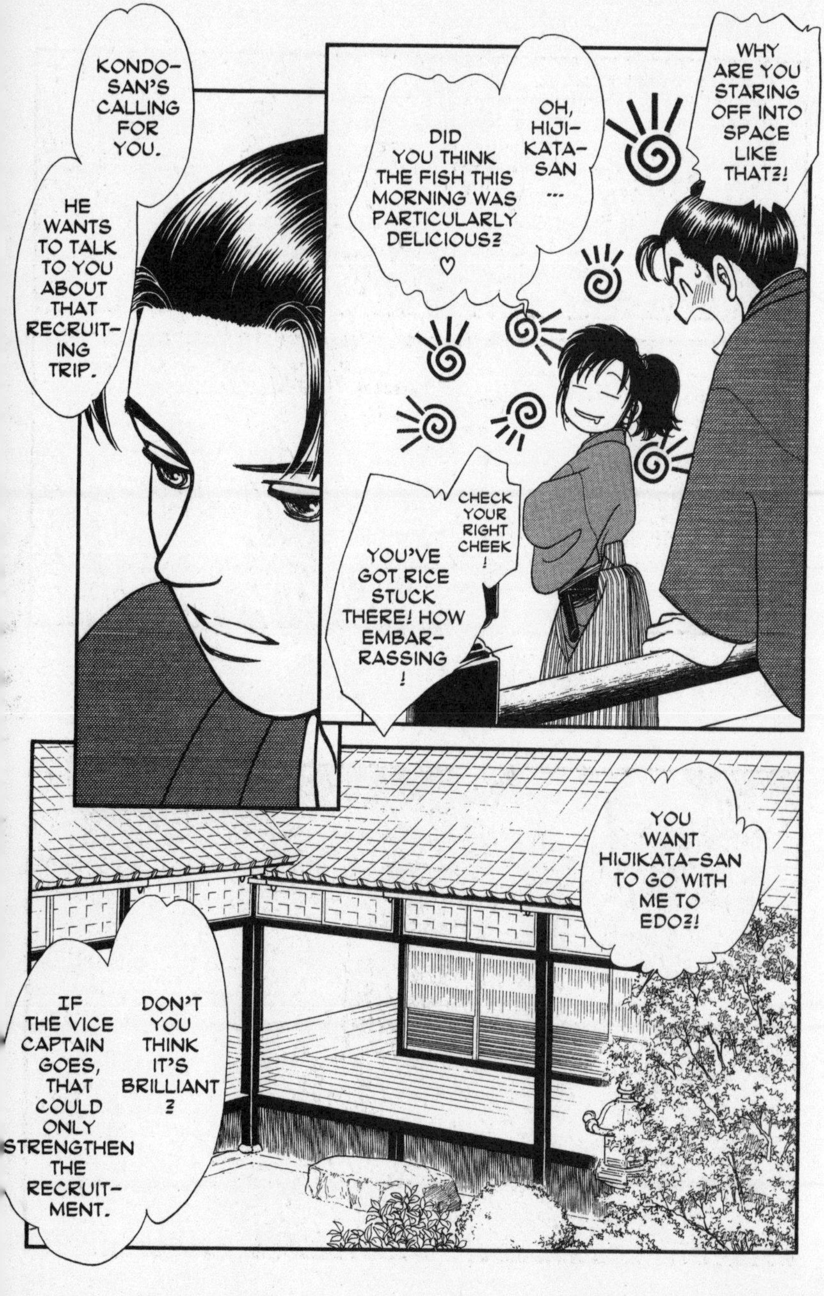
WHY ARE YOU STARING OFF INTO SPACE LIKE THAT?!
OH, HIJI-KATA-SAN ...
DID YOU THINK THE FISH THIS MORNING WAS PARTICULARLY DELICIOUS? ♡
CHECK YOUR RIGHT CHEEK!
YOU'VE GOT RICE STUCK THERE! HOW EMBAR-RASSING!
KONDO-SAN'S CALLING FOR YOU.
HE WANTS TO TALK TO YOU ABOUT THAT RECRUIT-ING TRIP.
YOU WANT HIJIKATA-SAN TO GO WITH ME TO EDO?!
DON'T YOU THINK IT'S BRILLIANT?
IF THE VICE CAPTAIN GOES, THAT COULD ONLY STRENGTHEN THE RECRUIT-MENT.

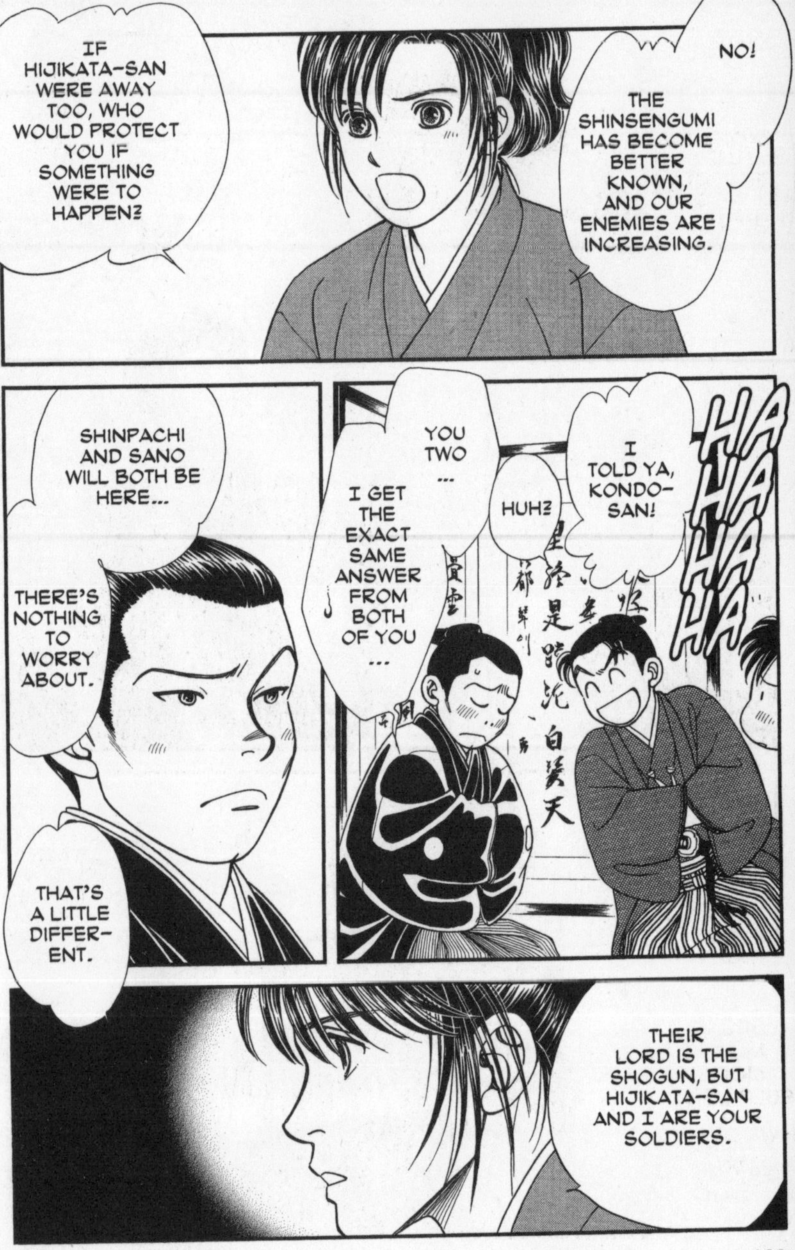
NO!
THE SHINSENGUMI HAS BECOME BETTER KNOWN, AND OUR ENEMIES ARE INCREASING.
IF HIJIKATA-SAN WERE AWAY TOO, WHO WOULD PROTECT YOU IF SOMETHING WERE TO HAPPEN?
I TOLD YA, KONDO-SAN!
HA HA HA HA
HUH?
YOU TWO ...
I GET THE EXACT SAME ANSWER FROM BOTH OF YOU ...
SHINPACHI AND SANO WILL BOTH BE HERE...
THERE'S NOTHING TO WORRY ABOUT.
THAT'S A LITTLE DIFFER-ENT.
THEIR LORD IS THE SHOGUN, BUT HIJIKATA-SAN AND I ARE YOUR SOLDIERS.

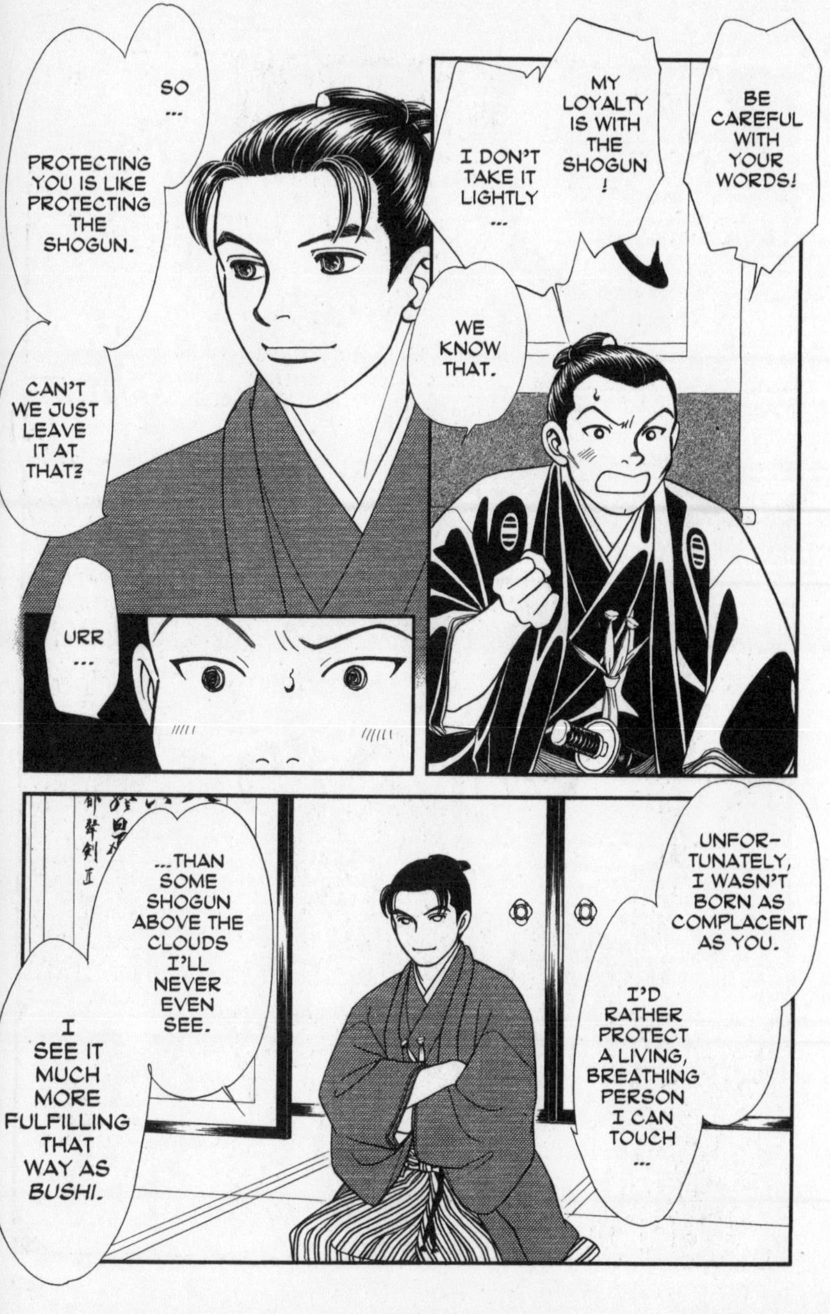
BE CAREFUL WITH YOUR WORDS!
MY LOYALTY IS WITH THE SHOGUN!
I DON'T TAKE IT LIGHTLY...
WE KNOW THAT.
SO... PROTECTING YOU IS LIKE PROTECTING THE SHOGUN.
CAN'T WE JUST LEAVE IT AT THAT?
URR...
UNFORTUNATELY, I WASN'T BORN AS COMPLACENT AS YOU.
I'D RATHER PROTECT A LIVING, BREATHING PERSON I CAN TOUCH...
...THAN SOME SHOGUN ABOVE THE CLOUDS I'LL NEVER EVEN SEE.
I SEE IT MUCH MORE FULFILLING THAT WAY AS *BUSHI*.

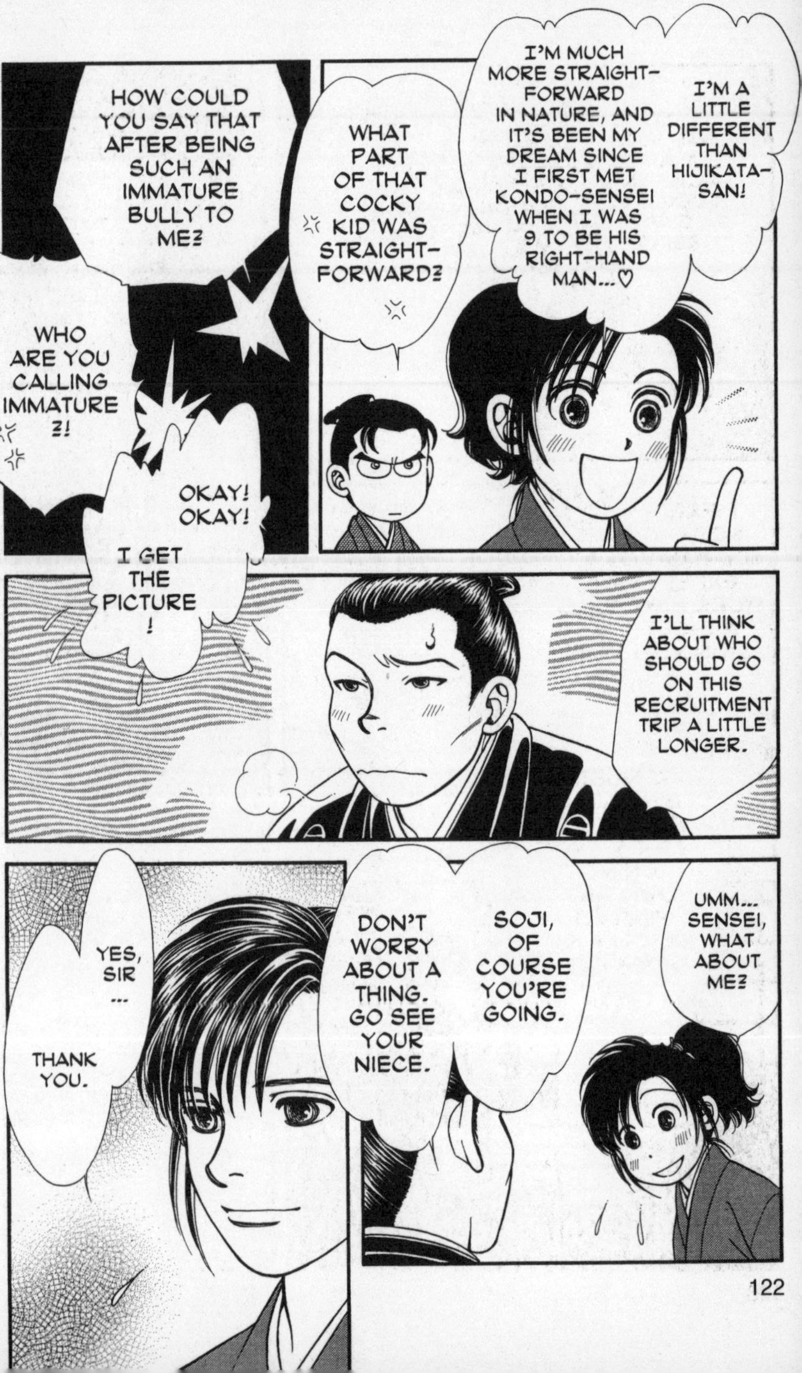
I'M A LITTLE DIFFERENT THAN HIJIKATA-SAN!
I'M MUCH MORE STRAIGHTFORWARD IN NATURE, AND IT'S BEEN MY DREAM SINCE I FIRST MET KONDO-SENSEI WHEN I WAS 9 TO BE HIS RIGHT-HAND MAN...♡
WHAT PART OF THAT COCKY KID WAS STRAIGHTFORWARD?
HOW COULD YOU SAY THAT AFTER BEING SUCH AN IMMATURE BULLY TO ME?
WHO ARE YOU CALLING IMMATURE?!
OKAY! OKAY!
I GET THE PICTURE!
I'LL THINK ABOUT WHO SHOULD GO ON THIS RECRUITMENT TRIP A LITTLE LONGER.
UMM... SENSEI, WHAT ABOUT ME?
SOJI, OF COURSE YOU'RE GOING.
DON'T WORRY ABOUT A THING. GO SEE YOUR NIECE.
YES, SIR...
THANK YOU.

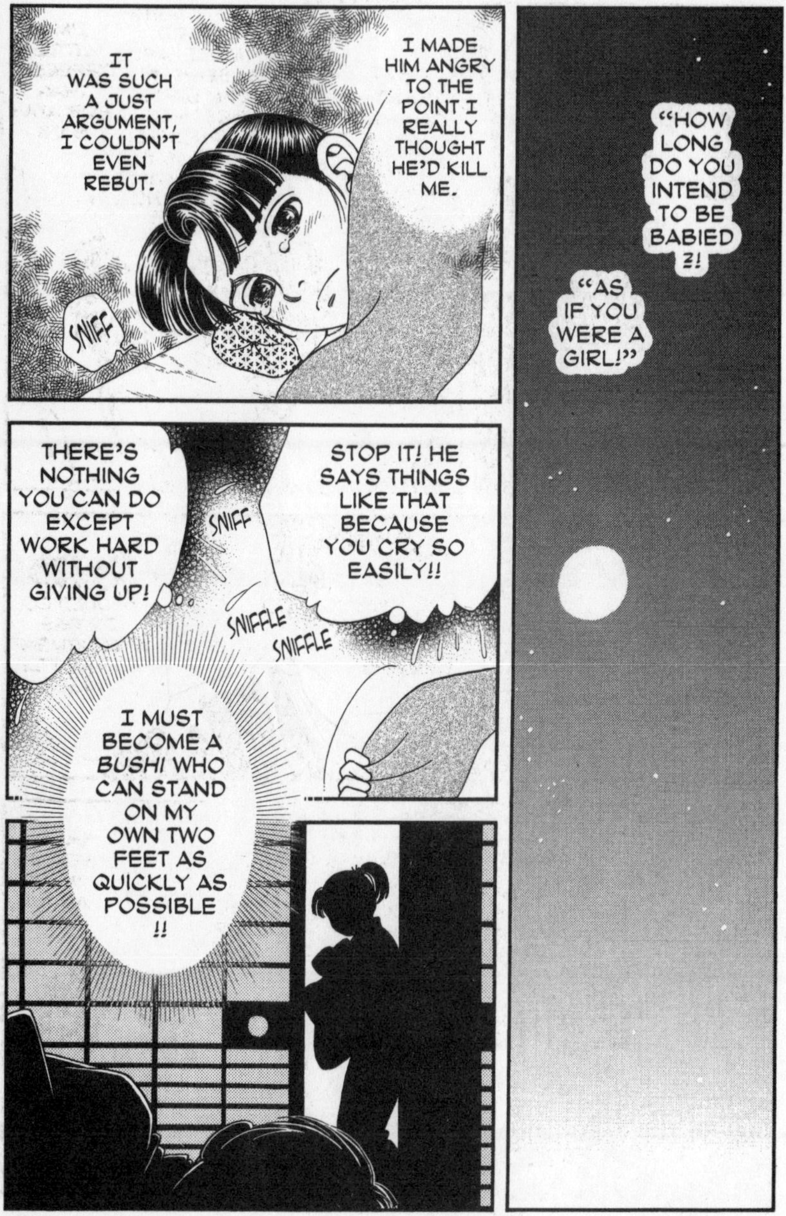
"HOW LONG DO YOU INTEND TO BE BABIED?!
"AS IF YOU WERE A GIRL!"
I MADE HIM ANGRY TO THE POINT I REALLY THOUGHT HE'D KILL ME.
IT WAS SUCH A JUST ARGUMENT, I COULDN'T EVEN REBUT.
SNIFF
STOP IT! HE SAYS THINGS LIKE THAT BECAUSE YOU CRY SO EASILY!!
THERE'S NOTHING YOU CAN DO EXCEPT WORK HARD WITHOUT GIVING UP!
SNIFF
SNIFFLE
SNIFFLE
I MUST BECOME A *BUSHI* WHO CAN STAND ON MY OWN TWO FEET AS QUICKLY AS POSSIBLE!!

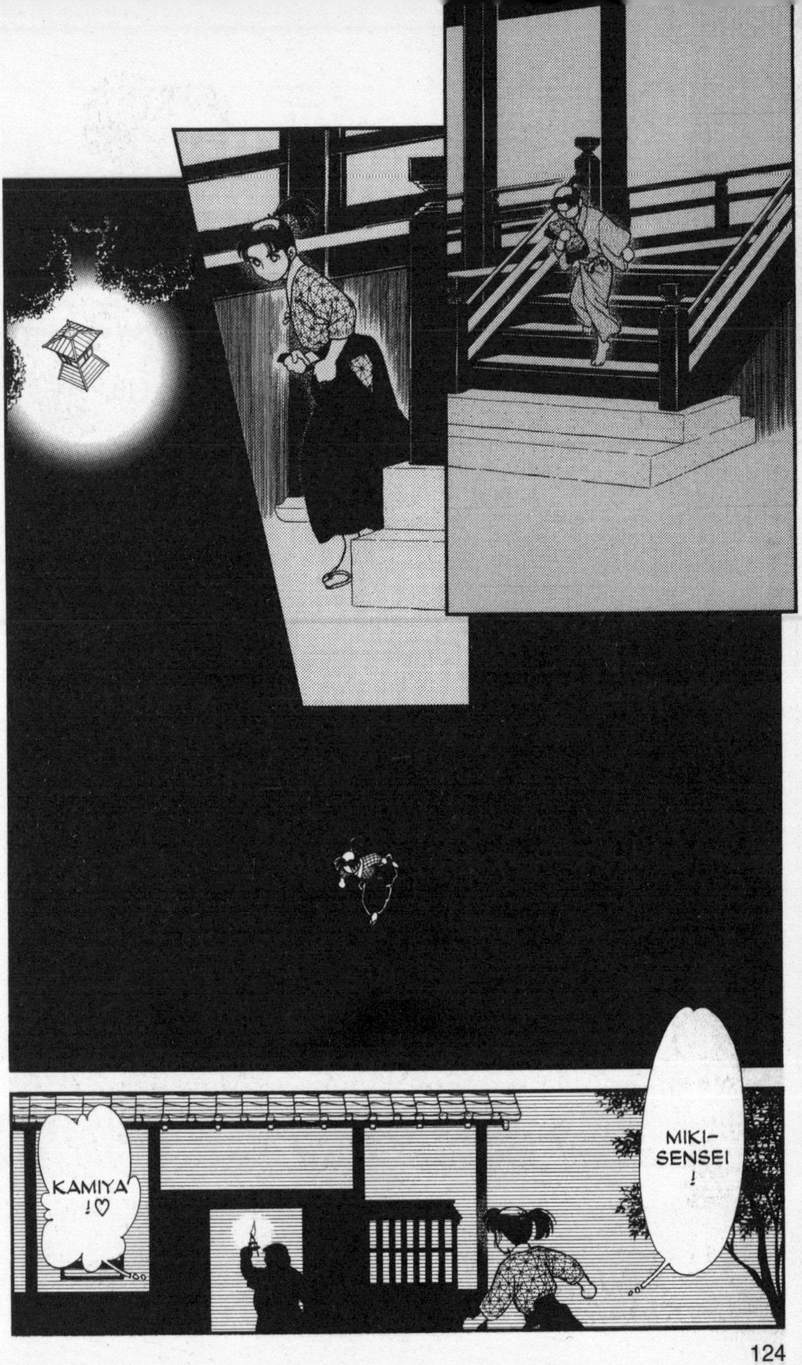
MIKI-SENSEI!
KAMIYA! ♡

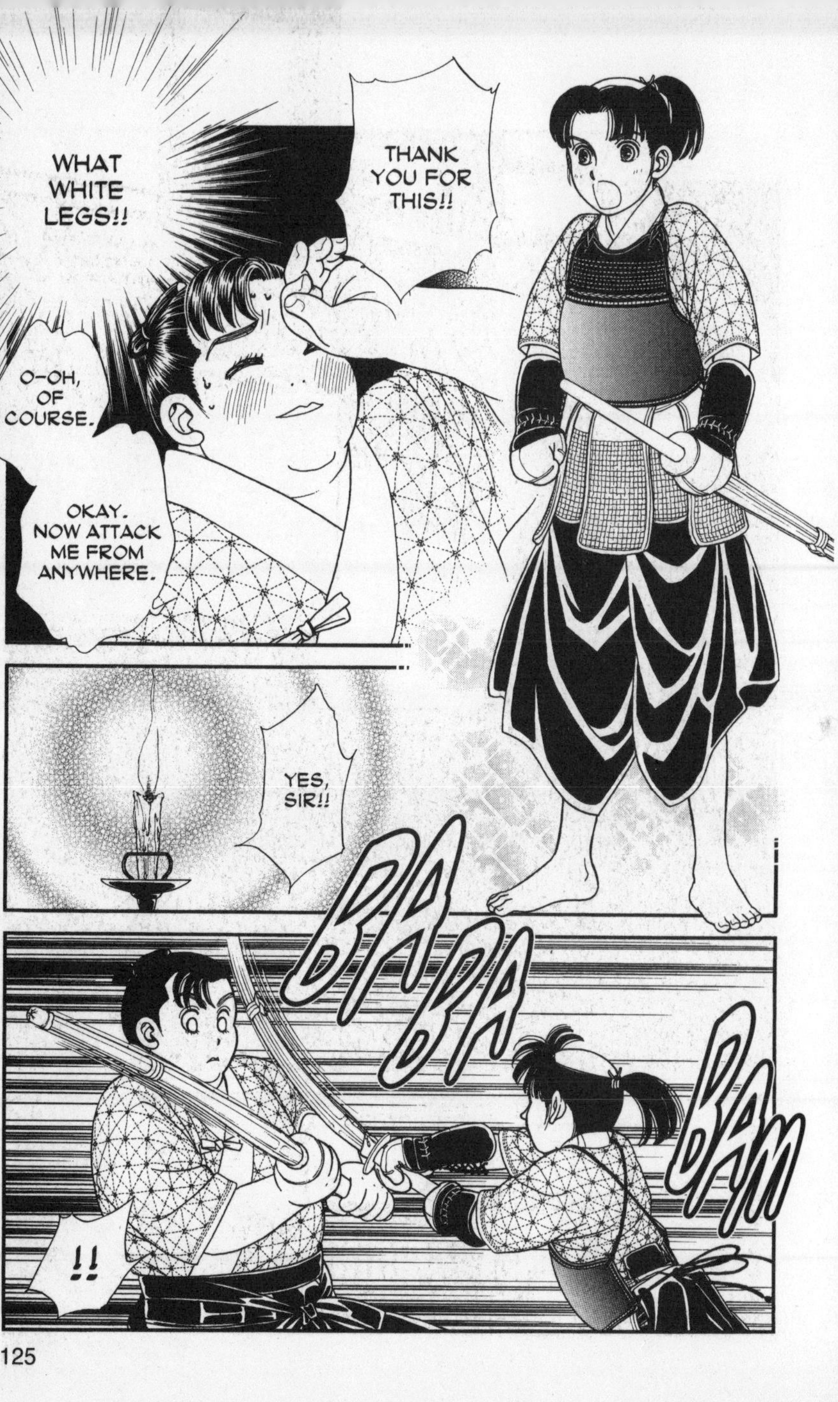
THANK YOU FOR THIS!!
WHAT WHITE LEGS!!
O-OH, OF COURSE.
OKAY. NOW ATTACK ME FROM ANYWHERE.
YES, SIR!!
BA BA BA
BAM
!!

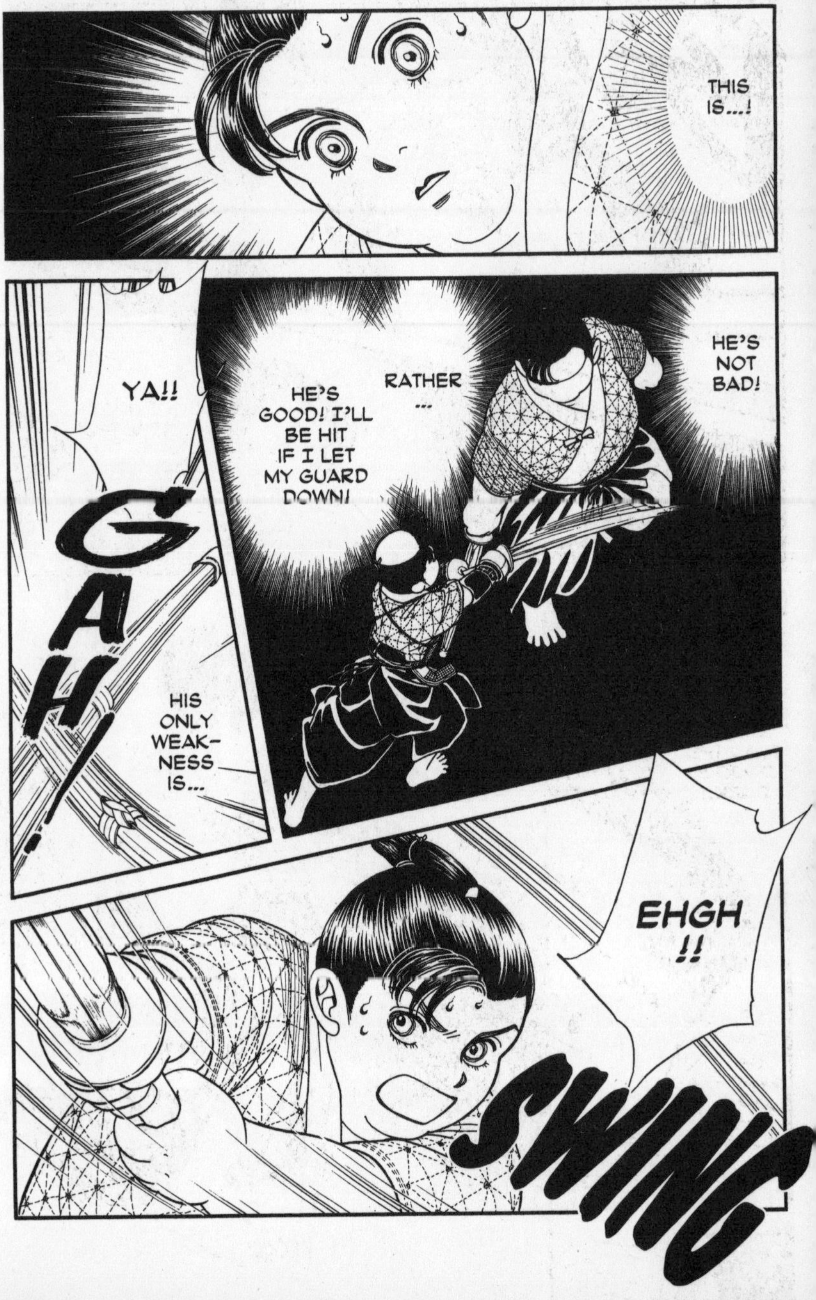
THIS IS...!
HE'S NOT BAD!
RATHER...
HE'S GOOD! I'LL BE HIT IF I LET MY GUARD DOWN!
YA!!
GAH!
HIS ONLY WEAKNESS IS...
EHGH!!
SWING

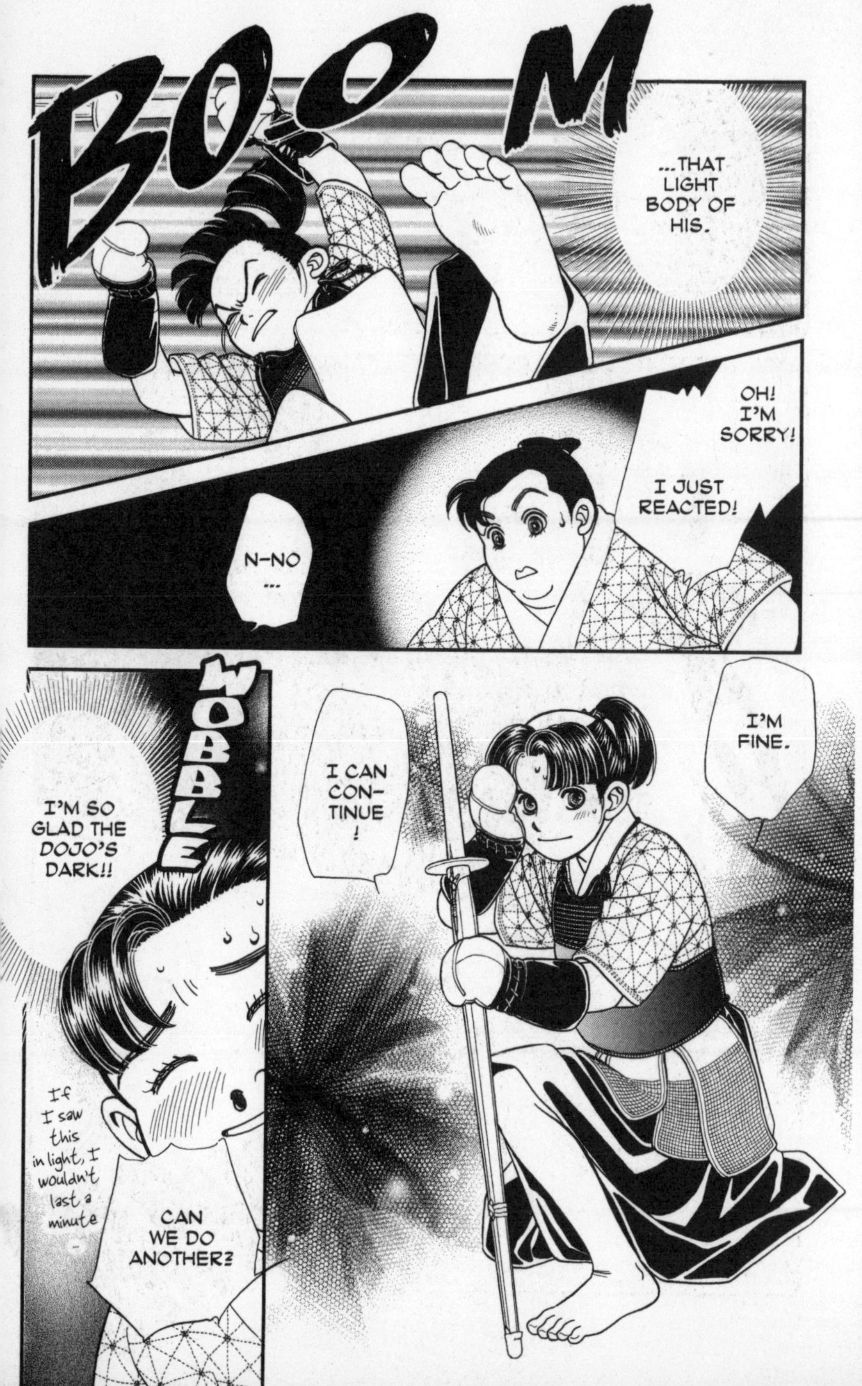
BOOM
...THAT LIGHT BODY OF HIS.
OH! I'M SORRY!
I JUST REACTED!
N-NO ...
I'M FINE.
I CAN CONTINUE!
WOBBLE
I'M SO GLAD THE DOJO'S DARK!!
If I saw this in light, I wouldn't last a minute ...
CAN WE DO ANOTHER?

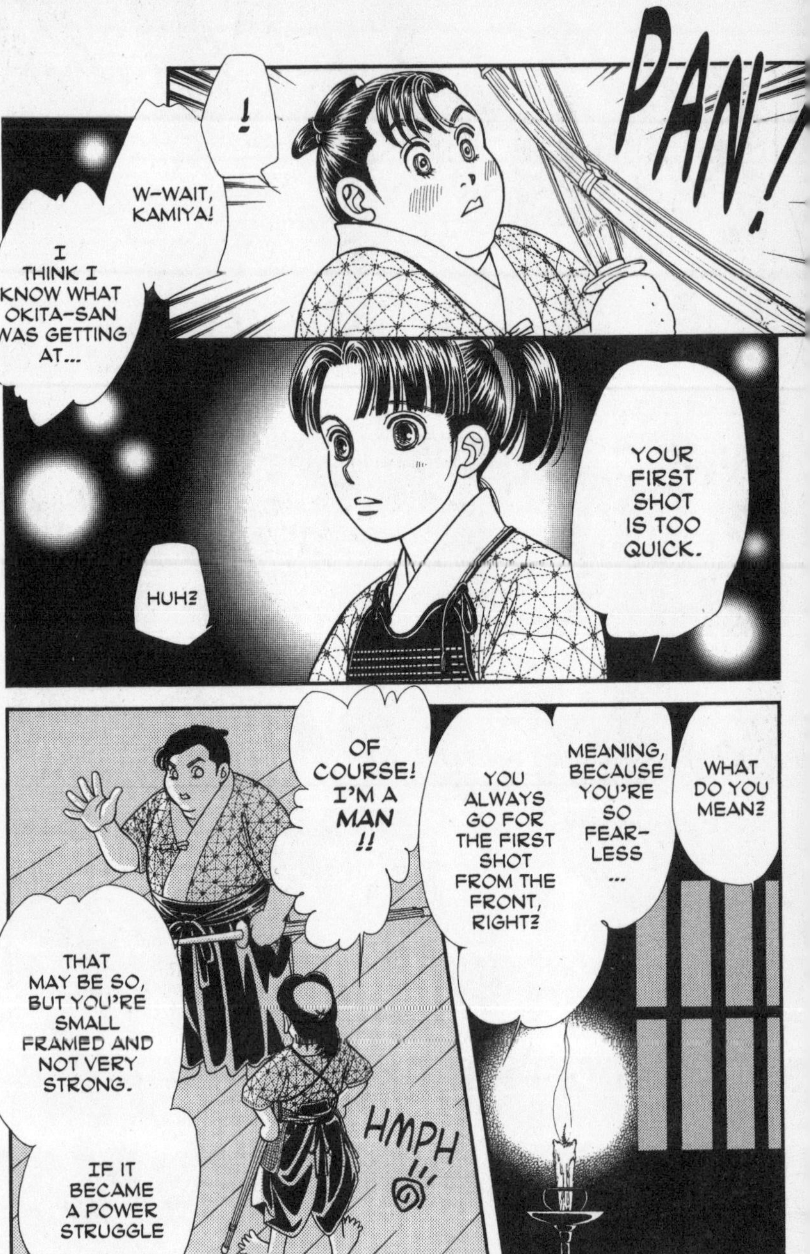
PAN!
!
W-WAIT, KAMIYA!
I THINK I KNOW WHAT OKITA-SAN WAS GETTING AT...
YOUR FIRST SHOT IS TOO QUICK.
HUH?
WHAT DO YOU MEAN?
MEANING, BECAUSE YOU'RE SO FEAR-LESS...
YOU ALWAYS GO FOR THE FIRST SHOT FROM THE FRONT, RIGHT?
OF COURSE! I'M A **MAN**!!
HMPH!!
THAT MAY BE SO, BUT YOU'RE SMALL FRAMED AND NOT VERY STRONG.
IF IT BECAME A POWER STRUGGLE...

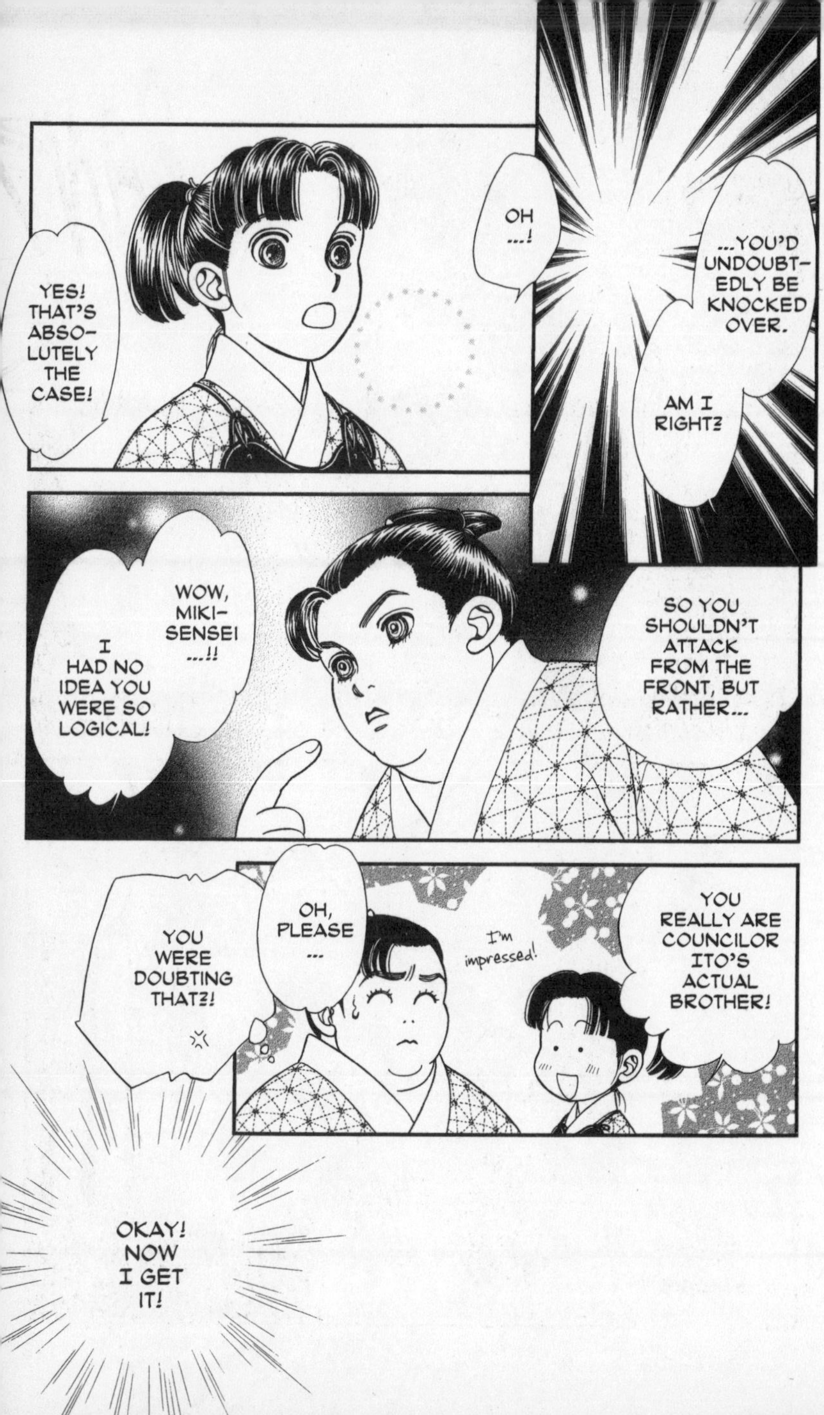
...YOU'D UNDOUBTEDLY BE KNOCKED OVER.
AM I RIGHT?
OH ...!
YES! THAT'S ABSOLUTELY THE CASE!
SO YOU SHOULDN'T ATTACK FROM THE FRONT, BUT RATHER...
WOW, MIKI-SENSEI ...!!
I HAD NO IDEA YOU WERE SO LOGICAL!
YOU REALLY ARE COUNCILOR ITO'S ACTUAL BROTHER!
I'm impressed!
OH, PLEASE ...
YOU WERE DOUBTING THAT?!
OKAY! NOW I GET IT!

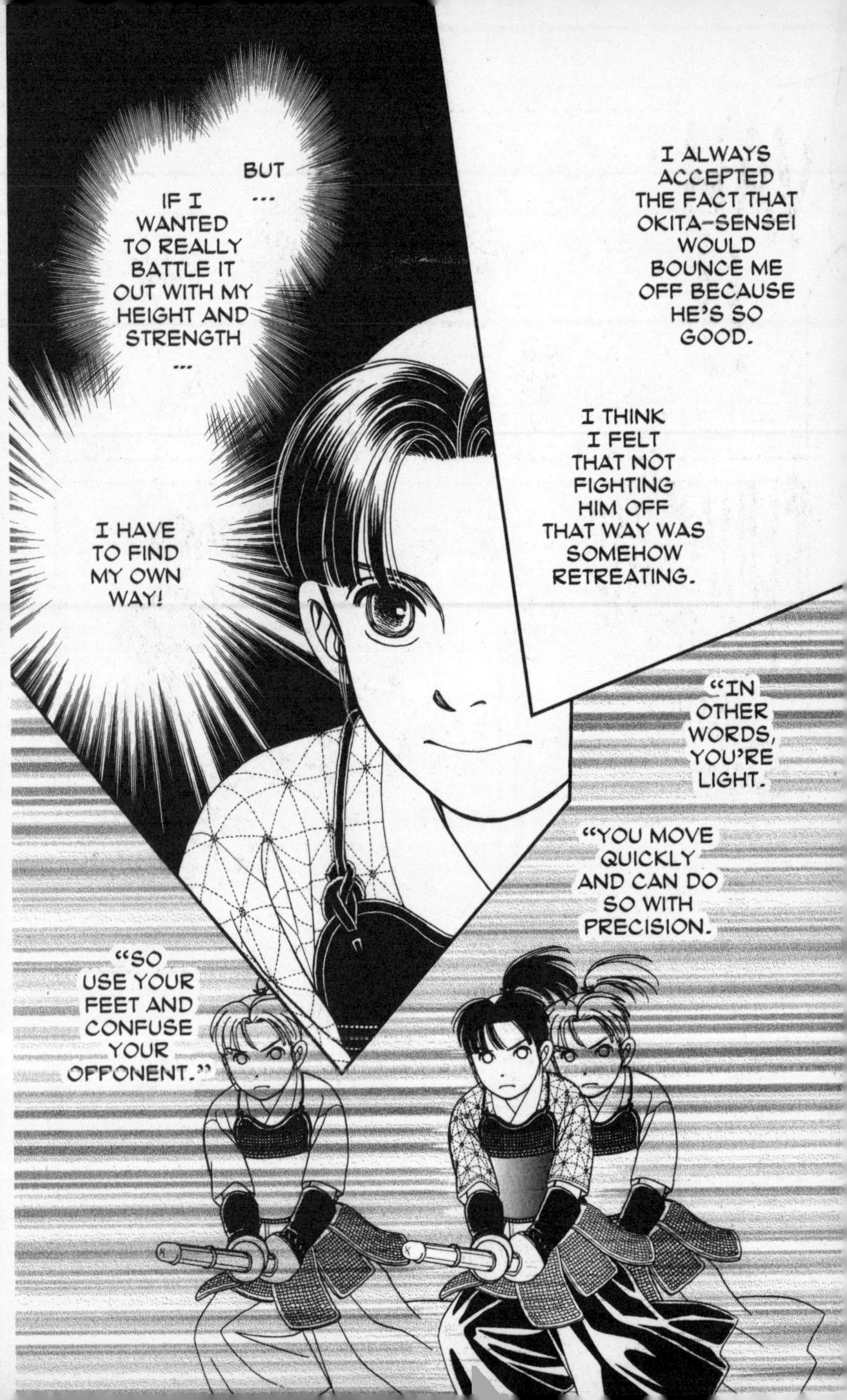
I ALWAYS ACCEPTED THE FACT THAT OKITA-SENSEI WOULD BOUNCE ME OFF BECAUSE HE'S SO GOOD.
I THINK I FELT THAT NOT FIGHTING HIM OFF THAT WAY WAS SOMEHOW RETREATING.
BUT ...
IF I WANTED TO REALLY BATTLE IT OUT WITH MY HEIGHT AND STRENGTH ...
I HAVE TO FIND MY OWN WAY!
"IN OTHER WORDS, YOU'RE LIGHT.
"YOU MOVE QUICKLY AND CAN DO SO WITH PRECISION.
"SO USE YOUR FEET AND CONFUSE YOUR OFFONENT."

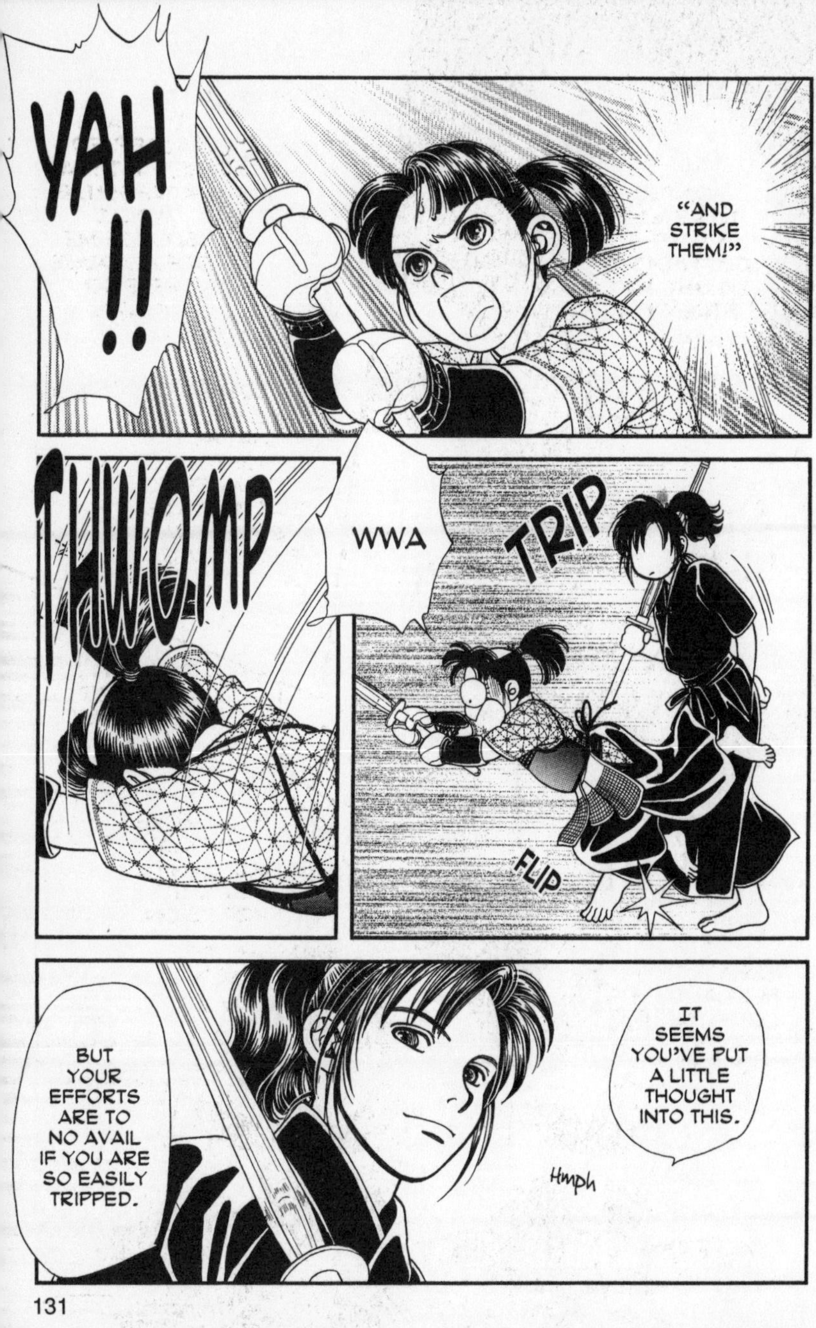
"AND STRIKE THEM!"
YAH!!
TRIP
WWA
FLIP
THWOMP
IT SEEMS YOU'VE PUT A LITTLE THOUGHT INTO THIS.
Hmph
BUT YOUR EFFORTS ARE TO NO AVAIL IF YOU ARE SO EASILY TRIPPED.

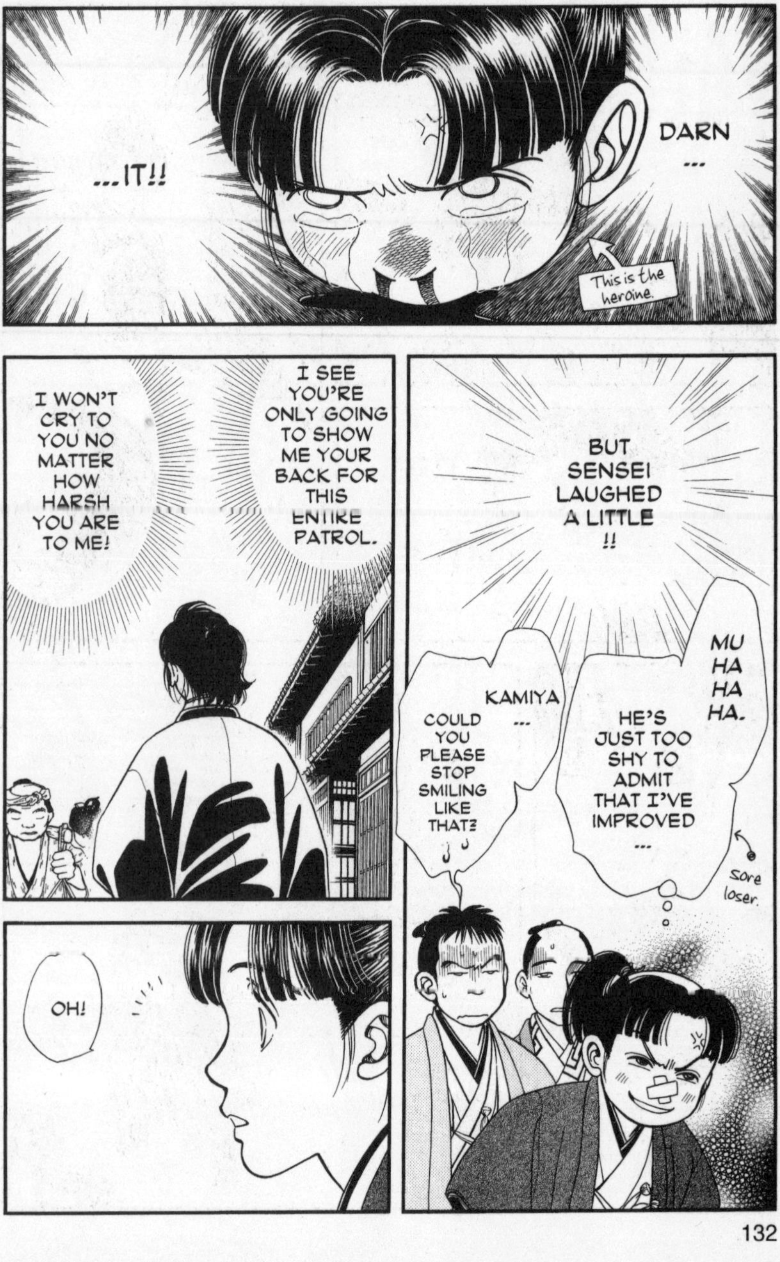
DARN ...
...IT!!
This is the heroine.
BUT SENSEI LAUGHED A LITTLE !!
MU HA HA HA.
HE'S JUST TOO SHY TO ADMIT THAT I'VE IMPROVED ...
Sore loser.
KAMIYA ... COULD YOU PLEASE STOP SMILING LIKE THAT?
I SEE YOU'RE ONLY GOING TO SHOW ME YOUR BACK FOR THIS ENTIRE PATROL.
I WON'T CRY TO YOU NO MATTER HOW HARSH YOU ARE TO ME!
OH!

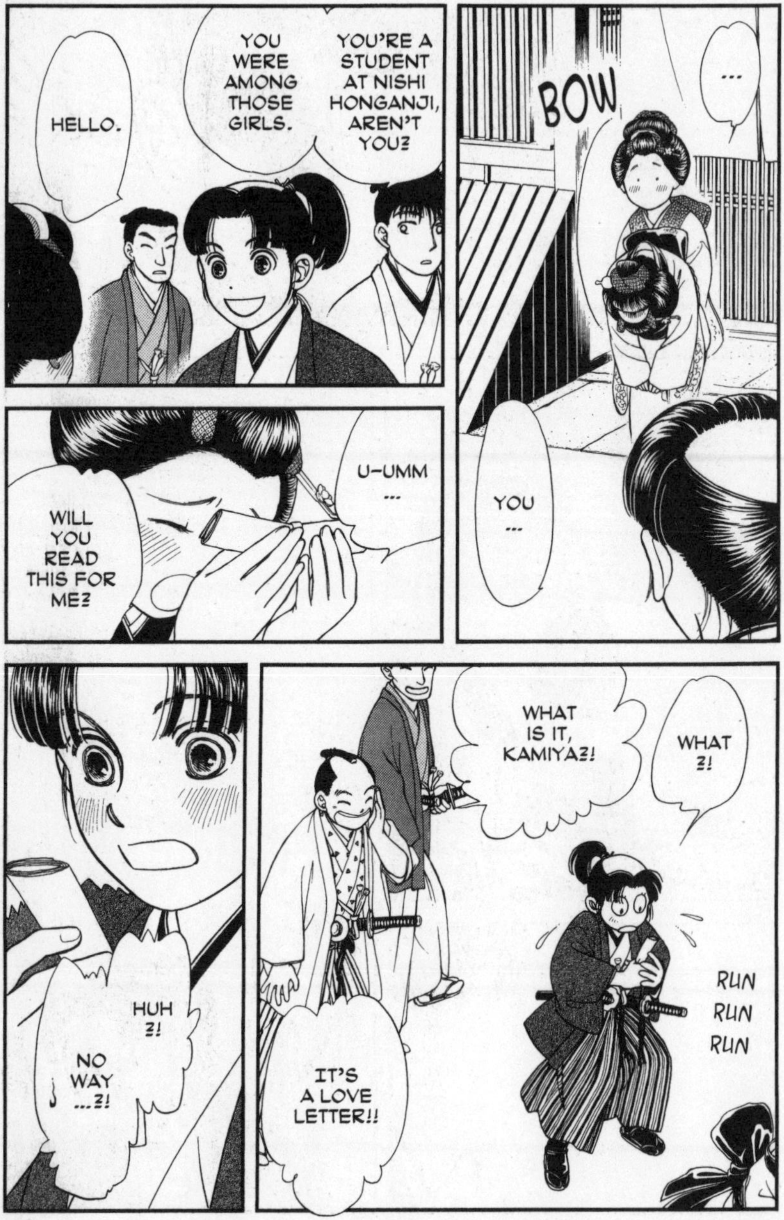
...
BOW
YOU ...
YOU'RE A STUDENT AT NISHI HONGANJI, AREN'T YOU?
YOU WERE AMONG THOSE GIRLS.
HELLO.
U-UMM ...
WILL YOU READ THIS FOR ME?
WHAT ?!
WHAT IS IT, KAMIYA?!
RUN RUN RUN
IT'S A LOVE LETTER!!
HUH ?!
NO WAY ...?!

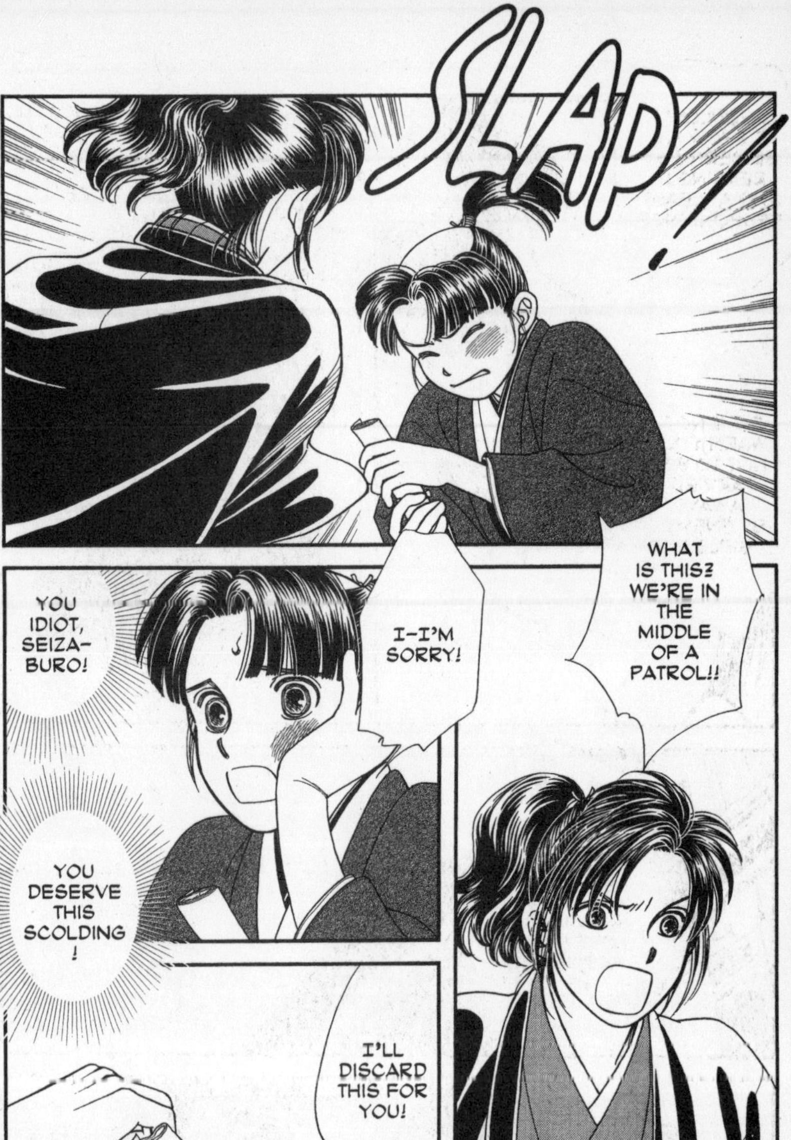
SLAP!!
WHAT IS THIS? WE'RE IN THE MIDDLE OF A PATROL!!
I-I'M SORRY!
YOU IDIOT, SEIZA-BURO!
YOU DESERVE THIS SCOLDING!
I'LL DISCARD THIS FOR YOU!

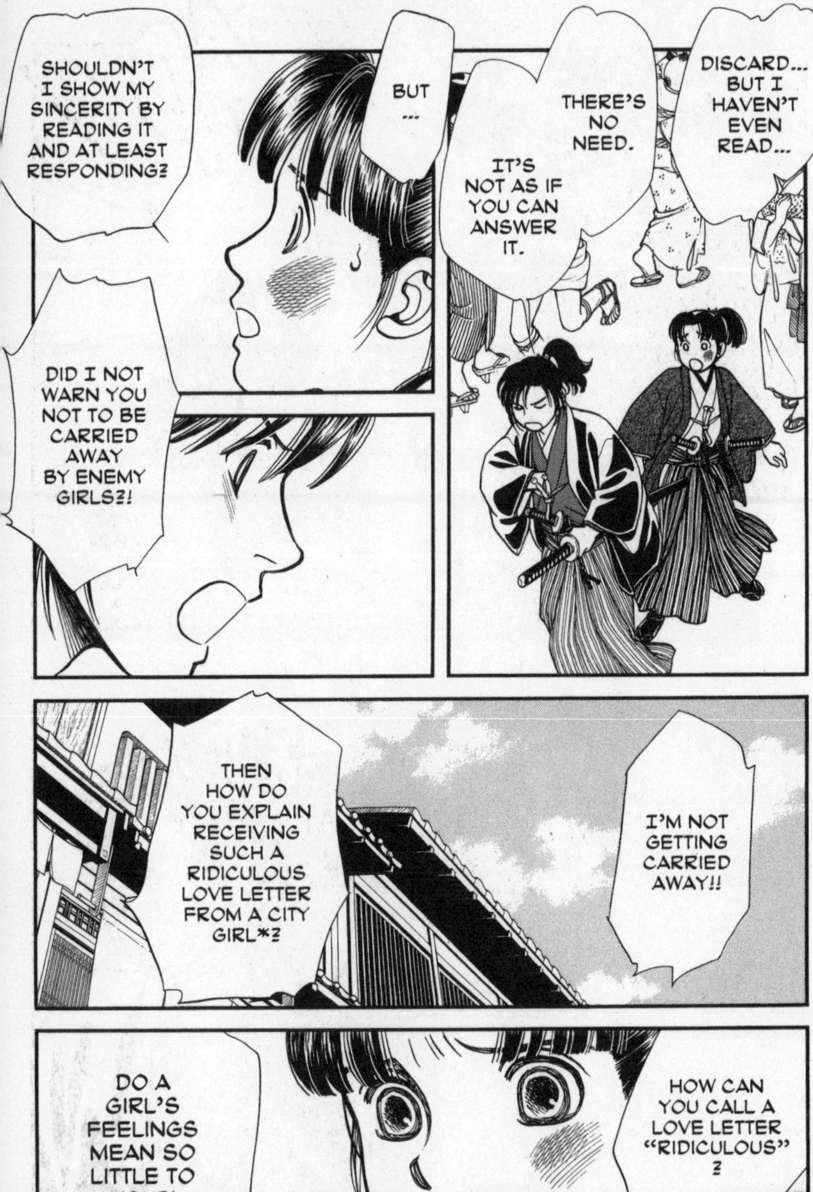
DISCARD... BUT I HAVEN'T EVEN READ...
THERE'S NO NEED.
IT'S NOT AS IF YOU CAN ANSWER IT.
BUT ...
SHOULDN'T I SHOW MY SINCERITY BY READING IT AND AT LEAST RESPONDING?
DID I NOT WARN YOU NOT TO BE CARRIED AWAY BY ENEMY GIRLS?!
I'M NOT GETTING CARRIED AWAY!!
THEN HOW DO YOU EXPLAIN RECEIVING SUCH A RIDICULOUS LOVE LETTER FROM A CITY GIRL*?
HOW CAN YOU CALL A LOVE LETTER "RIDICULOUS"?
DO A GIRL'S FEELINGS MEAN SO LITTLE TO YOU?!

*Due to the class system, marriage between *bushi* and merchants was banned. Any relations were considered scandals.

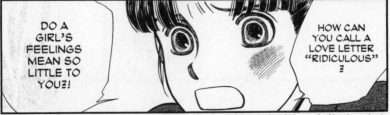

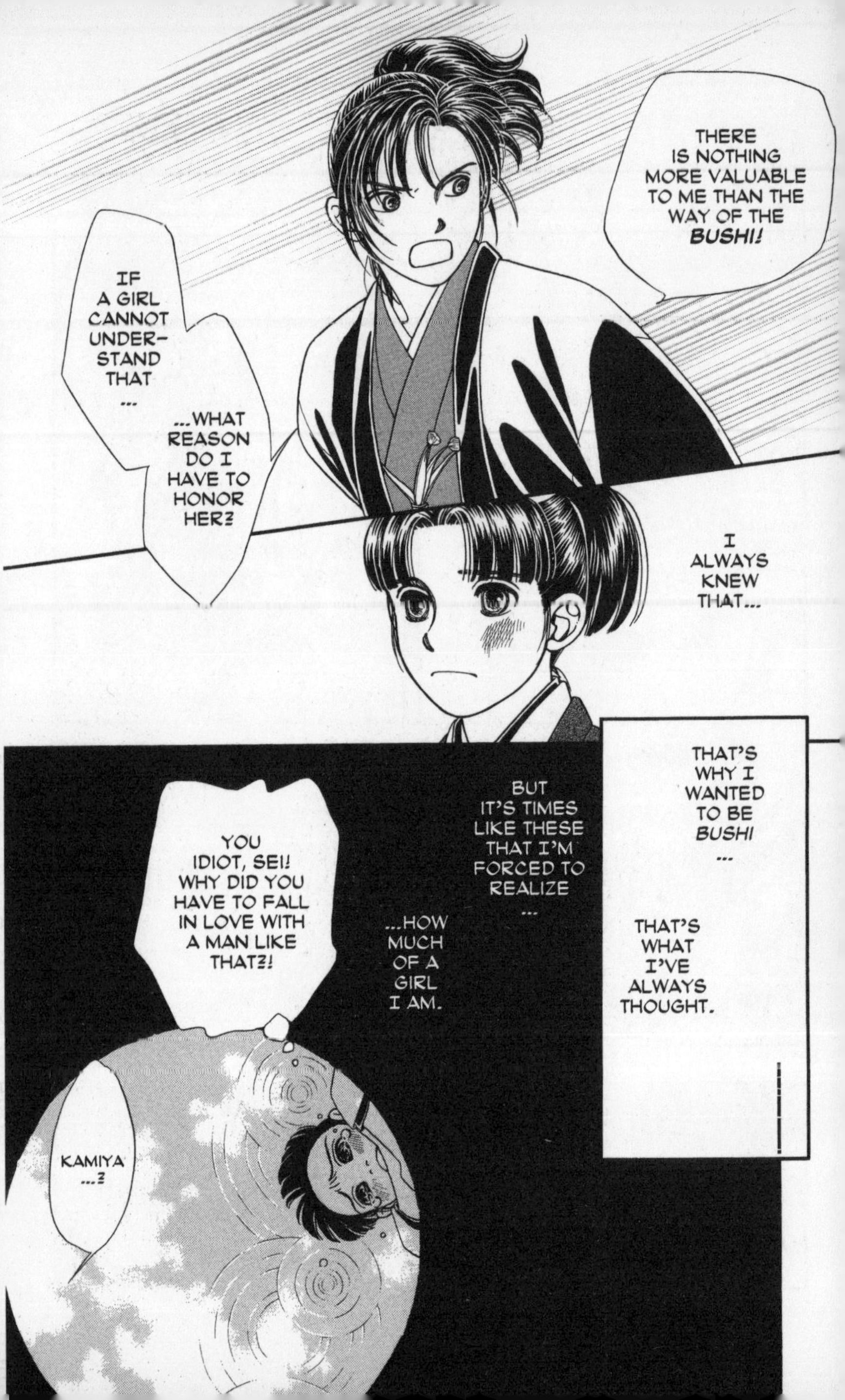
THERE IS NOTHING MORE VALUABLE TO ME THAN THE WAY OF THE *BUSHI!*
IF A GIRL CANNOT UNDER-STAND THAT ...
...WHAT REASON DO I HAVE TO HONOR HER?
I ALWAYS KNEW THAT...
THAT'S WHY I WANTED TO BE *BUSHI* ...
THAT'S WHAT I'VE ALWAYS THOUGHT.
BUT IT'S TIMES LIKE THESE THAT I'M FORCED TO REALIZE ...
...HOW MUCH OF A GIRL I AM.
YOU IDIOT, SEI! WHY DID YOU HAVE TO FALL IN LOVE WITH A MAN LIKE THAT?!
KAMIYA ...?

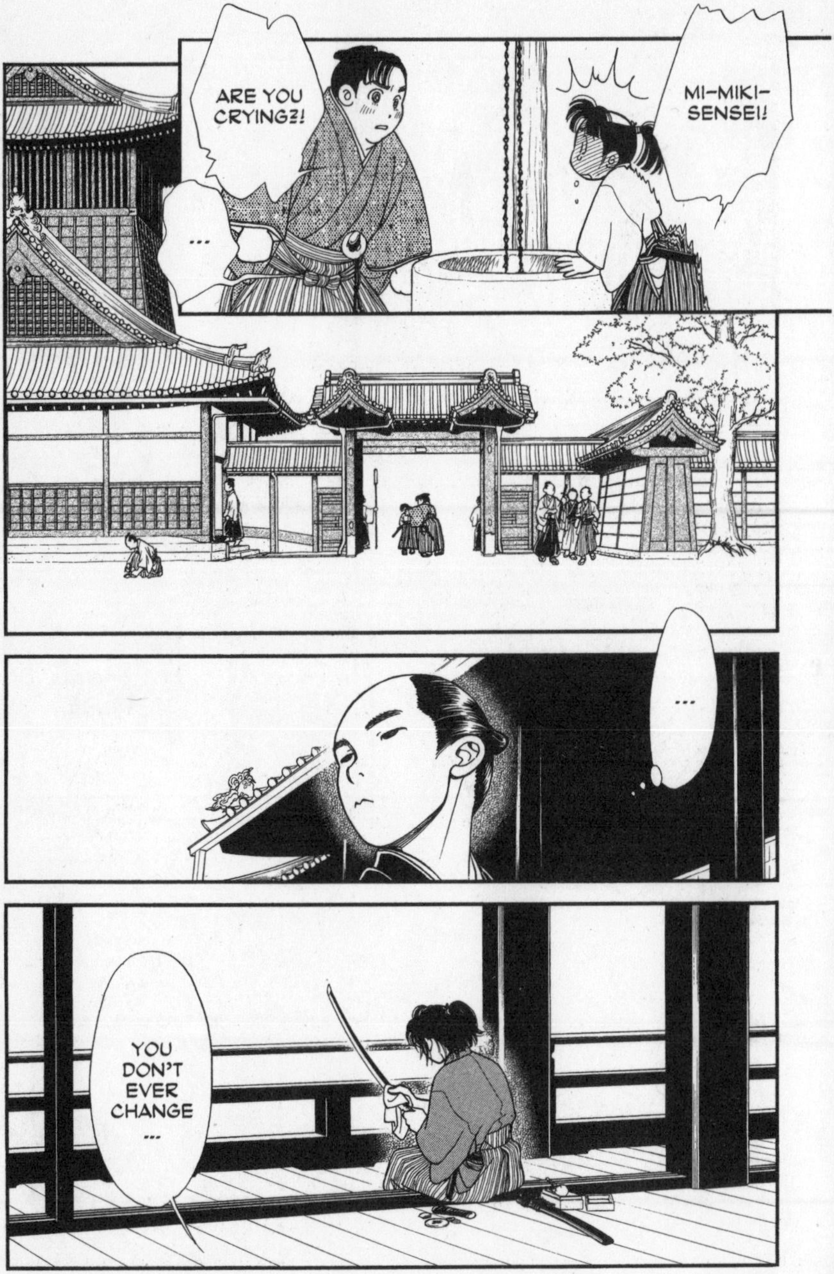
MI-MIKI-SENSEI!
ARE YOU CRYING?!
...
...
YOU DON'T EVER CHANGE ...

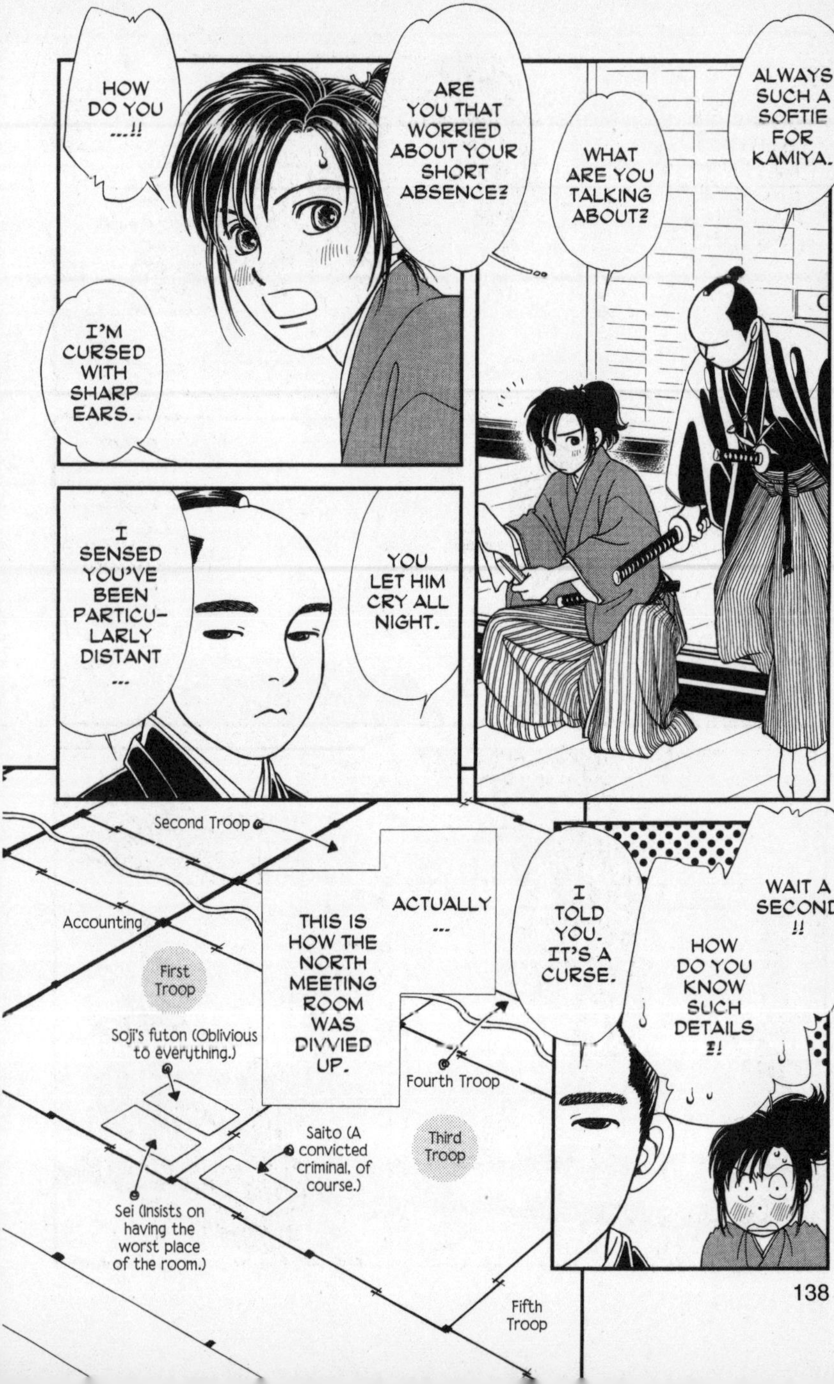
ALWAYS SUCH A SOFTIE FOR KAMIYA.
WHAT ARE YOU TALKING ABOUT?
ARE YOU THAT WORRIED ABOUT YOUR SHORT ABSENCE?
HOW DO YOU ...!!
I'M CURSED WITH SHARP EARS.
YOU LET HIM CRY ALL NIGHT.
I SENSED YOU'VE BEEN PARTICU-LARLY DISTANT ...
WAIT A SECOND!!
HOW DO YOU KNOW SUCH DETAILS?!
I TOLD YOU. IT'S A CURSE.
ACTUALLY ...
THIS IS HOW THE NORTH MEETING ROOM WAS DIVVIED UP.
Second Troop
Accounting
First Troop
Soji's futon (Oblivious to everything.)
Fourth Troop
Third Troop
Saito (A convicted criminal, of course.)
Sei (Insists on having the worst place of the room.)
Fifth Troop

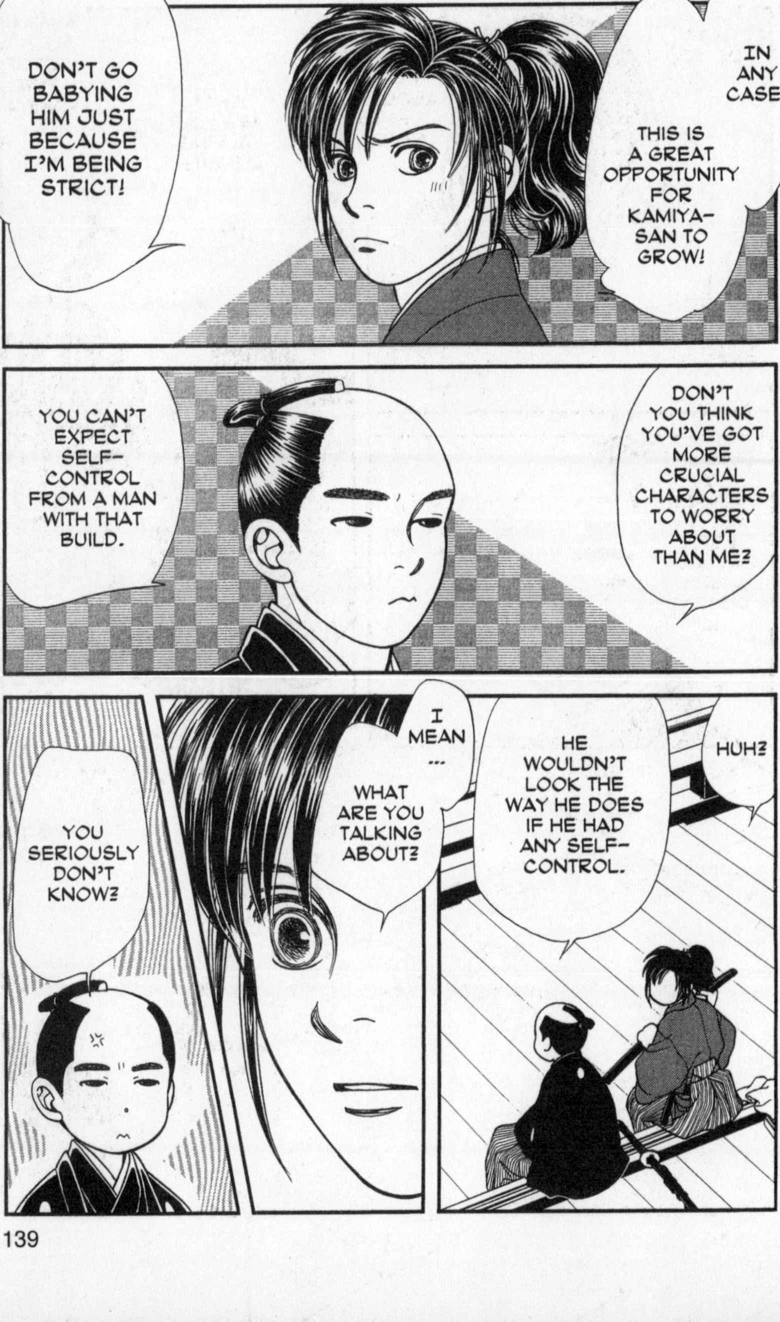
IN ANY CASE!
THIS IS A GREAT OPPORTUNITY FOR KAMIYA-SAN TO GROW!
DON'T GO BABYING HIM JUST BECAUSE I'M BEING STRICT!
DON'T YOU THINK YOU'VE GOT MORE CRUCIAL CHARACTERS TO WORRY ABOUT THAN ME?
YOU CAN'T EXPECT SELF-CONTROL FROM A MAN WITH THAT BUILD.
HUH?
HE WOULDN'T LOOK THE WAY HE DOES IF HE HAD ANY SELF-CONTROL.
I MEAN ...
WHAT ARE YOU TALKING ABOUT?
YOU SERIOUSLY DON'T KNOW?

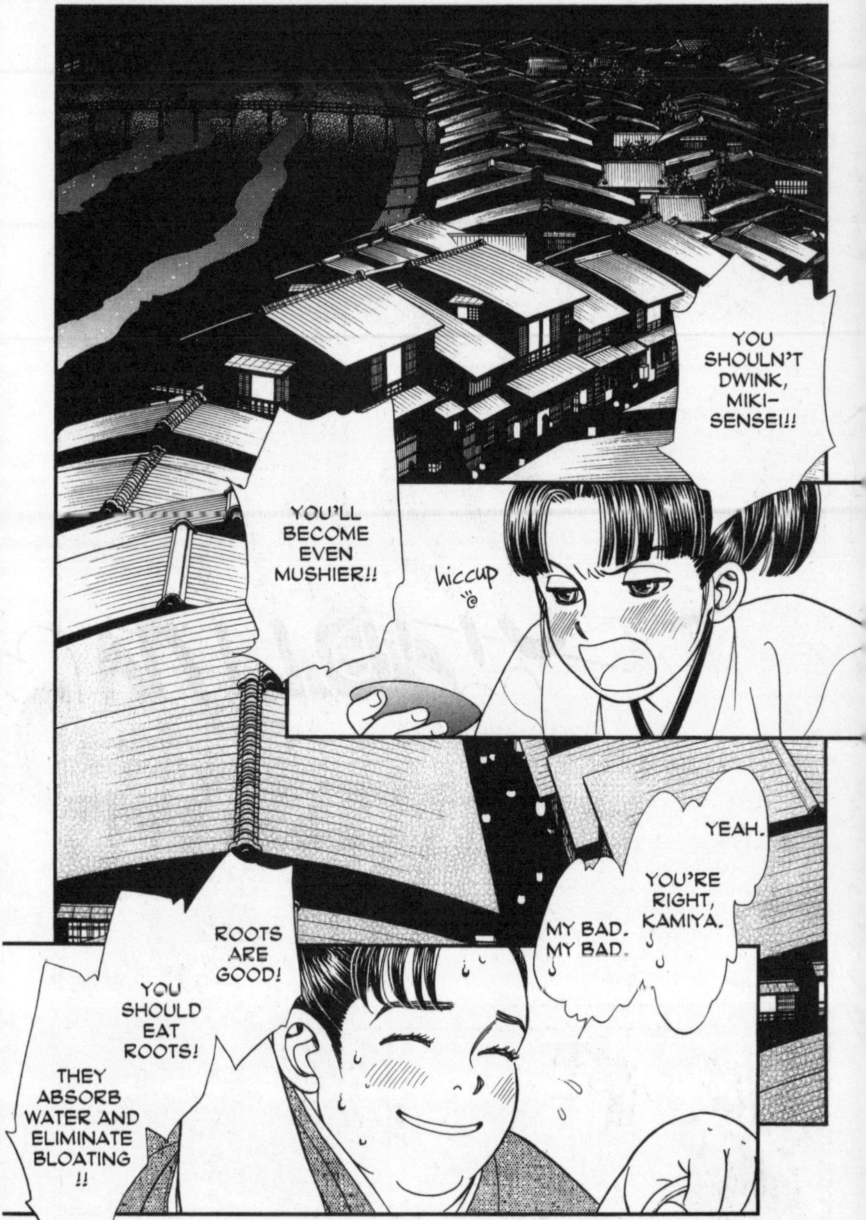
YOU SHOULN'T DWINK, MIKI-SENSEI!!
YOU'LL BECOME EVEN MUSHIER!!
hiccup
YEAH.
YOU'RE RIGHT, KAMIYA.
MY BAD. MY BAD.
ROOTS ARE GOOD!
YOU SHOULD EAT ROOTS!
THEY ABSORB WATER AND ELIMINATE BLOATING!!

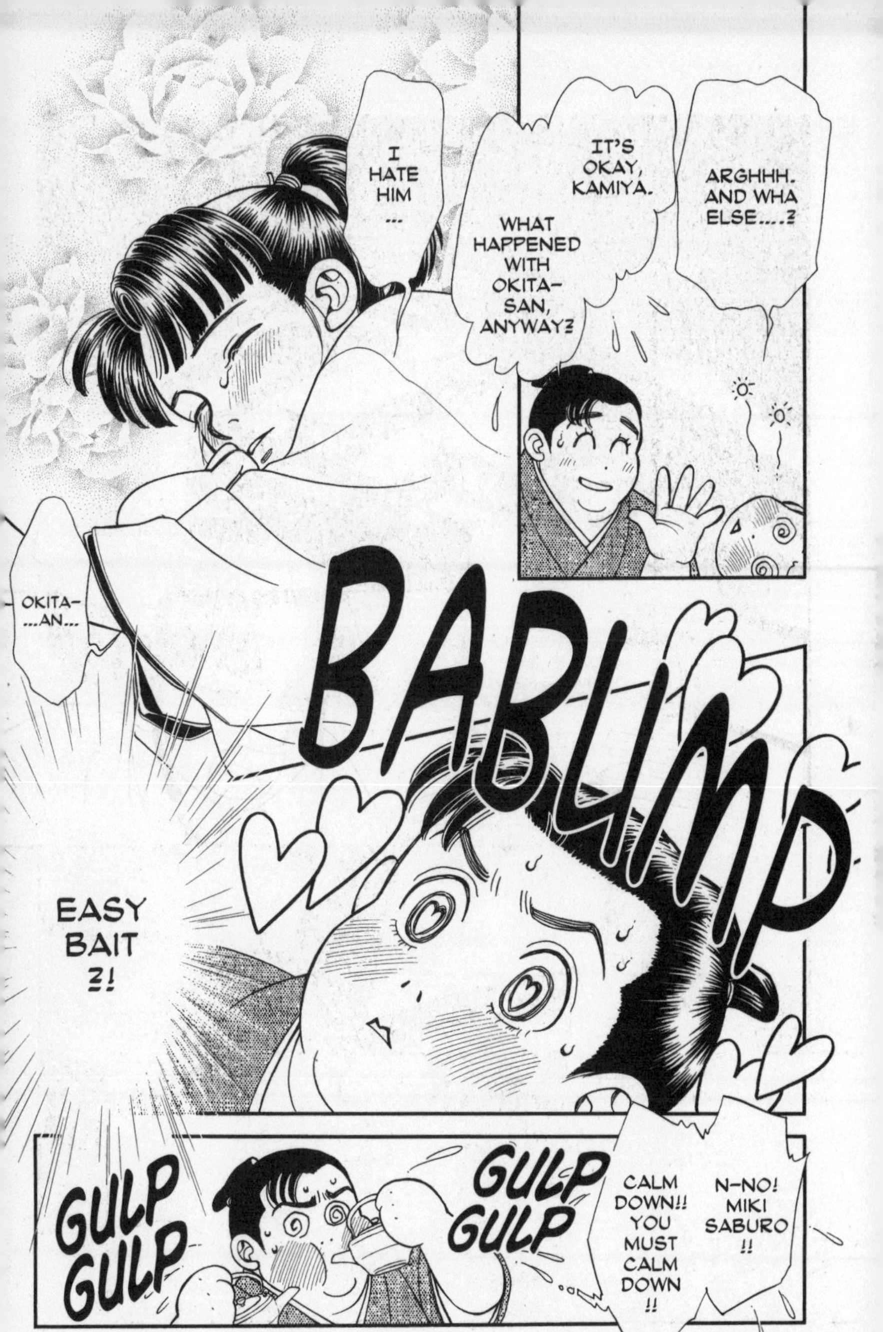
ARGHHH. AND WHA ELSE....?
IT'S OKAY, KAMIYA.
WHAT HAPPENED WITH OKITA-SAN, ANYWAY?
I HATE HIM ...
OKITA- ...AN...
BABUMP
EASY BAIT ?!
N-NO! MIKI SABURO !!
CALM DOWN!! YOU MUST CALM DOWN !!
GULP GULP
GULP GULP

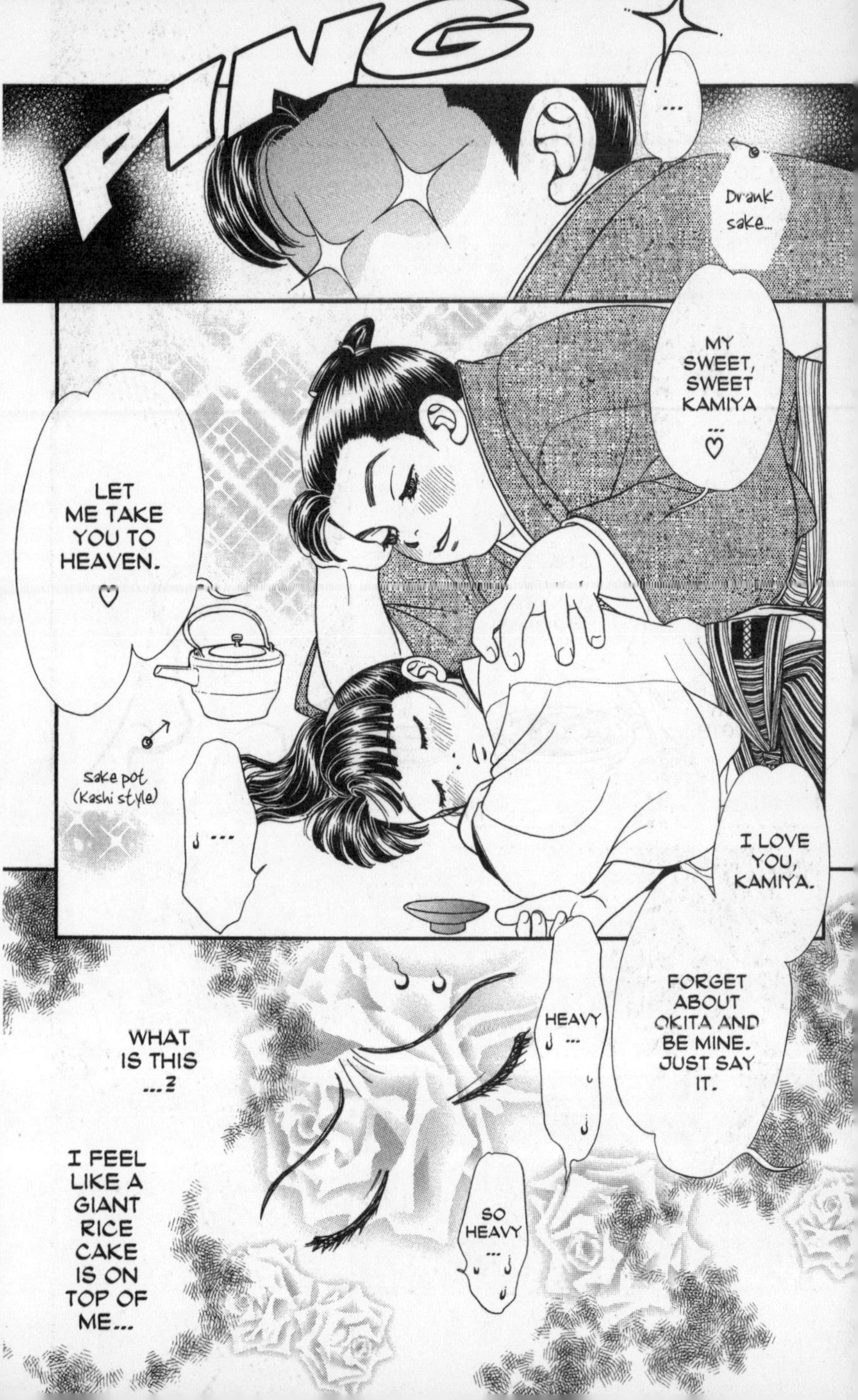
PING
...
Drank sake...
MY SWEET, SWEET KAMIYA... ♡
LET ME TAKE YOU TO HEAVEN. ♡
sake pot (Kashi style)
¿ ...
I LOVE YOU, KAMIYA.
FORGET ABOUT OKITA AND BE MINE. JUST SAY IT.
HEAVY ¿ ...
SO HEAVY ...
WHAT IS THIS ...?
I FEEL LIKE A GIANT RICE CAKE IS ON TOP OF ME...

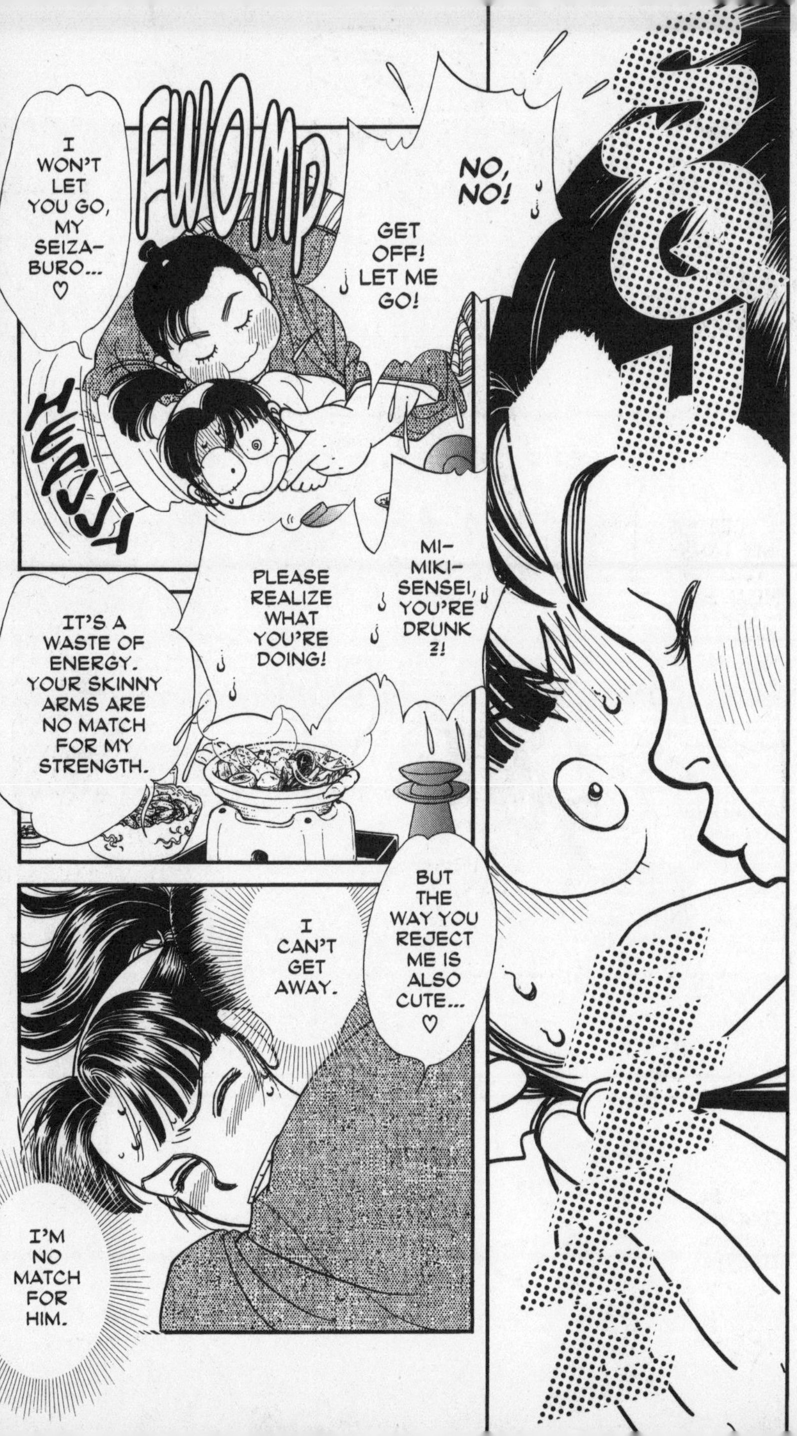
NO, NO!
GET OFF! LET ME GO!
FWOMP
I WON'T LET YOU GO, MY SEIZABURO... ♡
MI-MIKI-SENSEI, YOU'RE DRUNK?!
PLEASE REALIZE WHAT YOU'RE DOING!
IT'S A WASTE OF ENERGY. YOUR SKINNY ARMS ARE NO MATCH FOR MY STRENGTH.
BUT THE WAY YOU REJECT ME IS ALSO CUTE... ♡
I CAN'T GET AWAY.
I'M NO MATCH FOR HIM.

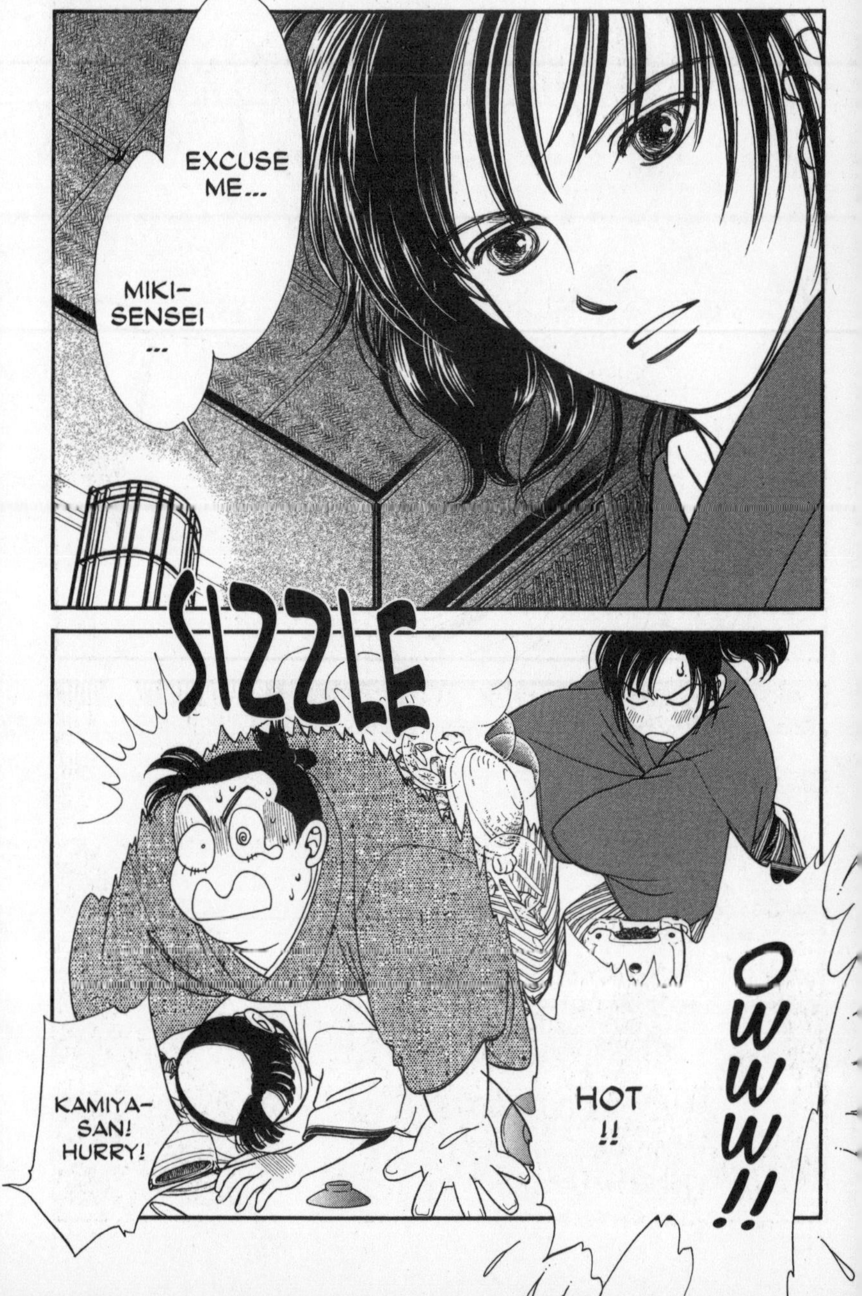
EXCUSE ME...
MIKI-SENSEI ...
SIZZLE
OWWW!!
HOT !!
KAMIYA-SAN! HURRY!

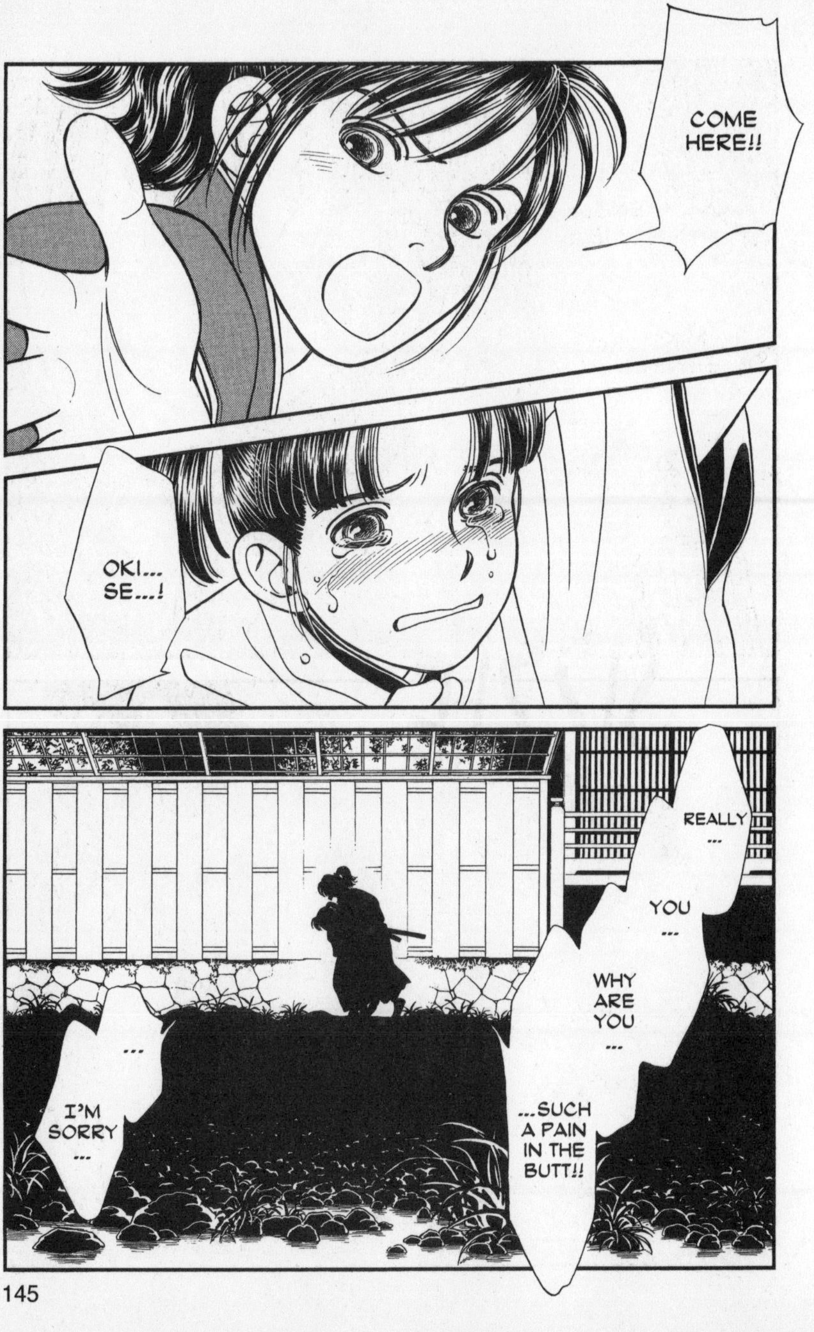
COME HERE!!
OKI... SE...!
REALLY ...
YOU ...
WHY ARE YOU ...
...SUCH A PAIN IN THE BUTT!!
...
I'M SORRY ...

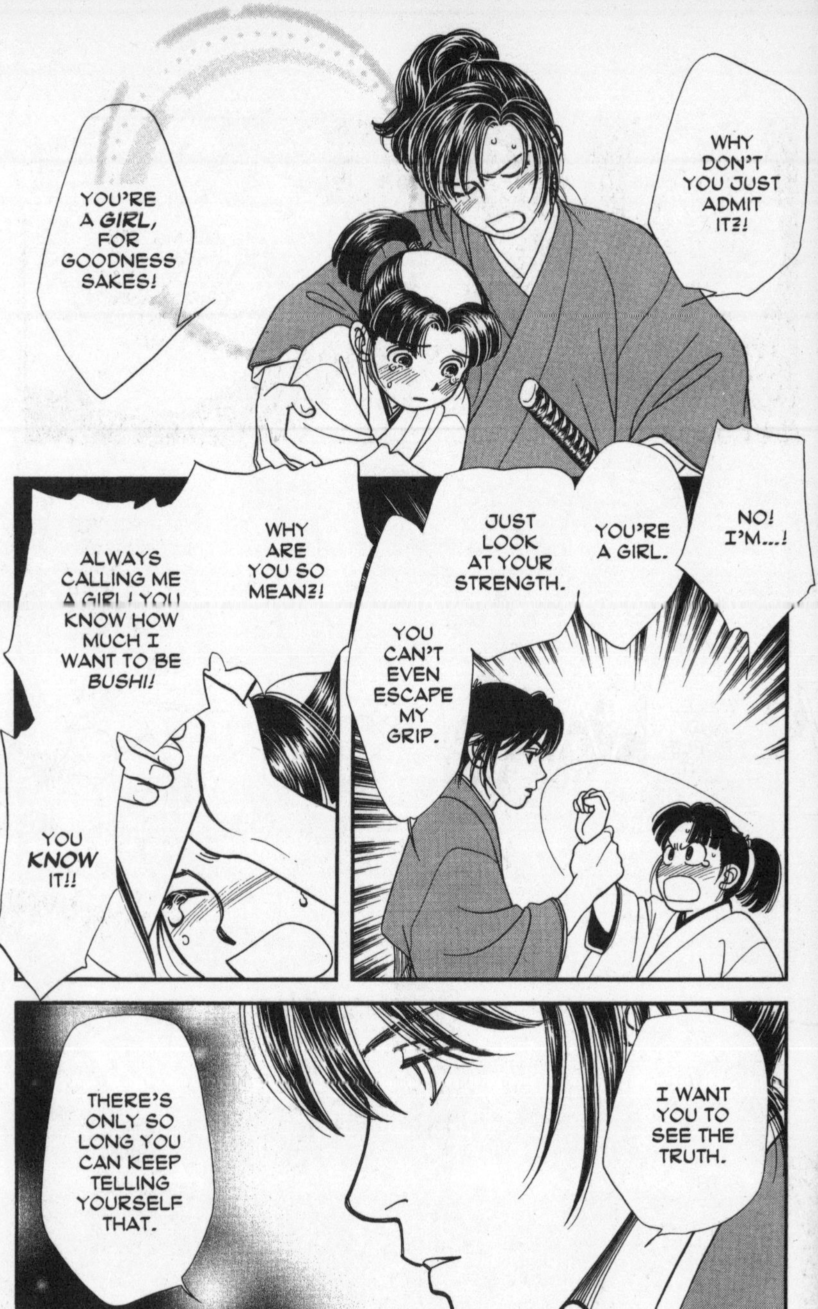
WHY DON'T YOU JUST ADMIT IT?!
YOU'RE A GIRL, FOR GOODNESS SAKES!
NO! I'M...!
YOU'RE A GIRL.
JUST LOOK AT YOUR STRENGTH.
YOU CAN'T EVEN ESCAPE MY GRIP.
WHY ARE YOU SO MEAN?!
ALWAYS CALLING ME A GIRL! YOU KNOW HOW MUCH I WANT TO BE BUSHI!
YOU KNOW IT!!
I WANT YOU TO SEE THE TRUTH.
THERE'S ONLY SO LONG YOU CAN KEEP TELLING YOURSELF THAT.

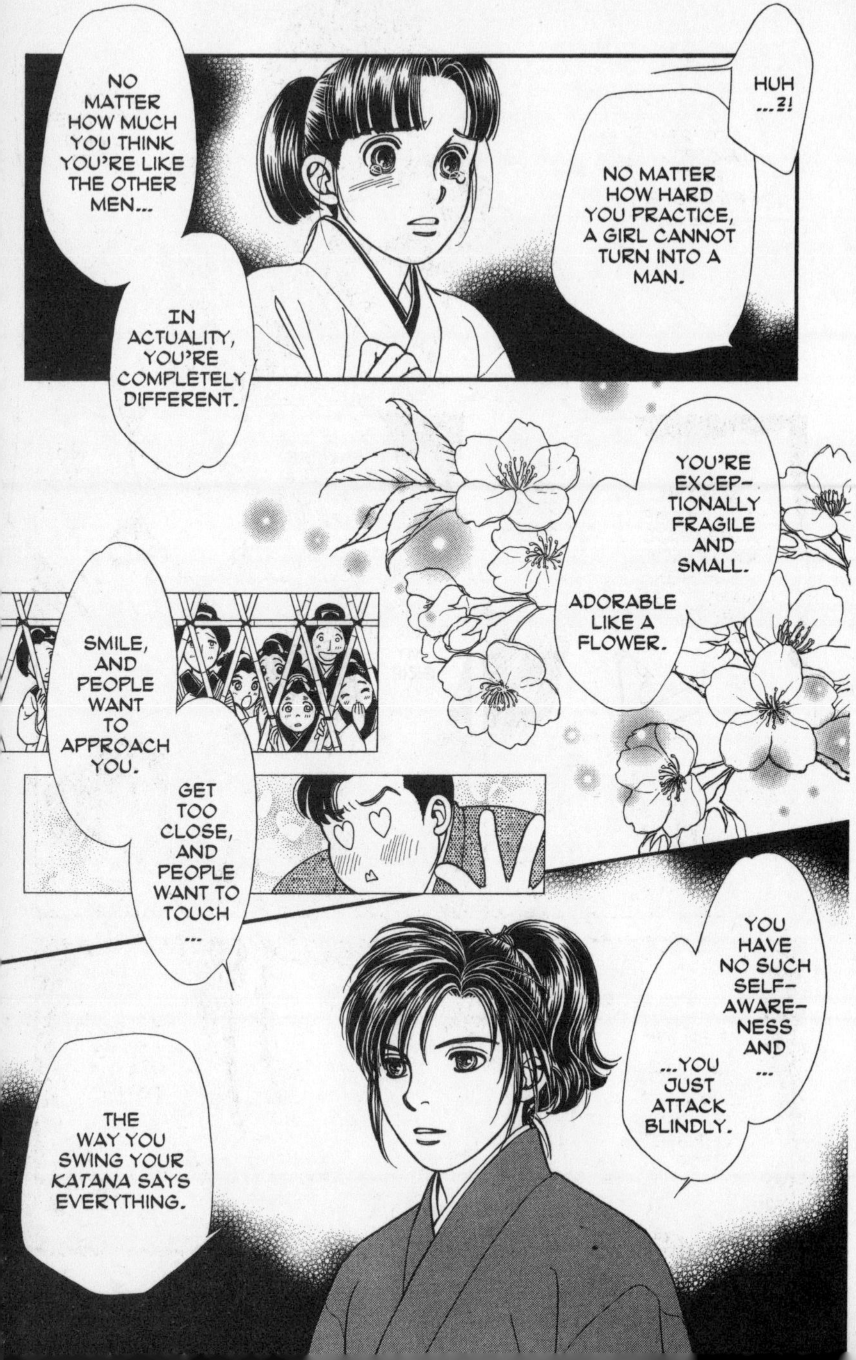
HUH ...?!
NO MATTER HOW HARD YOU PRACTICE, A GIRL CANNOT TURN INTO A MAN.
NO MATTER HOW MUCH YOU THINK YOU'RE LIKE THE OTHER MEN...
IN ACTUALITY, YOU'RE COMPLETELY DIFFERENT.
YOU'RE EXCEPTIONALLY FRAGILE AND SMALL.
ADORABLE LIKE A FLOWER.
SMILE, AND PEOPLE WANT TO APPROACH YOU.
GET TOO CLOSE, AND PEOPLE WANT TO TOUCH ...
YOU HAVE NO SUCH SELF-AWARENESS AND ...
...YOU JUST ATTACK BLINDLY.
THE WAY YOU SWING YOUR KATANA SAYS EVERYTHING.

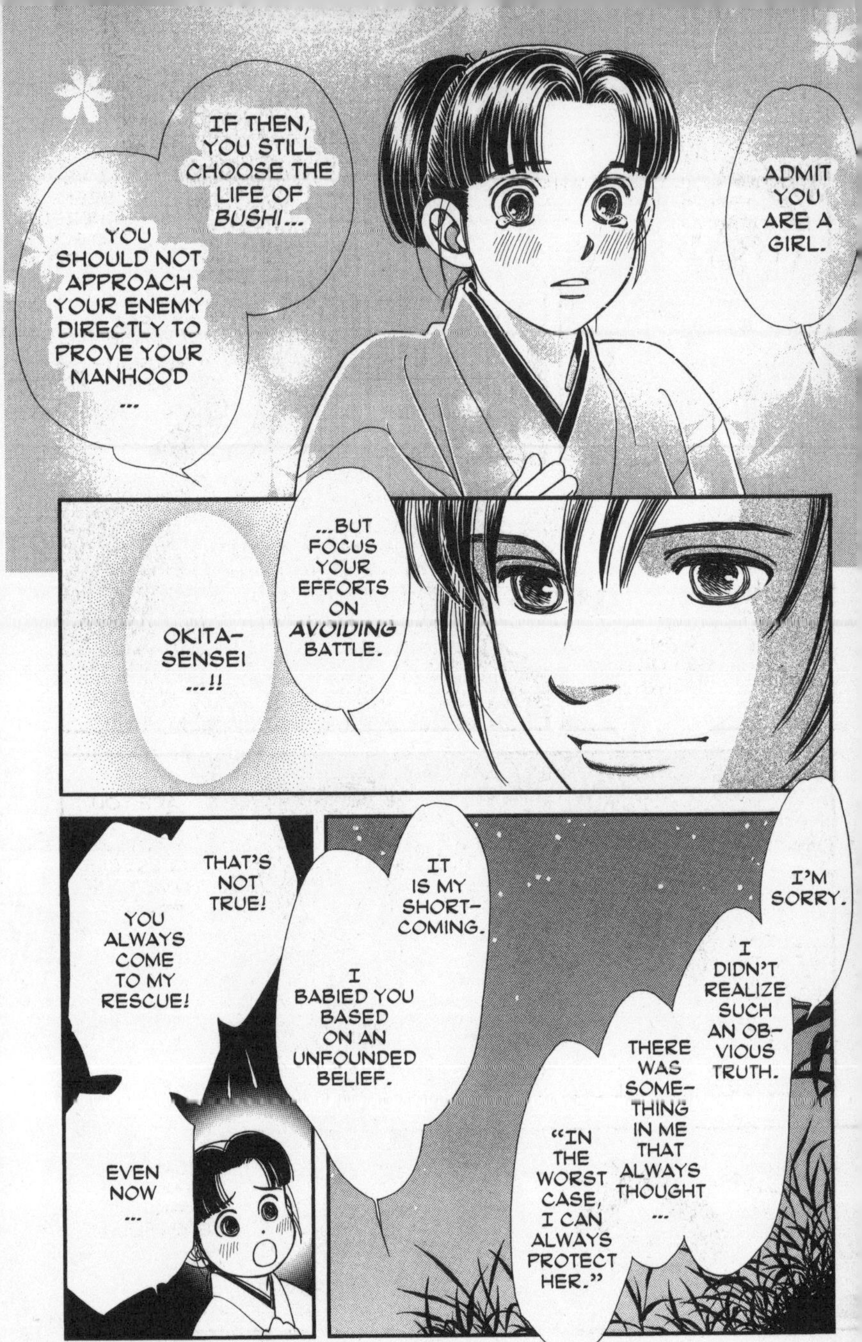
ADMIT YOU ARE A GIRL.
IF THEN, YOU STILL CHOOSE THE LIFE OF *BUSHI*...
YOU SHOULD NOT APPROACH YOUR ENEMY DIRECTLY TO PROVE YOUR MANHOOD ...
...BUT FOCUS YOUR EFFORTS ON ***AVOIDING*** BATTLE.
OKITA-SENSEI ...!!
I'M SORRY.
I DIDN'T REALIZE SUCH AN OB-VIOUS TRUTH.
THERE WAS SOME-THING IN ME THAT ALWAYS THOUGHT ...
"IN THE WORST CASE, I CAN ALWAYS PROTECT HER."
IT IS MY SHORT-COMING.
I BABIED YOU BASED ON AN UNFOUNDED BELIEF.
THAT'S NOT TRUE!
YOU ALWAYS COME TO MY RESCUE!
EVEN NOW ...

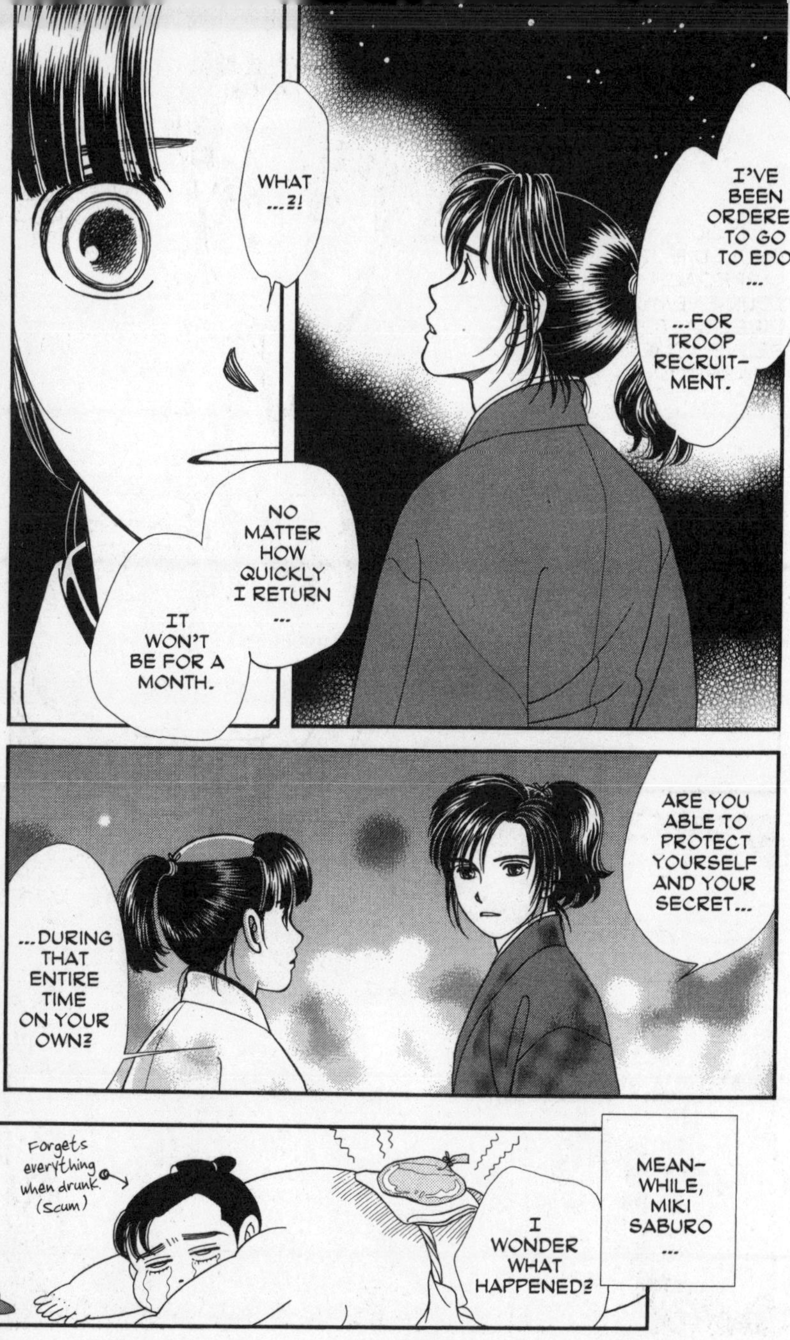
I'VE BEEN ORDERED TO GO TO EDO ...
...FOR TROOP RECRUIT-MENT.
WHAT ...?!
NO MATTER HOW QUICKLY I RETURN ...
IT WON'T BE FOR A MONTH.
ARE YOU ABLE TO PROTECT YOURSELF AND YOUR SECRET...
...DURING THAT ENTIRE TIME ON YOUR OWN?
MEAN-WHILE, MIKI SABURO ...
I WONDER WHAT HAPPENED?
Forgets everything when drunk. (Scum)

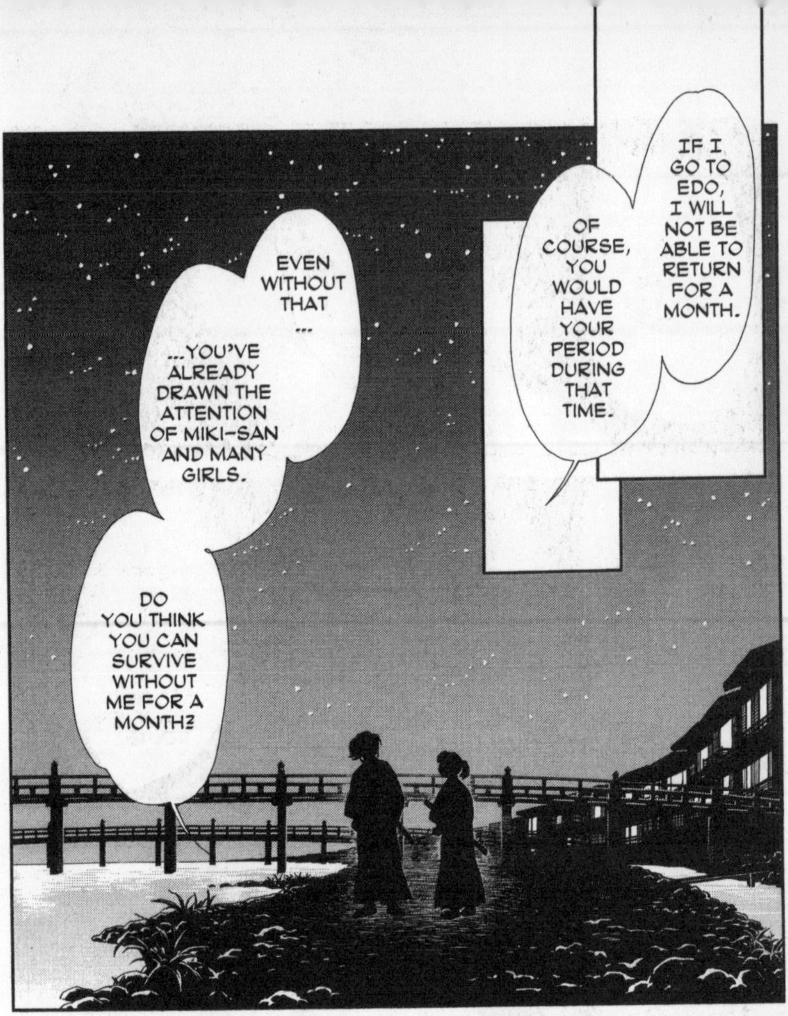
IF I GO TO EDO, I WILL NOT BE ABLE TO RETURN FOR A MONTH.
OF COURSE, YOU WOULD HAVE YOUR PERIOD DURING THAT TIME.
EVEN WITHOUT THAT ...
...YOU'VE ALREADY DRAWN THE ATTENTION OF MIKI-SAN AND MANY GIRLS.
DO YOU THINK YOU CAN SURVIVE WITHOUT ME FOR A MONTH?

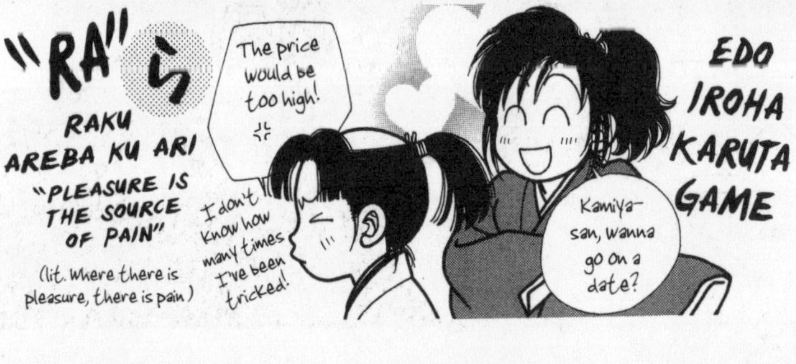
EDO IROHA KARUTA GAME
Kamiya-san, wanna go on a date?
The price would be too high!
I don't know how many times I've been tricked!
"RA" ら
RAKU AREBA KU ARI
"PLEASURE IS THE SOURCE OF PAIN"
(lit. Where there is pleasure, there is pain)

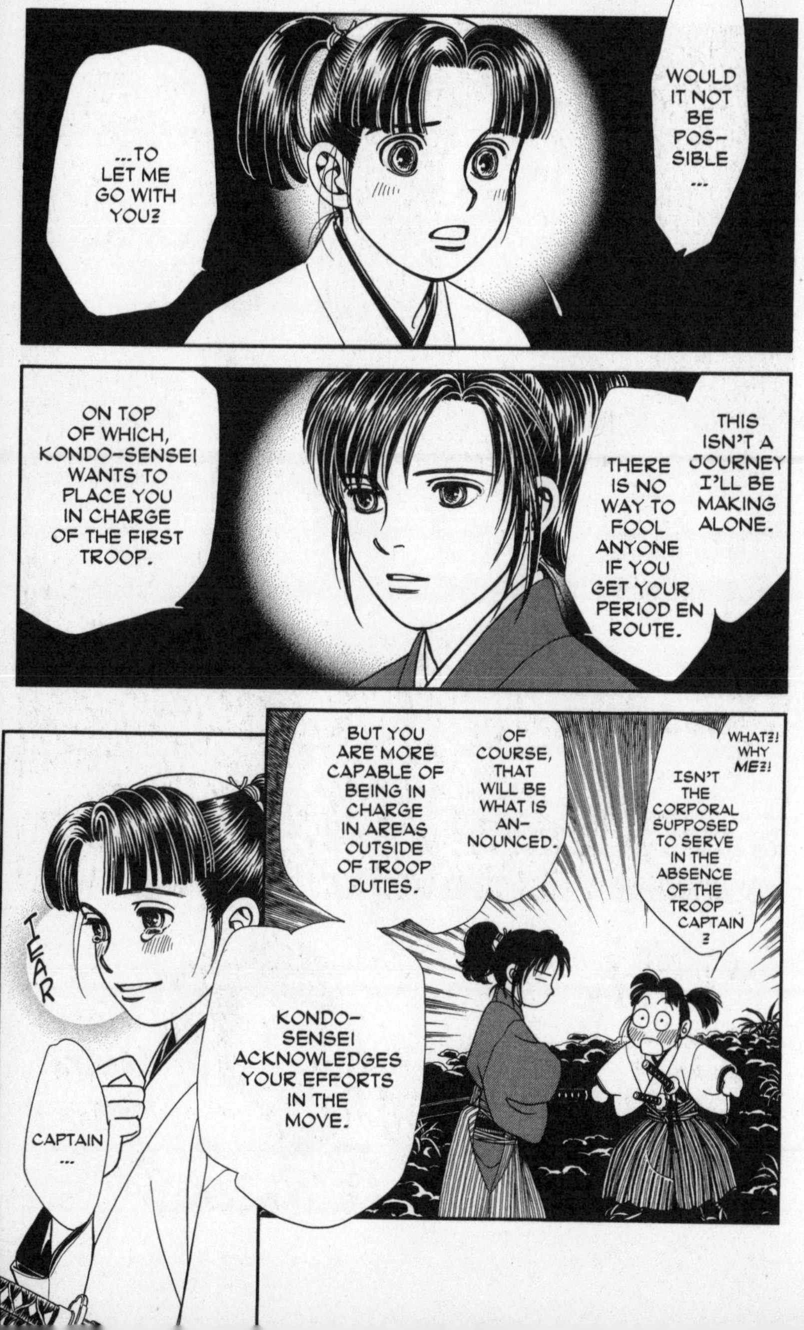
WOULD IT NOT BE POS-SIBLE...
...TO LET ME GO WITH YOU?
THIS ISN'T A JOURNEY I'LL BE MAKING ALONE.
THERE IS NO WAY TO FOOL ANYONE IF YOU GET YOUR PERIOD EN ROUTE.
ON TOP OF WHICH, KONDO-SENSEI WANTS TO PLACE YOU IN CHARGE OF THE FIRST TROOP.
WHAT?! WHY ME?!
ISN'T THE CORPORAL SUPPOSED TO SERVE IN THE ABSENCE OF THE TROOP CAPTAIN?
OF COURSE, THAT WILL BE WHAT IS AN-NOUNCED.
BUT YOU ARE MORE CAPABLE OF BEING IN CHARGE IN AREAS OUTSIDE OF TROOP DUTIES.
KONDO-SENSEI ACKNOWLEDGES YOUR EFFORTS IN THE MOVE.
TEAR
CAPTAIN...

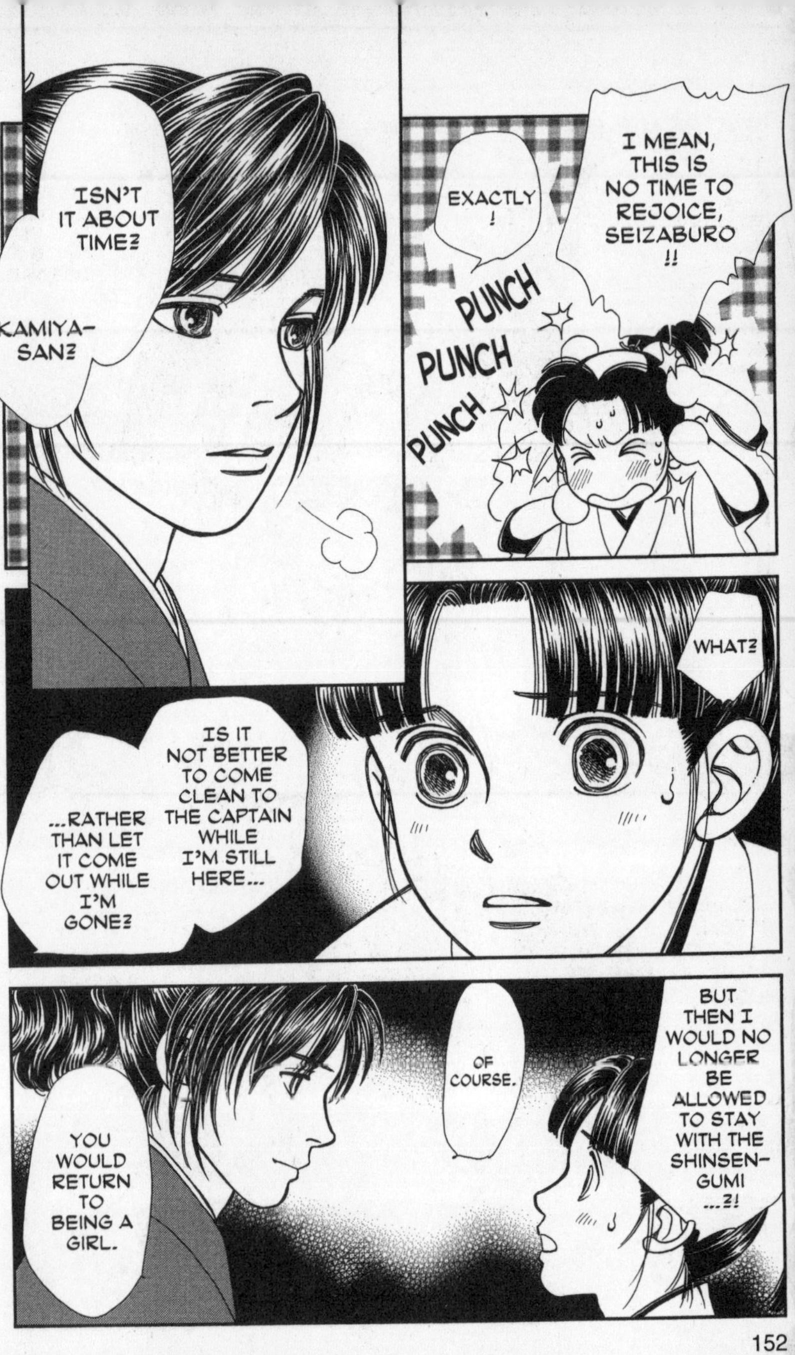
I MEAN, THIS IS NO TIME TO REJOICE, SEIZABURO!!
EXACTLY!
PUNCH
PUNCH
PUNCH
ISN'T IT ABOUT TIME?
KAMIYA-SAN?
WHAT?
IS IT NOT BETTER TO COME CLEAN TO THE CAPTAIN WHILE I'M STILL HERE...
...RATHER THAN LET IT COME OUT WHILE I'M GONE?
BUT THEN I WOULD NO LONGER BE ALLOWED TO STAY WITH THE SHINSEN-GUMI...?!
OF COURSE.
YOU WOULD RETURN TO BEING A GIRL.

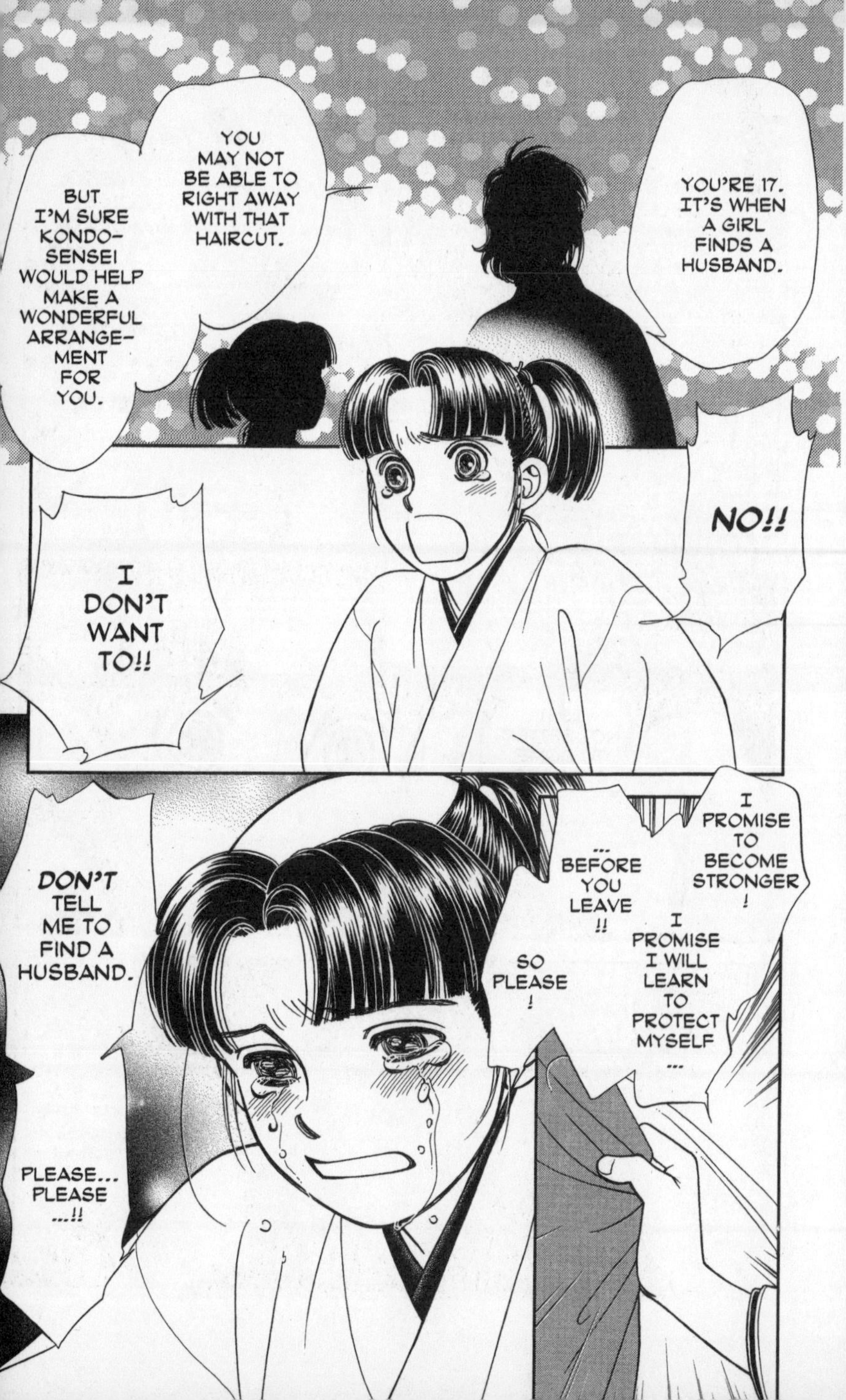
YOU'RE 17. IT'S WHEN A GIRL FINDS A HUSBAND.
YOU MAY NOT BE ABLE TO RIGHT AWAY WITH THAT HAIRCUT.
BUT I'M SURE KONDO-SENSEI WOULD HELP MAKE A WONDERFUL ARRANGEMENT FOR YOU.
NO!!
I DON'T WANT TO!!
I PROMISE TO BECOME STRONGER!
I PROMISE I WILL LEARN TO PROTECT MYSELF...
...BEFORE YOU LEAVE!!
SO PLEASE!
DON'T TELL ME TO FIND A HUSBAND.
PLEASE... PLEASE ...!!

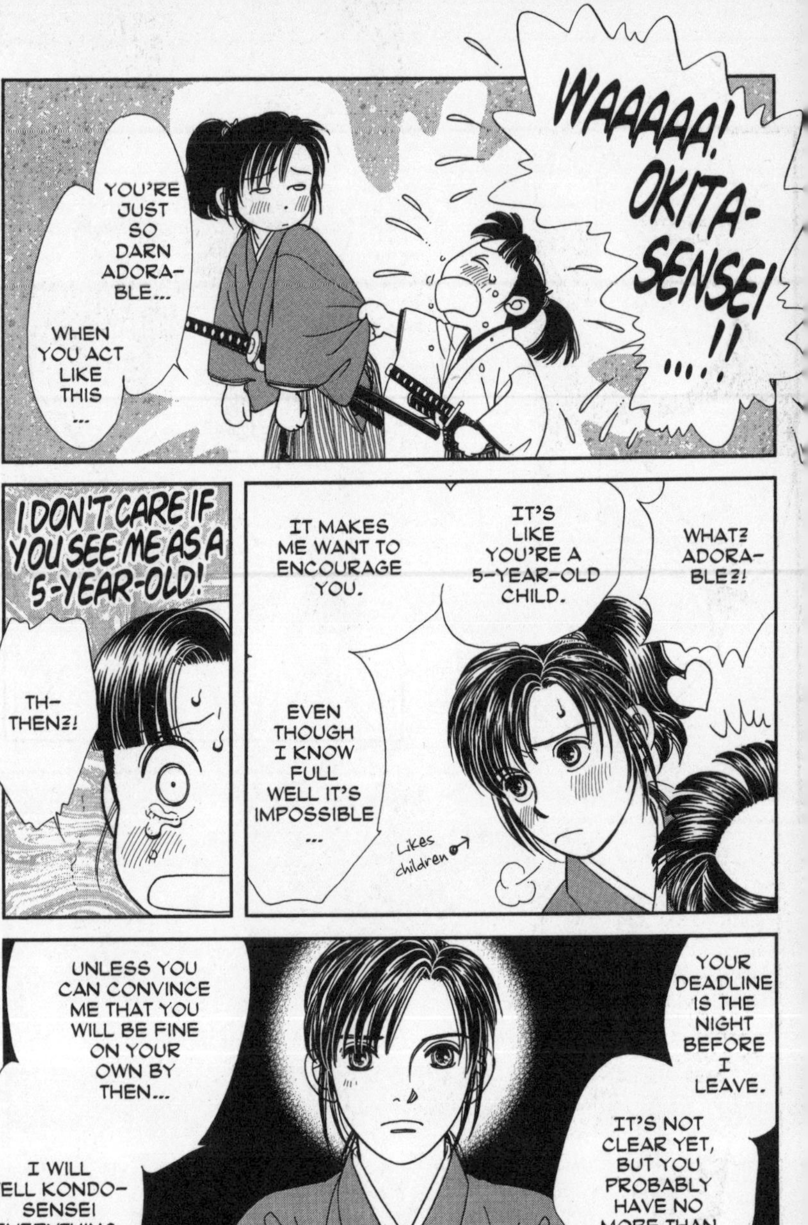
WAAAAA! OKITA-SENSEI ......!!
YOU'RE JUST SO DARN ADORABLE...
WHEN YOU ACT LIKE THIS...
WHAT? ADORABLE?!
IT'S LIKE YOU'RE A 5-YEAR-OLD CHILD.
IT MAKES ME WANT TO ENCOURAGE YOU.
EVEN THOUGH I KNOW FULL WELL IT'S IMPOSSIBLE...
Likes children
I DON'T CARE IF YOU SEE ME AS A 5-YEAR-OLD!
TH-THEN?!
YOUR DEADLINE IS THE NIGHT BEFORE I LEAVE.
IT'S NOT CLEAR YET, BUT YOU PROBABLY HAVE NO MORE THAN TEN DAYS.
UNLESS YOU CAN CONVINCE ME THAT YOU WILL BE FINE ON YOUR OWN BY THEN...
I WILL TELL KONDO-SENSEI EVERYTHING. ALL RIGHT?

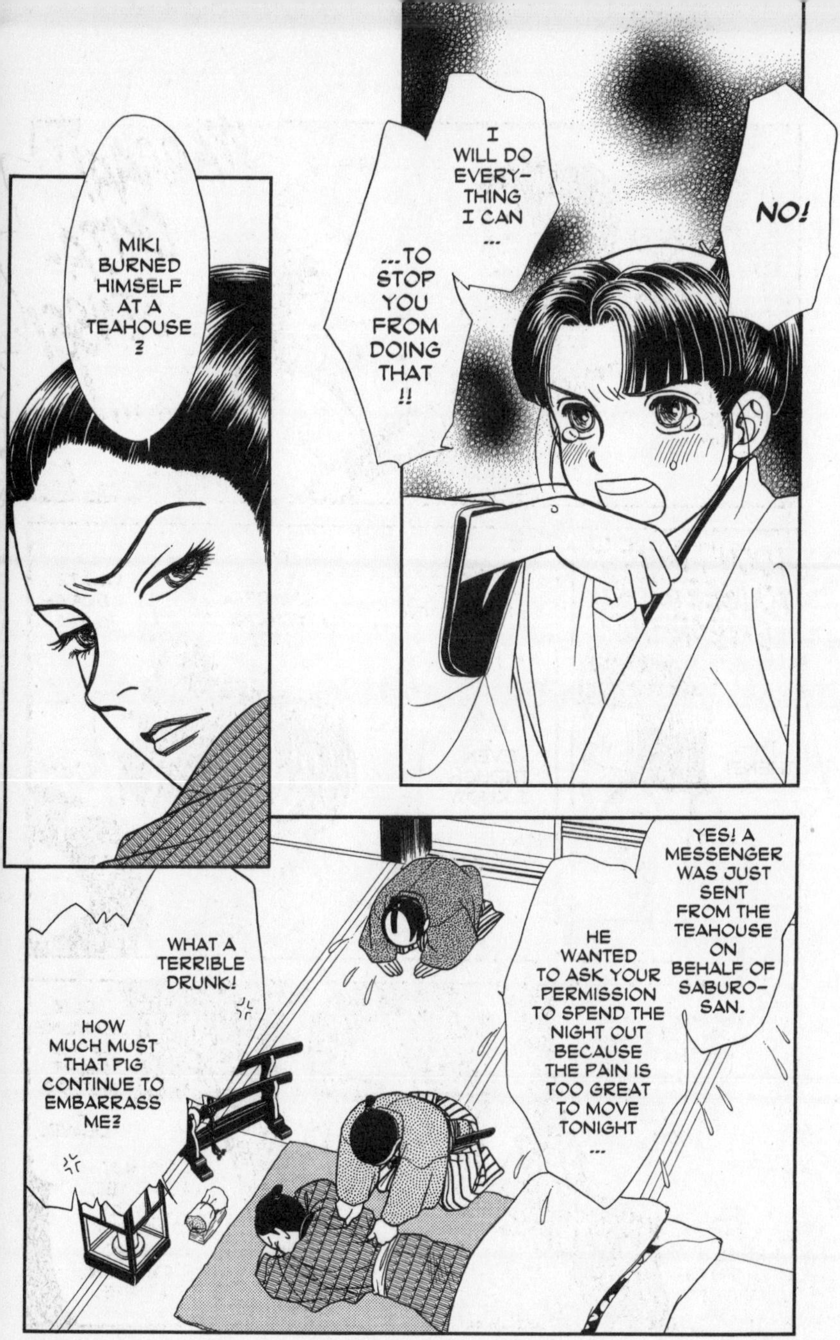
NO!
I WILL DO EVERY-THING I CAN ...
...TO STOP YOU FROM DOING THAT !!
MIKI BURNED HIMSELF AT A TEAHOUSE ?
YES! A MESSENGER WAS JUST SENT FROM THE TEAHOUSE ON BEHALF OF SABURO-SAN.
HE WANTED TO ASK YOUR PERMISSION TO SPEND THE NIGHT OUT BECAUSE THE PAIN IS TOO GREAT TO MOVE TONIGHT ...
WHAT A TERRIBLE DRUNK!
HOW MUCH MUST THAT PIG CONTINUE TO EMBARRASS ME?

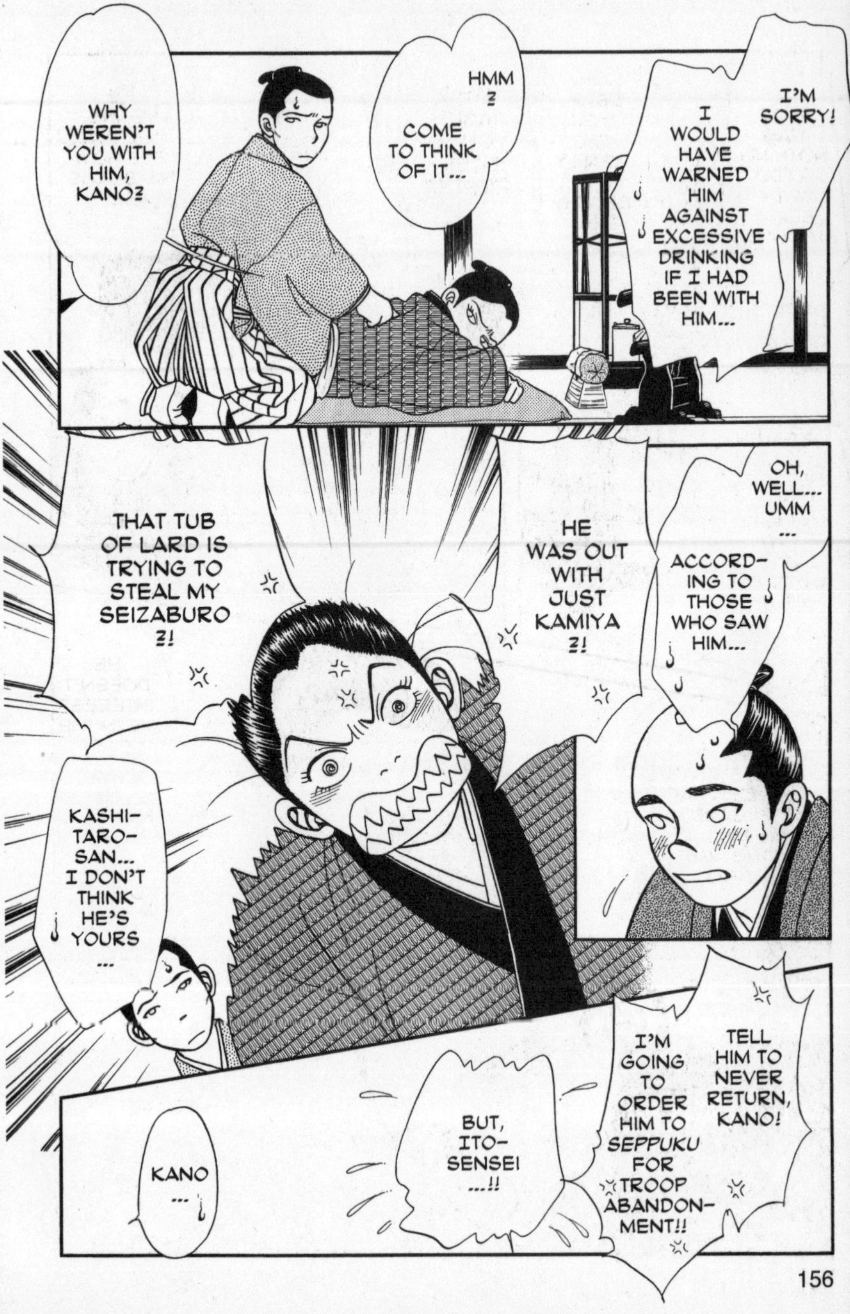
I'M SORRY!
I WOULD HAVE WARNED HIM AGAINST EXCESSIVE DRINKING IF I HAD BEEN WITH HIM...
HMM?
COME TO THINK OF IT...
WHY WEREN'T YOU WITH HIM, KANO?
OH, WELL... UMM ...
ACCORDING TO THOSE WHO SAW HIM...
HE WAS OUT WITH JUST KAMIYA?!
THAT TUB OF LARD IS TRYING TO STEAL MY SEIZABURO?!
KASHITARO-SAN... I DON'T THINK HE'S YOURS ...
TELL HIM TO NEVER RETURN, KANO!
I'M GOING TO ORDER HIM TO *SEPPUKU* FOR TROOP ABANDONMENT!!
BUT, ITO-SENSEI ...!!
KANO ...

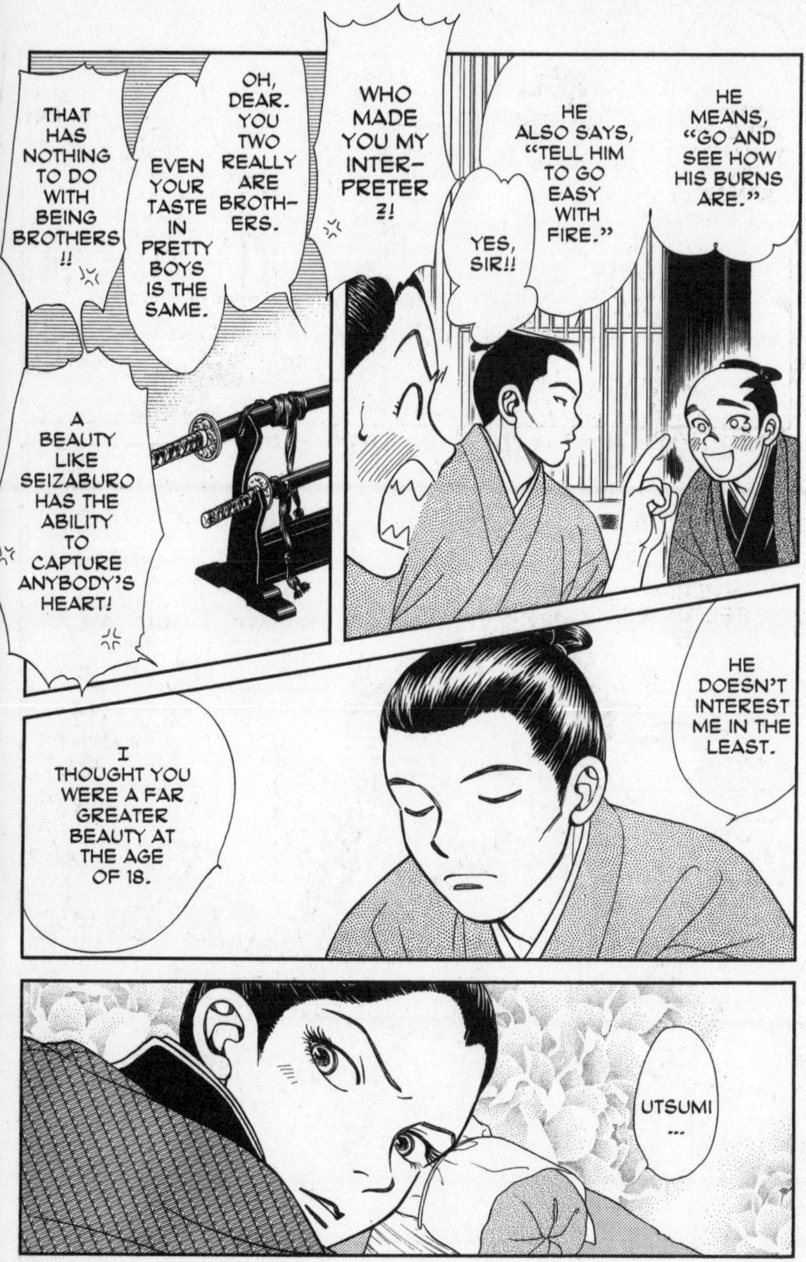
HE MEANS, "GO AND SEE HOW HIS BURNS ARE."
HE ALSO SAYS, "TELL HIM TO GO EASY WITH FIRE."
YES, SIR!!
WHO MADE YOU MY INTER-PRETER?!
OH, DEAR. YOU TWO REALLY ARE BROTH-ERS.
EVEN YOUR TASTE IN PRETTY BOYS IS THE SAME.
THAT HAS NOTHING TO DO WITH BEING BROTHERS!!
A BEAUTY LIKE SEIZABURO HAS THE ABILITY TO CAPTURE ANYBODY'S HEART!
HE DOESN'T INTEREST ME IN THE LEAST.
I THOUGHT YOU WERE A FAR GREATER BEAUTY AT THE AGE OF 18.
UTSUMI...

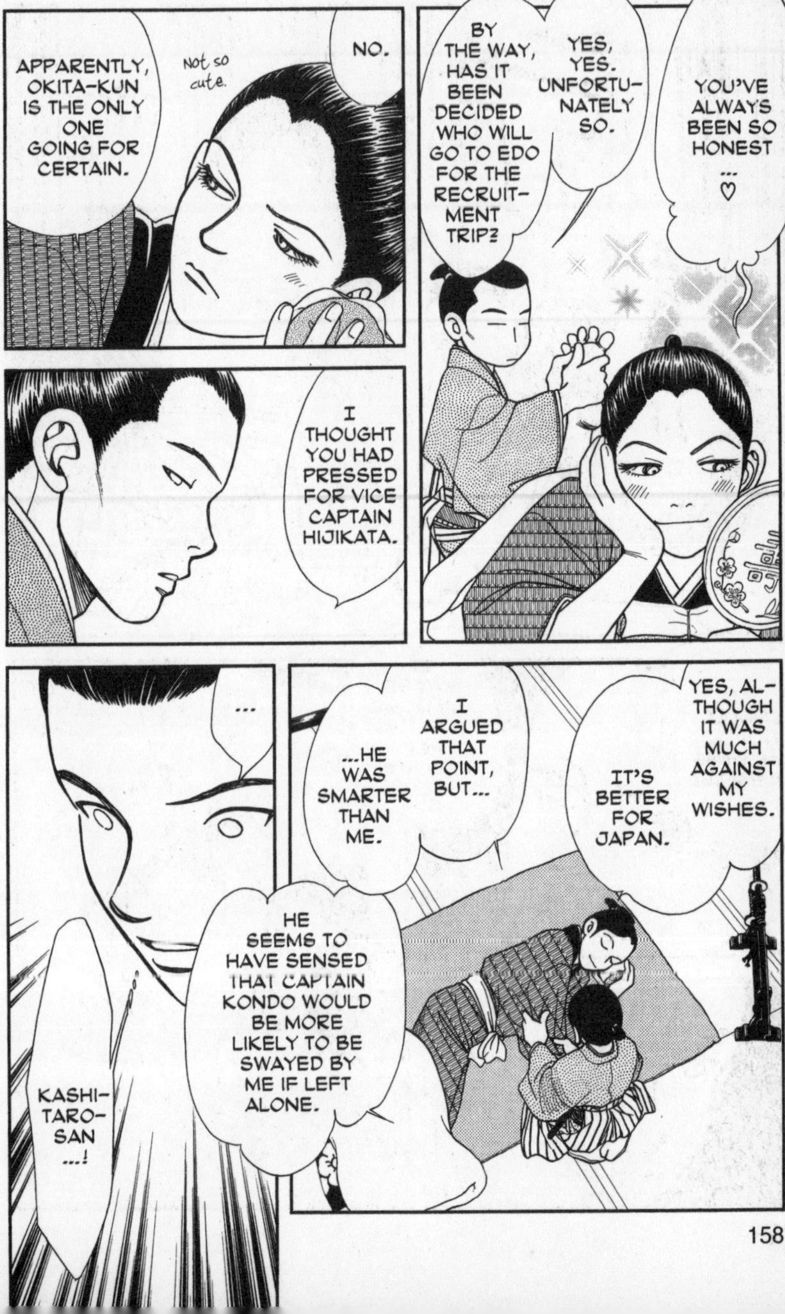
YOU'VE ALWAYS BEEN SO HONEST ... ♡
YES, YES. UNFORTUNATELY SO.
BY THE WAY, HAS IT BEEN DECIDED WHO WILL GO TO EDO FOR THE RECRUITMENT TRIP?
NO.
Not so cute.
APPARENTLY, OKITA-KUN IS THE ONLY ONE GOING FOR CERTAIN.
I THOUGHT YOU HAD PRESSED FOR VICE CAPTAIN HIJIKATA.
YES, ALTHOUGH IT WAS MUCH AGAINST MY WISHES.
IT'S BETTER FOR JAPAN.
I ARGUED THAT POINT, BUT...
...HE WAS SMARTER THAN ME.
HE SEEMS TO HAVE SENSED THAT CAPTAIN KONDO WOULD BE MORE LIKELY TO BE SWAYED BY ME IF LEFT ALONE.
...
KASHITARO-SAN ...!

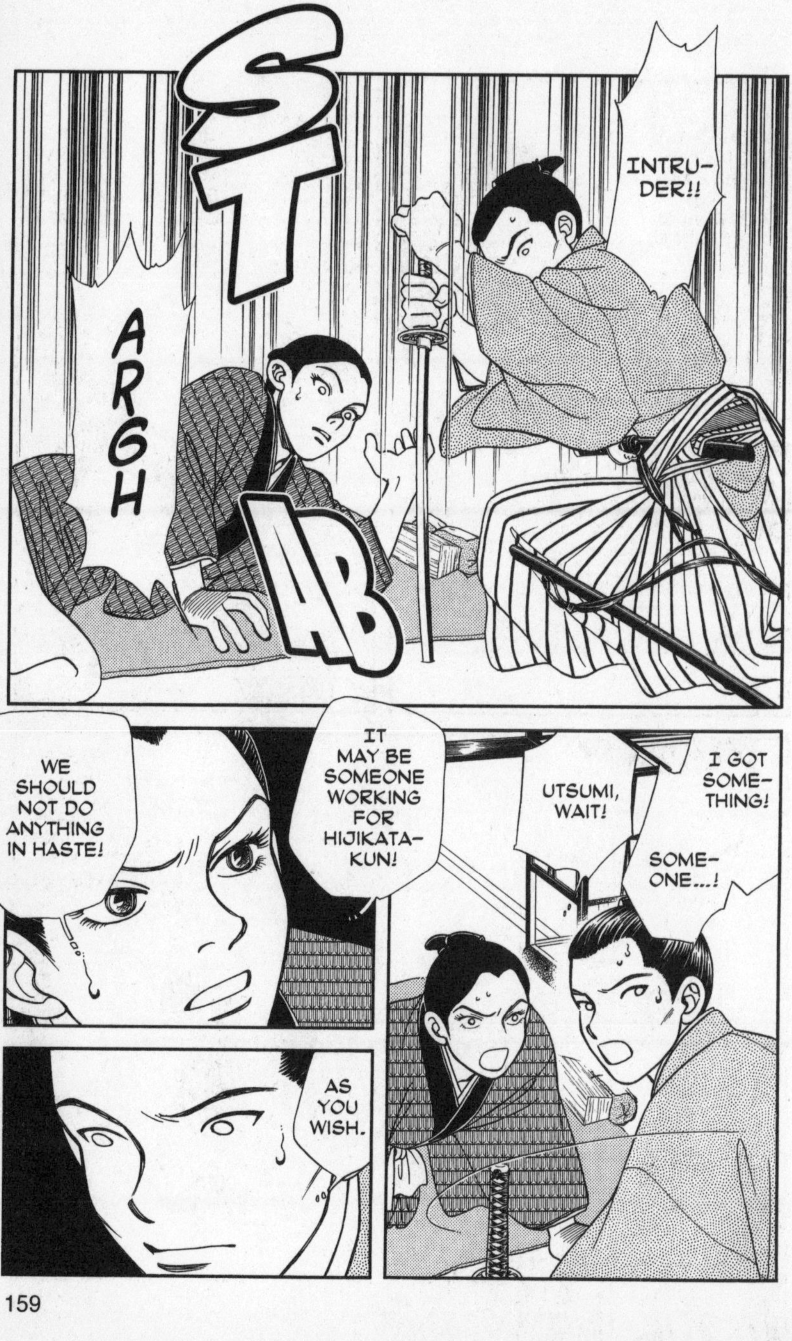
INTRU-
DER!!
ST
ARGH
AB
I GOT SOME-
THING!
SOME-
ONE...!
UTSUMI,
WAIT!
IT
MAY BE
SOMEONE
WORKING
FOR
HIJIKATA-
KUN!
WE
SHOULD
NOT DO
ANYTHING
IN HASTE!
AS
YOU
WISH.

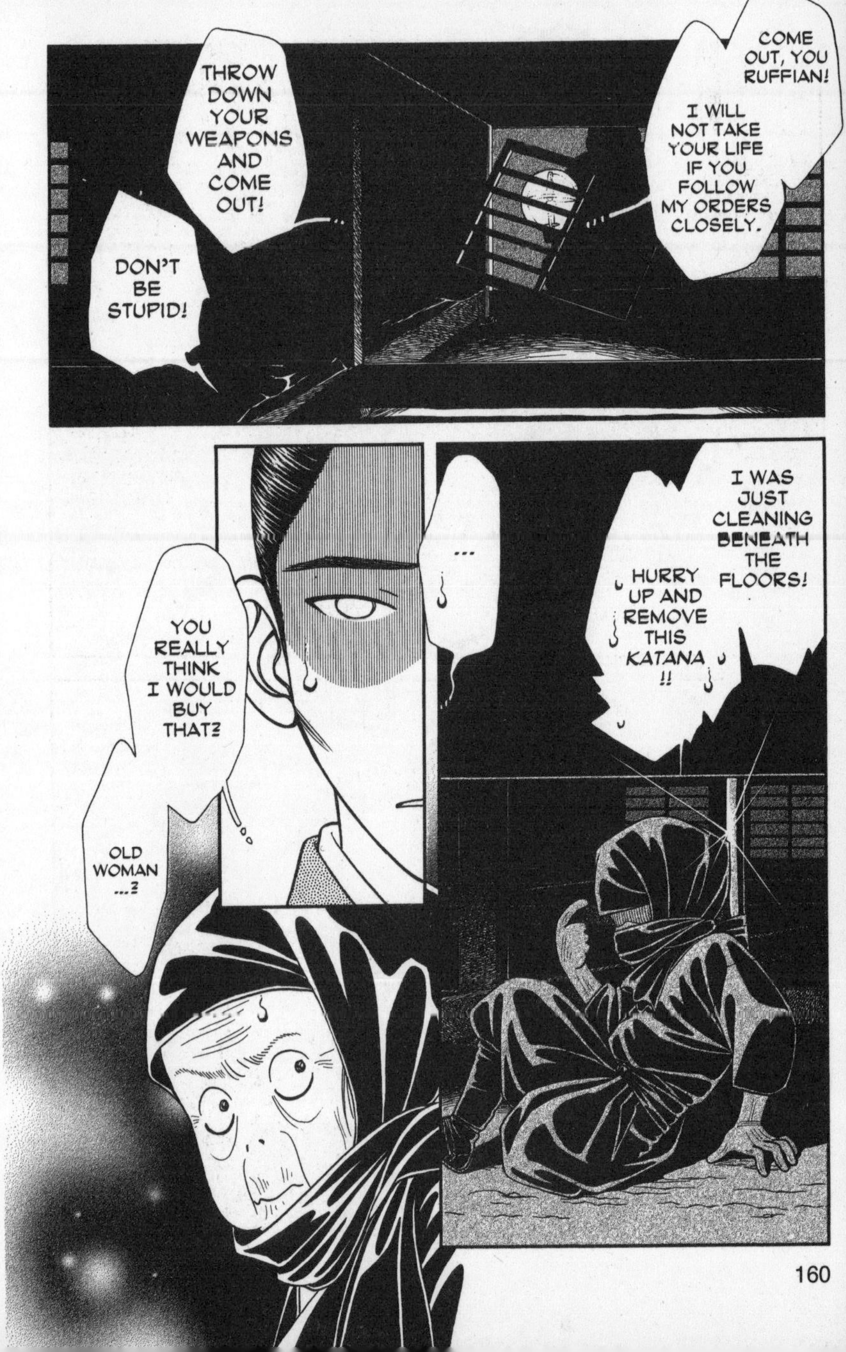
COME OUT, YOU RUFFIAN!
I WILL NOT TAKE YOUR LIFE IF YOU FOLLOW MY ORDERS CLOSELY.
THROW DOWN YOUR WEAPONS AND COME OUT!
DON'T BE STUPID!
I WAS JUST CLEANING BENEATH THE FLOORS!
HURRY UP AND REMOVE THIS KATANA!!
...
YOU REALLY THINK I WOULD BUY THAT?
OLD WOMAN...?

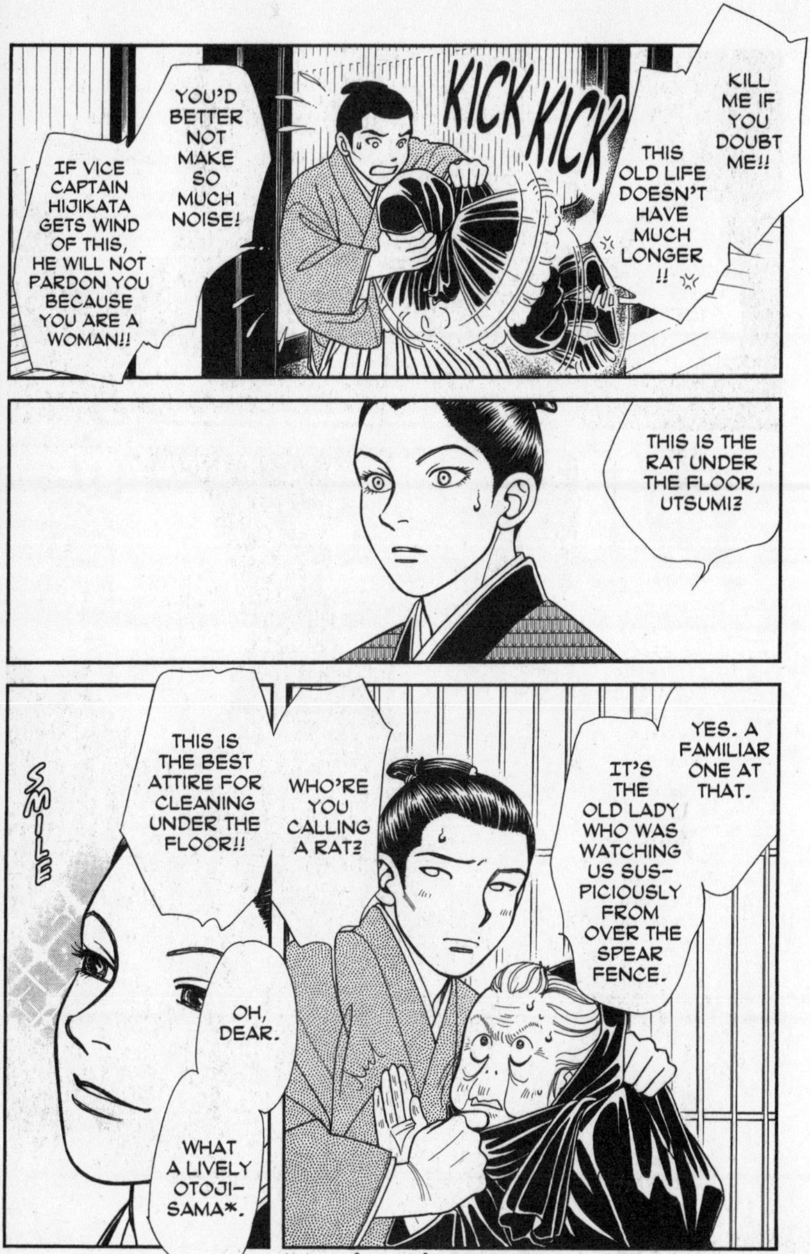
KILL ME IF YOU DOUBT ME!!
THIS OLD LIFE DOESN'T HAVE MUCH LONGER!!
KICK KICK
YOU'D BETTER NOT MAKE SO MUCH NOISE!
IF VICE CAPTAIN HIJIKATA GETS WIND OF THIS, HE WILL NOT PARDON YOU BECAUSE YOU ARE A WOMAN!!
THIS IS THE RAT UNDER THE FLOOR, UTSUMI?
YES. A FAMILIAR ONE AT THAT.
IT'S THE OLD LADY WHO WAS WATCHING US SUS-PICIOUSLY FROM OVER THE SPEAR FENCE.
WHO'RE YOU CALLING A RAT?
THIS IS THE BEST ATTIRE FOR CLEANING UNDER THE FLOOR!!
SMILE
OH, DEAR.
WHAT A LIVELY OTOJI-SAMA*.

*A term of respect for older women.

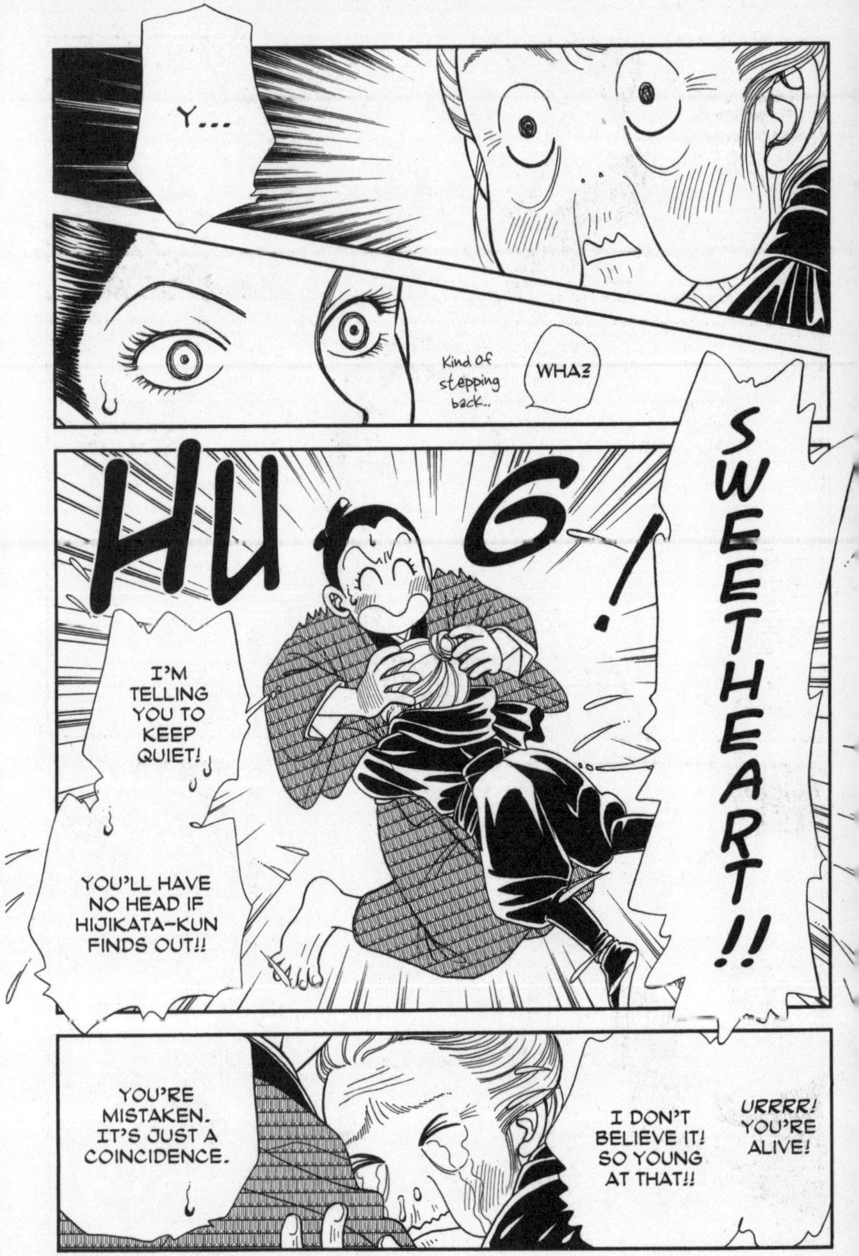
Y...
WHA?
Kind of stepping back..
SWEETHEART!!
HUG!
I'M TELLING YOU TO KEEP QUIET!
YOU'LL HAVE NO HEAD IF HIJIKATA-KUN FINDS OUT!!
URRRR! YOU'RE ALIVE!
I DON'T BELIEVE IT! SO YOUNG AT THAT!!
YOU'RE MISTAKEN. IT'S JUST A COINCIDENCE.

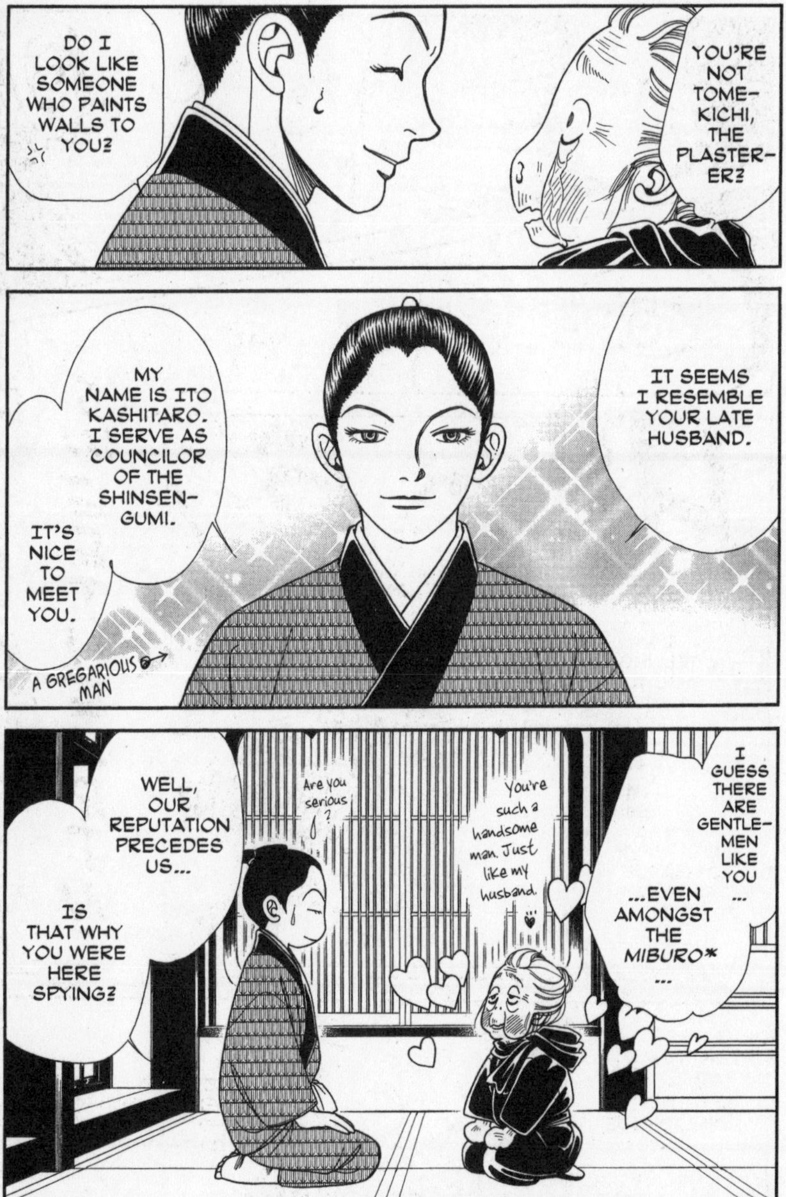
YOU'RE NOT TOME-KICHI, THE PLASTERER?
DO I LOOK LIKE SOMEONE WHO PAINTS WALLS TO YOU?
IT SEEMS I RESEMBLE YOUR LATE HUSBAND.
MY NAME IS ITO KASHITARO. I SERVE AS COUNCILOR OF THE SHINSEN-GUMI.
IT'S NICE TO MEET YOU.
A GREGARIOUS MAN
I GUESS THERE ARE GENTLE-MEN LIKE YOU ...
...EVEN AMONGST THE MIBURO* ...
You're such a handsome man. Just like my husband.
Are you serious?
WELL, OUR REPUTATION PRECEDES US...
IS THAT WHY YOU WERE HERE SPYING?

* "The wolves of Mibu;" a dirty name for the Shinsengumi.

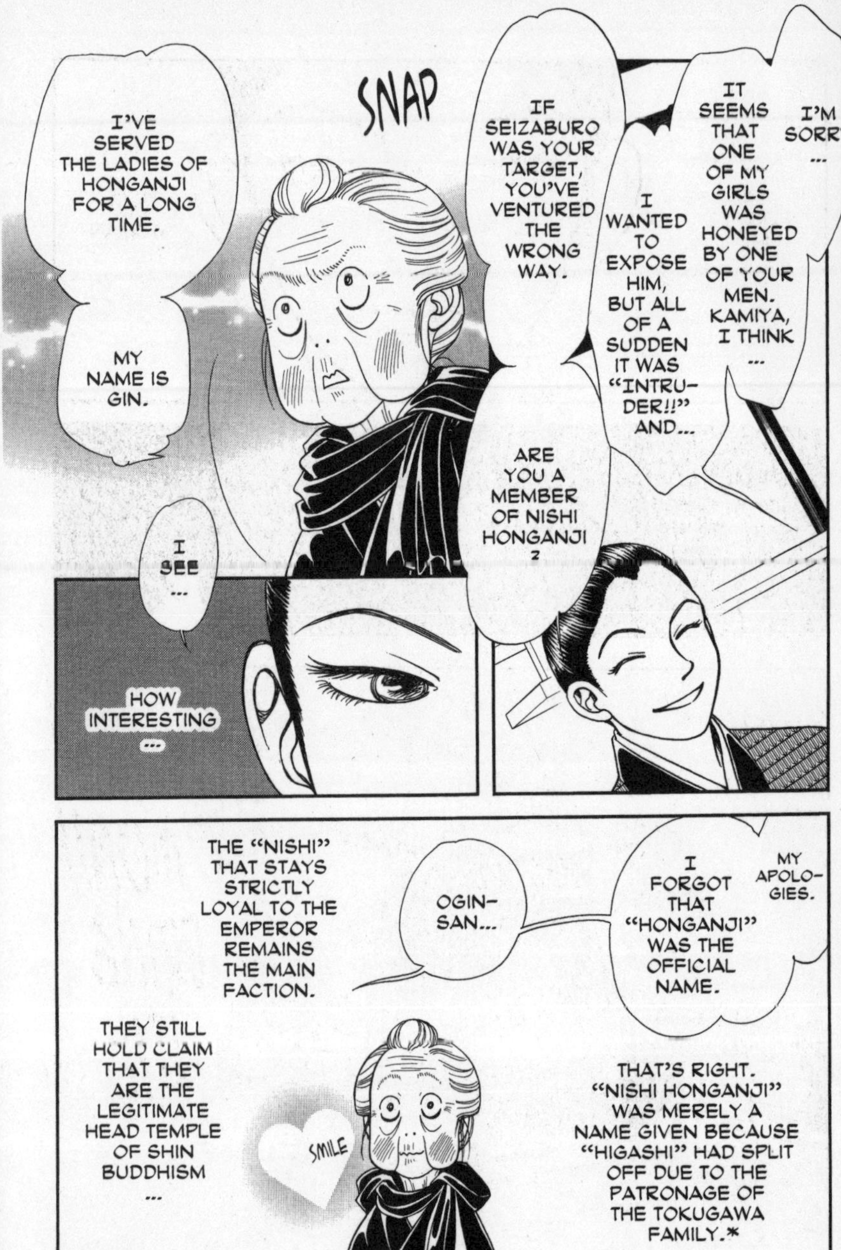
I'M SORRY...
IT SEEMS THAT ONE OF MY GIRLS WAS HONEYED BY ONE OF YOUR MEN. KAMIYA, I THINK...
I WANTED TO EXPOSE HIM, BUT ALL OF A SUDDEN IT WAS "INTRUDER!!" AND...
IF SEIZABURO WAS YOUR TARGET, YOU'VE VENTURED THE WRONG WAY.
SNAP
I'VE SERVED THE LADIES OF HONGANJI FOR A LONG TIME.
MY NAME IS GIN.
ARE YOU A MEMBER OF NISHI HONGANJI?
I SEE...
HOW INTERESTING...
MY APOLOGIES.
I FORGOT THAT "HONGANJI" WAS THE OFFICIAL NAME.
OGIN-SAN...
THE "NISHI" THAT STAYS STRICTLY LOYAL TO THE EMPEROR REMAINS THE MAIN FACTION.
THAT'S RIGHT. "NISHI HONGANJI" WAS MERELY A NAME GIVEN BECAUSE "HIGASHI" HAD SPLIT OFF DUE TO THE PATRONAGE OF THE TOKUGAWA FAMILY.*
SMILE
THEY STILL HOLD CLAIM THAT THEY ARE THE LEGITIMATE HEAD TEMPLE OF SHIN BUDDHISM...

*_Nishi_ means west and _higashi_ means east in Japanese.

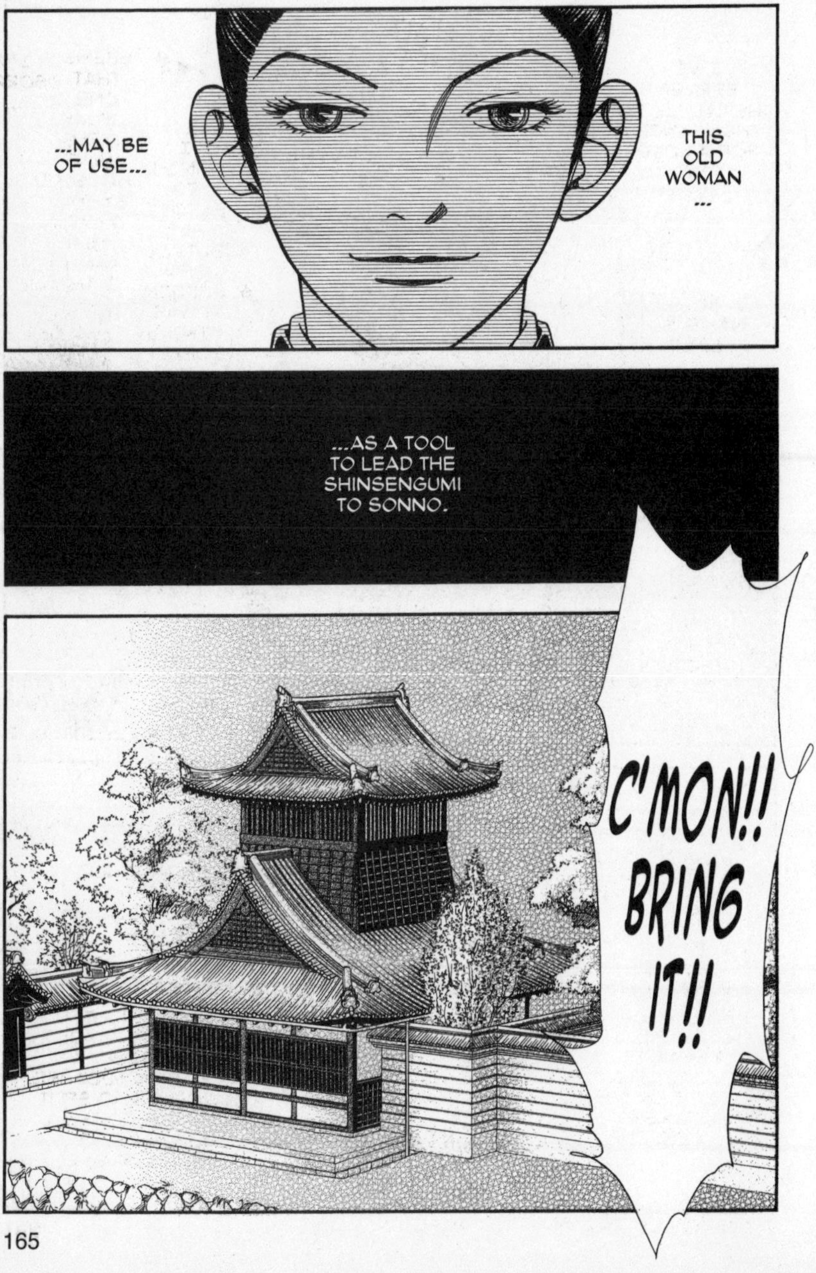
THIS OLD WOMAN ...
...MAY BE OF USE...
...AS A TOOL TO LEAD THE SHINSENGUMI TO SONNO.
C'MON!! BRING IT!!

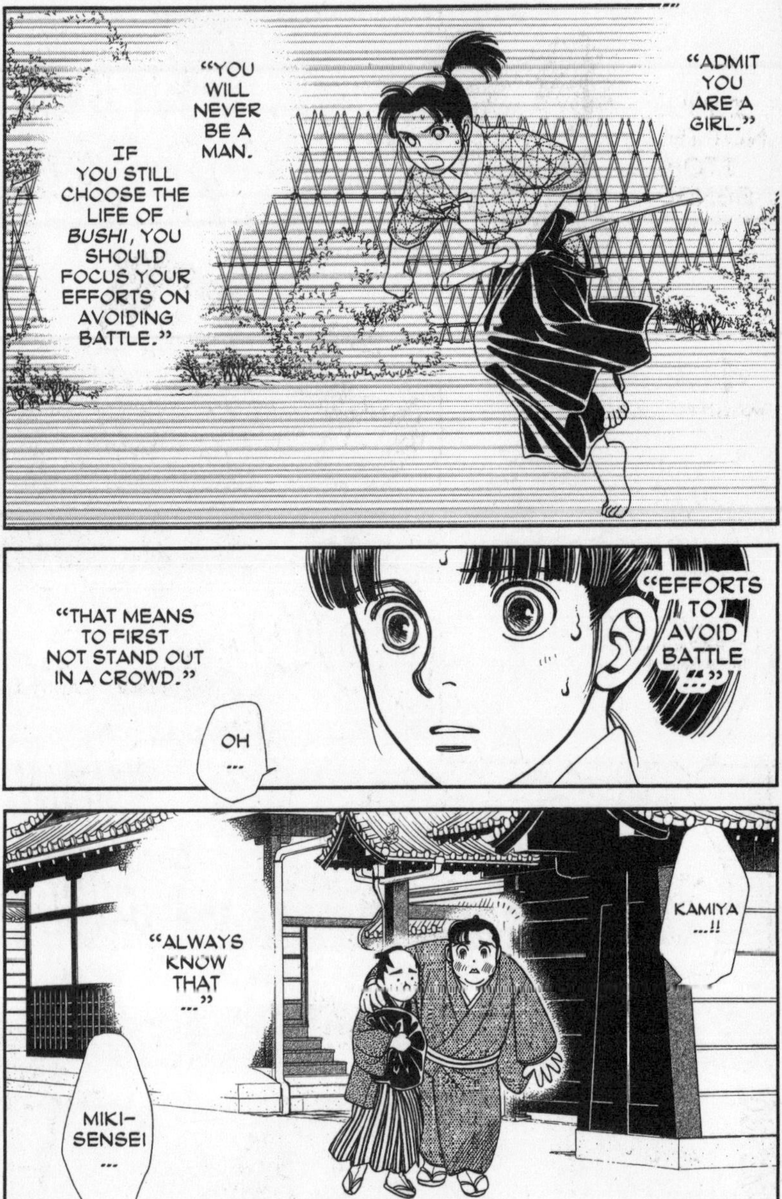
"ADMIT YOU ARE A GIRL."
"YOU WILL NEVER BE A MAN.
IF YOU STILL CHOOSE THE LIFE OF *BUSHI*, YOU SHOULD FOCUS YOUR EFFORTS ON AVOIDING BATTLE."
"EFFORTS TO AVOID BATTLE..."
"THAT MEANS TO FIRST NOT STAND OUT IN A CROWD."
OH...
KAMIYA...!!
"ALWAYS KNOW THAT..."
MIKI-SENSEI...

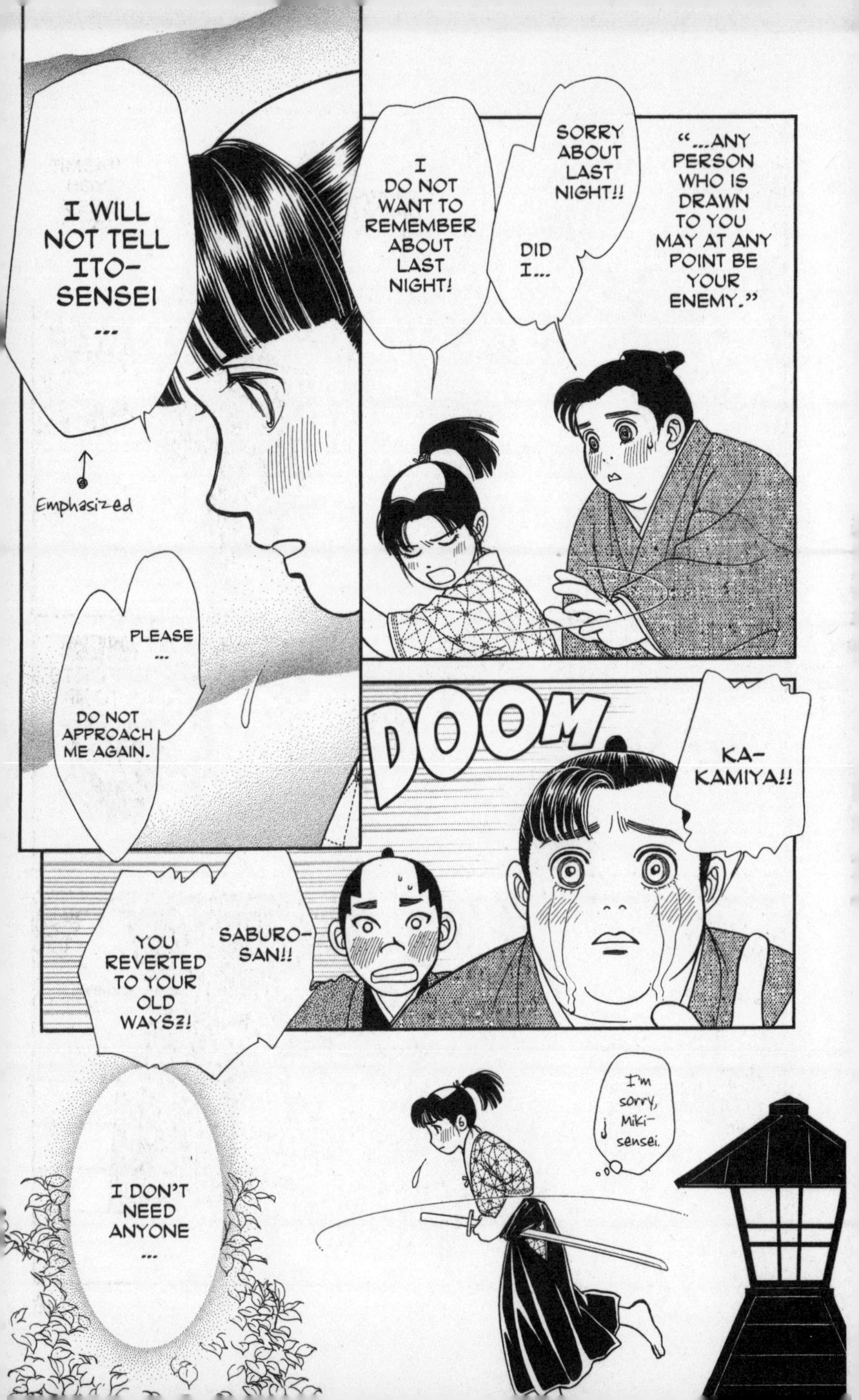
"...ANY PERSON WHO IS DRAWN TO YOU MAY AT ANY POINT BE YOUR ENEMY."
SORRY ABOUT LAST NIGHT!! DID I...
I DO NOT WANT TO REMEMBER ABOUT LAST NIGHT!
DOOM
KA-KAMIYA!!
SABURO-SAN!!
YOU REVERTED TO YOUR OLD WAYS?!
I WILL NOT TELL ITO-SENSEI ...
Emphasized
PLEASE ... DO NOT APPROACH ME AGAIN.
I'm sorry, Miki-sensei.
I DON'T NEED ANYONE ...

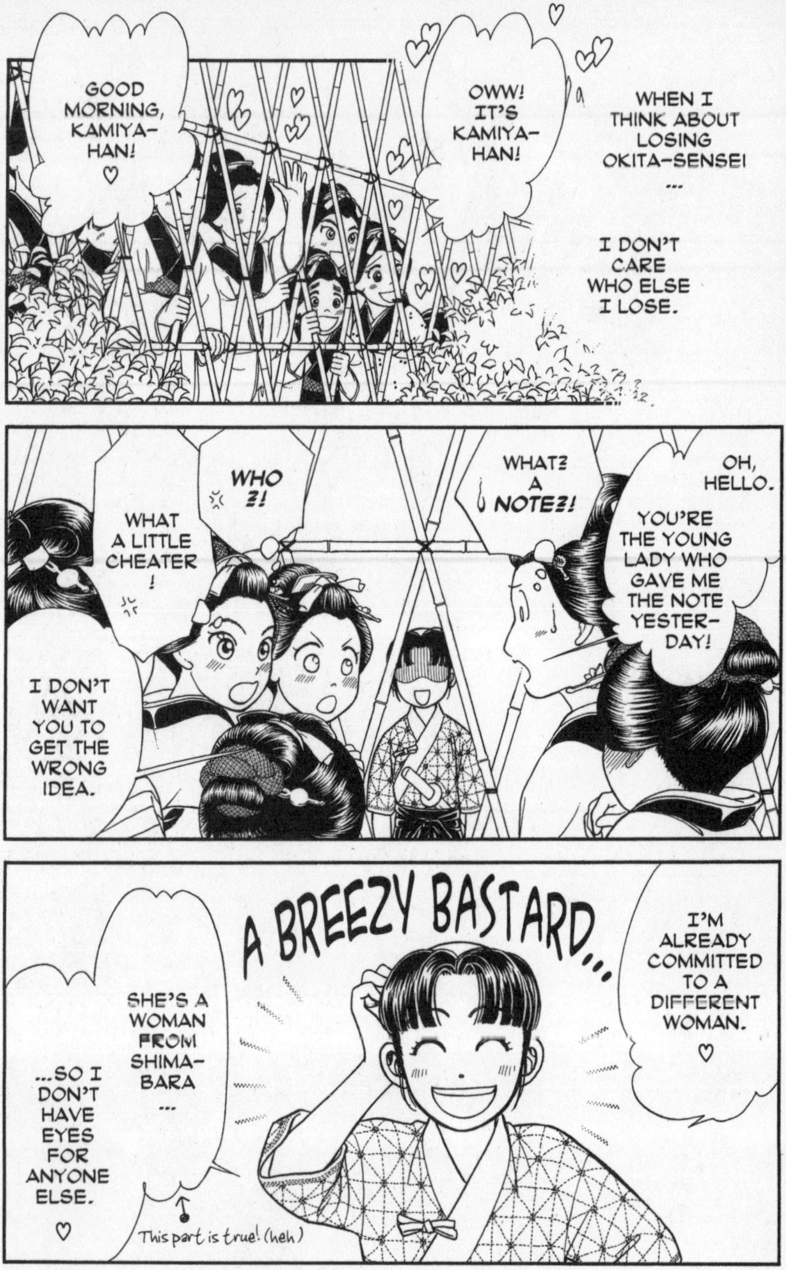
WHEN I THINK ABOUT LOSING OKITA-SENSEI ...
I DON'T CARE WHO ELSE I LOSE.
OWW! IT'S KAMIYA-HAN!
GOOD MORNING, KAMIYA-HAN! ♡
OH, HELLO.
YOU'RE THE YOUNG LADY WHO GAVE ME THE NOTE YESTERDAY!
WHAT? A NOTE?!
WHO?!
WHAT A LITTLE CHEATER!
I DON'T WANT YOU TO GET THE WRONG IDEA.
I'M ALREADY COMMITTED TO A DIFFERENT WOMAN. ♡
A BREEZY BASTARD...
SHE'S A WOMAN FROM SHIMABARA ...
This part is true! (heh)
...SO I DON'T HAVE EYES FOR ANYONE ELSE. ♡

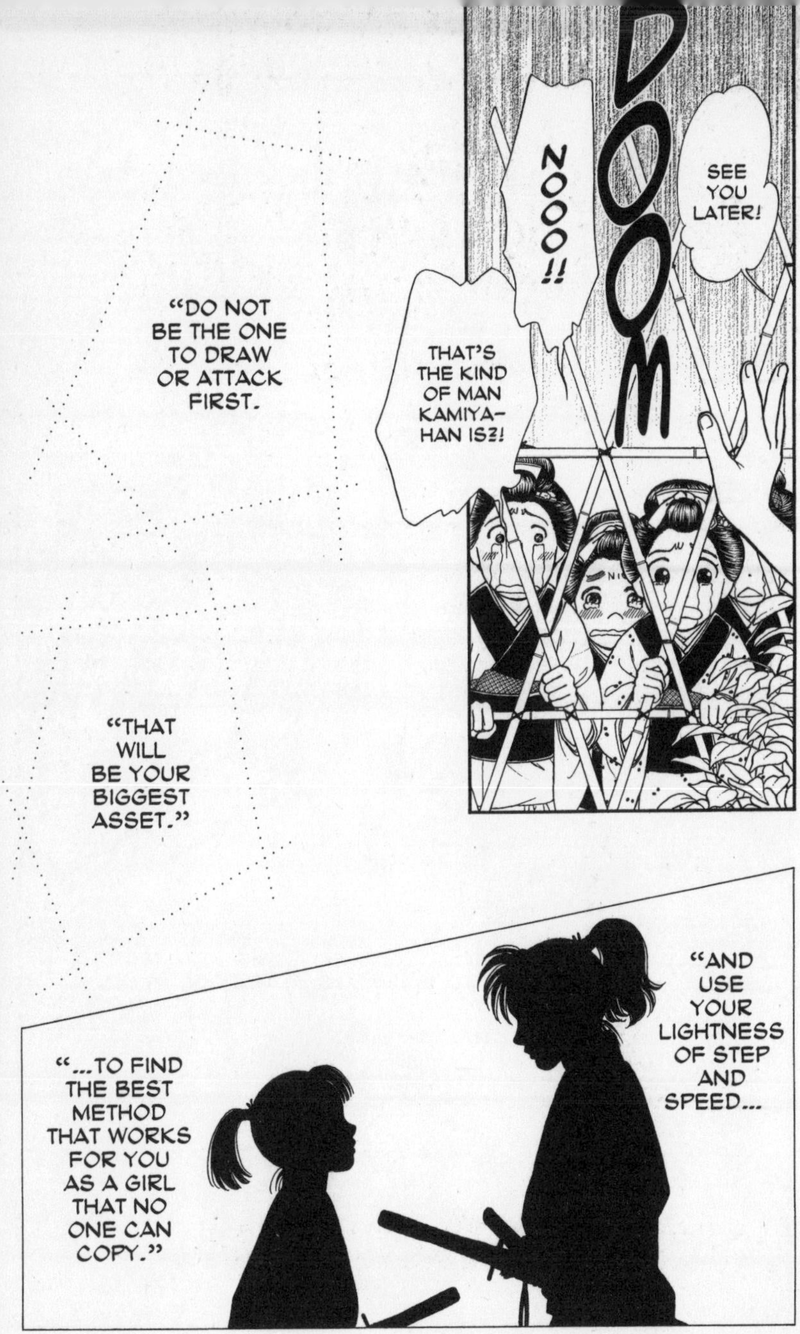
SEE YOU LATER!
DOOM
NOOO!!
THAT'S THE KIND OF MAN KAMIYA-HAN IS?!
"DO NOT BE THE ONE TO DRAW OR ATTACK FIRST.
"THAT WILL BE YOUR BIGGEST ASSET."
"AND USE YOUR LIGHTNESS OF STEP AND SPEED...
"...TO FIND THE BEST METHOD THAT WORKS FOR YOU AS A GIRL THAT NO ONE CAN COPY."

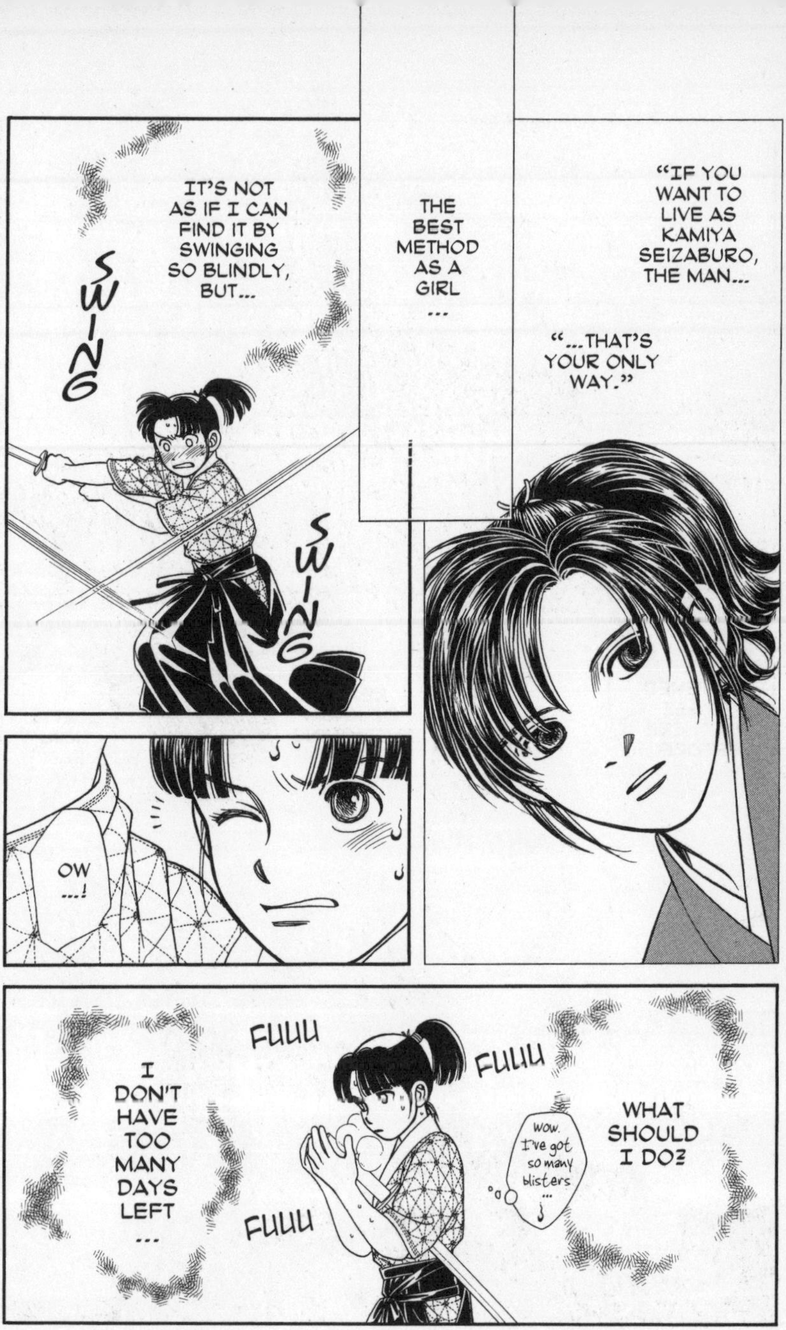
"IF YOU WANT TO LIVE AS KAMIYA SEIZABURO, THE MAN...
"...THAT'S YOUR ONLY WAY."
THE BEST METHOD AS A GIRL ...
IT'S NOT AS IF I CAN FIND IT BY SWINGING SO BLINDLY, BUT...
SWING
SWING
OW ...!
FUUU
WHAT SHOULD I DO?
Wow. I've got so many blisters ...
FUUU
FUUU
I DON'T HAVE TOO MANY DAYS LEFT ...

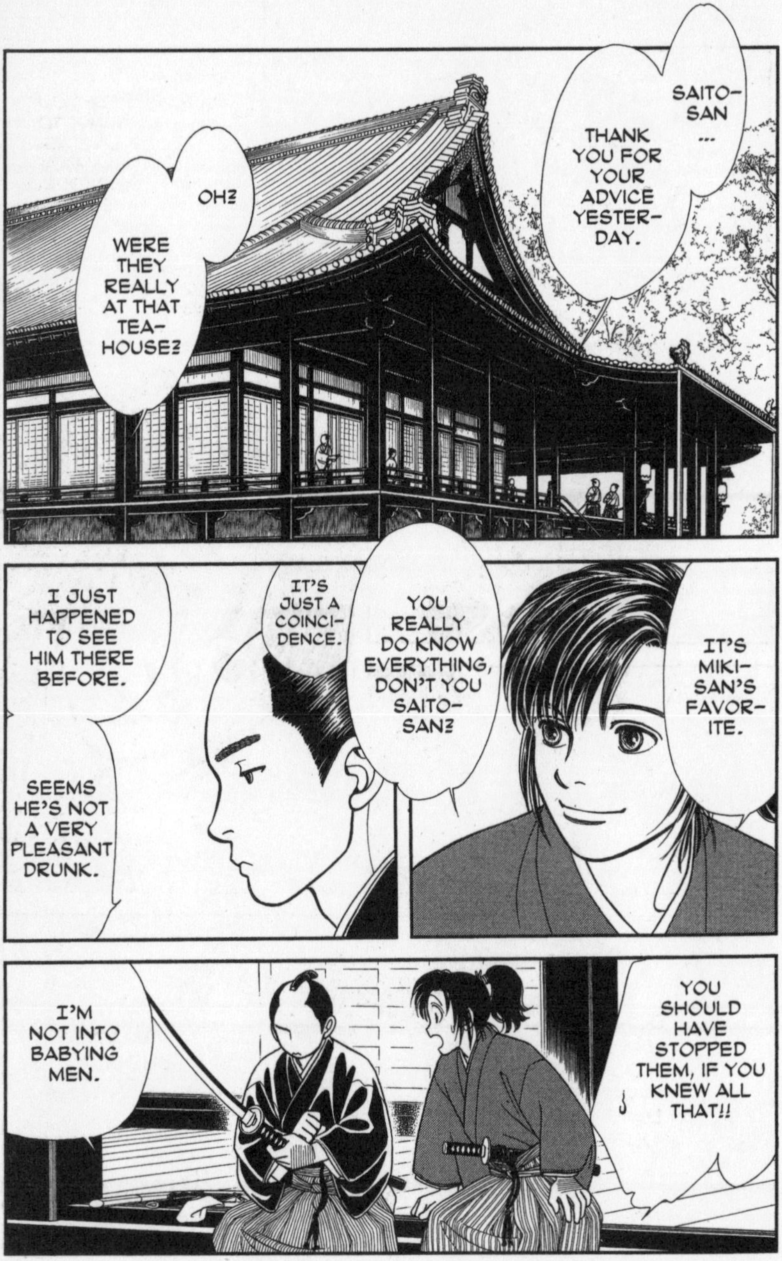
SAITO-SAN...
THANK YOU FOR YOUR ADVICE YESTERDAY.
OH?
WERE THEY REALLY AT THAT TEAHOUSE?
IT'S MIKI-SAN'S FAVORITE.
YOU REALLY DO KNOW EVERYTHING, DON'T YOU SAITO-SAN?
IT'S JUST A COINCIDENCE.
I JUST HAPPENED TO SEE HIM THERE BEFORE.
SEEMS HE'S NOT A VERY PLEASANT DRUNK.
YOU SHOULD HAVE STOPPED THEM, IF YOU KNEW ALL THAT!!
I'M NOT INTO BABYING MEN.

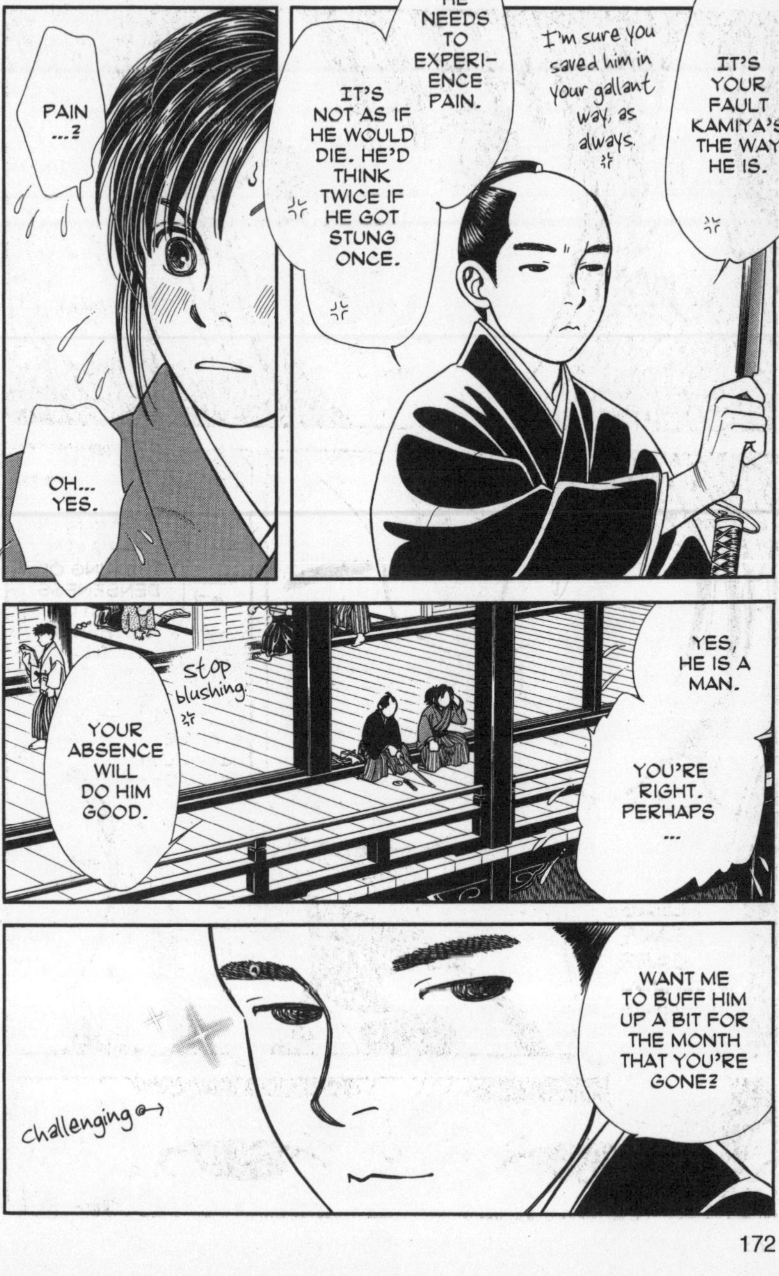
IT'S YOUR FAULT KAMIYA'S THE WAY HE IS.
I'm sure you saved him in your gallant way, as always.
HE NEEDS TO EXPERIENCE PAIN.
IT'S NOT AS IF HE WOULD DIE. HE'D THINK TWICE IF HE GOT STUNG ONCE.
PAIN...?
OH... YES.
YES, HE IS A MAN.
YOU'RE RIGHT. PERHAPS...
stop blushing.
YOUR ABSENCE WILL DO HIM GOOD.
WANT ME TO BUFF HIM UP A BIT FOR THE MONTH THAT YOU'RE GONE?
Challenging

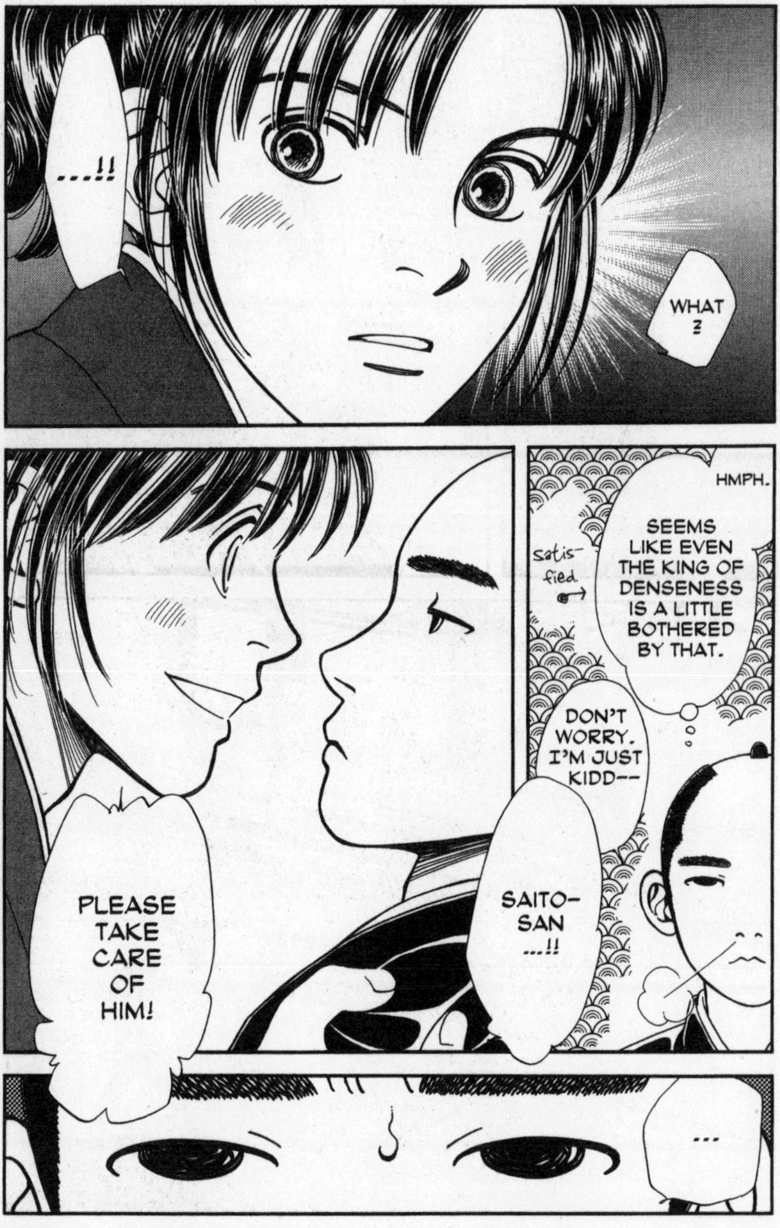
WHAT?
...!!
HMPH.
SEEMS LIKE EVEN THE KING OF DENSENESS IS A LITTLE BOTHERED BY THAT.
satis-fied
DON'T WORRY. I'M JUST KIDD--
SAITO-SAN ...!!
PLEASE TAKE CARE OF HIM!
...

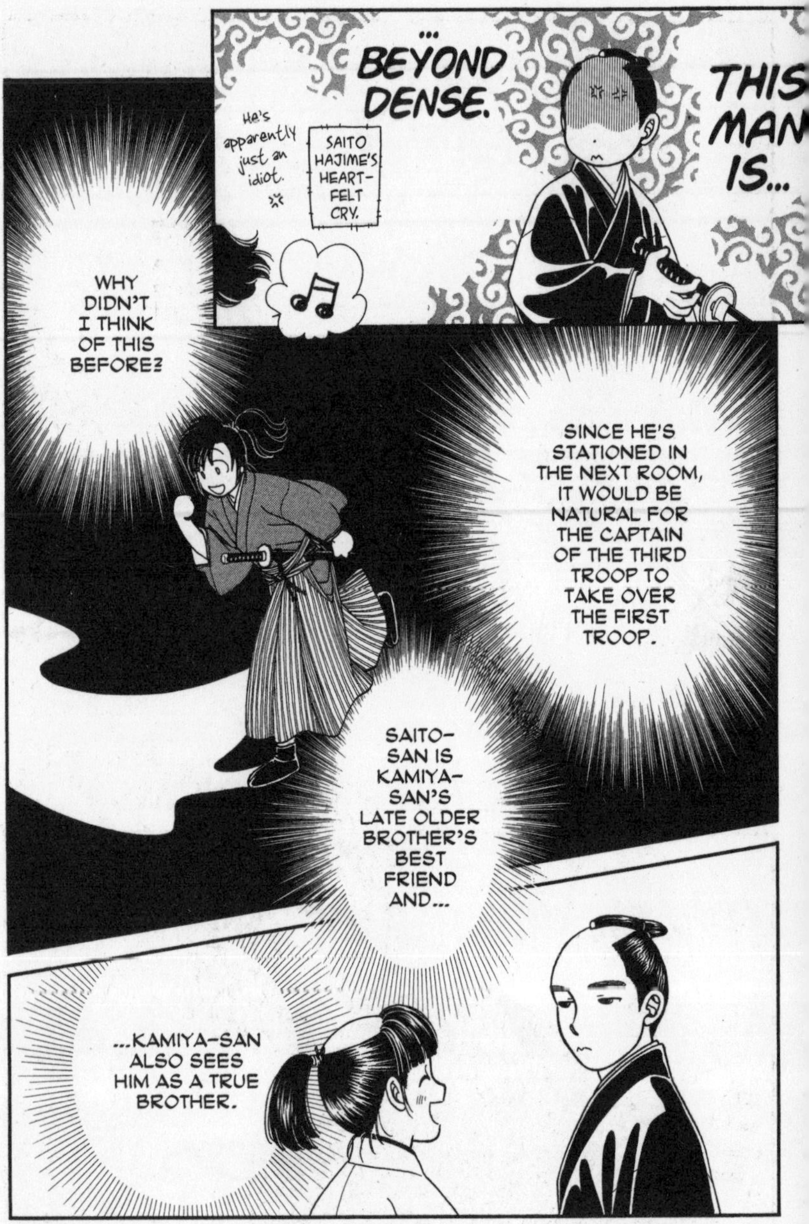
THIS MAN IS...
... BEYOND DENSE.
SAITO HAJIME'S HEART-FELT CRY.
He's apparently just an idiot.
SINCE HE'S STATIONED IN THE NEXT ROOM, IT WOULD BE NATURAL FOR THE CAPTAIN OF THE THIRD TROOP TO TAKE OVER THE FIRST TROOP.
WHY DIDN'T I THINK OF THIS BEFORE?
SAITO-SAN IS KAMIYA-SAN'S LATE OLDER BROTHER'S BEST FRIEND AND...
...KAMIYA-SAN ALSO SEES HIM AS A TRUE BROTHER.

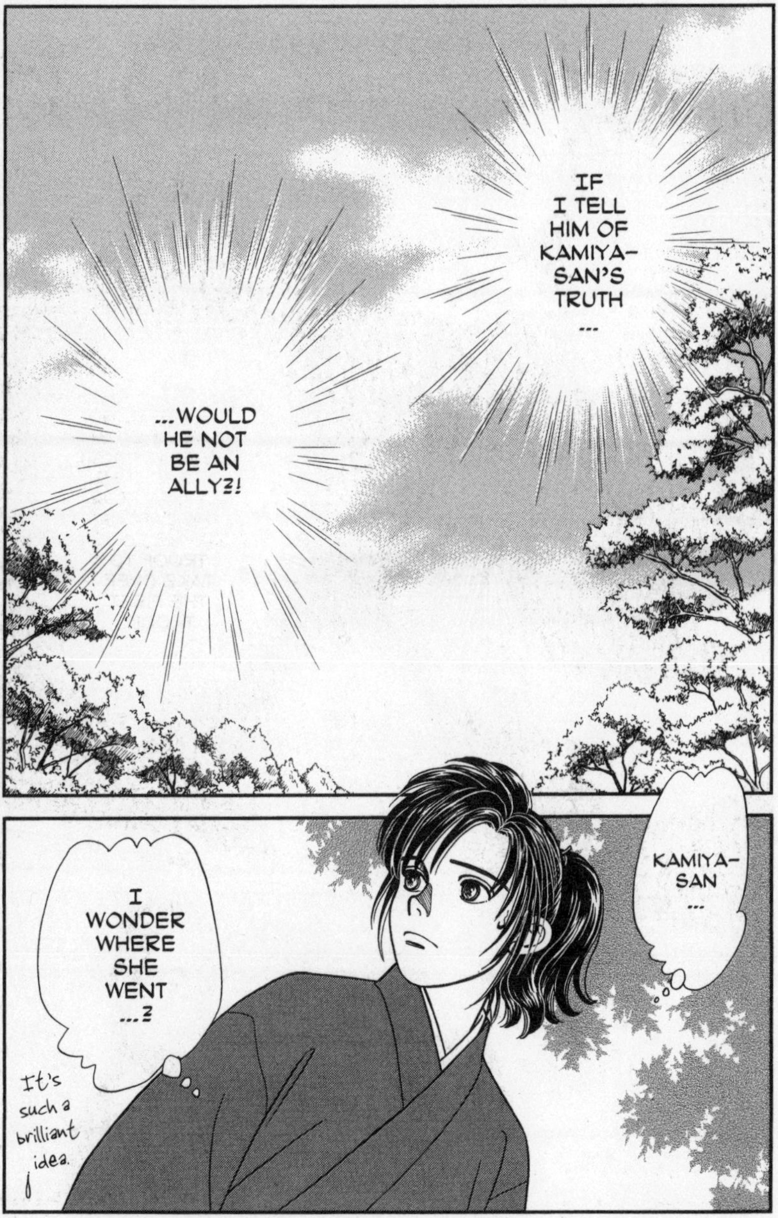
IF I TELL HIM OF KAMIYA-SAN'S TRUTH ...
...WOULD HE NOT BE AN ALLY?!
KAMIYA-SAN ...
I WONDER WHERE SHE WENT ...?
It's such a brilliant idea.

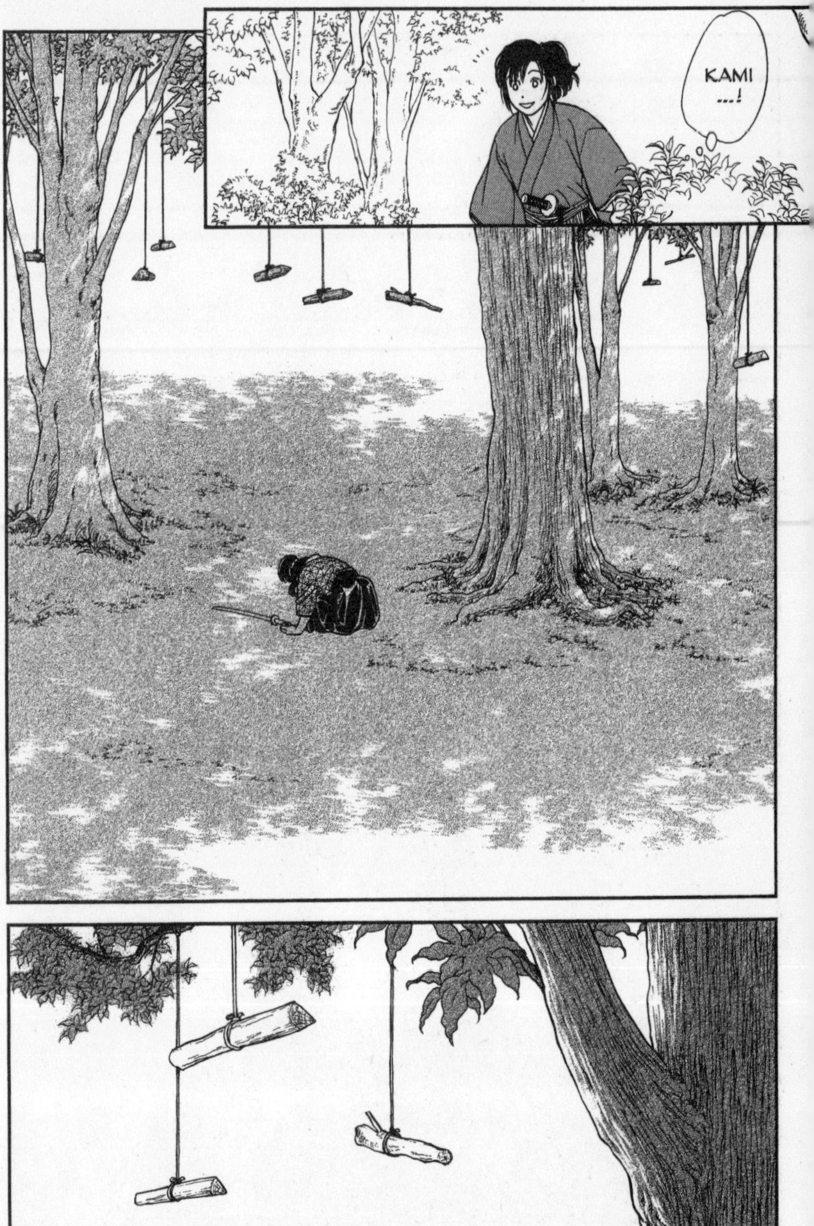
KAMI
...!

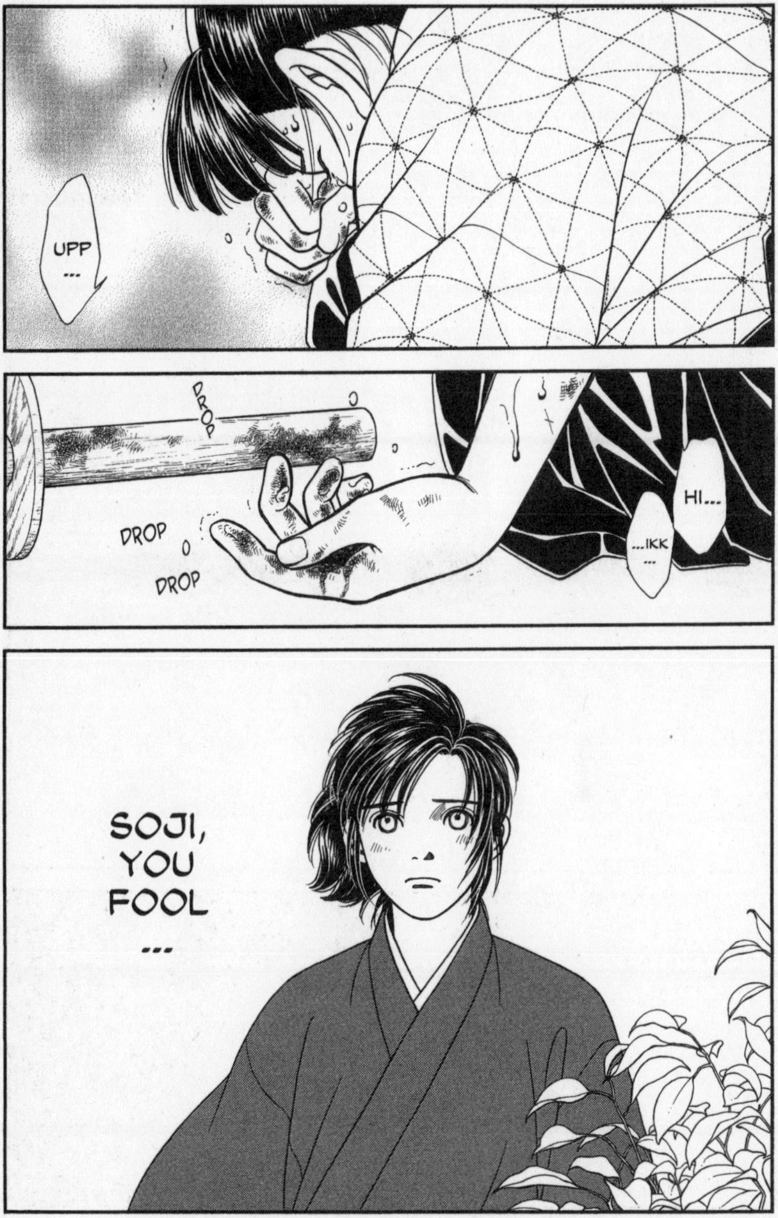
UPP ...
HI...
...IKK ...
DROP
DROP
DROP
SOJI, YOU FOOL ...

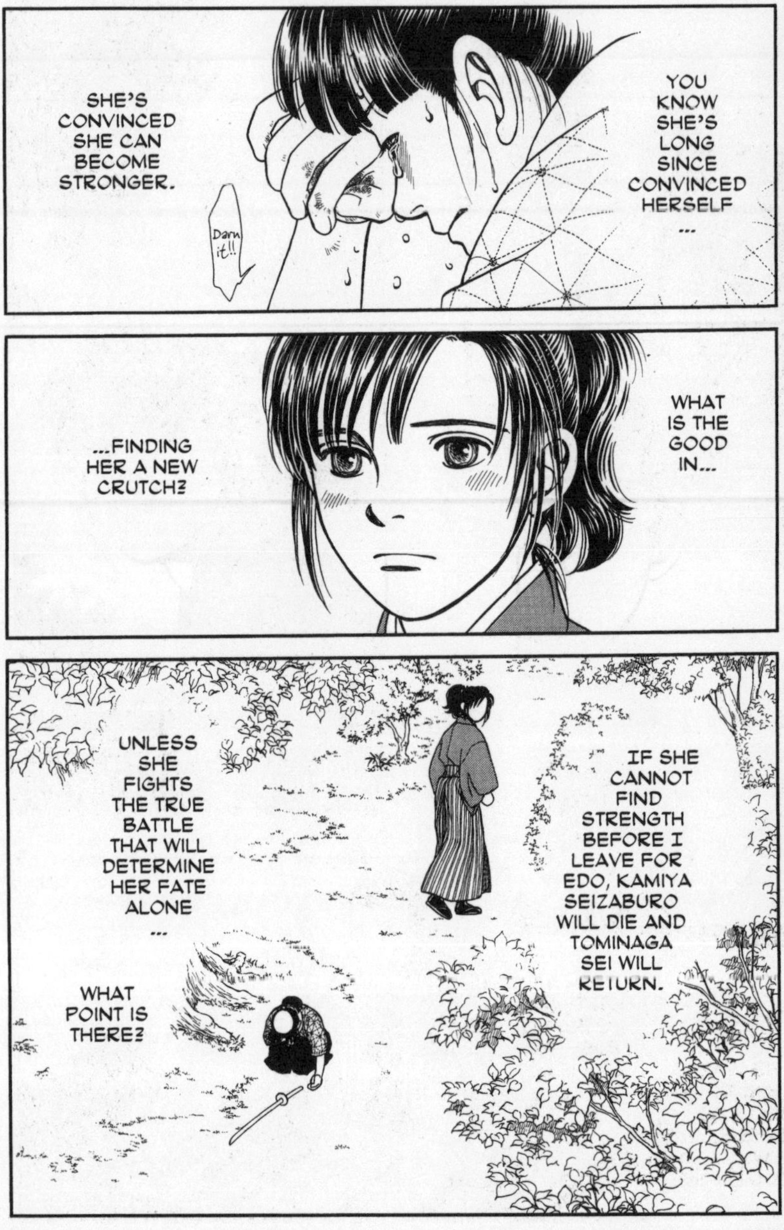
YOU KNOW SHE'S LONG SINCE CONVINCED HERSELF ...
SHE'S CONVINCED SHE CAN BECOME STRONGER.
Darn it!!
WHAT IS THE GOOD IN...
...FINDING HER A NEW CRUTCH?
IF SHE CANNOT FIND STRENGTH BEFORE I LEAVE FOR EDO, KAMIYA SEIZABURO WILL DIE AND TOMINAGA SEI WILL RETURN.
UNLESS SHE FIGHTS THE TRUE BATTLE THAT WILL DETERMINE HER FATE ALONE ...
WHAT POINT IS THERE?

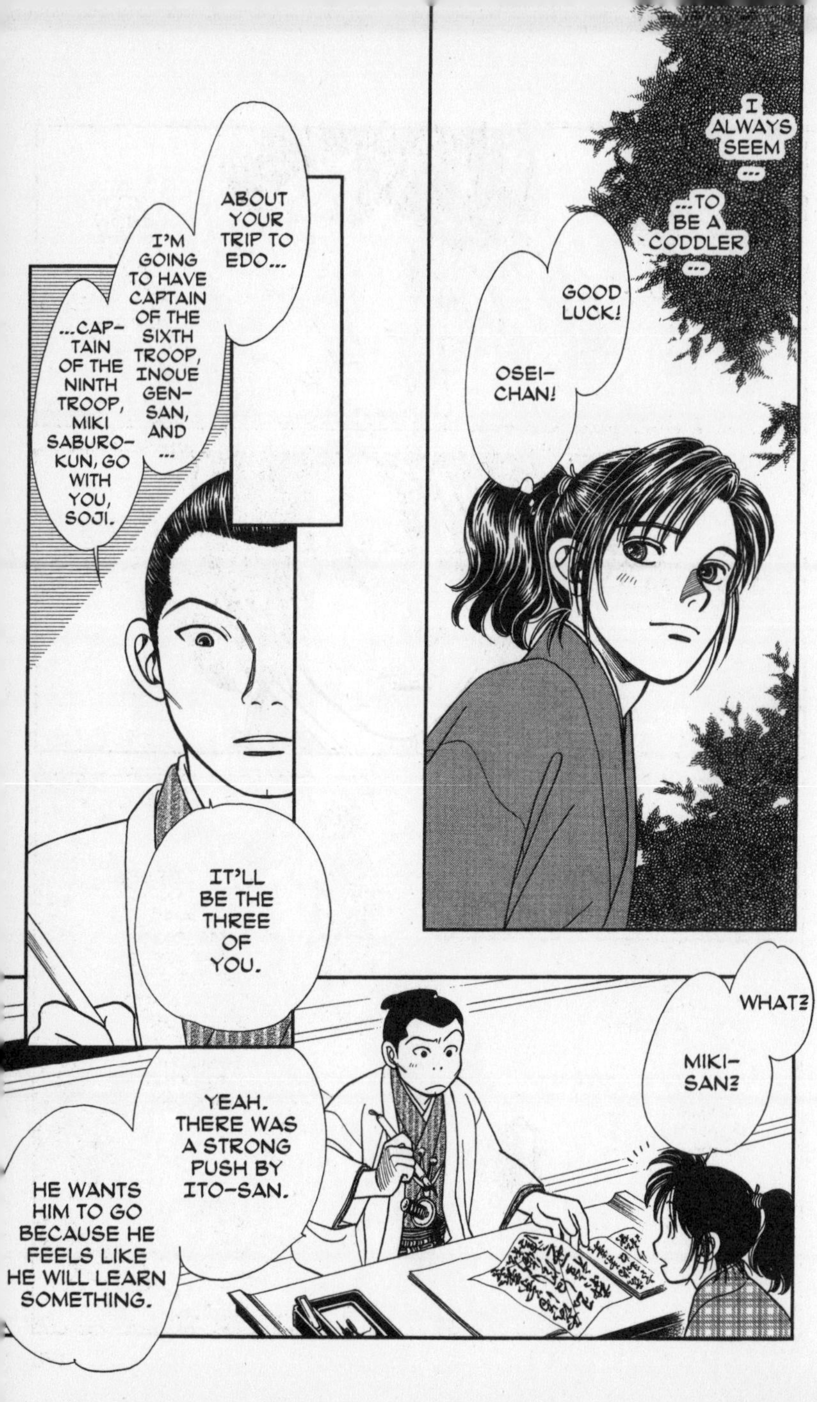
I ALWAYS SEEM...
...TO BE A CODDLER...
GOOD LUCK! OSEI-CHAN!
ABOUT YOUR TRIP TO EDO...
I'M GOING TO HAVE CAPTAIN OF THE SIXTH TROOP, INOUE GEN-SAN, AND...
...CAPTAIN OF THE NINTH TROOP, MIKI SABURO-KUN, GO WITH YOU, SOJI.
IT'LL BE THE THREE OF YOU.
WHAT? MIKI-SAN?
YEAH. THERE WAS A STRONG PUSH BY ITO-SAN.
HE WANTS HIM TO GO BECAUSE HE FEELS LIKE HE WILL LEARN SOMETHING.

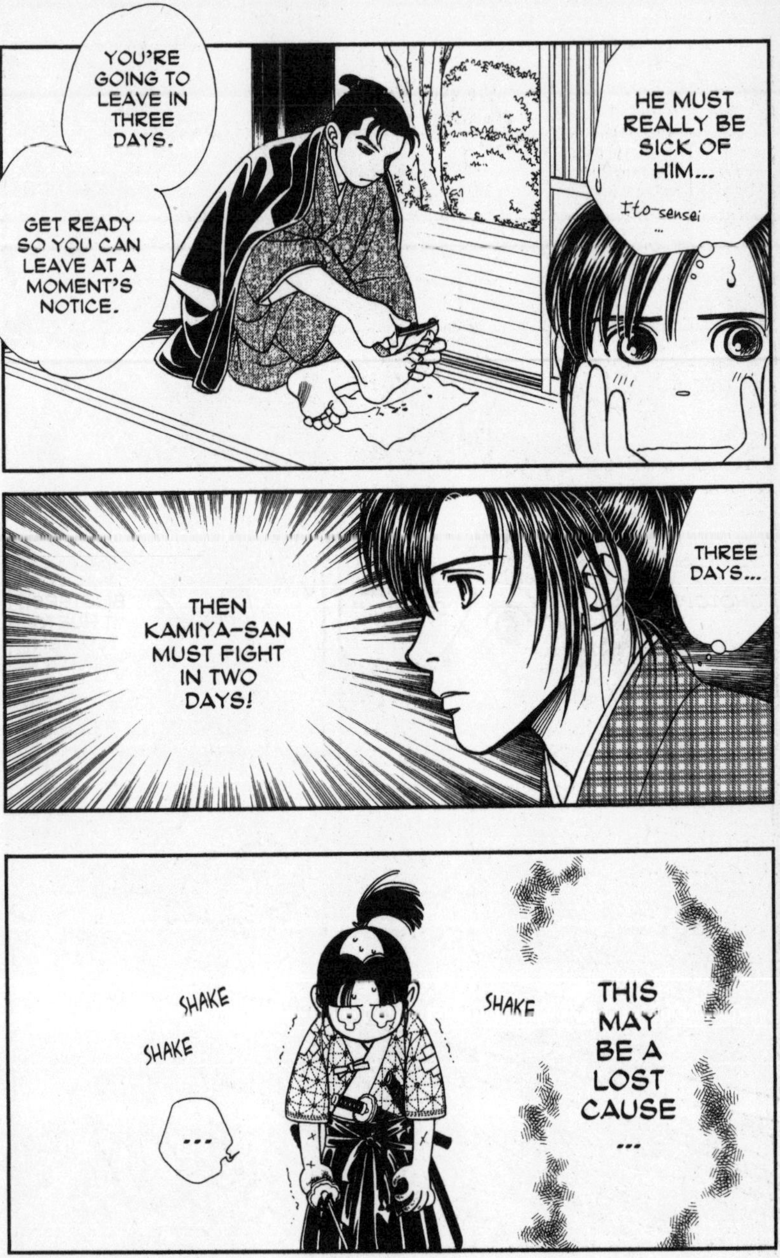
YOU'RE GOING TO LEAVE IN THREE DAYS.
GET READY SO YOU CAN LEAVE AT A MOMENT'S NOTICE.
HE MUST REALLY BE SICK OF HIM...
Ito-sensei ...
THREE DAYS...
THEN KAMIYA-SAN MUST FIGHT IN TWO DAYS!
THIS MAY BE A LOST CAUSE ...
SHAKE
SHAKE
SHAKE
...

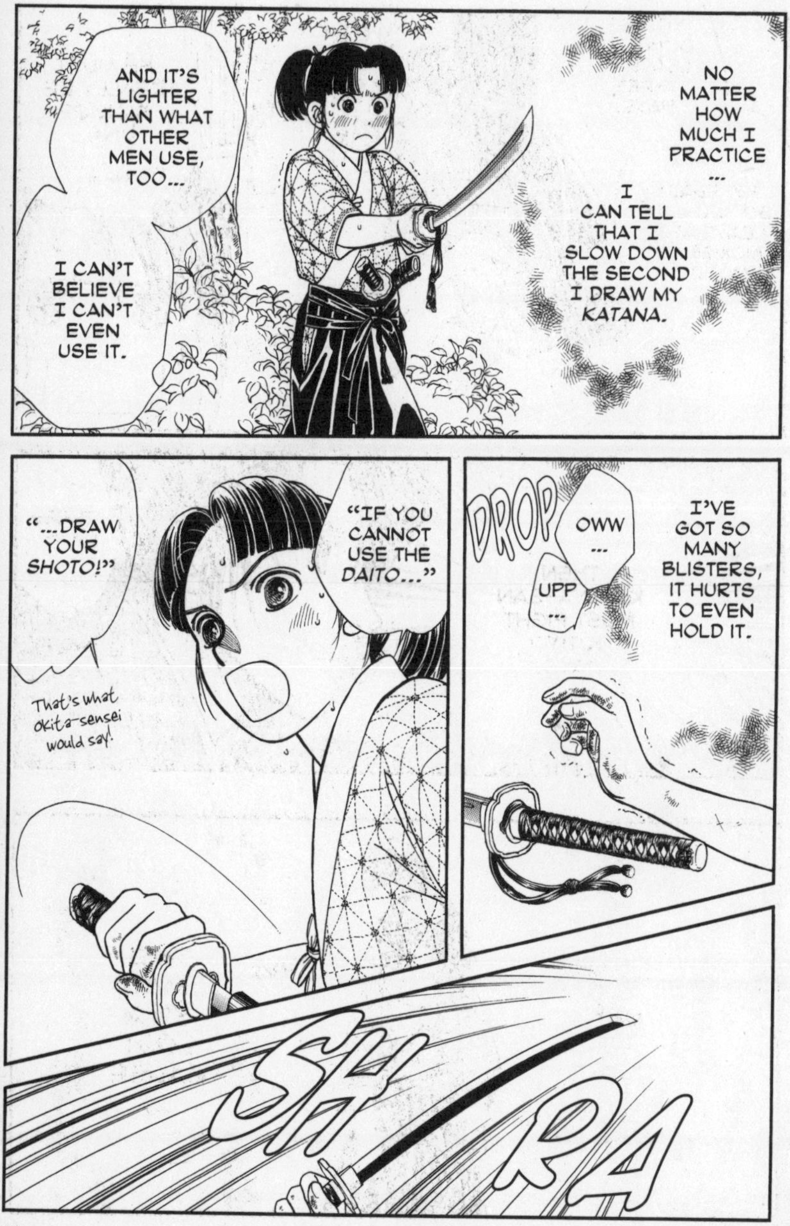
NO MATTER HOW MUCH I PRACTICE ...
I CAN TELL THAT I SLOW DOWN THE SECOND I DRAW MY *KATANA.*
AND IT'S LIGHTER THAN WHAT OTHER MEN USE, TOO...
I CAN'T BELIEVE I CAN'T EVEN USE IT.
I'VE GOT SO MANY BLISTERS, IT HURTS TO EVEN HOLD IT.
OWW ...
UPP ...
DROP
"IF YOU CANNOT USE THE *DAITO...*"
"...DRAW YOUR *SHOTO!*"
That's what Okita-sensei would say!
SH RA

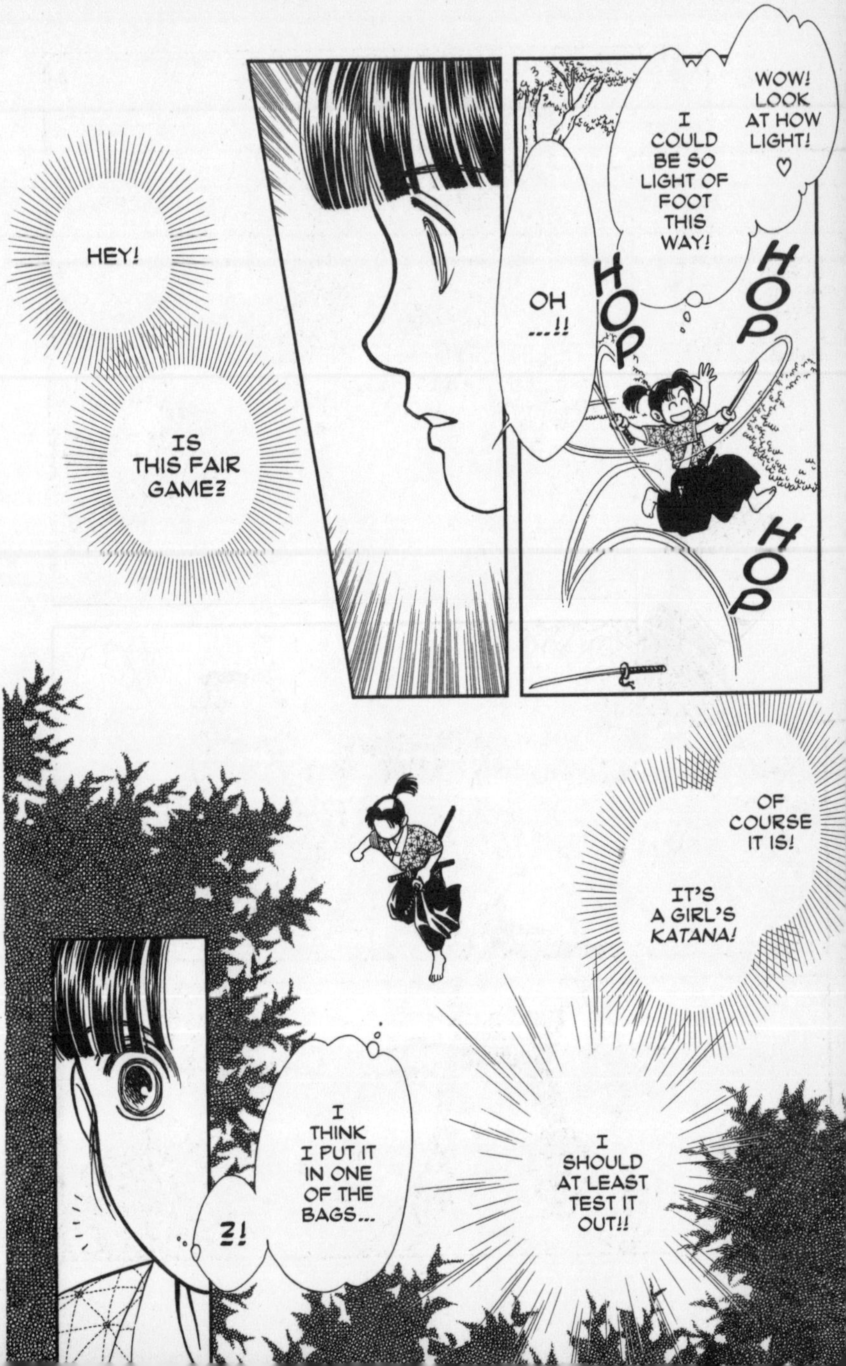
WOW! LOOK AT HOW LIGHT! ♡
I COULD BE SO LIGHT OF FOOT THIS WAY!
HOP HOP
HOP
HOP HOP
OH ...!!
HEY!
IS THIS FAIR GAME?
OF COURSE IT IS!
IT'S A GIRL'S KATANA!
I SHOULD AT LEAST TEST IT OUT!!
I THINK I PUT IT IN ONE OF THE BAGS...
?!

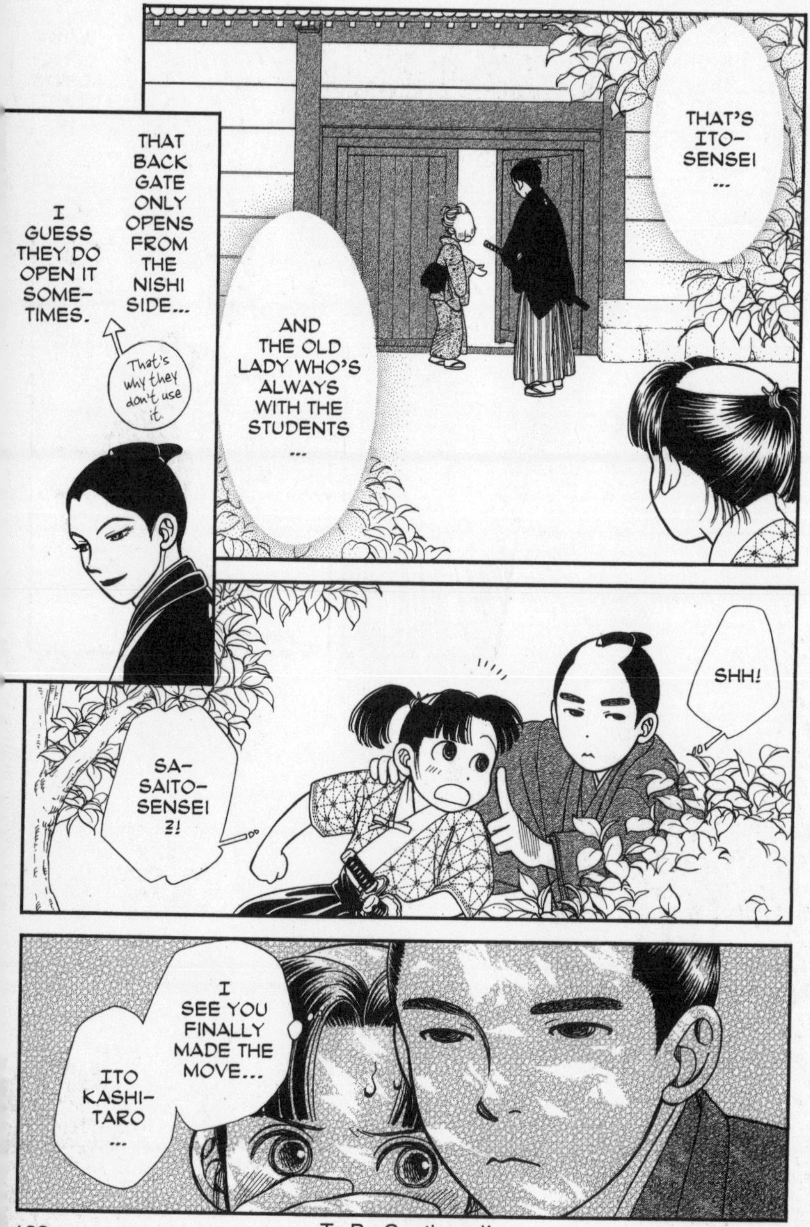
THAT'S ITO-SENSEI ...
AND THE OLD LADY WHO'S ALWAYS WITH THE STUDENTS ...
THAT BACK GATE ONLY OPENS FROM THE NISHI SIDE...
I GUESS THEY DO OPEN IT SOME-TIMES.
That's why they don't use it.
SHH!
SA-SAITO-SENSEI ?!
I SEE YOU FINALLY MADE THE MOVE...
ITO KASHI-TARO ...

To Be Continued!

TAEKO WATANABE PRESENTS

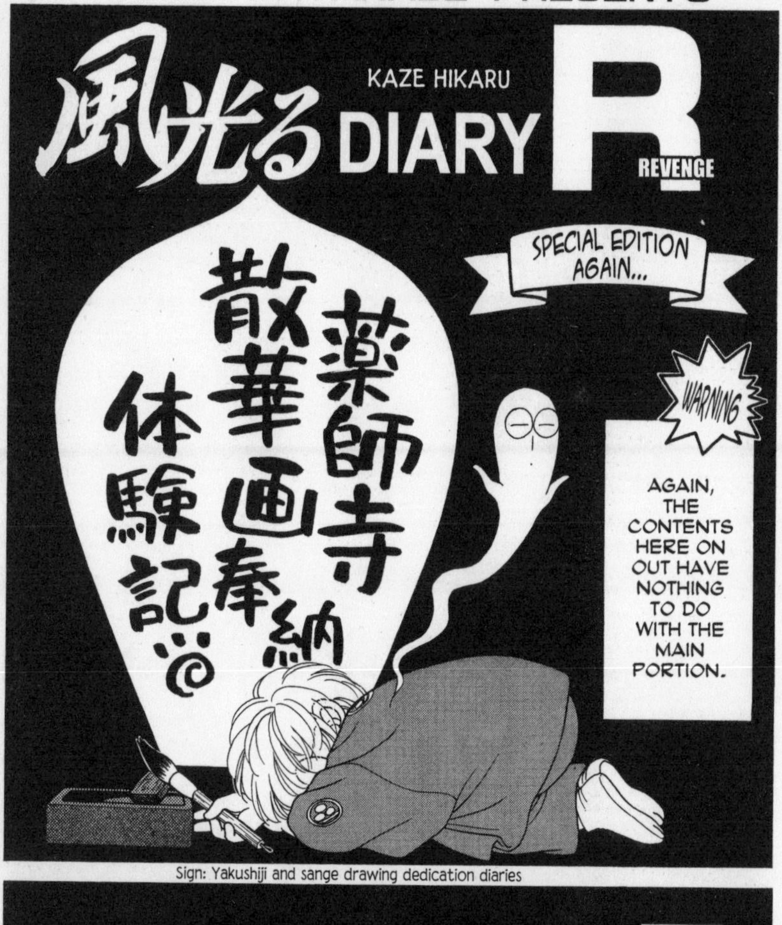

風光る
KAZE HIKARU
DIARY R
REVENGE
SPECIAL EDITION AGAIN...
薬師寺
散華画奉納
体験記
WARNING
AGAIN, THE CONTENTS HERE ON OUT HAVE NOTHING TO DO WITH THE MAIN PORTION.

Sign: Yakushiji and sange drawing dedication diaries

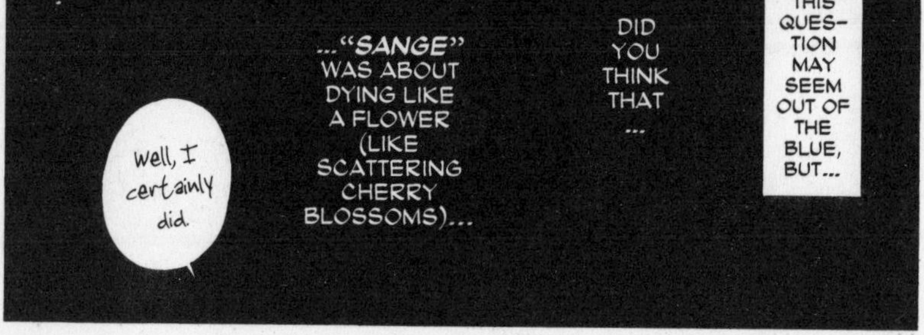

THIS QUESTION MAY SEEM OUT OF THE BLUE, BUT...
DID YOU THINK THAT...
..."SANGE" WAS ABOUT DYING LIKE A FLOWER (LIKE SCATTERING CHERRY BLOSSOMS)...
Well, I certainly did.

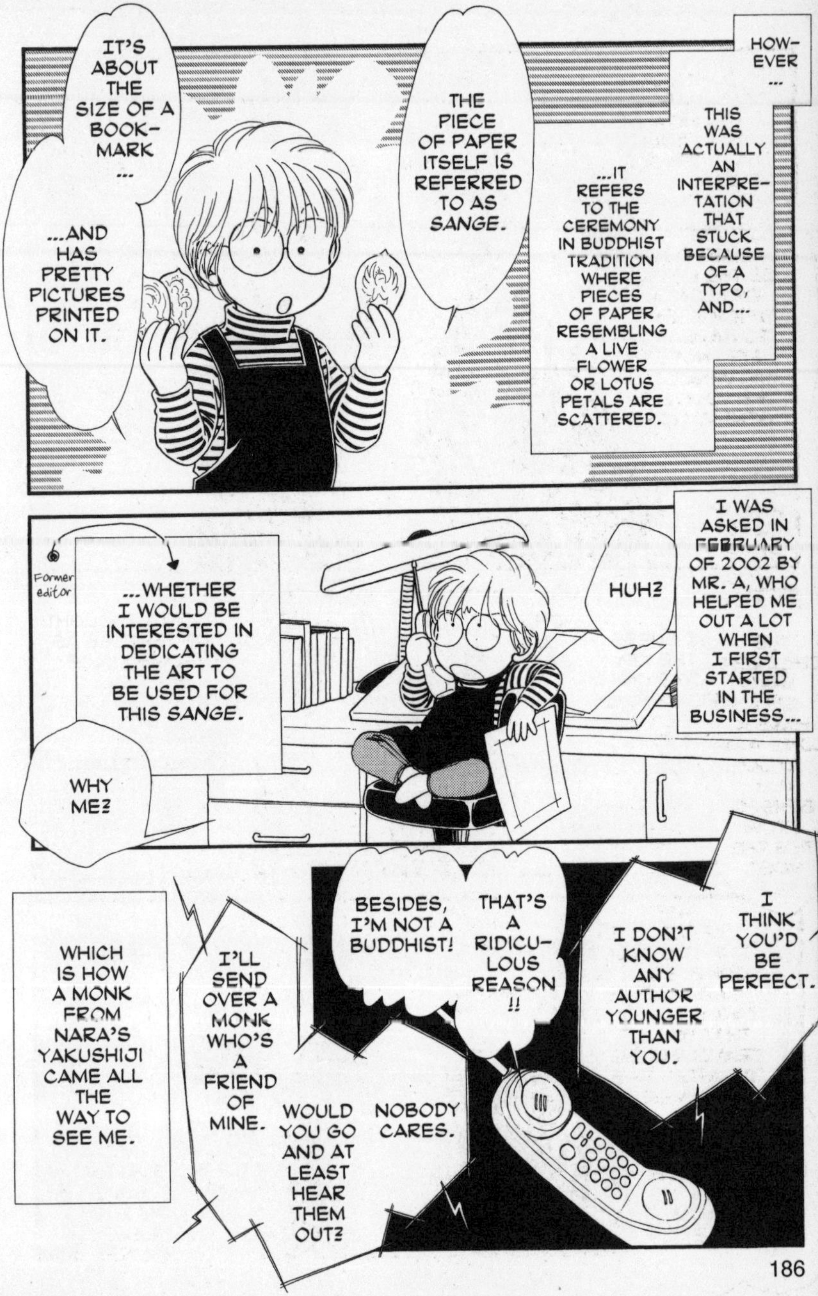
HOW-EVER...
THIS WAS ACTUALLY AN INTERPRE-TATION THAT STUCK BECAUSE OF A TYPO, AND...
...IT REFERS TO THE CEREMONY IN BUDDHIST TRADITION WHERE PIECES OF PAPER RESEMBLING A LIVE FLOWER OR LOTUS PETALS ARE SCATTERED.
THE PIECE OF PAPER ITSELF IS REFERRED TO AS *SANGE*.
IT'S ABOUT THE SIZE OF A BOOK-MARK...
...AND HAS PRETTY PICTURES PRINTED ON IT.
I WAS ASKED IN FEBRUARY OF 2002 BY MR. A, WHO HELPED ME OUT A LOT WHEN I FIRST STARTED IN THE BUSINESS...
HUH?
Former editor
...WHETHER I WOULD BE INTERESTED IN DEDICATING THE ART TO BE USED FOR THIS *SANGE*.
WHY ME?
I THINK YOU'D BE PERFECT.
I DON'T KNOW ANY AUTHOR YOUNGER THAN YOU.
THAT'S A RIDICULOUS REASON!!
BESIDES, I'M NOT A BUDDHIST!
NOBODY CARES.
I'LL SEND OVER A MONK WHO'S A FRIEND OF MINE.
WOULD YOU GO AND AT LEAST HEAR THEM OUT?
WHICH IS HOW A MONK FROM NARA'S YAKUSHIJI CAME ALL THE WAY TO SEE ME.

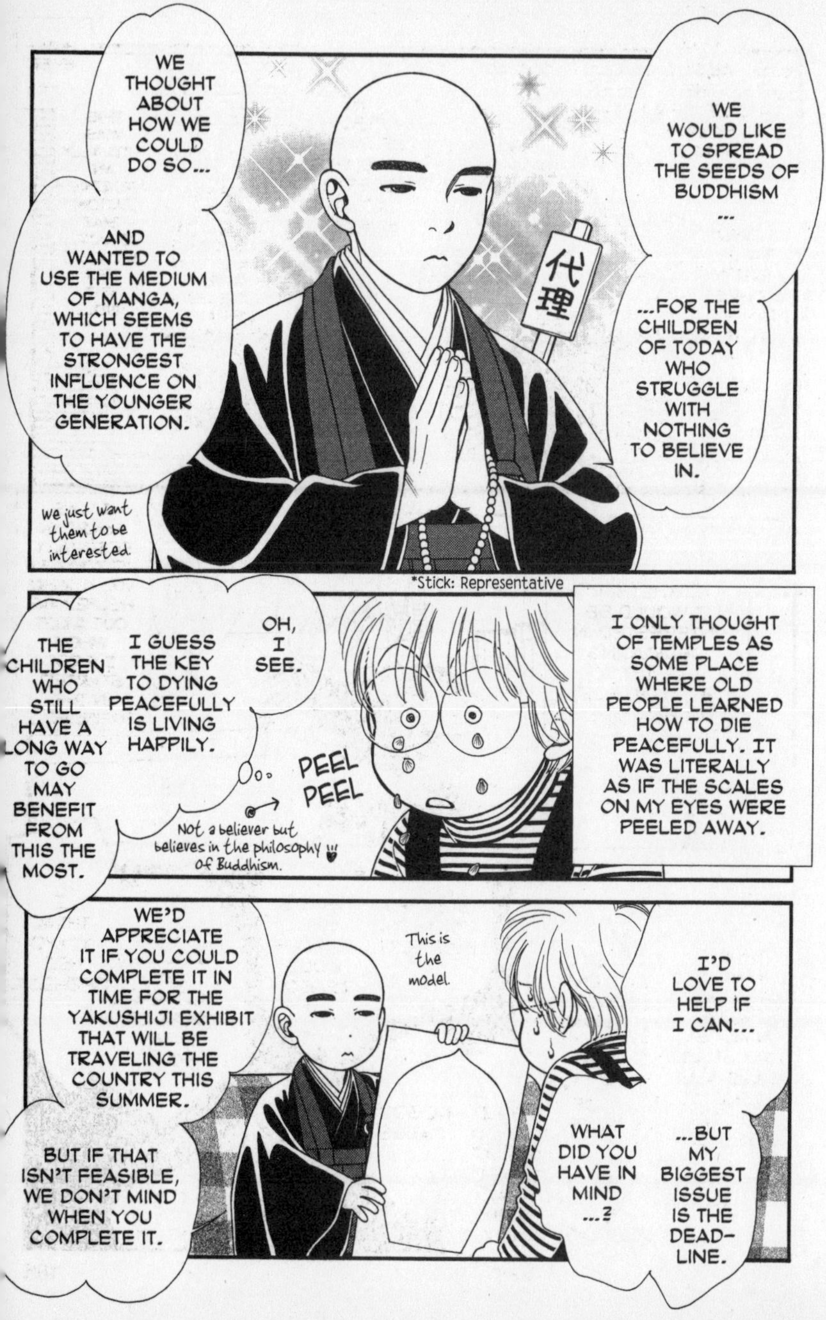
WE WOULD LIKE TO SPREAD THE SEEDS OF BUDDHISM ...
...FOR THE CHILDREN OF TODAY WHO STRUGGLE WITH NOTHING TO BELIEVE IN.
代理
WE THOUGHT ABOUT HOW WE COULD DO SO...
AND WANTED TO USE THE MEDIUM OF MANGA, WHICH SEEMS TO HAVE THE STRONGEST INFLUENCE ON THE YOUNGER GENERATION.
we just want them to be interested.
*Stick: Representative
I ONLY THOUGHT OF TEMPLES AS SOME PLACE WHERE OLD PEOPLE LEARNED HOW TO DIE PEACEFULLY. IT WAS LITERALLY AS IF THE SCALES ON MY EYES WERE PEELED AWAY.
PEEL PEEL
OH, I SEE.
I GUESS THE KEY TO DYING PEACEFULLY IS LIVING HAPPILY.
THE CHILDREN WHO STILL HAVE A LONG WAY TO GO MAY BENEFIT FROM THIS THE MOST.
Not a believer but believes in the philosophy of Buddhism.
I'D LOVE TO HELP IF I CAN...
...BUT MY BIGGEST ISSUE IS THE DEAD-LINE.
WHAT DID YOU HAVE IN MIND ...?
This is the model.
WE'D APPRECIATE IT IF YOU COULD COMPLETE IT IN TIME FOR THE YAKUSHIJI EXHIBIT THAT WILL BE TRAVELING THE COUNTRY THIS SUMMER.
BUT IF THAT ISN'T FEASIBLE, WE DON'T MIND WHEN YOU COMPLETE IT.

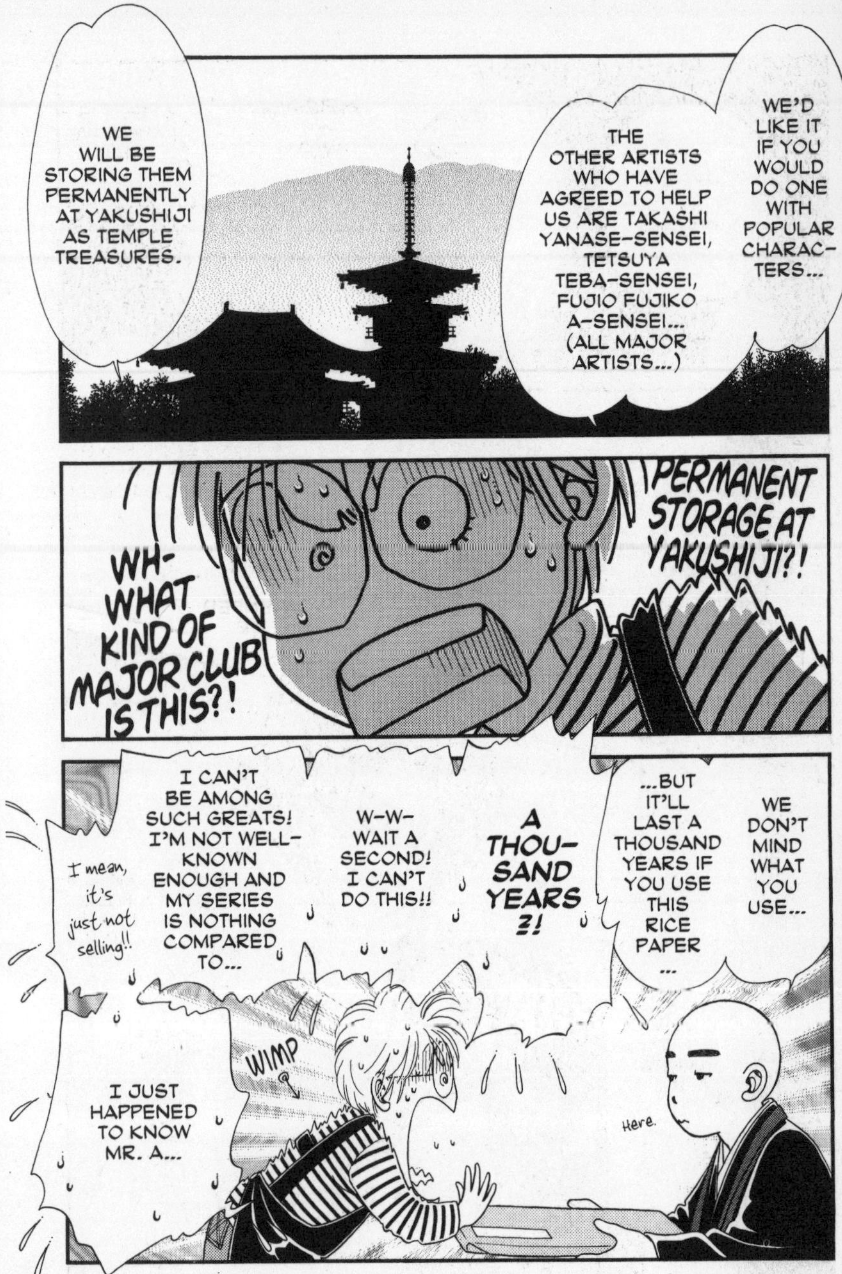
WE'D LIKE IT IF YOU WOULD DO ONE WITH POPULAR CHARAC-TERS...
THE OTHER ARTISTS WHO HAVE AGREED TO HELP US ARE TAKASHI YANASE-SENSEI, TETSUYA TEBA-SENSEI, FUJIO FUJIKO A-SENSEI... (ALL MAJOR ARTISTS...)
WE WILL BE STORING THEM PERMANENTLY AT YAKUSHIJI AS TEMPLE TREASURES.
PERMANENT STORAGE AT YAKUSHIJI?!
WH-WHAT KIND OF MAJOR CLUB IS THIS?!
WE DON'T MIND WHAT YOU USE...
...BUT IT'LL LAST A THOUSAND YEARS IF YOU USE THIS RICE PAPER...
A THOU-SAND YEARS?!
W-W-WAIT A SECOND! I CAN'T DO THIS!!
I CAN'T BE AMONG SUCH GREATS! I'M NOT WELL-KNOWN ENOUGH AND MY SERIES IS NOTHING COMPARED TO...
I mean, it's just not selling!!
Here.
WIMP
I JUST HAPPENED TO KNOW MR. A...

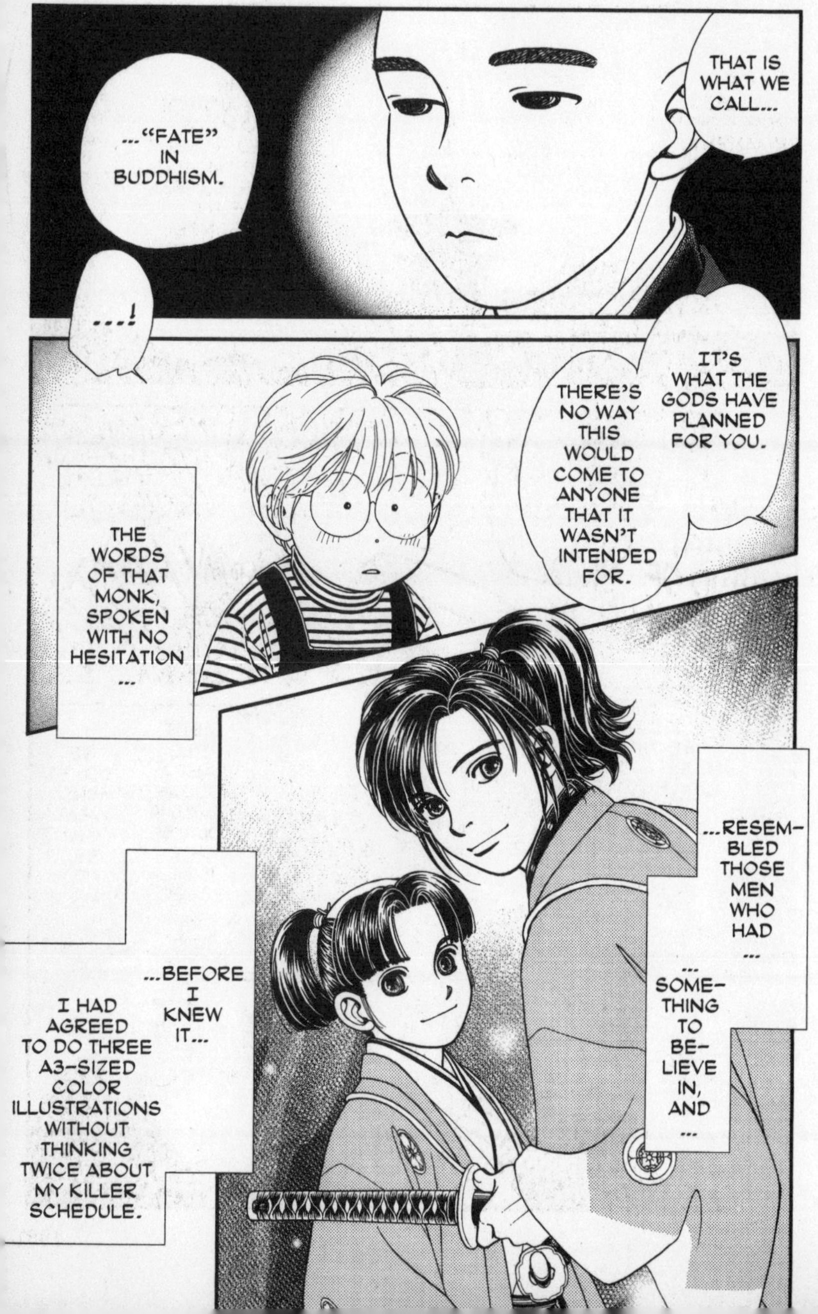
THAT IS WHAT WE CALL...
...“FATE” IN BUDDHISM.
...!
IT’S WHAT THE GODS HAVE PLANNED FOR YOU.
THERE’S NO WAY THIS WOULD COME TO ANYONE THAT IT WASN’T INTENDED FOR.
THE WORDS OF THAT MONK, SPOKEN WITH NO HESITATION...
...RESEMBLED THOSE MEN WHO HAD...
...SOMETHING TO BE-LIEVE IN, AND...
...BEFORE I KNEW IT...
I HAD AGREED TO DO THREE A3-SIZED COLOR ILLUSTRATIONS WITHOUT THINKING TWICE ABOUT MY KILLER SCHEDULE.

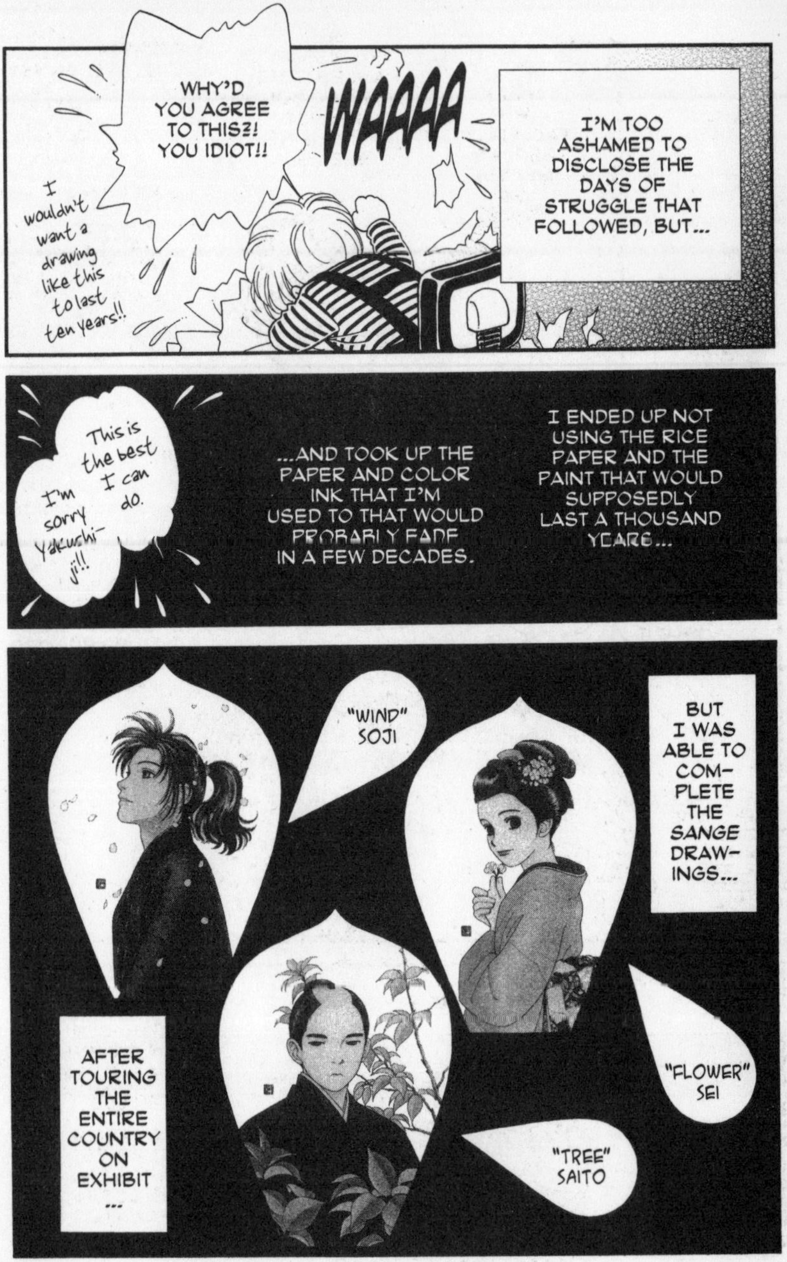
I'M TOO ASHAMED TO DISCLOSE THE DAYS OF STRUGGLE THAT FOLLOWED, BUT...
WAAAA
WHY'D YOU AGREE TO THIS?! YOU IDIOT!!
I wouldn't want a drawing like this to last ten years!!
I ENDED UP NOT USING THE RICE PAPER AND THE PAINT THAT WOULD SUPPOSEDLY LAST A THOUSAND YEARS...
...AND TOOK UP THE PAPER AND COLOR INK THAT I'M USED TO THAT WOULD PROBABLY FADE IN A FEW DECADES.
This is the best I can do.
I'm sorry Yakuchi-ji!!
BUT I WAS ABLE TO COMPLETE THE SANGE DRAWINGS...
"WIND" SOJI
"FLOWER" SEI
"TREE" SAITO
AFTER TOURING THE ENTIRE COUNTRY ON EXHIBIT...

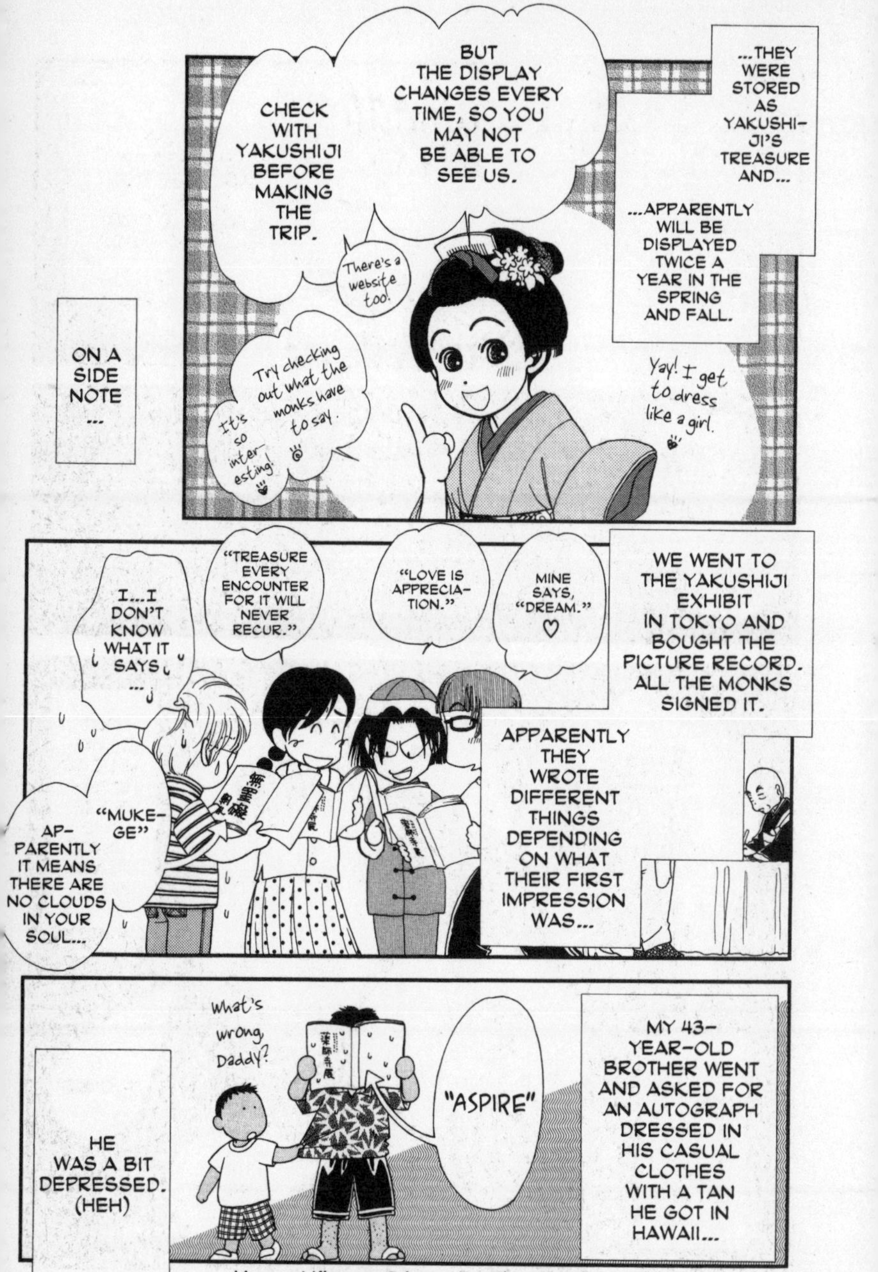
...THEY WERE STORED AS YAKUSHIJI'S TREASURE AND...
...APPARENTLY WILL BE DISPLAYED TWICE A YEAR IN THE SPRING AND FALL.
Yay! I get to dress like a girl.
BUT THE DISPLAY CHANGES EVERY TIME, SO YOU MAY NOT BE ABLE TO SEE US.
CHECK WITH YAKUSHIJI BEFORE MAKING THE TRIP.
There's a website too!
Try checking out what the monks have to say.
It's so interesting!
ON A SIDE NOTE...
WE WENT TO THE YAKUSHIJI EXHIBIT IN TOKYO AND BOUGHT THE PICTURE RECORD. ALL THE MONKS SIGNED IT.
APPARENTLY THEY WROTE DIFFERENT THINGS DEPENDING ON WHAT THEIR FIRST IMPRESSION WAS...
MINE SAYS, "DREAM."
"LOVE IS APPRECIATION."
"TREASURE EVERY ENCOUNTER FOR IT WILL NEVER RECUR."
I...I DON'T KNOW WHAT IT SAYS...
"MUKEGE"
APPARENTLY IT MEANS THERE ARE NO CLOUDS IN YOUR SOUL...
MY 43-YEAR-OLD BROTHER WENT AND ASKED FOR AN AUTOGRAPH DRESSED IN HIS CASUAL CLOTHES WITH A TAN HE GOT IN HAWAII...
"ASPIRE"
What's wrong, Daddy?
HE WAS A BIT DEPRESSED. (HEH)

Kaze Hikaru Diary R: The End

Decoding Kaze Hikaru

Kaze Hikaru is a historical drama based in 19th century Japan and thus contains some fairly mystifying terminology. In this glossary we'll break down archaic phrases, terms, and other linguistic curiosities for you, so that you can move through life with the smug assurance that you are indeed a know-it-all.

First and foremost, because *Kaze Hikaru* is a period story, we kept all character names in their traditional Japanese form—that is, family name followed by first name. For example, the character Okita Soji's family name is Okita and his personal name is Soji.

AKO-ROSHI:
The ronin (samurai) of Ako; featured in the immortal Kabuki play *Chushingura* (Loyalty), aka *47 Samurai*.

ANI-UE:
Literally, "brother above"; an honorific for an elder male sibling.

BAKUFU:
Literally, "tent government." Shogunate; the feudal, military government that dominated Japan for more than 200 years.

BUSHI:
A samurai or warrior (part of the compound word *bushido*, which means "way of the warrior").

CHICHI-UE:
An honorific suffix meaning "father above."

DO:
In kendo (a Japanese fencing sport that uses bamboo swords), a short way of describing the offensive single-hit strike *shikake waza ippon uchi*.

RONIN:
Masterless samurai.

RYO:
At the time, one *ryo* and two *bu* (four bu equaled roughly one ryo) were enough currency to support a family of five for an entire month.

-SAN:
An honorific suffix that carries the meaning of "Mr." or "Ms."

SENSEI:
A teacher, master, or instructor.

SEPPUKU:
A ritualistic suicide that was considered a privilege of the nobility and samurai elite.

SONJO-HA:
Those loyal to the emperor and dedicated to the expulsion of foreigners from the country.

-HAN:

The same as the honorific –SAN, pronounced in the dialect of southern Japan.

-KUN:

An honorific suffix that indicates a difference in rank and title. The use of *kun* is also a way of indicating familiarity and friendliness between students or compatriots

MEN:

In the context of *Kaze Hikaru, men* refers to one of the "points" in kendo. It is a strike to the forehead and is considered a basic move.

MIBU-ROSHI:

A group of warriors that supports the Bakufu.

NE'E-SAN:

Can mean "older sister," "ma'am," or "miss."

NI'I-CHAN:

Short for *oni'i-san* or *oni'i-chan*, meaning older brother.

OKU-SAMA:

This is a polite way to refer to someone's wife. *Oku* means "deep" or "further back," and comes from the fact that wives (in affluent families) stayed hidden away in the back rooms of the house.

ONI:

Literally "ogre," this is Sei's nickname for Vice-Captain Hijikata.

RANPO:

Medical science derived from the Dutch.

I confess I'm terrible at drawing close-ups. I don't know if I just get nervous, but I've never been able to draw something that I liked. So why would someone like that choose to draw a close-up? It is for no other reason than the popularity of the distant landscape series. It's inevitable that people will tell me "the old ones were better," so why not go for my weakest drawing? Knowing well that the livelihood of shojo manga is based on facial expression, I've avoided this basic skill. I wanted to return to my roots and really face my nemesis. The magazine just changed and I figured there's no harm in posing as a rookie. There's a lot facing the characters in this volume, so I thought that it would be fitting. (Heh).

Taeko Watanabe debuted as a manga artist in 1979 with her story *Waka-chan no Netsuai Jidai* (Love Struck Days of Waka). *Kaze Hikaru* is her longest-running series, but she has created a number of other popular series. Watanabe is a two-time winner of the prestigious Shogakukan Manga Award in the girls category—her manga *Hajime-chan ga Ichiban!* (Hajime-chan Is Number One!) claimed the award in 1991 and *Kaze Hikaru* took it in 2003.

Watanabe read hundreds of historical sources to create *Kaze Hikaru*. She is from Tokyo.

KAZE HIKARU VOL. 13
The Shojo Beat Manga Edition

STORY AND ART BY
TAEKO WATANABE

Translation & English Adaptation/Mai Ihara
Touch-up Art & Lettering/Rina Mapa
Cover Design/Izumi Evers
Interior Design/Julie Behn
Editor/Jonathan Tarbox

Editor in Chief, Books/Alvin Lu
Editor in Chief, Magazines/Marc Weidenbaum
VP, Publishing Licensing/Rika Inouye
VP, Sales & Product Marketing/Gonzalo Ferreyra
VP, Creative/Linda Espinosa
Publisher/Hyoe Narita

Printed in Canada

Published by VIZ Media, LLC
P.O. Box 77010
San Francisco, CA 94107

Shojo Beat Manga Edition
10 9 8 7 6 5 4 3 2 1
First printing, May 2009

www.viz.com

store.viz.com

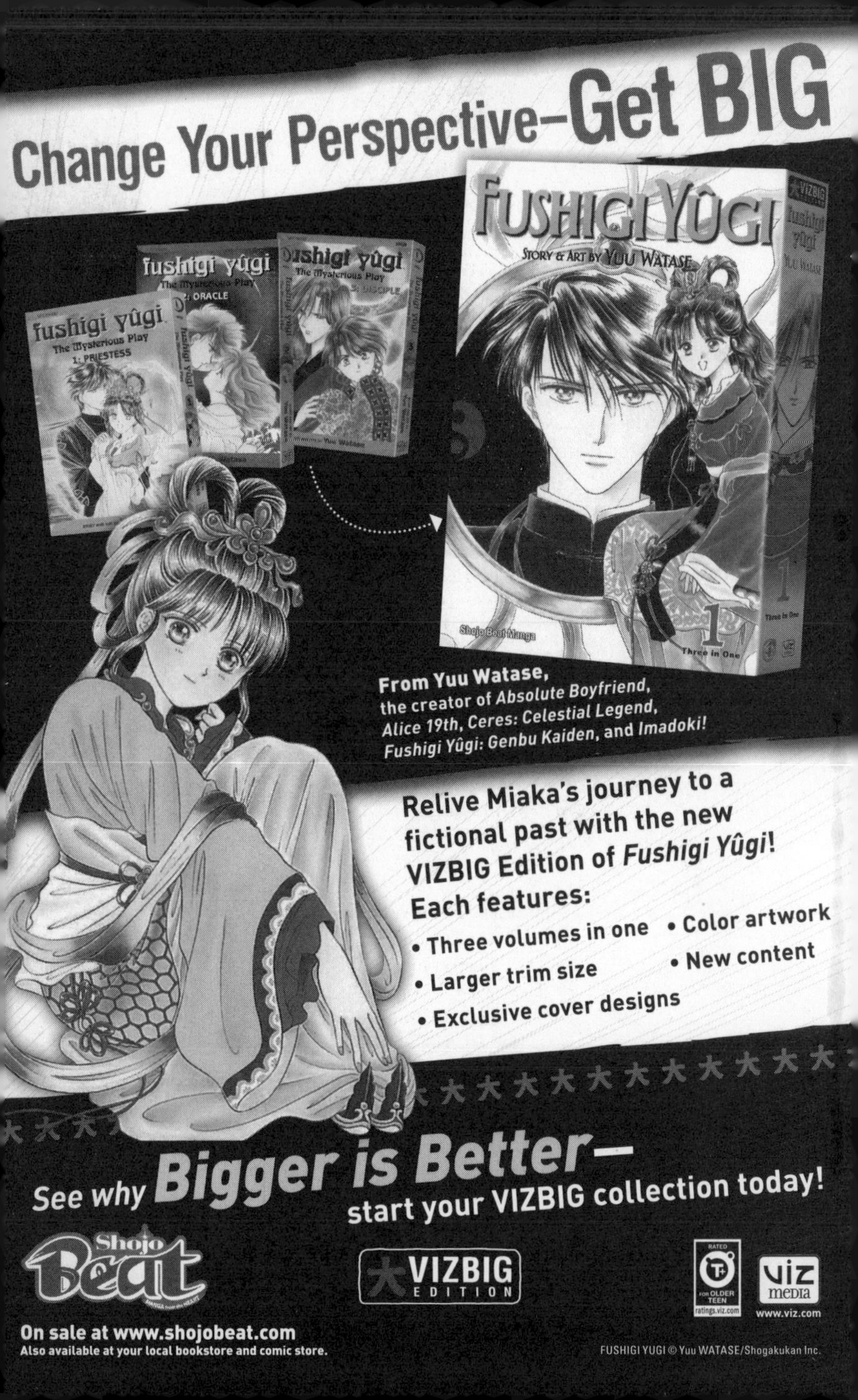

Change Your Perspective–Get BIG
fushigi yûgi The Mysterious Play 1: PRIESTESS
fushigi yûgi The Mysterious Play 2: ORACLE
fushigi yûgi The Mysterious Play 3: DISCIPLE
FUSHIGI YÛGI
STORY & ART BY YUU WATASE
Shojo Beat Manga
1 Three in One
VIZBIG EDITION
From Yuu Watase, the creator of Absolute Boyfriend, Alice 19th, Ceres: Celestial Legend, Fushigi Yûgi: Genbu Kaiden, and Imadoki!
Relive Miaka's journey to a fictional past with the new VIZBIG Edition of Fushigi Yûgi!
Each features:
• Three volumes in one
• Color artwork
• Larger trim size
• New content
• Exclusive cover designs
See why Bigger is Better— start your VIZBIG collection today!
Shojo Beat MANGA from the HEART
VIZBIG EDITION
RATED T+ FOR OLDER TEEN ratings.viz.com
VIZ media
www.viz.com
On sale at www.shojobeat.com
Also available at your local bookstore and comic store.
FUSHIGI YUGI © Yuu WATASE/Shogakukan Inc.